Public Performances

Public Performances

Studies in the Carnivalesque and Ritualesque

Edited by
Jack Santino

Volume 4
Ritual, Festival, and Celebration
A series edited by
Jack Santino

Utah State University Press
Logan

© 2017 by University Press of Colorado

Published by Utah State University Press
An imprint of University Press of Colorado
1580 North Logan Street, Suite 660
PMB 39883
Denver, Colorado 80203-1942

All rights reserved
First paperback edition 2024

 The University Press of Colorado is a proud member of
The Association of University Presses.

The University Press of Colorado is a cooperative publishing enterprise supported, in part, by Adams State University, Colorado State University, Fort Lewis College, Metropolitan State University of Denver, University of Alaska Fairbanks, University of Colorado, University of Denver, University of Northern Colorado, University of Wyoming, Utah State University, and Western Colorado University.

Cover illustration by Will Kiley Santino

ISBN: 978-1-60732-634-2 (cloth)
ISBN: 978-1-64642-624-9 (paperback)
ISBN: 978-1-60732-635-9 (ebook)

Library of Congress Cataloging-in-Publication Data

Names: Santino, Jack, editor.
Title: Public performances : studies in the carnivalesque and ritualesque / edited by Jack Santino.
Other titles: Ritual, festival, and celebration ; v. 4.
Description: Logan : Utah State University Press, 2017. | Series: Ritual, festival, and celebration ; volume 4 | This volume is written by scholars who have presented research at the Conference on Holidays, Ritual, Festival, Celebration, and Public Display. The papers themselves are not necessarily the same as their original presentations, and represent only a few of the authors who have presented at this annual conference over the years. This annual conference began in 1997 and the 15th was held in 2011 at the Sorbonne.This book reflects on the field of Ritual Studies, and the role and influence of the conference—Paraphrase from the introduction. | Includes bibliographical references and index.
Identifiers: LCCN 2016049464| ISBN 9781607326342 (cloth) | ISBN 9781646426249 (paperback) | ISBN 9781607326359 (ebook)
Subjects: LCSH: Political customs and rites. | Holidays—Political aspects. | Parades. | Processions. | Festivals. | Annual Conference on Holidays, Ritual, Festival, Celebration and Public Display.
Classification: LCC GN293.3 .S88 2017 | DDC 306—dc23
LC record available at https://lccn.loc.gov/2016049464

To Roger D. Abrahams,
scholar extraordinaire

Contents

Introduction   ix

1   From Carnivalesque to Ritualesque: Public Ritual and the Theater of the Street
    Jack Santino   3

2   Locality, Spectacle, State Politics: Comparative Study of Carnival Traditions in Renaissance Nuremberg and Modern Trinidad
    Samuel Kinser   16

3   Conflict Displays in the Black Atlantic
    Roger D. Abrahams   49

4   Protesting and Grieving: Ritual, Politics, and the Effects of Scale
    Beverly J. Stoeltje   66

5   Political Percussions: Cork Brass Bands and the Irish Revolution, 1914–1922
    John Borgonovo   93

6   ¡Que Bonita Bandera! Place, Space, and Identity as Expressed with the Puerto Rican Flag
    Elena Martínez   113

7   The Lives of Processions in Bali and Lombok, Indonesia
    David Harnish   133

8   The Anthropology of Festivals: Changes in Theory and Practice
    Laurent Sébastien Fournier   151

9   The Politics of Cultural Promotion: The Umthetho Festival of Malawi's Northern Ngoni
    Lisa Gilman   164

10 Music as Activist Spectacle: AIDS, Breast Cancer, and LGBT Choral Singing
    Pamela Moro   *189*

11 The "Days of Scanzano": The Carnivalesque and the Ritualesque in an Antinuclear Protest
    Dorothy L. Zinn   *205*

12 "Some Are Born Green, Some Achieve Greenness": Protest Theater and Environmental Activism
    Scott Magelssen   *222*

13 The Material Culture of Remembrance in Ireland: Roadside Memorials as Contested Spaces
    Barbara Graham   *239*

14 The Politics of Junk: Social Protest, "Outsider" Environments, and Ritualesque Display at the Heidelberg Project in Detroit
    Daniel Wojcik   *254*

About the Authors   278
Index   283

Introduction

The chapters in this volume are written by scholars who have presented research at the Conference on Holidays, Ritual, Festival, Celebration, and Public Display. The essays are not necessarily the same as their original presentations, and the authors represent a very small percentage of the total number of scholars who have presented at this conference over the years. I initiated the Conference on Holidays, Ritual, Festival, Celebration, and Public Display in 1997; in 2011, we held the fifteenth annual conference in Paris at the Sorbonne. Fifteen years is a good chunk of time; by now the conference had its own history and impact. It is, I think, a good time to pause and reflect on the field of ritual studies, and the role and influence of the conference.

The title of the conference, while unwieldy, is intentionally inclusive. It too, in a sense, has a history. I first heard the term *public display* from Roger D. Abrahams, who has used it often in his writings as a way of capturing a variety of events (see, for example, 1982, 1987). *Ritual, festival,* and *celebration* may seem self-evident choices, but I was directly influenced here by their use in an exhibition at the Smithsonian Institution's Renwick Gallery in 1982. At that time I was on staff as a folklorist and program coordinator for the Smithsonian's Office of Folklife Programs, in charge of coordinating a series of "Living Celebrations" to be held in conjunction with the exhibition of ritual objects at the gallery (Santino 1988). This exhibition was guest-curated by Victor Turner, the great anthropologist whose work on ritual was and is internationally lauded. He was already a great influence on me through his published work, and I had begun to apply some of his ideas to the contemporary celebrations of American holidays such as Halloween. Thus, I wanted the word *holidays* in the title of the conference (see, for example, Turner 1967, 1982; Santino 1983, 1994, 1998).

However, there is a more important, more theoretical underpinning to this inclusive title. It refers to a number of interrelated genres or types of events. They tend to share many characteristics. The terms often overlap and are frequently used interchangeably. A calendar holiday such as New Year's Eve, for example, is also an annual rite of passage; religious rituals are frequently components of larger festivities, such as a saint's day procession during a patronal feast day. Most of these are public displays of symbolic action; and almost all can be described as celebration (or commemoration, which can be thought of as a form of celebration.)

It is the awareness of the overlapping elements and dimensions of such public performances, their interchangeability, the "inter-share-ability" of their components, that has led to the development of certain ideas throughout the period of the conferences. Certainly, components such as procession may be found in a number of different types of events—a political protest march, a college football homecoming celebration, or a pilgrimage to a healing site, for instance. Thus, these all "share" procession as a component, or element, of the event. On a broader level of conceptualization, so do political demonstration, festival, and ritual. In addition, qualities such as an organization of time and space or the fact of public spectatorship are also "shared" among events. Context is a crucial distinguishing feature. Also, questions of intention and reception—why the event, which is always polysemic, is enacted and how its meanings and purposes are interpreted and constructed by those involved, either actively or passively—are also important considerations when attempting to understand a public action.

Throughout the collection, we see research on ritual, carnival, parades and processions, festivals with political dimensions and political acts with festive dimensions. We see performance events purposed toward social issues, such as the LGBT choir described by Pamela Moro, and theatrical performances as activist acts, as seen in the chapter by Scott Magelssen. Hopefully we can begin to develop a unified theory of public display— that is, folk and popular public ritual—that can address these various and disparate examples. The intent is not to reduce these very different events and multiple contexts to a single, simplistic paradigm, but rather to sketch out the similarities and differences among them, the ways in which the generic associations of one may be used for different situations and goals. Of course we must recognize that the individual events have contexts both immediate and historical, and are used for and speak to very specific needs and situations, Padlocks on public display on the Paris bridges are not the same as the rags left at an Irish holy well, but there are connections. At the very least, both acts manifest a traditional paradigm of ritual action, and one might well be a model for the other. The items at the holy wells are not the same as the materials left at the Vietnam Veterans Memorial Wall in Washington, DC, but there are performative similarities and at least some overlap in motivations, having to do with making anonymous, deeply personal, socially communicative statements. To what extent can the same be said of, for instance, the display of flags in the context of a Puerto Rican

Day festival (see Elena Martínez's chapter in this volume) or the use of brass bands in nationalist Ireland (John Borgonovo)? Both of these are very different from the processions in Lombok (David Harnish)—what qualities of performative social action are shared among them? Going further, can we compare the public display at the wells, bridges, and memorials to these parades, as actions relying on traditional paradigms of public display in particular social situations, perhaps reflecting some sort of common human sociocultural behavior in situations of differential identity? As innovative as some of the emergent forms we see today are, they continue to give witness to deeply shared traditions of communal structures of communication that allow for personal self-expression. Parades, processions, padlocks on a bridge all call attention to themselves; they call attention to people in action or are material reminders of people having acted.

Along with theatrical and choral performances (Magelssen, Moro), political demonstrations (Dorothy Zinn), and heavily politicized parades (Martínez), Daniel Wojcik contributes the very useful idea of the "performative environment" in his study of so-called outsider art projects that are receiving attention from scholars in many disciplines. Many, though not all, of these projects are performative insofar as they are created to influence public behavior and social attitudes. In the case of Tyree Guyton, the artist is explicitly using both recycled materials and his own work to create environments that will directly change peoples' habits. He wants to drive out drug dealers, to inspire people to take pride in their neighborhood, and to become involved in their community. As Wojcik documents, Guyton's efforts have frequently been met with resistance, opposition, and even hostility from politicians and residents of Detroit.

This book's arrangement moves from traditional carnival through ritual to ritualesque events both political and theatrical in nature, ending with the consideration of performative art environments. My initial essay sets forth the ideas of carnivalesque and ritualesque public display performances. Samuel Kinser's study of carnival in early modern Nuremberg and in contemporary Trinidad is followed by Roger D. Abraham's examination of African-centric and African-derived festive and ritual events. Both of these essays show how elements of social conflict are embedded in these performances, whether in the European rites of reversal or the African-derived positioning of alternative systems of power and conflict display events within the carnivals. From there we move to a study of ritual theory and the political dimensions of ritual by Beverly Stoeltje. Following are three case studies of parades and processions: in Ireland in the early twentieth century by Borgonovo, the Puerto Rico parade in New York today by Martínez, and processions in Indonesia by Harnish. All of these demonstrate the active roles such events play in their societies: as social agents and as means of asserting power, identity, and positionality. Laurent Sébastien Fournier provides a consideration of festivals, including those sponsored by local authorities, and this is followed by Lisa Gilman's study of the Umtheto festival of the northern Ngoni of Malawi, which was organized to promote local language and culture. From there we move to studies of public performances that are overtly ritualesque, beginning with Moro's chapter on choirs singing to raise consciousness concerning the AIDS epidemic and breast cancer. Zinn studies a public protest event in Scanzano, Italy, While the earlier essays indicate the ways various events display issues of conflict, here the event is focused on specific grievances in order to bring attention to and rectify them. From theatrical protest events we move to protest theater, with Magelssen's chapter on activist theatrical events. His essay discusses with theatrical, ritualesque public actions and actual dramatic presentations presented in a theater.

The final two chapters deal with material culture. If conflict has been a theme throughout the collection, Barbara Graham examines a different kind of social clash. In her study of roadside memorials in Ireland, she has found that the general public often disapproves of these displays and considers them inappropriate ways to commemorate the dead. What are the conditions for acceptance of an emergent popular ritual concerning death? Finally, Wojcik presents a study of the outsider art of Detroit's Tyree Guyton. Guyton, a self-taught artist, has made it his job to challenge urban evils with bold public art displays aimed at cleaning up the neighborhood of drug dealers and calling attention to other social problems as well. Here we see grassroots art creation as activist ritualistic public display.

It is my intention in this collection to suggest relationships among the various ritual genres (Stoeltje 1993) and further, to uncover ways and means by which the political dimensions present in them can be understood. Beyond the particular motivations of participants, there is a level of analysis that allows us to say that when these events are organized from the ground up—that is, when not institutionally sponsored (by church, state, or commerce)—the very doing, performing, and enacting of them is a political act. Whether one's politics are left or right, radical or libertarian, the very taking to the streets, declaring public space open to citizens to march in, parade through, or mark with symbols of popular and topical significance, is an act of asserting power (see, for instance, de Certeau 1984). For this reason, such actions are closely regulated, met with resistance from "above"—by representatives of official institutions who consider regulation of public activity their domain. Conversely, when a public space is dedicated to celebrating a normative institution such as the military or the church, this too is a enactment of political power in public.

The essays in this book range in topic from traditional carnival to formal ritual, with many chapters examining events that fall outside that binary, dealing with both carnivalesque and ritualesque actions. These parameters, along with the unauthorized use of public space, suggest themselves as qualities found in public display generally. These events and actions are always emergent from social context, always political in some sense of the word. It is hoped that the ensemble collection will help point the way, if not to a unified theory, then to a unified field of public display as emergent political popular culture, and to an understanding of public performance events as expressions of politics, of grief, of grievance, of laughter, and of protest—often all at the same time.

REFERENCES

Abrahams, Roger. 1982. "The Language of Festivals: Celebrating the Economy." In *Celebration: Studies in Festivity and Ritual*, ed. Victor Turner, 161–77. Washington, DC: Smithsonian Institution Press.

Abrahams, Roger. 1987. "An American Vocabulary of Celebrations." In *Time out of Time: Essays on the Festival*, ed. Alessandro Falassi, 173–83. Albuquerque: University of New Mexico Press.

de Certeau, Michel. 1984. *The Practice of Everyday Life*. Trans. Steven Rendall. Berkeley: University of California Press.

Santino, Jack. 1983. "Halloween in America: Contemporary Customs and Performances." *Western Folklore* 62 (1): 1–20. http://dx.doi.org/10.2307/1499461.

Santino, Jack. 1988. "The Tendency to Ritualize: The Living Celebrations Series as a Model for Cultural Presentation and Validation." In *The Conservation of Culture: Folklorists and the Public Sector*, ed. Burt Feintuch, 118–31. Lexington: University Press of Kentucky.

Santino, Jack. 1994. *Halloween and Other Festivals of Death and Life*. Knoxville: University of Tennessee Press.

Santino, Jack. 1998. *The Hallowed Eve: Dimensions of Culture in a Calendar Festival in Northern Ireland*. Lexington: University Press of Kentucky.

Stoeltje, Beverly J. 1993. "Power and the Ritual Genres: American Rodeo." *Western Folklore* 52 (2/4): 135–56. http://dx.doi.org/10.2307/1500083.

Turner, Victor. 1967. *The Forest of Symbols: Aspects of Ndembu Ritual*. Ithaca: Cornell University Press.

Turner, Victor, ed. 1982. *Celebration: Studies in Festivity and Ritual*. Washington, DC: Smithsonian Institution Press..

Public Performances

1

From Carnivalesque to Ritualesque
Public Ritual and the Theater of the Street

Jack Santino

Ritual, festival, celebration, carnival, holiday, *public display event*—these terms and others are used to refer to a variety of public performances. Often the terms overlap. Sometimes they are used interchangeably. In part, this is due to the porous, shifting nature of the events themselves, heavily dependent on context and intended purpose. It is the intention of this essay to examine public performances in order to tease out shared qualities and to set forth ways of apprehending these events in a way that allows us to more fully grasp their purposeful meanings and to articulate ways that they differ. By approaching performance events as carnivalesque and ritualesque, we are able to understand the multiple modes of communication; the simultaneity of joy and anger, of politics and fun; and how "fun" in some contexts equals protest.

Carnival, strictly speaking, refers to the pre-Lenten festival that represents an opportunity for sensual abandon in advance of the deprivations of the forty-day period of Lent. This festive occasion is known in several guises and in fact sometimes occurs outside of reference to the Western Christian church calendar: for instance, Fastnacht is celebrated in some Protestant areas after Ash Wednesday, the beginning of Lent (Tokofsky 2004); and as European colonizers and settlers brought the tradition with them to the New World, it became heavily synthesized with African masquerade traditions, resulting in a New World Afro-Caribbean and South American carnival complex. As West Indian populations in turn migrated to North America and Europe, Trinidadian-style carnival is often celebrated in summer in these new locations (Allen 1999). No longer tied to a Christian calendar and heavily Africanized, these Trinidad- and Rio-styled

Figure 1.1. Carnival at Dunkirk, France, 2011

performances are being taken up in Europe. In any case, however, carnival refers to celebrations of great abandon, social inversion, public excess, sensuality, and the temporary establishment of an alternate society, one free of or even in opposition to the norm.

Ritual, conversely, in its true sense of "sacred ceremony," is about constructing and reinforcing social categories, even if those categories represent a minority position or a marginalized group. Rites of passage are the means by which individuals and groups transition from one category to another. The categories in question are usually culturally constructed, for example, "husband," "wife," "president," and so on. Even those rites associated with physical and biological realities, such as birth, puberty, or death, are contained deeply within webs of cultural meaning, having to do with perceptions of an afterlife, the presence or absence of beliefs concerning the world of the supernatural, and the nature of the universe. Death, it would seem, is death. But is there a concept of the soul? If so, when does it take leave of the body? In Roman Catholic ritual, a person's soul requires the rituals of the church to usher it into the other world, possibly as late as three days after the physical death. Even something as apparently objective as the onset of puberty is seen to vary across cultures. Thus, ritual constructs and validates the very categories it deals in.

Because it is the way society validates its fundamental categories, ritual is the means for creating and reinforcing power structures, as presidential inaugurations, the installation of queens, or a commencement exercise demonstrate. Ritual is symbolic in nature but felt to be very real by those who are engaged with it; thus, among the transformations that ritual accomplishes, it is a means by which social categories are made real. Ritual actions are thought to have real power; ritual is instrumental, not expressive. As John MacAloon would say, that which occurs in ritual is thought to be real and to partake of unquestionable truths (MacAloon 1984; see also Rappaport 1999). Ritual, then, is instrumental symbolic behavior. The transformations accomplished by ritual are essentially permanent.

Carnival, by contrast, remains expressive rather than instrumental. It is a temporary period. The understanding is that after the world is turned upside down, it will be turned right side up again. Carnival very often features parody and social critique, but the carnival frame remains expressive. Again following MacAloon, the carnival frame says: "Everything that happens here is fun and temporary, without lasting effect."

However, these terms—*carnival* and *ritual*—are idealized constructions. Carnival often leads to riot, as seen from sixteenth-century Rome to 1970s Notting Hill in London. (LeRoy Ladurie 1979; Cohen 1993). Moreover, festive celebrations often serve as rites of season, and a great many sacred ceremonies the world over are very merry and inversive. Finally, a great many events, such as Jonkonnu or the medieval Feast of Fools, fall outside of the Lent-Easter calendrical restrictions, yet seem to be carnivals in their own right.

Mikhail Bakhtin's work on the "carnivalesque" has allowed us to move beyond generic essentialism to understand elements or dimensions of public events as sharing certain characteristics (1984). We identify the carnivalesque in Pride Day celebrations, in spontaneous street celebrations following sports victories, or in protest rallies.

The distinction between ritual and festival (carnival has been called the festival par excellence; Falassi 2004, 71), then, is blurred and porous. Sometimes an event is distinctly one or the other. Often it is a little bit of both. This problematic is due at least in part to the shared use of standardized symbolic frames (certain ways of marking time or space), kinesics (parades, dances, house visitations), sound (noise, rough music, song, chants), and so on. However, we can develop a way of viewing symbolic public events as partaking more or less in the carnivalesque and/or the ritualesque. Thus, we can get past the absolutism and essentialism of assuming or assigning a single type of communication according to genre: for example, if it is ritual (understood as such by the participants), it is sacred; therefore, it is perceived as sacred by the participants in all its aspects (see MacAloon 1984). Most events will have elements of the ritualesque along with the carnivalesque, and the latter does not negate the former. The two are not antithetical, and the genre frames are multivocal. In the ongoing spontaneity of real-time enactments, public performances can signify many things at once.

Yet another important consideration when examining symbolic public events is the question of instrumentality versus expressivity. Ritual can be said to be public symbolic action that is thought to be instrumental—it is done primarily to make something happen. Transformation and transcendence are typically associated with ritual; rituals rely on some sense of transcendent authority in order to accomplish the change, whether that is a rite of passage of the life cycle, a religious service, a healing ceremony, or a commencement exercise. The "ritualesque" refers to those aspects of a symbolic event that are meant to lead to extra-ceremonial change, or transformation. Events such as Halloween celebrations or carnivals are clearly expressive and festive, but will also have ritualesque elements of social critique and political parody. Other events, such as the Parisian *manifestations*, are primarily intended to bring about social change, and yet they contain carnivalesque elements of costume, music, and inversion. As ritual transformations are meant to continue after the ritual is completed, ritualesque actions are those that are intended to have a permanent effect on society. Ritualesque events aim for change beyond the "time out of time" of the event itself. This ritualesque dimension is not in opposition to the carnivalesque; indeed, it is often with carnivalesque events (such as Pride Day) that the ritualesque is constructed.

We need this concept of the ritualesque to sharpen our understanding of public festivity. When the Halloween masquerade is over, the rules and norms of everyday life are expected by most to resume. But when Earth Day or Pride Day or a Take Back the Night march is over, participants hope they have made a difference in that everyday world.

MATERIAL CULTURE

A through-line in public display events and/or street theater at the folk and popular levels of organization is the claiming of public space by people not in any official way authorized to do so. When one erects a cross on the highway to commemorate a fatality, this is a popular usage—that is, something done by "the people." I am not referring here to official memorials, but rather the self-motivated, self-generated shrines that emerged as a ritual of mourning violent, untimely death in the latter decades of the twentieth century. If such a shrine is created at the entrance to a fast food restaurant or a commercial shopping center, the proprietors might fear that the shrine will discourage customers. Likewise, local and state governments wrestle with the increase in roadside shrines and memorials, some banning them outright, others turning a blind eye, and still others trying to accommodate them in some way (Everett 2002). Here, issues of traffic safety are said to be paramount.

Figure 1.2. Padlocks on the Pont Echevrin behind Notre Dame Cathedral, Paris

We see in these examples uses of public space (or, if privately owned, space that is publicly accessed and used repeatedly by members of the public) in ways that the owners or the proprietary officials have not sanctioned. In short, people reclaim public space in order to use it symbolically and ritualistically, to make public statements in their own terms. Very often the space is not neutral; it may have important cultural associations of it own (for example, the use of the Place de la Bastille in Paris as a staging site for *les manifestations*), or it may have been rendered numinous, powerful, and sacred by more recent events that have occurred there, such as is the case of the Charlie Hebdo offices.

An interesting example of this contestation of public space can be seen in the padlock phenomenon that appears to be sweeping the world (I first encountered it in Kemerovo, Siberia). Paris has become noted for the padlocks along the Pont des Arts over the Seine, in front of the Louvre. The custom is for couples to place a lock, often inscribed with their names, on the bridge, then toss the key into the river. The lock represents a permanent relationship. When I first saw these in 2010, on the Pont des Arts and also the nearby Pont Echevren, there were frequent official announcements that the locks must be taken down. Supposedly, city officials did in fact cut locks off the bridges on several occasions. By 2014, however, not only had the custom continued to grow in popularity, the number of locks was now voluminous. Locks were attached to other locks, several inches thick. In February 2015, a panel on the Pont des Arts collapsed from the weight and was removed. Finally, in June 2015, the City of Paris removed all the padlocks from the Pont des Arts, though not from the Pont Echevren, saying that the weight of them threatened the structural integrity of the bridge.

As in the case of roadside crosses, the rationale of safety very well may be the immediate impetus for the removal of the padlocks. But as I stated, they had been viewed as problematic by city officials long before they reached the point of danger to the bridge. I see here again a popular custom—that is, an emergent tradition of everyday people, in which public space is claimed as available for unofficial actions and communications and for uses unintended by the officials. And here again, this is met with resistance from the authorities, who eventually suppress the activity and reinforce their own control.

The padlocks are most often found at liminal spaces, such as bridges or other places overlooking a body of water. Very often it would appear that the view available, suitably romantic, is the significant factor in the choice of location. In Paris, for example, on a bridge near Notre Dame, only the side facing the cathedral is covered with the padlocks.

The padlocks are also interesting because they differ from many other forms of public display activities that also involve people personally but anonymously leaving signs of their participation, their presence. I am reminded of rag trees and rag wells in Ireland, Scotland, and other places; the spontaneous shrines mentioned above; cairns of stones in Jewish death traditions, and so on. In these cases, the rituals and symbols address serious problems—death and sickness (rag trees and rag wells are primarily sites of healing). The locks reference love. In all instances, however, we see the materialization of hope and the theatricalization of intention (as ritual). As with most votive offerings, the action represents a desired future condition. The objects bear witness to actions intended to influence the future. The padlocks suggest the intention and the hope for permanence, and in that sense they are positive, not negative. They are a form of true popular culture—not popular culture as created by the corporate-owned and corporate-controlled mass media. They are actions and customs initiated and understood by everyday people—and as such, are viewed suspiciously by authorities.

CARNIVALS OF GRIEF

Spontaneous shrines, which have become an international phenomenon, represent the development of a mourning practice from folk precedents. Decorative gravesite elaboration is well known and ancient in Europe, Asia, and Africa. Most likely Catholic Spanish colonizers, soldiers, and priests brought with them to the New World the custom of marking deaths that occurred on the roads with crosses. The custom has flourished in the American Southwest, Mexico, and Central America among peoples of Spanish, Anglo, and Native ancestries ever since. Roadside crosses, or other items such as flowers and messages, have become an all-too-common sight on the highways of the United States.

It was perhaps with the creation of the Vietnam Veterans Memorial Wall in Washington, DC, that people began to evolve the custom to contexts beyond road fatalities. While no one either died or is buried at this site, the monument is not unlike a massive gravestone—slabs of granite inscribed with the names of the deceased. Its design was groundbreaking for war memorials, among other reasons because it lists the name of every person killed, in chronological order. Conventions of military hierarchy were not primary concerns. Also, many of the deceased were lost in battle, their bodies never recovered. For whatever reasons, the memorial has become a site of personal grieving, as individuals leave tokens of significance to them and to the deceased at the wall (see Haas 1998).

As in the case of highway memorials, this type of ritual is different from the grieving traditions engaged in by families and friends at home or in churches, mosques, synagogues, and other sacred places; these are acts that are simultaneously public and personal; anyone visiting the National Mall or driving on an interstate highway may see and comprehend the assemblages that have been created, but the individuals who created them remain anonymous. This reflects and communicates the nature of the deaths involved: violent, untimely, and related to reasons that may have been avoided. There is controversy regarding the Vietnam War; highway deaths sometimes signal unsafe roads or drunk driving. The resultant shrines and commemorative assemblages, then, both address these social issues and commemorate the deceased. They are performative commemoratives; their performativity is like a performative utterance (Austin 1962); they are active social forces themselves. The shrines are meant to have an effect, make a difference, cause a result. Thus, they are not only expressive (of love, of grief), they are also instrumental. And as instrumental symbolic creations, they are very like formal ritual (Santino 2006).

I was in Paris in 2015, three weeks after the attacks and killings at the Charlie Hebdo offices. I was in the city in part to witness the Paris *boeuf gras* carnival, which has been revived in recent years. The procession led to the Place de la République, a plaza central both geographically and symbolically. The mass manifestation on the Sunday following the Charlie Hebdo killings was centered there. I saw that the statue of Marianne, the national symbol of France, was covered with memorabilia dedicated to the Charlie Hebdo victims, along with calls for *liberté, egalité,* and *fraternité*. Not only was the monument itself covered with flowers and wreaths; it was written upon directly in ways that signaled how extraordinary the occasion was. I noticed that some candles were lit, and while I was there a woman brought a wreath. It was still an active site of mourning, weeks after the event. People were writing—with paint—on the plaza itself. The entire plaza had become a canvas for displays of mourning, celebrations of freedom of expression, and demonstrations of solidarity.

The next day I took the Métro to the Charlie Hebdo headquarters. Upon leaving the station a few blocks from the offices, I saw that both sides of the boulevard had extensive shrines. One was dedicated to Ahmed Merabet, the Muslim police officer who was killed in the attack. The phrase "Je suis Charlie" had become a primary semantic component of the collective responses; here, the handmade signs read, "Je suis Ahmet."

The offices themselves were under armed guard, and pedestrians were not allowed to approach. However, the end of the short street, which ended in a T intersection with another, was covered with shrine memorabilia. Because the people at the newspaper had been killed for their drawings of the Prophet Muhammad, the pencil (or pen) had emerged as a primary symbol. Pencils—real pencils, replica pencils, inflatable pencils, drawings of pencils—were the fundamental building blocks of these symbolic statements.

In this context I want to draw attention to such organic emergence of symbols specific to the occasions. In late 2014 and early 2015, the United States was roiled by police killings of unarmed African American men. In many cases police officers were not found to be guilty of any wrongdoing. As these situations seemed to occur with increasing frequency, African American communities took to the streets to protest. Violence erupted. And again, we saw the emergence of primary symbols of protest rooted to the specific events in question—"Hands up—don't shoot," supposedly said by the victim (Michael Brown), led to the subsequent use of hands—real or pictured—in reference to those words, to chants of; "I can't breathe," as said by Eric Garner as he choked to death. Here we can see how protests rely on traditional paradigms (processions, effigies, rough music, etc.) and simultaneously involve emergent, situationally specific symbolic language.

At Charlie Hebdo central, I was struck not only by the pencils, but also by the very riot of objects, symbols, concepts referenced, and messages expressed, as well as by the multitude of media used for these expressions. People had covered the official street name signs with official-looking imitations that read, "Place de la Liberté d'Expression." Official bouquets and banners from the mayors of Paris and New York, ambassadors, and an international array of journalists were intermingled with handmade signs, cartoons, flowers, candles (many of them still lit at this time) and, of course, pencils. I found it all very moving. There were several people there, and conversations began easily. People from Paris and other parts of France were intrigued and I think impressed that I, an American professor, was there to

Figure 1.3. Pencils and pens at the Charlie Hebdo office

Figure 1.4. The image of the pencil accompanies this message at Charlie Hebdo: "The Republic is stronger than hatred."

pay witness. There was a kind of liminality and communitas present, both in the democratic mélange of the objects and items and among the people present (how people would have responded if a Muslim had been present, I cannot say). Certainly there was a popular use of public space, and with the street signs especially, a usurpation of official hegemony. As was shown in the United States after the events of September 11, 2001, liminality and communitas are not exclusively limited to festive events.

In her essay in this volume, Beverly Stoeltje cites Barbara Babcock (1978, 297), who describes carnivals as a "surplus of signifiers." That was what I experienced on the streets of Paris that day, a riot of color and texture—objects, images drawn and photographed, the smell of candles and flowers, all with individual meanings, intentions, and cultural associations. But carnivals are festive events: ludic, popularly associated with joyful effervescence. This space was sacred and solemn—a carnival of grief.

THE CARNIVALESQUE AND THE RITUALESQUE

Carnivals, properly speaking, may not always be such happy events. Most certainly the license of carnival allows for and even encourages the expression of forbidden sentiments, including the political. The paradox of festive license, of course, is that it is sanctioned by the entrenched authorities. License is limited, and at times those limits are contested (Fabre 2007). Carnivalesque political parody can be very pointed, but must not spur actual direct action or be seen to spur direct action, or it will be curtailed or violently suppressed. Yet some carnivals do lead to revolts (Bercé 1977; LeRoy Ladurie 1979); and some public protests utilize traditional frames found in festivals to address and express grief, grievance, and outrage. As stated above, roughly coterminous with the Charlie Hebdo killings in Paris, the United States was dealing with people taking their grief and grievances with their police forces to the streets of Ferguson, Missouri, and Baltimore, Maryland. Certainly the participants in those protests would never refer to their actions as carnivals in any sense, but we can see in them a kind of darker carnival, as people claim their own streets, chant, burn effigies, parade, and sometimes destroy commercial property as a sign of their rejection of the status quo. Perhaps it is possible to view such events as points on a continuum, with these being assigned a position toward the ritualesque pole. The events referred to here as "carnivals of grief" are intended to have immediate and long-term effects on society. They are not contained within a frame of carnivalesque parody or of permitted, tolerated license, after which the world is turn right side up again.

This is the distinction I wish to draw between carnivalesque and ritualesque: that which occurs within carnival and festival is allowed because the liminal frame is understood as social permission to defy the norms. These norms will be safely returned to—at least, that is the social bargain. For this reason researchers have often seen carnival as a social safety valve that allows participants to express deviant behavior occasionally so as to enable them to tolerate the normative rules otherwise. The ritualesque, as I see it, refers to those actions that are intended to have direct effects and consequences that will be maintained after the event itself is a memory. I am referring here to symbolic actions, undertaken with the intention of making a difference, causing a change. Ritual, as sacred ceremony, is the agent of transformation—rites of passage most famously, as well as healing rituals, religious ceremonies, and so on. Ritual is symbolic action that is considered by its adherents to be instrumental, not merely expressive. Likewise, the events that I am referring to as "ritualesque" are symbolic public actions that are enacted to cause social change, not merely performed as ends in themselves. A protest demonstration, a rally for a candidate, or the placing of a memorial at the site of a traffic fatality where alcohol was involved are all examples of ritualesque actions.

Figure 1.5. Young female, black participant embodies resistance at a *manifestation* in Paris, 2011

"Carnivalesque" and "ritualesque" are not oppositional terms. Carnival is capacious and may frequently include ritualesque dimensions. Likewise, ritualesque events often use carnivalesque elements to make their point, as in a Gay Pride celebration. The point is to distinguish these two aspects of public display, not to suggest that they are oppositional. Quite the opposite is true. The carnivalesque is often, but not necessarily, put to ritualesque purposes.

PROCESSION

Spontaneous shrines, rag wells, healing shrines, padlock bridges—all are forms of public ritualesque activities of which the focus is material culture. The material culture is stationary; the spectators come and go. Procession has its own special properties Here, the spectators are more or less stationary, while the procession passes by (Ashley 2001). In all cases of processions, public ritual, public votive offerings, and so on, it is important to do something, to be seen doing something, and to see evidence that something has been done. The visual and the performative are combined in these kinds of cultural actions. If one is participating in a parade, march, or procession, it is a journey with a specific route (often past significant sites to the purpose of the march) and a specific beginning and endpoint. If one is a spectator, one experiences the passing of the parade in a manner that may be intended to be understood narratively: Who leads the parade? How are the elements distributed throughout? Who or what culminates it? (Ashley 2001; see also Twycross 1996). Here, the moving through territory is of paramount importance. In Northern Ireland, for instance, parades are often viewed—and objected to—as "triumphal" occasions, claiming territory as British, though this is invariably denied by those who organize the parades.

* * *

While I acknowledge the innate and contextual differences of the many examples cited throughout this essay, at one level they all share a political dimension in that they all involve the taking, claiming, and use of public space as a right, an act of popular sovereignty and agency, regardless of the specific discourse, which may be thought to be apolitical by those expressing it. Often the event is for purely festive purposes, as when people flood the streets to celebrate a sports victory. Other times, these popular events share the basic trait of rituals—the use of expressive, symbolic activity to achieve instrumental ends. Many of these may not be sacred ceremonies per se, but share these characteristics as ritualesque occasions. Equally, certain events will share the characteristics of carnival, including inversion, mocking authority or ignoring it altogether, or celebrating taboo subjects. These dynamics may or may not be directly applied to social change. Often identifying the carnivalesque elements obscures the ritualesque qualities of an event (here again, I point to Pride Day celebrations; see also Bercé 1977, 65). Thus we move from a carnival/ritual binary to a continuum ranging from the carnivalesque to the ritualesque as a means of apprehending and comprehending the multiple modes of communication—hidden transcripts, anger masked as fun—used in public performances (Scott 1992). In doing so, we wish to acknowledge and respect peoples' serious intentions expressed in festivity and play.

REFERENCES

Allen, Ray. 1999. "J'Ouvert in Brooklyn Carnival: Revitalizing Steel Pan and Ole Mas Traditions." *Western Folklore* 58 (3/4): 255–78. http://dx.doi.org/10.2307/1500461.

Ashley, Kathleen. 2001. "Introduction: The Moving Subjects of Processional Performance." In *Moving Subjects: Processional Performance in the Middle Ages and the Renaissance*, 7–34. Amsterdam: Rodopi.

Austin, J. L. 1962. *How to Do Things with Words*. Oxford: Clarendon.

Babcock, Barbara A. 1978. "Too Many, Too Few: Ritual Modes of Signification." *Semiotica* 23 (3/4): 291–302. http://dx.doi.org/10.1515/semi.1978.23.3-4.291.

Bakhtin, Mikhail. (Original work published 1965) 1984. *Rabelais and His World*. Trans. Helene Iswolsky. Bloomington: Indiana University Press.

Bercé, Yves-Marie. 1977. *Fête et révolte: Des mentaliés populaires du XVIe siècle*. Paris: Hachette.

Cohen, Abner. 1993. *Masquerade Politics: Explorations in the Structure of Urban Cultural Movements*. Berkeley: University of California Press.

Everett, Holly. 2002. *Roadside Crosses in Contemporary Memorial Culture*. Denton: University of North Texas Press.

Fabre, Daniel. (Original work published 1992) 2007. *Carnaval; ou, La fête à l'envers*. Paris: Gallimard.

Falassi, Alessandro. 2004. "The Masks, the Mist, and the Mirror: Carnevale in Venice, Italy." In *Carnival*, ed. Jane Kepp, 64–91. Seattle: University of Washington Press.

Haas, Kristin Ann. 1998. *Carried to the Wall: American Memory and the Vietnam Veterans Memorial*. Berkeley: University of California Press.

Le Roy Ladurie, Emmanuel. 1979. *Carnival in Romans*. New York: George Braziller.
MacAloon, John. 1984. *Rite, Drama, Festival, Spectacle: Rehearsals toward a Theory of Cultural Performance*. Philadelphia: ISHI.
Rappaport, Roy A. 1999. *Ritual and Religion in the Making of Humanity*. Cambridge: Cambridge University Press. http://dx.doi.org/10.1017/CBO9780511814686.
Santino, Jack. 2006. "Performative Commemoratives, Spontaneous Shrines, and the Public Memorialization of Death." In *Spontaneous Shrines and the Public Memorialization of Death*, ed. Jack Santino, 5–15. New York: Palgrave MacMillan. http://dx.doi.org/10.1007/978-1-137-12021-2_2.
Scott, James C. 1992. *Domination and the Arts of Resistance: Hidden Transcripts*. New Haven: Yale University Press.
Tokofsky, Peter. 2004. "Fastnacht in Basel, Switzerland: A Carnival of Contradictions." In *Carnival*, ed. Jane Kepp, 92–119. Seattle: University of Washington Press.
Twycross, Meg. 1996. *Festive Drama*. Cambridge: D. S. Brewer.

2

Locality, Spectacle, State Politics
Comparative Study of Carnival Traditions in Renaissance Nuremberg and Modern Trinidad

Samuel Kinser

MASKING, COSTUMING, AND PERFORMING ARTS HAVE rarely flowered as luxuriantly as in Trinidad Carnival in the twentieth century, the founding epoch for many of the spectacles dotting Caribbean diasporic communities in England and North America today.[1] A similar efflorescence of broadly participatory festive innovations, combining visual effects with great kinetic and dramatic variability, occurred during the same early springtime occasion of Carnival in western Europe. In Europe in the fifteenth century as in the Americas in the late nineteenth and early twentieth centuries, urban areas experiencing modest but stable growth expanded and innovated their Carnival traditions. Such was the case after the 1450s in Venice and Florence, in Dijon and Metz, in Hamburg and Nuremberg. Such was also the case after the 1870s in Salvador de Bahia, Brazil, and New Orleans, Louisiana, as well as in the capital of Trinidad, Port of Spain. Do common traits underlie the performative power in these two temporally and spatially distant, as well as ethnically contrasting, areas? If they do, what causes their augmentation or diminution? This essay outlines and explores three such traits in two locales in the above-named areas: Nuremberg between the 1450s and 1540s and Port of Spain during the course of the earlier twentieth century. This limited exploration, if its conclusions are sound, may offer a way of understanding why the festive arts cultivated in Carnival spread widely and enduringly in some cases and not in others.[2]

The traits that I shall consider can be phrased as porosity, spectacularization, and politico-social conciliation. The traits act in interlaced fashion to favor Carnival innovations in midsized stable communities whose population and ethnic makeup do not change dramatically and suddenly. Given these conditions, I offer three hypotheses. First, augmenting geographical and social contacts (here called porosity or receptivity to non-locally centered conditions) stimulates local self-awareness, which finds one outlet in carnivalesque games and inventions. Second, as the spectators for festivities like Carnival increase, revelers' self-representations move toward expressing their collectively shared fears, desires, and dreams in spectacularized modes. Third, state aims and the desires of different groups are always at odds in a complex society. When such dissonance is repressively disregarded or demagogically disguised as equivalent to perfect harmony, Carnival arts falter. Openly permitted and discussed, on the other hand, such disharmony between political calculations and socially segmented strivings engenders a tension that increases carnivalesque invention. Stated baldly in this fashion, these traits and hypotheses appear as little more than sociological truisms. They require historical clothes. In the two cases to be considered, the "clothes" not only illustrate but complicate the abstracting generalizations just made.

Choosing Nuremberg to test the effect of these traits on its Carnival tradition was easy to do because of this town's unusually varied and numerous sources of information. We know about artisan guilds' parades and merchant-elites' parading, about neighborhood-located skits and plays, and at least a little bit about informal masking games by unorganized individuals. Eighty lavishly illustrated manuscripts (*Schembartbücher*), the texts of over one hundred Carnival plays (*Fastnachtspiele*), and several hundred years of city council and police ordinances have been preserved and partially studied by historians, literary scholars, and folklorists for over two hundred years.[3]

Port of Spain's earlier twentieth-century Carnival sources are nearly as numerous, but they are not so well archived, nor have they been so repeatedly studied from different angles. Two kinds of sources are, however, available that offer information entirely absent in the case of Nuremberg. First, along with extensive contemporary newspaper commentaries, we possess photographs and phonograph records of contemporary music. And second, historians can imitate anthropological methods by going to the area, questioning participants, and even engaging in the festive arts being studied.[4] The chief features of those arts were and remain the following: first and foremost is massive masking and costuming prepared and practiced in fiercely competitive fashion by groups and individuals for many months before Fat Tuesday (Mardi Gras), and then displayed in parade after parade in streets and grandstand venues during the last two days of Carnival. Music making in a variety of genres is scarcely less important, ranging from purely percussive drumming to melodically and rhythmically complex orchestral effects played on steel barrelheads, not to mention a singing tradition blossoming from something like "playing the dozens" into calypso-competitive rhyme-songs, soca, chutney soca, rapso, and so on. From the very beginning of the festivity's elaboration—and today increasingly so—partying has been integrated with these costuming, parading, and music-making preparations for the climactic last two days. We know very little about anything analogous in Nuremberg to such Trinidadian semipublic, commercially encouraged party occasions for drinking, dancing, and fooling around, although such affairs must have existed.

POROSITY

In Port of Spain as in Nuremberg, expansion and innovation drew on familiar and popular urban modes of entertainment. The creators of new Carnival forms sought to please the many, not the elite or the officious few. In Nuremberg the Carnival plays and poems treated themes of sex and bodily functions (especially adultery and defecation) and of social pretension and exclusion (especially victimizing women, Jews, and peasants) with the complacent humor of shared prejudice. German literary scholars have shown parallels to such Carnival play themes in the genres called *Meistergesang* ([guild]master [competitive] singing) and *Spruchgedichte* (poeticized proverbial sayings). Enterprising authors like the barber and printer Hans Folz (1435–1513) and the cobbler poet Hans Sachs (1494–1576) began publishing such compositions, including in them their writing about Carnival. The common core of popular beliefs and feelings upon which Nuremberg's Carnival makers drew was a mélange of Christian and pre-Christian myths and legends, salted with the circumstances of contemporary life.

From the mid-nineteenth century onward, the maskers of Port of Spain's Carnivals had at hand many sorts of commercialized reiterations of traditional beliefs in newsprint, periodicals, and pulp literature. From the 1920s, radio and motion pictures added new types of popularization. The deep wells of mythology here were not only Euro-Christian but pan-African and naturalistic in tone; the most important makers of Trinidad's twentieth-century Carnival tradition were ex-slaves from many parts of that vast continent.

Slavery had been abolished in 1834 in Trinidad, but Africans—and later the indentured servants brought from India to replace their plantation labor—continued to suffer political, social, and economic inequality. So a double system of festivity also continued. Among colonial white elites,

Carnival retained European forms after 1834 as it had before. These groups imagined Carnival as an emanation from a would-be, should-be homogenous (although stratified by social class) society. Therefore, on Mardi Gras the rich and powerful might very properly celebrate their condition with banqueting and dancing while the colonized powerless should look on and strive little by little to imitate these superiors. But the African slaves who watched such self-congratulatory celebrations and later the ex-slaves who left such scenes behind had a different idea of Carnival; few among them entertained a homogenizing vision of the few leading the many. For them Carnival was a day of liberation, a moment to flourish their own version of life in this colonial place. As early as the 1850s a second kind of Carnival began to appear on Fat Tuesday in the central streets of Port of Spain to shock, disgust, and fascinate whatever white folk deigned to peer from balconies. In the barrack-yard habitations of the ex-slaves, drumming went on for weeks in preparation for Mardi Gras's eruption. Dramatic skits began to emerge as people developed their costuming into weirdly festooned devils and warriors, kings, queens, and clowns, throwing a strange light on colonial pretensions by means of their own dreams of collective power.[5]

This second festival, developing on the sidelines of the Carnival celebrated by French Creole elites and some members of the newer English ruling classes, was not only exuberant but outrageous in many of its fantasies. It was regularly condemned in the press and several aspects of it were outlawed in the 1880s and 1890s: nighttime drumming and parading with lighted torches (the so-called *canboulay* parades); street brawls between rival barrack-yard bands; one-against-one "stick-fighting" employing heavy baton-like weapons and accompanied by cadenced drumming; and obscenities associated with cross-dressing and costumes like that called *pisse-en-lit* ("piss-in-the-bed"; maskers exhibited wet nightgowns smeared with mustard).[6]

These repressive measures had two unexpected consequences. The first is that the French Creole class and an incipient middling "colored" class joined forces against those in church and state who were clamoring for entire suppression of the Carnival. The subsequently emergent, somewhat chastened Carnival created space for new inventions that launched it on its way to becoming a vehicle for nationalizing aspirations in the twentieth century; it became a day of both liberation and circumspect resistance for persons emanating from a diversity of classes and ethnicities. Second, although Port of Spain's twentieth-century Carnival advertised itself as multiethnic, multireligious, and multiclass in spirit, its practices identified it as an essentially Afro-American interpretation of the old European festivity. So the old fracture between two Carnivals, European-derived and African-derived, scarcely concealing a set of mutually developing racist preconceptions, has gradually been submerged, although certainly not entirely healed today.[7] This is due no doubt to Carnival's predominantly popular cultural rather than either elite-cultural or folk-cultural character.

By "popular cultural" I mean the primacy of oral over written and printed modes of communication in the elaboration of its forms. Popular culture, thus defined, arises from the exchange of expressions, bodily gestural no less than verbal, by people conducting their daily business in frequent face-to-face interaction with each other. Such daily business of course occurred in twentieth-century Port of Spain's black quarters, as in fifteenth-century Nuremberg's working-class quarters, amid some measure of contact with written messages. By the fourteenth century in Europe, as later in the Americas, official and elite classes increasingly communicated with each other in ways that gave primacy to written and later to printed modes of expression, although of course they also carried on their daily lives using oral and gestural communication.

These distinctions are relevant to the assessment of the three traits that I am comparing in Nuremberg and Port of Spain. Consider this alternative: does localized sentiment develop *versus* porosity, or is localism *reinforced* by regional and more-than-regional openness to Carnival traditions further afield? The two factors most directly influencing this alternative are the timing and effectiveness of education systems inculcating literacy (and hence openness to messages from afar) and the legal systems sanctioning social class distinctions in largely written terms but largely unwritten enforcements, enforcements that nonetheless prevail by means of mostly non-written, custom-based behaviors. Nuremberg and Port of Spain both had programs of public education. But neither city had effective means of carrying out educational programs for all their citizens, nor were officials much interested in doing so during the time periods compared here. How many of the Nuremberg butchers, goldsmiths, or cutlery craftsmen who danced during Carnival in the marketplace were literate cannot even be guessed. The same is true of the Port of Spain maskers flooding the streets during the last days of Carnival. We can only assert this: Nuremberg dancers, maskers, and actors in neighborhood Carnival plays played with each other by means of a common language and affirmed the same social class system as the city's chief officers. Most of the early twentieth-century lower-class Afro-Trinidadian players in Carnival, however, spoke dialectal forms of English or French (the large majority of ex-slaves had come to Trinidad between the 1780s and 1810 from French-speaking islands) strongly influenced by underlying African languages of which their white superiors had little idea. Also unlike the Nuremberg artisans, most Afro-Trinidadians would never have imagined affirming wholeheartedly a social class system, sustained and enforced politically by British overlords, that made them automatically inferior because of their race and their past status as slaves. Why, then, did these two societies, distant not only in time and space but in ethno-politico-social disposition, nevertheless burgeon with similar popular cultural carnivalesque inventions during a similar short period of two to three generations?

Before attempting to answer that question by means of more detailed comparison of the two Carnivals' paths of invention, let me suggest that part of the overall similarity in those paths derives from the special nature of Carnival. Carnivalesque festivity contrasts with the orderly and ordering ceremonial gaiety that dominates large-gauged happy occasions like saints' days, coronations, and celebrations of nationhood. The essence of Carnival is rather to reformulate people's everyday experience in phantasmic, inversive, excessive forms. In this process of changing experience into something tangential or opposed to what is "normal," Carnivals succeed best when they utilize local experience: social and individual foibles, cultural sins and successes, political scandals, collective fortune good and bad. Local experience feeds Carnival's performative fantasies by means of the social dynamics that it displays in one-to-one or small-group encounters. Every Carnival habitué knows that the best moments in the festival occur during half-planned encounters, in confrontations and repartees that are sprinkled with wit, lubricated with inebriating substances, and broken open by unpredictable actions. These are the moments that one remembers, laughs over, and works into the performance skills that will brighten next year's holiday. Carnival is a set of traditions that are ever variable, not only because personnel varies from year to year and not only because the performers who come back annually get better at their roles, but also because the games people play retain, at their best, a maximum of improvisation exercised in predictably unpredictable circumstances. Local knowledge both stabilizes and destabilizes the careening games, for everyone has shared in the weaving of the fabric that is being wildly torn. Meaning and significance are dislocated but not destroyed. The repartee of challenge and response maintains commonly acknowledged parameters of form, even as these matters of common knowledge are pulled and pummeled into ever-unfinished permutations.[8]

The importance of local knowledge in stimulating richly inventive Carnival performance, and in audience understanding of that performance, is self-evident. Carnival requires people who share a universe of discourse, of everyday subjects and objects to toss back and forth. But how are these here-and-now features mixed with elements further distant in space and time? The contrast between Nuremberg's early modern and Port of Spain's modern times is easy to define in this respect. In the earlier period knowledge and its sharing traveled along short and narrowly conceived communicative lines, mostly face-to-face between artisans or commercial trading partners or ambulant clerics. But by the later eighteenth century communicative lines had stretched and multiplied. Pamphlets, broadsheets, newsletters, and books found ever-increasing numbers of readers. Today telephone, radio, television, and the now ubiquitous, doubly misleading appellation, "Face"-"Book" move "challenge" and "response" across continents. Expanded porosity in the nineteenth and twentieth centuries, multiplied as much by mechanized travel as by mechanized communication, has shredded localism ever more rapidly. In the fifteenth century the porosity of European locales increased greatly with the printing press, but the effects were still small compared to the situation four centuries later. Even in twentieth-century Trinidad, equipped with newspapers and railroads, most people's worlds of understanding were limited to a few neighboring villages or to a few neighborhoods in the case of the burgeoning capital, Port of Spain. Insofar as new media penetrated these places, they worked as stimulants to improvisatory invention rather than as sieves emptying Carnival of locally anchored meaning.

It is obvious that answering the question as to whether porosity stimulates or stifles localism demands time- and space-specific measures of change in order to move beyond such generalizations as those just made. To establish useful measures of change would require in turn estimating shifts in "climates of opinion," the controversial, easily mishandled Zeitgeist of German cultural-historical tradition. This cannot be established with any surety for early modern Nuremberg, where few individual voices commenting on Carnival are extant.[9] Even for twentieth-century Port of Spain we have only whiffs of opinion about changing conditions in hot spots of invention like the neighborhoods of Belmont, Laventille, East Dry River, or even in more middle- and upper-class areas.

With respect to the role of small-gauged but gradually loosening porosity, the remarkable parallelism between these two time-spaces subsists, although the gradually evolving sociopsychological specificities of this parallelism cannot be unraveled. In the short space of two generations there appeared a galaxy of new ways to "play Carnival" across previously isolating social class boundaries. As we will see, there are parallels as well in the use and meaning of spectacle, and in the nature of state-political interventions.

NUREMBERG

In 1500 the city of Nuremberg was the third-largest urban agglomeration in Germany, following Cologne and Augsburg. About 40,000 citizens lived inside its walls; it dominated a surrounding hinterland of some 200 villages with an estimated additional population of 25,000. It is thought that 50 percent of the city population were artisanal families engaged in over fifty craft specialties. In 1561 a government table lists 1,370 artisans with master status. No useful statistics are available concerning artisans with nonmaster status, nor are there any for lower-class groups, these latter estimated as amounting to about 40 percent of the whole population. Forty-two families dominated politics, society, and cultural patronage. About 400 other "named" families (*die Genannten*) had some marriage ties to the forty-two-family patriciate, and some of them served in minor offices. These two upper-class groups amounted to between 6 and 8 percent of the total population. A city that began in the twelfth and thirteenth centuries as an urban center struggling to free itself from feudal power by acquiring privileges step by step from the German emperors had achieved status as a "free imperial city" with self-governing powers by the mid-fourteenth century. In the process its political makeup narrowed toward hereditary mercantile oligarchy. The shift away from a time of widely shared mercantile and artisanal political power was marked by a craftsmen's revolt in 1347–1349 against the domination in the city council by the town's richest merchants. The revolt was suppressed with the aid of the emperor's military forces, and the city council henceforth attempted to regulate citizen behavior more strictly, in moral as well as physical ways. Official records include recurrent denunciations by the council of alleged "improper" or "dishonest" conduct by persons or groups.

City council records before 1450 have been lost, whether by fire or malfeasance, but local chronicles report that from 1377 the city paid its official fifers and drummers to play for the dance of butchers in Carnival. By the late fifteenth century city historians asserted that the butchers' thus-favored role was due to their loyalty to the city council during the artisans' revolt. Whether this interpretation was legendary or true, the necessary prominence of meat provisioners during Carnival is self-evident (a prominence found in many parts of Europe), and this government largess was maintained until the 1470s. At that time there was a significant expansion in carnivalesque activities—expansion, but not change in the fundamental forms long used. Thus, for example, although precise documentation cannot establish it, most students of this Carnival date the earliest neighborhood theatrical pieces (Fastnachtspiele) no later than the

1390s, but a few references to current events suggest that the heyday of Fastnachtspiele was 1470 to 1510. Masking, running in and out of houses without permission, throwing ashes and feathers provoked city council prohibitions in 1434, 1469, 1477, and 1495. These activities were common across Europe from the thirteenth century, along with the custom of accosting strangers with requests for money or comestibles (a widespread custom that in Carnival scholarship is often called *quête*, or "questing"). Do the council's repeated denunciations indicate that such activities intensified in the period chiefly studied in this chapter, 1450–1540? Artisans certainly began dancing in occupational groups before the governmentally favored butchers secured semiofficial status for their Carnival dance in the mid-fifteenth century, but this favoritism perhaps stimulated competition by other occupations to develop dancing parades. Post-1450 documents show four other groups in addition to the butchers parading now and then with government permission: cutlery makers, drapers, cabinet makers, and metal workers.[10]

The sixteenth-century Schembartbücher (masking books) illustrate the probable appearance of the butchers' dance in the 1450s. In them one sees not only the city-employed fifers but four animal figures and a structure like a Christmas tree with glistening mirror-like ornaments (see figure 2.1).[11]

The dancers, arranged in an elliptically interweaving circle in a large open space, which is probably the town's marketplace, hold their place in the circle by means of rounded leather rings that perhaps evoked their sausage-making. The ensemble evinces a homely collective spirit, a small-town warmth and jollity that the city council found worthy of emphasizing. Repeated entries in city council minutes emphasize the obligation of all masters in the butchers' trade to participate, and one such official entry mentions rewarding the dancers with donuts and wine at city hall.

Insofar as one can estimate a matter as inchoate and shifting as public opinion, it seems that Nuremberg elites were proud of their widely known artists and intellectuals, such as Albrecht Dürer and Willibald Pirckheimer. But they were perhaps even more proud of Nuremberg's artisan renown because it affected their prestige and prosperity directly. Like other such urban elites across Europe, members of the governing elite made much of their money from international trade. But it was the skill of metal workers in making armor and cutlery as well as the skill of cabinet makers and print makers that etched Nuremberg's special fame. The poetic endeavors of the shoemaker and *Meistersinger* Hans Sachs have something to do with this long tradition of prideful support of craftsmanship, a tradition contrasting strongly with that of Venice, Nuremberg's nearby rival in urban Carnival

Figure 2.1. Butchers' dance in 1449(?), Schembart book, State and University Library, Hamburg

expansion during the later fifteenth and sixteenth centuries. In Venice a more aristocratic bent in social and political customs and institutions was beginning at this very time to stifle Carnival's popular aspects.[12] Hans Sachs, like his artisan predecessor Hans Folz, wrote Carnival plays and published them during the century of expansion after 1450; they are works written with a few exceptions in a spirit of easygoing, humorous moralism. It seems likely that some of Sachs's pungent songs and easy rhyming lines were sung and spoken in the streets during Carnival.

What, then, was the general import of carnivalesque expansion after 1450, if the genres of expression remained largely the same? Expansion meant more people gathering here and there to produce more disorder, and that was an abomination in the eyes of the vigilant oligarchy, as they emphasized in the reprimand of 1469 mentioned earlier. After prohibiting fireworks, masking, and throwing actions, this edict primly concluded: "In the last Carnival various people used lightheaded, luxurious, immodest, impolite words and gestures both in plays and rhymes [*spil- und reymensweise*], not only inside houses, but elsewhere, both day and night. Such behavior is . . . sinful, annoying, and shameful."[13]

Such earnest entreaties and blanket prohibitions proved worse than useless because they were contradicted by the council's swerving policies. In 1482 it gave permission to everyone to mask as they wished on Fat Tuesday. But in 1483 it granted the leaders of a group of twelve the right to parade, but only without masks and only using "proper" rhymed verses (*zuchtig Reimen*). Again in 1511 it permitted one named group to go inside houses with masks on, but in 1512 an unidentified miscellany of youthful Carnival players (*die Bursen*), on the other hand, were forbidden to use masks and costumes when they conducted quêtes from house to house.[14]

The government wanted order and control, but in such a manner that Carnival could go on accommodating those who behaved modestly and politely. Those on whose conduct the council thought that it could most count were members of a group made up of none other than sons of the ruling caste. Perhaps as early as the 1450s and certainly by the 1470s these elite young men began parading together in rivalry with artisan groups like the butcher dancers. They called themselves "masked runners" (*Schembartlaüfer*). The name is first officially documented in 1475, when it is used in a familiar, commonplace way, so the group must have begun using it before that date.[15]

Its appearance accompanied that of other new formations. In 1476 "the honorable council allowed thirteen groups to run," that is, to parade across the central marketplace and perhaps to move through associated areas. This is a previously unheard-of number of permitted parades. It may have had to do with a new device introduced the year before by the Schembart group, a so-called hell (*Hölle*) that for that year had the shape of a dragon and was pulled across the marketplace on sled runners. Green in color, it is shown in the colored Schembart book manuscripts with a long red tongue from which fireworks erupted sporadically. Such a newfangled spectacle certainly drew new crowds and perhaps stimulated new groups to organize. By the late 1480s the Schembart group paid a fee to the butchers for the right to precede them in their parade. The starring role in the marketplace parades had by then been entirely usurped by these young men with their gleaming, costly costumes (see figure 2.2).[16]

Wearing masks molded to show sweetly bland expressions, twelve or more of them, depending on the year of the parade, followed a leader (*Hauptmann*) in similar costumes, carrying long pikes made entirely of wood instead of being tipped with iron (a city antiviolence regulation) and waving a bundle of bushy evergreen twigs out of which came intermittent bursts of gunpowder. Jingling bells girdled waist and knees. The declining attractiveness of the butchers and other guild dancers was accelerated in

Figure 2.2. Schembart leader, 1488, Schembart book, State and University Library, Hamburg.

the 1490s through the 1520s by increasingly elaborate hell constructions: dragons appeared again in 1507 and 1511, but then more dreadful monsters emerged in the form of giants devouring little children (*Kinderfresser*) in 1508, 1516, and 1522. Castle towers appeared, only to be besieged and burned in the marketplace for the delectation of spectators, once in 1493, twice during three consecutive days of Carnival in 1495, again in 1496, and finally in 1504. Fools began to sprout in the hells, especially after publication in 1494 of Sebastian Brant's famous book, *Ship of Fools*: they pranced about, sometimes on ships and sometimes in towers, in 1496, 1504, 1506, 1513, and finally, most explosively, in 1539.

Nuremberg Carnival after 1480 continued to be heterogeneous and multifaceted socially and culturally. Carnival plays continued to flourish; unauthorized masking and importunate quêting continued to trouble the council. But Nuremberg now had a centering spectacle, a big show with three facets: gorgeous costumes, the extraordinary hells, and a steadily expanding repertoire of masking figures. Until the 1480s few costumed players are named in the sources except "wildmen." In 1479, however, persons dressed as peasants, Moors, and old women were noted. Wildmen emerged in many forms, not just as hairy giants carrying off little puppet children or peasant-clothed mannequins. They were all developed by the Schembart runners: a goat-horned, bird-beaked, furry-skinned creature with ordinary hands carrying a wooden box with a miniature replica of itself/himself fighting an old woman; a pig-headed figure whose furry clothing reached to bare human knees, cradling in his arms an ordinarily clothed child of five or six; a stork-headed figure also costumed in skins with the fur turned outward, exhibiting naked drooping breasts and naked legs below the knees.

Figuration expanded luxuriantly, especially in 1504 and 1518, to the point where such characters must have paraded almost independently from the dances of artisans and from the pageantry surrounding the hells. Each of the figures just described as well as those mentioned below received in the Schembart books an independent page like that shown in figure 2.2, with coats of arms at the base to indicate the claims to patrician ancestry of the annually changed leaders.[17] A man clothed entirely in evergreen boughs with nuts attached, another covered with playing cards or dice to gaily satirize the popularity of games of chance, a woman grimly bent forward with the weight of a basket on her back in which a man screams piteously for help, dancing peasants, prancing Moors: these characters offered material for social reflection as well as for folktale dreaming. They were the culmination of Nuremberg's Carnival tradition, and in terms of cultural invention the costuming verve displayed in them was the tradition's most signal quality, for it showed a move away from spectacles as self-expression toward spectacle as the mirror of fears and desires, whimsical projections of half-conscious thoughts.

The glittering costumes and constructions of the men who first created a central focus for Carnival and then expanded upon it, overshadowing the neighborhood plays and the helter-skelter quêtes and masking, served to dissipate the self-centering vindication of "you" encountering "me." Representations of personal engagement were being replaced by shimmering reflections of interiority. "We" as communally bound persons, as represented in our occupational attachments and in our genealogically engendered security, began supplementing these bonds. "We" began chasing our dreams.

The operator of this specular change was the shared experience of assured prosperity—three, four, or five generations of it among the upper class, and among artisans just as much time in a steadily maturing interregional guild system. It was a system that fed artisans well and surely underlay their support for the merchant-led regime. The annual changes in Schembart costumes from the 1480s onward, like their approximately biennial constructions and conflagrations of costly hells, advertised the assurance of youthful merchants that they would surely inherit their fathers' preeminence. The blandly sweet facial masks chosen for their costumes in the 1480s express to perfection this assumption. If any voices were raised at the time to question this conspicuous consumption, their voices have not reached us—with one strange exception, since it comes from a group playing a Carnival game of potlatch excess similar to that which the Schembart runners had played against the butchers.

Imagine the shock to the Schembart entrepreneurs when in 1507 a group of seven Walloon ("Welschen" or "Weschen," depending on the manuscript) merchants in the city mounted a masquerade that in terms of wealth and magnificence outshone anything that they had done. The presence of these Walloons can probably be explained by the fact that they came from the French-speaking part of a region governed in 1507 by the Hapsburg emperor Maximilian as Duke of Burgundy.[18] Maximilian was also lord of Nuremberg, since it was one of the "free imperial cities" under his direct suzerainty, and he had visited Nuremberg on several occasions. Commercial relations with the Burgundian area probably flourished because of this political connection. Certainly if the Walloons in question were familiar with affairs at the imperial court they knew, as any educated Nuremberger would have known, about this emperor's concern with the Turkish suzerain's growing power in the Balkans, moving in the direction of Maximilian's domains in Austria, which were little more than 100 miles southeast of Nuremberg. And now on Fastnacht in 1507 there appeared at the very gate of Nuremberg "a great Turkish Emperor" clothed in "gold, satin and silks" that were fashioned in a "Turkish way." He was followed into the city by sixty Turkish "servants" dressed with similar magnificence; they carried long pikes, presumably made only of wood like those allowed to Schembart runners. Then came horses pulling trunks full of gold rings, jewels, and precious Oriental bolts of cloth. They moved to the sound of loud drumming across the marketplace to city hall, where they were received with all honor by city councilmen (whether by all or by only a few is unclear), to the consternation of the anonymous Schembart reporter whose description of this event is the only account that has survived. Not only were these Turkish maskers received with reverent bows by the councilors and invited to display their magnificence on tapestry-covered tables, the councilors chatted with them during "a whole hour."[19]

The laws of Nuremberg forbade anyone to mask without permission of the council. Yet this company marched in without warning just at the time when the Schembart runners were gathering for their parade. One of the Schembart leaders boldly went to them as they were packing up their display—to them, let us note, not to members of the council—and demanded on what authority they had appeared there, usurping the Schembarts' place. Instead of answering, so this Schembart report implies, they turned and gathered together to defend themselves. The Schembart runners, sensing their inferior numbers vis-à-vis that array, retired to a nearby house that seems to have been one of their regular gathering places. There they waited until "wildmen" had "opened up some space" and had gathered together before bursting out to attack the Turkish maskers.[20]

The ensuing riot went on for most of the day all across the city. The Schembart reporter ran here and there, observing, fighting, offering stereotypes: "There are seven Walloons among them"; "They have no heart, the wildmen are running forward." "The Honorable Council [*Ehrbare Rat*: the usual way to refer to the city council] became furious with the Schembart," and one councilman even struck the reporter on the ankle, but he fought on. "They yelled at me 'the Schembart are nothing but useless wretches, [they are] doing wrong to good people!'" Nuremberg's Carnival players made a fine day of it, shouting, cursing, running, pushing, pulling, and punching, while neither the city militia nor the numerous guildsmen, neither wildmen nor Schembart men, seems to have been able or willing to quell the uproar. No one was killed, and no one was reported as seriously hurt. A few of the Schembart men, but none of the Walloon party, were arrested and sentenced to three days in jail, but then "by grace" were excused by the Honorable Council without undergoing imprisonment. Nonetheless, writes the reporter, concluding his story as a good Schembart should, "those masquerading as Turks did so without the Honorable Council being informed about it beforehand."[21]

Worse was to come for the Schembart runners. After 1524 the city council, yielding to the sharp criticism of Carnival by Lutheran ministers in

Locality, Spectacle, State Politics

Figure 2.3. Schembart hell, 1539, Schembart book, Universitätsbibliothek Kiel

the city led by Andreas Osiander, no longer permitted the Schembart parade. The suspension continued until 1538. Some Carnival plays and the butchers' dance continued in this turbulent period, during which Lutheranism gained ground in Nuremberg and across Germany, but texts of the plays have not survived.[22] There is only one mention in surviving council minutes of the butchers' dance and no mention of the donuts and wine that used to be offered to them at city hall to honor their preparations and performance. But then in 1539, for reasons that have never been documentarily established, the Schembart maskers as well as the butchers were permitted to parade again. What the Schembart maskers then prepared and performed was fatal to their way of celebrating Carnival.

Enthusiasm was high. According to some Schembart books, 150 butchers performed their dance, no doubt including many who had retired during the intervening fifteen years since their last performance in 1524. In an illustration of the performance, fifteen wildmen and ten devils can be seen among some 120 paraders.[23] The devils and a grand number of fools are milling about a large ship on wheels, recalling the ship of fools displayed long ago in 1506, and harking back to Sebastian Brant's famous book of 1494. A preacher stands on deck in black costume next to the mast, adjacent to which a fool holds up not the sacred Bible but what the Schembart books call a "board game" (*pred spiel*). It is configured like a present-day backgammon board, the sort of dicing game pastime in which people indulged without fear of official repression during Carnival. There was no mistaking this figure; it was none other than the Lutheran leader Andreas Osiander. In some illustrations of the scene it is not a fool but a grinning devil who presents to the preacher this anything but holy object.

The Schembart players were apparently evenhanded in their mockery. In some copies of Schembart books, this ship of fools makes reference with equal iconographic verve to one of the Protestants' favorite objects of satire, the power attributed to Catholic priests to influence people's access to heaven. On the masthead of the ship hangs an image of keys, a symbol of the Catholic Church's alleged possession of "the power of the keys," that is, its sacramental control of the gates of heaven and hell.[24] This lighthearted carnivalesque manner of satirizing extremists in the religious dissensions dividing Nurembergers was lost, predictably enough, on many witnesses of the parade. A mob stormed out of the marketplace to attack Osiander's house (but not, it seems, to attack any Catholic theologian). Although, as in the 1507 riot, no one was killed or seriously injured, the city council promptly outlawed the Schembart parades.

In 1540 the city council declined to allow performance of the butcher dance, but invited them to come and enjoy donuts "in accord with old custom." The council in this ruling made no mention of the previous year's Osiander uproar. Butcher dances are intermittently recorded up to 1570, and the sword dance executed by the cutlery guild was also performed from time to time. But the imaginative and costly displays, the parading and occasional riotous uproars implying widespread popular participation apparently all disappeared after 1539.

Two divergent segments of Nuremberg opinion found an outlet in the bold allegories of 1539. Both segments had begun accumulating resentment at the Protestant offensives in the town even before Osiander's arrival in 1522. On one hand were the young patricians who chiefly resented repression of their free-flowing, wide-ranging annual exhibition. On the other was popular middle- and lower-class dislike of the new moralism, intent on banning board games and every other kind of foolishness that found free play once a year in Carnival. Neither of these segments of opinion could satisfy the doctrinal stalwarts who wanted elimination of anything without biblical authority, such as Lenten fasting. But eliminating Lent should mean also eliminating Carnival, in the opinion of these Protestants opposed to both the aforesaid easygoing segments of opinion, both of them concerned to conserve an old and enjoyable tradition, however morally questionable.

The city council, which had tried to strike an enduring balance by banning extremists like the Anabaptists from Nuremberg in August 1525, did not achieve its goal, but the councilors did not entirely abandon this ideal.

That the riot victimizing Osiander in 1539 was easily quelled reflects the continuing ascendancy of middle-of-the-roaders among the political elite. These probably included many of the Schembart participants, as already revealed by their avoidance of accusations of the city council in the case of the riot of 1507. Consider the consequences of that riot compared to what action was taken in 1539. When in the Carnival of 1507 the "Turks" marched in, paying no attention to the people gathering in the marketplace to watch the butchers, wildmen, and assorted other maskers in the Schembart presentations, they marched straight to the agents of power at city hall. And the city councilors responded to this appeal to their entwined economic and political interests, letting lapse a network of legalities (no masking without permission, no marching, no bearing of arms, no overluxurious display of riches, etc.) designed to hold their own subjects—but not their trading partners—within bounds. The Schembart players understood this. They did not go to the councilors to assert legalities but instead went up to the offending Walloons and picked a fight. And the Schembart players were rewarded for this sidestep. Their rioters were given no jail time and the Schembarts received permission for their parade the very next year. A magnificent new hell was built and burned, constructed no doubt in the most sensational manner to prove that after all they were the very best at Carnival.[25]

Yes, the "Turks" played Carnival marvelously in that year of 1507, displaying mercantile magnificence in harmony with dreamy politics. Council members standing on the city square clapped their hands, whatever their real opinions, and the Schembarts subsequently vented their spleen in side streets without serious consequences. It was safe to do so in 1507; the Turkish sultan Bayazet II was not at that time pursuing his predecessor's march up through the Balkans. What, then, prompted the city council in 1539 to change its policy of orderly compromise, a change that proved to herald the end of the era of expanding Carnival invention in Nuremberg? Something—in fact, two things—slipped out of control between 1507 and 1539. In the opinion of the city's political elite, the amiable jousts previously conducted between popular demands and state supervision could no longer be maintained in the case of Carnival. Bayazet had been replaced by Suleiman the Magnificent and in 1529 his army began a siege of Vienna. It was no longer amusing to imagine Turks arriving with silks and gems in the Nuremberg marketplace to offer congenial trading relations. Emperor Maximilian, meanwhile, had been replaced by Emperor Charles V, his grandson, who was a conscientious Catholic determined to quell the religious dissent stimulated by Luther's followers. His army was not far away, and he had a permanent castle in the city. The militias being organized since 1530 by emergent Protestant princes were also nearby, gathering strength to defend their occasional confiscations of Catholic properties by means of a new alliance, the so-called Smalkaldic League. Thus the porosity of this city to grandiose and growing foreign forces had increased dramatically at the same time as internally destabilizing religious dissent rocked and split local opinion. The council's compromising attitude to Carnival spectacles had become too dangerous to the city's social and political elites. No more Schembart satires, however seemingly evenhanded in their depiction of dissent, could be permitted in the marketplace.

PORT OF SPAIN

Unlike my procedure in describing Nuremberg's Carnival expansions, I shall proceed in a less documentarily specific way in the case of Port of Spain because development of the African underclasses' different aesthetic, religious, and ethnic presuppositions into Trinidad's musico-dancing and costuming arrays is not, and could not be, documentable in step-by-step or person-place ways. This development took place in oral-gestural, person-to-person, and neighborhood-bound ways. There were no literate and interested observers on hand. The few outsiders who took note of what was happening in Trinidad's Carnivals before the twentieth century had little interest in the intricate features of their genesis and production. The few insiders—upper-class residents of Port of Spain, for example, like those staring and sneering at parading blacks below their balconies in Melton Prior's great 1888 engraving—wanted to have nothing to do with Afro-Trinidadians except to see that they did their work and behaved properly.

The refusal to recognize, let alone to accept, non-Europeans as part of one polity endured for at least two generations after 1834, the date of juridical emancipation of the slaves. Afro-Trinidadians, East Indians, Chinese, and other non-European ethnic fractions were not seen as equal political and social partners in a society exclusively ruled by the British upper class and the descendants of French and Spanish Creole governors. Given this situation, it was inevitable that the basic social cleavage outlined at the beginning of this chapter—between Euro-Trinidadian and Afro-Trinidadian—continued to dominate Carnival merrymaking for a long time. Upper-class Euro-Trinidadians held on to elite customs centered on elegant balls and fancy dress, imitating their slave-holding ancestors. Everyone else used the popular cultural, Afro-Trinidadian street-centered displays to create self-affirming, nonexclusive forms that proved to be not only embracing and inventive but reconciling, even among parts of the upper classes, who were gradually becoming ethnically mixed. Two important turning points can be distinguished in this roiling, disjointed development, the first around the beginning of the twentieth century and the second in the 1950s and 1960s as political independence from Great Britain became a reality.

During the first decades after slavery ended, African traditions of drumming, parading, and stick-fighting were adapted to carnivalesque street play and backyard rivalries, in which fighting, costuming, and verbalizing prowess were equally prized. Although "canboulay" parades were suppressed in the 1880s, flamboyant group play and competition took ever-new forms. Meanwhile, an emergent middle class incorporating many ethnicities seized upon a politically diversifying public press to argue about how to make and keep Carnival respectable. Widening cultural porosity in the port city accompanied military and economic openings that brought to it sailors from all parts of the world. Public education for all began, which meant that Afro-Trinidadians, who had in most cases developed a French dialect during slavery, began around 1900 to communicate mainly in English.

The first calypso tent appeared in 1898. Rhyming rivalries in English emerged, set to drums and singsong syncopated rhythms, rivalries that were repeated day after day during the several-month Carnival season. The event was advertised, audiences were charged a tiny fee, and "coloreds" of middle-class status soon sought the tents. Minstrel-style singing also entered Carnival in the 1890s. In 1900 a businessman said to be a French Creole, one Ignatius Bodu, organized a different kind of competition, one among costumed, parading bands of revelers, at the downtown's main public space, Marine Square. The profitability of such exhibitions was immediately apparent; by 1911 they took a competitive form for cash prizes. Just as cowboy troupes in American circuses always included Amerindian counterheroes, so the Afro-Trinidadians did not fail to add "Wild Indians" to their parades from as early as the 1840s; by 1912 this masking genre had metamorphosed into half a dozen forms of rivalrous confrontation in the streets as well as in the mounting number of costume competitions.[26]

In the first two decades of the sixteenth century, as we noticed, applause for the spectacular hells produced by the Schembart players apparently had the side effect of creating an augmented set of folktale-tinged figures like the "child eater," "giant," and "acorn-man." In the two or three decades before World War I in Trinidad, the slow growth of grudging admiration for carnivalesque ingenuity and prowess among middle-class "coloreds," and even among some upper-middle-class whites, led to similar folktale-tinged multiplication.[27] Those visiting Trinidad Carnival today may see these elaborately costumed, verbosely gesticulating players only in special venues for "traditional characters": Midnight Robbers, Jab-Jab, Jab Molassi, Pierrot, Pierrot-Grenade, Bat, Beast, Dragon, Devil, Moko Jombie, Bad Behavior Sailor, King Sailor, Fancy Sailor, and so on.[28]

The politico-social significance of this panoply of characters, costumes, and song had already been affirmed in a San Fernando newspaper in 1881: Carnival is the only "national" festival because it is the only one that people can claim as their own (Brereton 1979, 172). World War I and the beginning of large-scale petroleum industrial investment with its concomitant labor organization heightened discontent with colonial rule and its exclusive elite. The main ingredients—ethnic, economic, and cultural—of a Trinidadian national identity, with Carnival as one of its signal expressions, were beginning to stir and mix by 1915.

The coming of independence from Great Britain arrived on a wave of repercussive movements of liberation throughout the world in the 1950s and 1960s, movements that stimulated a national élan among all Trinidadians, an opening wide of the nets of porous receptivity, far beyond anything that humanist and Reformation movements provided Nurembergians. The once secondary Carnival, enlivened by the characterological inventions of once-enslaved Afro-Trinidadians, was now the only Carnival of consequence. The Afro-Trinidadian political elite leading the nation after 1956 found eminently useful the Carnival's socially conciliatory, alliterative slogan, "All o' we is one." Thus, from very different although parallel beginnings, Nuremberg and Port of Spain commoners arrived at the same goal of centering Carnival on the provision of occasionally astonishing, always pleasurable transformations of everyday experiences to an ever-more dominant middle-class majority. In Nuremberg artisans and lower-class elements had played their plays, dreamed up their masks, sung their songs, and flung ashes and dust separately from the upper classes until the mid-fifteenth century. Then the wealthy Schembart group developed parades and costuming that pleased everyone. In the same way, first Trinidadian businessmen and later American companies (recording companies like Victor and Decca from the 1920s, Pan Am Airlines and Amoco Oil from the 1960s) invested in competitions that attracted participation from middle-class as well as lower-class social elements. Finally too—and here, more noticeably in Port of Spain than in Nuremberg—the Carnival fever touched the minds and hearts of highly trained artists well aware of international tastes and styles. Masking-group creators such as Harold Saldenha, George Bailey, Wayne Berkeley, and after 1970 Peter Minshall drew their ideas from the most heterogeneous and deep-lying layers of their nation's integrating culture.[29]

After many other nations' seamen had left their mark on carnivalesque imaginations, sailors from Port of Spain's nearby American naval base began to roam the capital in great numbers during and after World War II, producing almost immediately among Carnival maskers a series of exaggerated, mocking imitations: Bad Behavior Sailors, but then also King Sailors in glittering array, performing with their crew well-coordinated sea-weather weaving steps and drunkenly imitative ones. Soon appeared the Fireman character, who pretended to push with a metal rake imaginary coals into an imaginary ship's furnace (see fig. 2.4).[30] Sometimes the maskers adorned this masquerade (called "Sailor mas'") with a whole array of firemen, scarcely recognizable any longer as sailors in their dazzling costumes but still pushing with rakes down the middle of a street imaginary embers, while jostling and gesturing to sidewalk throngs.

As remarkable as the surreal imagination exhibited in the sailor bands is what seems to be an African-derived preoccupation with clashing colors and juxtaposed textures. Glittering beads and waving feathers adorn thickly woven, velvet-like black and indigo materials placed next to bright yellows and oranges. Figural contours, preeminent in European Carnival modeling, take second place to sensuous surfaces in this tradition.

Like the sailor bands, the calypso singers also developed new dimensions between the 1920s and 1950s. By the latter date a whole group of singers instead of one or two might stand in a row trading rhymed couplets in a witty "war" that produced high excitement among the listeners, who clapped hands and yelled encouragement. The singers adopted exotic names to accent their renown (Growler, Roaring Lion, Mighty Sparrow, Executor, Lord Kitchener). The tents became more expensive and expansive, record companies brought singers to and from New York for recording sessions and performances, the singers organized themselves into a self-governing association, and the competitions became part of the nationally promoted and governmentally supervised Port of Spain Carnival after 1956. Performers became more and more attentive to expanded audiences, finally becoming isolated star performers, so remote from their auditors that gestures and nearly acrobatic moves became as important as the words and the rhythm.[31]

Nothing is as important as rhythm when you move in great groups through the streets. The way that steel barrelhead drumming evolved into the third major aspect of Port of Spain's Carnival by the 1960s is a demonstration of this assertion. Drumming was limited in various ways by colonial authorities ever since its notorious use in the so-called Canboulay riots of the 1880s. But music makers found a way to circumvent the rules

Figure 2.4. Fireman from Sailor mas' band, Traditional Characters Competition, Port of Spain, 2002 (Photograph courtesy of Hélène Bellour, custodian, Jeffrey Chock Photography Archive)

with rhythmic beating on large biscuit tins and rhythmic pounding on street cobbles or bare earth with large bamboo logs. Then came World War II. The American naval base produced great quantities of fifty-gallon oil barrels during the war that were afterward discarded. All that was needed was

Figure 2.5. Lord Kitchener singing at financial complex, Port of Spain, 1980s (Photograph courtesy of Hélène Bellour, custodian, Jeffrey Chock Photography Archive)

to saw off the heads and pound them into assorted spaces and sizes. The impulse arose to put isolated tones in isolated spaces, for thus a tunable rhythm section could move through the streets. But drumming in groups, even done with the tinkling sound of steel drums, continued to be regarded as suspect because it so easily led to fights between the groups of impoverished, unemployed players. Then in 1962, building on the swell of interest all over the new nation in the emergent ensembles of these "steelpan" bands, the government wisely instituted a steel-band "Panorama" contest in the Queen's Park Savannah pavilion to serve as the climax of the Carnival, accompanying the final competition of masking groups (see fig. 2.6 and Bellour et al. 2002).[32] The government also then encouraged foreign companies to sponsor the steelpan bands, so as to offer the players money, regular spaces, or "panyards," in which to conduct practices, and uniforms.[33]

* * *

In this exploration of what common factors there might be in a short, two- to three-generational surge in sociocultural expansiveness among some well-known, long-lasting urban Carnivals, I have used the metaphor of a porous-like membrane that lets in some but not too many outside influences and does not let out, dilute, or dissolve much of a festive tradition's enduring features. A "healthy" Carnival maintains carefully restrained relations with potentially rivalrous neighbors and menacing overlords, filtering what it borrows as it goes along. Sooner or later, however, the filtering membrane starts to shred. The outside floods in, overturning a Carnival's integrity.

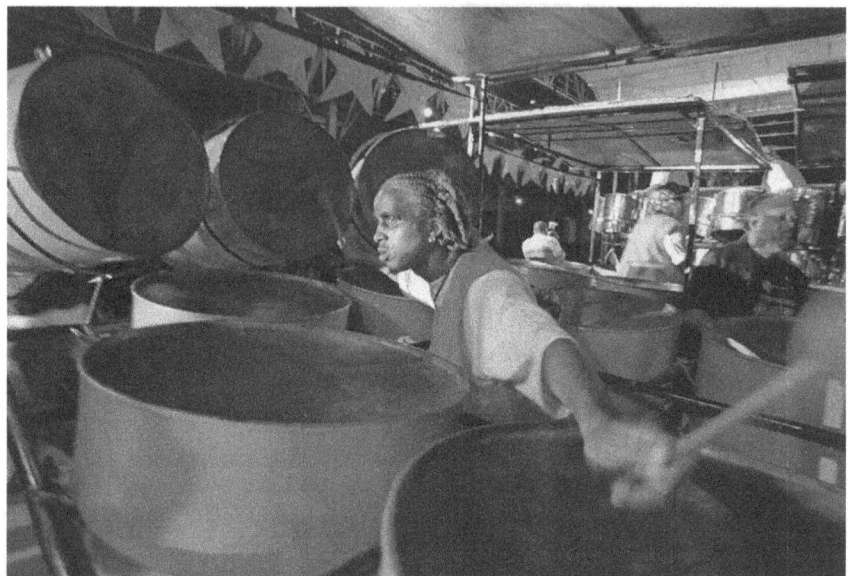

Figure 2.6. Steelpan player in his band, Panorama Competition, circa 2010 (Photograph courtesy of Hélène Bellour, custodian, Jeffrey Chock Photography Archive)

In Nuremberg the filtering nets were torn open by Reformation fervor and an international big-power politics that was rapidly ending the golden age of urban self-government in the later Middle Ages. In Port of Spain excess porosity has come from long-existing tendencies within the Carnival as much as from outside pressures, and has proceeded less precipitously. One of these tendencies is the receptivity to sensory values exhibited in the love of thickly mixed and often clashing (perhaps only to Euro-American eyes) colors, textures, and materials. This receptivity has been quickly accommodated by technological innovations that make the surfaces of costumes and the broadcasting of music ever bigger, louder, and of course also more expensive. The Carnival has become more spectacular because audiences have become larger in a spiral of reciprocal influence.

Thus in Trinidad hyper-technological solutions to the task of winning competitions before increasingly larger, louder, and more crowded audiences began asphyxiating the older modes of invention that between 1900 and 1930 had concentrated on making costumes and songs, rhythms and gestures in ever-more intricate and locally contextualized ways. At a cultural level, sexy, glittering costumes became less and less different from nightclub versions found any night of the week in London or New York, or in the grandiose Carnival finales in Rio or Nice. At the social level, by the

1960s and 1970s the change meant participants moved through the streets no longer on foot but on large flat-bed trucks equipped with food and drink for a now self-enclosing group above the sidewalk crowds. The occupants of the trucks all wore bikini costumes of little variation and danced as sexily as they could to blaring music from a sound system leading their procession. The idea, so it was said, was to protect these nice people from offensive interaction with drunks or worse, but the effect was to reduce the parades to boring repetition. These aims and maneuvers have continued to evolve since the 1970s in the same directions, with ever-greater technology and policing. So the middle classes' enduring anxieties about "security," at odds as always with the age-old Carnival desire for show-off "fun" in unanticipated encounters, reduce chances for the latter almost to zero. But the anxieties are right in line with state aims of such massive control that incident-free festivity can be guaranteed. Tension between state politics and social factions is reduced to whispers.

In spite of these tendencies, Port of Spain's Carnival, every year more widely advertised, increasingly imitated in Caribbean immigrant communities as well as in other Caribbean islands, continues to summon the imagination, producing around unlikely corners and out of sight new costuming, new gestures, and small tinkling and percussive sounds that astonish and delight. Can it be that this happens because of a sharply continuing mix and clash of ethnicities, with their residues of prejudice, their persistent sense of communal and neighborhood isolation, suspicion, and mutual dependence? I don't know. In another context I have called this unlikely inspiration in unlikely places a kind of "dreaming with others" (Kinser 1990, xv.) It is a kind of excited sharing with others of at first private dreams of reckless glory, an energy that then orients collective invention and carries a group along right up to its testing, rivalrous, and delighted enactment onstage or in the streets.

Carnival is particular among festivals, I suggested earlier, in its pursuit of a rule-free moment of joyful interaction. But of course the pursuit entails many unfree, dreary days spent in organizing, ruminating and reconsidering, arousing and settling conflicts, and practicing the skills necessary for perfect interaction. The three traits to which attention has been drawn in this essay are operators and facilitators of such dreaming and practice. They are exterior. They merely indicate on one hand the geohistorically accidental and incidental, and on the other hand the institutionally generic factors that channel and ignite certain groups to begin and then maintain over a long period this joyful collectivism. In Nuremberg and Port of Spain the period of preparation for the seventy-year eras of expansion was at least the hundred years preceding those eras. This too—this preparatory historical hesitancy, with its scarcely traceable moments of trial and error, its hidden circumstances of organization and production—should be cited as one of the traits prompting such expansions.

NOTES

1. No one has yet surveyed in historical detail the astonishing spread of Trinidad-style Carnivals in North America, the Caribbean islands, and Europe. In 1999 K. Nurse published a list of sixty-one such Carnivals in the course of a study looking at the relation of such "diasporic Caribbean Carnivals" to present-day "globalization" (2004, esp. 246–47; this article is a reformulation of his 1999 study). In 2006 I listed twenty-some Trinidad-style celebrations in the United States alone, emphasizing the diversity of their sociocultural origins and contexts (70–76; my list differs in details from Nurse's, and some of those that Nurse and I listed no longer exist).

2. Few broadly comparative scholarly studies of European Carnivals with Carnivals in the Americas have been made. Peter Burke's essay of 1996 (reprinted in 1997 with slight changes at the beginning and end) sketches a four-stage model of comparable historical development in the two areas: Europe from 1500 to 1900 and the Americas from 1800 to 1990 (Burke 1997, 159–61). My study is not so broad, limiting discussion to only two Carnival traditions that are more chronologically limited and geographically specific than Burke's comparisons. His four stages do not apply well to my chosen traditions, based as his stages are on assumptions of essentially unbroken cultural-historical development. One other comparative cross-cultural study should be mentioned, a study almost predicted by Burke when he suggests a developmental connection between Rio's twentieth-century Carnival and Nice's nineteenth-century mode of festivity: Ferreira 2013 derives Rio's Carnival not only from Nice but from Paris's nineteenth-century Carnivals. These studies, like mine here, treat Carnival only as performance. As Bakhtin 1968 has preeminently shown, the festivity can also be historicized, compared, and contrasted less as a date-and-place manifestation than as a "spirit," a "carnivalesque" spirit entering into many festive and nonfestive occasions, and expressed in many genres of literature and visual art.

3. The first reproductions from a Schembart manuscript were made in 1765. The Carnival plays were edited by Adelbert von Keller from 1853 to 1858. New editions of Keller's manuscript-based texts began in 2005 (Nöcker and Schuler 2009). City council minutes and police records were partially published by several researchers in the course of the twentieth century. E. Simon (2003) has published especially complete excerpts from such records pertaining to dramatic activities in Nuremberg, including much material touching on Carnival. Scholarly treatments of Nuremberg in this period, sociopolitically focused but including important sections on cultural affairs, have been published by Jeffrey Chipps Smith (1983), Gerald Strauss (1966), and Gerhard Pfeiffer (1971).

4. The summary that follows here as well as the materials in the section devoted to Port of Spain in this study derive in part from this opportunity for contemporary historians. I have visited the Port of Spain Carnival as well as Carnivals in other parts of Trinidad seven times in monthly or longer stays between 1996 and 2015. Understanding the material and experience thus acquired has depended above all on ongoing conversation and collaborative work with Hélène Bellour (see, e.g., Bellour and Kinser 2004). Bellour is the custodian of Jeffrey Chock's (d. 2013) photographic archive, an invaluable collection of Carnival forms,

Trinidadian customs, and daily realities. Other important students of Trinidadian Carnival are cited later in this essay. Trinidadians' unusually open-hearted reception to inquiries and interviews has also been essential to carrying out this work.

5. The classic visualization of the early appearance of this second Carnival is Melton Prior's engraving of an Afro-Trinidadian parade down Port of Spain's main business street, first published in the *Illustrated London News* in 1888 and since then republished in nearly every historically oriented study of this Carnival, including Cowley 1996 and Bellour and Kinser 2004. Barrack yards were narrowly partitioned rows of rooms ranged behind the city blocks with an open space awkwardly placed adjacently where dancing, drumming, fighting, and much else went on, in and out of Carnival.

6. See Brereton 2004, 58–61, for an equitable discussion of this still-controversial part of the development of Carnival in later nineteenth-century Port of Spain.

7. A second breach, that between the Afro-Trinidadian and East Indian–Trinidadian sense of festivities, including Carnival, has been harder to heal, although the relatively recent form of chutney soca music and the Carnival dancing parties where it is played has brought these two groups together in easeful circumstances. The important question of African–East Indian relations in Trinidad, including their divergent contributions to Carnival, must, regretfully, be omitted from this study.

8. The skills involved in executing on-the-spot improvisations have been explained and illustrated in exemplary terms by Martin Walsh (2004) and Jeffrey Chock (2004) in Riggio 2004. Both essays treat the Port of Spain group called the Paramin Blue Devils.

9. One such individual voice was that of Hans Sachs, who denounced Nuremberg's Carnival in pungent terms in 1540, both before and after participating in it by writing some Carnival plays. I have commented on Sachs' poem "A Conversation with Carnival about Her Characteristics" in Kinser 1986, 19–22; 1999, 68–70. Another one of these rare personal voices commenting on Nuremberg's Carnival tradition is treated later in this study. Of course, one can count the verbal and visual texts and pictures produced as records of Carnival performance as also comments on the festivity. But such records are only inferentially personal, having been adapted to anticipated audiences in ways derived from the modes of production peculiar to their genre.

10. Roller 1965 cites these artisanal participations after 1450, emphasizing in particular that the cutlery guild normally executed its sword dance only at seven-year intervals. The custom of periodic rather than yearly repetition of certain Carnival customs continues to be characteristic today in small-town European celebrations, where manpower and practice time for required roles have only become more difficult.

11. The illustration shown, Hamburg, Staats- and Universitätsbibliothek Cod. ms. 55b, fols. 10v–11r (manuscript dated circa 1650 in Roller 1965, 235), is available for viewing online. The alleged date of the depicted dance, said to be 1449, is questionable. See Roller 1965, 24. The illustrations in the roughly eighty Schembart book manuscripts, made at different times over more than two centuries (mid-sixteenth to late eighteenth), show differences in content as well as style. See note 24 for examples of such differences. Even the first Schembart books are thus thought to have been composed about one hundred years after the date ritually repeated in the manuscripts as the date of the first butcher dance.

12. Bertrand 2013 and Muir 1981 trace this shift in orientation of Venice's Carnival tradition, more attractive to tourists and longer enduring than the Carnival at Nuremberg, but also less hospitable to nonelite components.

13. Kinser 1986, 3–4, translates and interprets this denunciation. Simon 2003, 421, prints the whole German text.

14. Simon 2003, 427–28 and 440–41, cites these back-and-forth attempts at control.

15. How and exactly when were these Schembart runners given sanction to parade through the main public square or marketplace, eventually to precede the previously favored butchers? The answers to these questions have not been found, nor has the precise meaning of their name: *Schem-* (meaning "shadow," but also occasionally "mask," already found in thirteenth-century sources) plus *-bart* or *-part*, the contemporary Nuremberg mode of writing it (possibly meaning "beard," but this particle may be merely an adjectival suffix meaning "-like," so that "schembart" could mean "shadow-like" or "mask-like"). The suffix *-lauf* (run), often added in contemporary records to their name in order to refer to their performance (*Schembartlauf*), may indicate that their performance was considered, at least at first, as a short and swift parade rather than as a dance, although it must have soon included short halts, especially after the addition of the Hölle (hell) in 1475.

16. The illustration of a Schembart runner in 1488 is taken, like figure 2.1, from the Hamburg manuscript cited in note 11. The half-and-half decoration of his costume (often called *mi-parti* costuming) may have been an adaptation of the leggings worn by young men who were members of the Compagnie della Calza in Venice, whose costumes included decorations on the right leg. The Compagnie were associations of young men who organized balls, banquets, and other festivities during Carnival. If the costume seen here resulted from Nuremberg traders' acquaintance with the Carnival activities of the Compagnie, developed from the 1440s in Venice, it is a good example of how nonlocally circumscribed elite-cultural sensibility began to find entry into Nuremberg's popular cultural Carnival tradition. See Bertrand 2013, 69. The mi-parti mode of costuming was occasionally used by Schembart paraders for many years, as shown in illustrations in Roller 1965 and Sumberg 1941.

17. Are the blackamoor on the left and the self-admiring monkey on the right in figure 2.2 appropriately carnivalesque versions of authentic coats of arms? The question has not to my knowledge been investigated. One should keep in mind in any case that no painter has ever depicted what really happened with utter fidelity; compositional models always intervene. It is also well to keep in mind that, as mentioned in note 11, all Schembart manuscripts were illustrated many decades after the alleged dates. No manuscripts dated from before 1540 have been found. Verbal details accompanying the illustrations, however, indicate that at least some illustrator or illustrators had at some unknown time some oral source or even written notes, now lost, on which to rely.

18. Dialectal "Weschen" is "Welschen" in "educated" German; it has been used for centuries to refer to the Romance-language speakers bordering German areas to the west, that is, the Italians and the French. My translation of Welschen as Walloons, that is, as French-speaking Belgians living in the area called Burgundy in Maximilian's time, is based on the reasoning in this paragraph.

19. Sumberg 1941, 15–17, following up the work of earlier German scholars, has identified the author of this anonymous description, found in at least five Schembart manuscripts, as Pankraz Bernhaupt Schwenter (1481–1555), who was for many years master of ceremonies for the city council at patrician dances, weddings, and other functions. Schwenter also wrote and compiled local chronicles after his official retirement in 1547. He not only participated in the 1507 riot (at age twenty-six, before his employment by the city council) but was masked as a devil in the hell constructed in 1539, which is discussed below. He was thus an ardent and eventually long-term supporter of the group and its elegant, pretentious displays. His admiration of the Turkish group's masking invention is nonetheless offered without qualification: "Der gleichen Inn Nuernberg nieht gesehen wordten." I cite here and in following quotations Roller 1965, 218–19, following the orthography and punctuation found there.

20. "Ihr in Rauhen Kleidern" is the reporter's synonym for "wildmen," for "raw clothes" meant leather skins with the fur turned outward, as were worn by a number of the wildmen and wildwomen playing in Schembart parades: "Unnd Ihr in Rauhen Kleidern, Laufft zuvor math raum Under Dem Volckh, beharrt bis sie alle zusammen Khammen."

21. Mezger 1991, 40, reproduces a drawing of two Turkish maskers from Codex germ. 2083, fol. 330r, a drawing also shown in at least one other Schembart manuscript, according to Mezger 1991, 521n24. Are these two of the invasive maskers of 1507? As Mezger points out (41), Turks were a military threat to southeast Germany for over 200 years (circa 1480s–1680s). Turkish costuming has continued to appear in varied Carnivals to the present day.

22. See Simon 2003, 342, 443. The text of a school play called *Susanna* does survive, apparently performed circa 1530, but circumstances of presentation are not clear (313). The butcher dance was expressly permitted in 1536 (342).

23. The illustration used in this essay and discussed in this paragraph is taken from Kiel's Schembart book, which can also be viewed online (KB395, p. 189). It shows fewer devils and wildmen than the numbers I cite here in the text; those numbers derive from study of Ms. Nor. K.444 in Nuremberg's Stadtbibliothek, reproduced in color in Ayala and Boiteux 1988, 100.

24. Figure 2.3 shows the dangling keys. Authority for their presence also comes from an anonymous note inserted in the Vienna Nationalbibliothek manuscript of the Schembart runs, Ms. Ser. Nova 2977. Roller 1965, 207, prints this note, which describes how Osiander is mocked by a "fool" holding a "board game" up to him "as if [it were] a book," that is, mocking literal-minded Protestant insistence on fetishlike regard for a mere object, "the book," the Bible. Similarly, continues the note, there was a doctor with a urine bottle ("doctor mit einem harnglass") and above, hanging out of the crow's nest on the masthead, "hung a knavish doctor's [theologian's?] keys" ("hiengen doctor Wentzels schluessel"). Another manuscript shows a well-dressed man in the crow's nest manipulating a quadrant. A third shows a similarly well-dressed man holding in one hand a globe or celestial sphere—or is it a urine bottle?—and raising his other hand as if in instruction. Still other manuscripts show only jesters in the crow's nest who blow trumpets. Such variability lays stress on the need for a new and more detailed comparative study of the illustrations, since that should, among other things, make more probable the reconstruction of what happened in 1539. My decision to emphasize evenhanded mockery rather than simply anti-Protestant fervor does go against the dominant mode of interpreting what happened, but I think this interpretation has been overly swayed by the riot against Osiander alone (described in the following paragraph).

25. Aside from its comparative value, there is a second reason to describe in some detail the report of the so-called Scharmützel riot against pseudo-Turk maskers in 1507. Other extant evidence about Nuremberg Carnival in this era is either bureaucratic, like the city council's edicts, or designed for general dissemination, like the Fastnachtspiele, the poems and songs by Hans Sachs, and the words and illustrations in the Schembart books. But the Scharmützel report was, it seems, written out of a need to convey an intense experience, in which the expression of emotion played as important a role as the desire to represent the situation so as to justify the actions of the author and his Schembart friends. Admiration for the pseudo-Turks' display of wealthy costumes and accouterments and the conscientious reporting of the pseudo-Turks' insults (e.g., that the Schembart are "useless idlers") alternate with ill-concealed indignation at the city council's treatment of the Schembart. Finally, however, the author's sense of his group's dependency on continuing political favor overcomes his sense of indignation. The Schembarts were an elite group whose Carnival panache was inseparable from maintaining the sociopolitical status quo. So we have a voice here that tells us in personal terms how tension between state aims, social class differences, and festive

traditions was felt and acted upon. This is the kind of source material for which sociocultural historians always hope and rarely find. Commonplace sentiments about Carnival are sometimes made by characters in the Carnival plays, but such sentiments are inflected by the plays' traditions of theatrical representation and festive gaiety (see, e.g., Kinser 1986 on a play by Hans Folz concerning such thoughts about Carnival).

26. These references to the first of the two periods of expansion in Port of Spain's Carnival are taken from Anthony 1989; Bellour and Kinser 2004; Brereton 1979, 1981, 2004; Cowley 1996; D. Hill 1993.

27. Throughout the period there were some outreaching gestures, mostly by upper-middle-class whites who costumed themselves in historically grand European ways. "At a Queen's Park Oval pageant organized for the 1906 Carnival several small parties of well-to-do maskers wearing costumes of Greek, Roman, Louis XIV, and Victorian times, promenaded in decorated floats and carriages" (cited in E. Hill 1997, 95).

28. All these characters and others are defined in the "Trinidad Carnival Glossary" at the conclusion of Riggio 2004, 282–94, compiled by Carol Martin.

29. Minshall's international renown eventually resulted in his selection to design the staging of the opening and closing ceremonies of the 1996 Olympics in Atlanta, Georgia. Minshall went to London to study art in 1960 and found himself writing a thesis on stage design starring two of the Carnival's costumed transformations of Trinidadian life, Bat and Fancy Sailor. The way these characters were being reimagined in the 1950s and 1960s, Minshall declared in an interview, was "surreal" and gave him a point of departure. "Imagine a man coming down the street in Port of Spain, and where his head should be is a giant slice of paw paw [papaya], or a cash register with a drawer that actually works . . . I did not choose the mas'—it held me by the foot and pulled me in. Three weeks after that experience I met Elise Rondo. Put those two things together. I was finding myself. I was so proud to be from where I was. There was . . . an art that we knew how to make. We have a voice to add to the song of the universe" (quoted in Schechner and Riggio 1998, 174, 178). Minshall's pageants and individual costuming for Port of Spain are listed on 176–77. Like other Trinidadians, he refers to both on-the-street costuming and his grandstand pageants as "mas'"—"mask" or "Masque," with the final consonantal sound dropped, a Trinidadian convention.

30. See Chock 2006, for a dazzling photo of a firemen group in the streets (99) and a glittering King Sailor (38) and female King Sailor (see Chock's caption, 186) with a brightly colored phallic nose headdress, the latter with a "junior" King Sailor at her side (38), all undated. All the costumes have gold brocade accents. While colors and embroidery have steadily increased since the 1940s, basic structural components have persisted, especially the division of the costume into headdress, blouse, and wide-cuffed trousers.

31. See figure 2.5. Chock offers a wide variety of 1980s and 1990s calypsonians (58–62). I have chosen Chock's photograph of Lord Kitchener because this singer has conserved an older costume style (see, e.g., D. Hill 1993, 98) even while developing more showman antics.

32. E. Hill, 1997, unnumbered page following p. 52, reprints a 1965 photograph of a steelpan orchestra sponsored by Pan American Airlines showing these now large-scale orchestra-like bands in proper uniforms. Some steelpan bands eventually enjoyed sponsored foreign tours during noncarnival season.

33. The date is questionable because Bellour states (personal communication) that this undated, unlocalized photograph was "worked over" by Chock in 2010, but may have been first photographed earlier. The three illustrations of Trinidad used in this essay are all by Chock, who photographed the Carnival in the streets as well as in the grandstands, in the mud-mas' mornings of Jouvay and the corn-soup evenings of steelband practices during

thirty years (1980–2013). If there had been someone like Chock to record the realities of Nuremberg's Carnival, a lot of the observations made here would no doubt acquire a new brightness and perhaps a different weight and value.

REFERENCES

Anthony, Michael. 1989. *Parade of the Carnivals of Trinidad, 1839–1989.* Port of Spain: Circle.
Ayala, Pier Giovanni d', and Martine Boiteux, eds. 1988. *Carnavals et mascarades.* Paris: Bordas.
Bakhtin, Mikhail. 1968. *Rabelais and His World.* Cambridge, MA: MIT Press.
Bellour, Hélène, Jeffrey Chock, Kim Johnson, and Milla Riggio. 2002. *Renegades: The History of the Renegades Steel Orchestra of Trinidad and Tobago.* Oxford: Macmillan Education.
Bellour, Hélène, and Samuel Kinser. 2004. "Amerindian Masking in Trinidad's Carnival: The House of Black Elk in San Fernando." In *Carnival: Culture in Action—The Trinidad Experience,* ed. Milla Cozart Riggio, 129–45. New York: Routledge.
Bertrand, Gilles. 2013. *Histoire du carnaval de Venise: Xie–Xxie siècle.* Paris: Pygmalion.
Brereton, Bridget. 1979. *Race Relations in Colonial Trinidad, 1870–1900.* Cambridge: Cambridge University Press.
Brereton, Bridget. 1981. *A History of Modern Trinidad, 1783–1962.* Portsmouth, NH: Heinemann.
Brereton, Bridget. 2004. "The Trinidad Carnival in the Late Nineteenth Century." In *Carnival: Culture in Action—The Trinidad Experience,* ed. Milla Cozart Riggio, 53–63. New York: Routledge.
Burke, Peter. 1997. "The Translation of Culture: Carnival in Two or Three Worlds." In *Varieties of Cultural History,* ed. Peter Burke, 148–61. Ithaca: Cornell University Press.
Chock, Jeffrey. 2004. "Paramin Blue Devils." In *Carnival: Culture in Action—The Trinidad Experience,* ed. Milla Cozart Riggio, 157–61. New York: Routledge.
Chock, Jeffrey. 2006. *Trinidad Carnival: Photographs by Jeffrey Chock.* Trinidad and Tobago: Medianet.
Cowley, John. 1996. *Carnival, Canboulay and Calypso: Traditions in the Making.* Cambridge: Cambridge University Press.
Ferreira, Felipe. (Original work published 2005) 2013. *L'invention du carnaval au dix-neuvieme siècle.* Paris: L'Harmattan.
Hill, Donald R. 1993. *Calypso Calaloo: Early Carnival Music in Trinidad.* Gainesville: University Press of Florida.
Hill, Errol. (Original work published 1972) 1997. *The Trinidad Carnival: Mandate for a National Theatre.* London: New Beacon Books.
Kinser, Samuel. 1986. "Presentation and Representation: Carnival at Nuremberg, 1450–1550." *Representations (Berkeley, Calif.)* (13): 1–41. http://dx.doi.org/10.2307/2928492.
Kinser, Samuel. 1990. *Carnival, American Style: Mardi Gras at New Orleans and Mobile.* Chicago: University of Chicago Press.
Kinser, Samuel. 1999. "Why Is Carnival So Wild?" In *Carnival and the Carnivalesque: The Fool, the Reformer, the Wildman, and Others in Early Modern Theatre,* ed. Konrad Eisenbichler and Wim N. M. Hüsken, 43–87. Amsterdam: Rodopi.
Kinser, Samuel. 2006. "Mardi Gras and Carnival." In *Encyclopedia of American Holidays and National Days,* ed. Len Travers, 61–76. Westport, CT: Greenwood.
Mezger, Werner. 1991. *Narrenidee und Fastnachtbrauch: Studien zum Fortleben des Mittelalters in der Europäischen Festkultur.* Konstanz: University Publishing House.

Muir, Edward. 1981. *Civic Ritual in Renaissance Venice*. Princeton: Princeton University Press.
Nöcker, Rebekka, and Martina Schuler. 2009. "Überlieferung, Edition, Interpretation." In *Fastnachtspiele: Weltliches Schauspiel in Literarischen und Kulturellen Kontexten*, ed. Klaus Ridder, Rebekka Nöcker, and Martina Schuler, 363–80. Tübingen: Max Niemeyer. http://dx.doi.org/10.1515/9783110230178.6.363.
Nurse, Keith. 2004. "Globalization in Reverse: Diaspora and the Export of Trinidad Carnival." In *Carnival: Culture in Action—The Trinidad Experience*, ed. Milla Cozart Riggio, 245–54. New York: Routledge.
Pfeiffer, Gerhard, ed. 1971. *Nürnberg, Geschichte Einer Europäischen Stadt*. Munich: Beck.
Riggio, Milla Cozart, ed. 2004. *Carnival: Culture in Action—The Trinidad Experience*. New York: Routledge.
Roller, Hans Ulrich. 1965. *Der Nürnberger Schembartlauf; Studien zum Fest- und Maskenwesen des späten Mittelalters*. Tübingen: Tübinger Vereinigung für Volkskunde.
Schechner, Richard and Milla Cozart Riggio. 1998. "Peter Minshall: A Voice to Add to the Song of the Universe: An Interview." *Drama Review* 42 (3): 170–93. http://dx.doi.org/10.1162/105420498760308544.
Simon, Eckehard. 2003. *Die Anfänge des Weltlichen Deutschen Schauspiels, 1370–1530: Untersuchung und Dokumentation. Münchener Texte und Untersuchungen zur Deutschen Literatur des Mittelalters*. Tübingen: Max Niemeyer Verlag.
Smith, Jeffrey Chipps. 1983. *Nuremberg, a Renaissance City, 1500–1618*. Austin: University of Texas Press.
Strauss, Gerald. 1966. *Nuremberg in the Sixteenth Century*. New York: John Wiley & Sons.
Sumberg, Samuel. 1941. *The Nuremberg Schembart Carnival*. New York: Columbia University Press.
Walsh, Martin. 2004. "The Blue Devils of Paramin: Tradition and Improvisation in a Village Carnival Band." In *Carnival: Culture in Action—The Trinidad Experience*, ed. Milla Cozart Riggio, 146–56. New York: Routledge.

3

Conflict Displays in the Black Atlantic

Roger D. Abrahams

Wherever Africans and Europeans converged as the mercantile transatlantic world developed, a lively exchange of stylized forms of public display emerged. Not least of these were the costumed battles featuring stick-fighting, and others that called for improvised songs or speeches. Many festivities took place at the holidays marked by the Roman Catholic or Protestant church calendars. Using European customary practices as a baseline for describing these display events as they occurred in the New World, it is possible to see to just what extent African styles and practices entered into their new formulations.

In the anglophone sphere of the black New World, the most self-evident alterations revolve around the development of organizations which, because they were given warrior names and motives and carried out play battles, civic authorities worried would turn into rebellions. Ritualized confrontations at Christmas, carnival, midsummer, and the various harvest holidays are found throughout the black Atlantic, often showing contrasts to western European and trans-Mediterranean festive forms and practices. The calendar, in other words, may have been dictated by the colonizers' customary ritual celebrations, but the vocabulary of the practices is generated out of essentially African styles, especially in the areas of dress, song, dance, and competitive play. All of the dimensions of the aesthetic of the cool animate the events, So too are rites of passage, especially death and burial practices, infused with this aesthetic organization, under the otherwise repressive conditions of plantation slavery. In the form of voluntary self-help organizations that seize upon European holidays and make them their own, intimations of a black style of self-fashioning become clear. In the system of slave Sunday markets, which is found throughout the New World, slaves and free blacks were often drawn to the "plays" that arose after the selling occurred. During the slave holidays, which featured processional organizations "showing out" and contending with each other, a stylistic and moral consistency between African American enclaves is made manifest. In these activities, slaves discovered a number of ways of seizing liberties for themselves. An essential element of this African American style of festive forms is the number and intensity of song and dance competitions that erupt as costumed organizations from specific locales encounter each other, draw a line, and wage "war" creatively.

* * *

Black vernacular creativity thrives in commercial hub cities to which large ex-slave populations were drawn after emancipation. The pattern of African and European cultural blending, already in place during the plantation era, saw the abrupt growth of intensified cultural production in these borderland areas of jerry-built housing. Mutual assistance clubs and fraternal societies produced local lodges and clubs in which neighborhood pride came to be invoked. The voluntary organizations, the fraternal lodges, and secret societies emerged as commercial empires developed in the eighteenth century. City after city reports the plethora of lodges. As the great piano entertainer Jelly Roll Morton noted of his hometown during the late nineteenth and early twentieth century—the era in which jazz came into being—"Everybody in the city of New Orleans was always organization-minded." As Morton remembered of these celebrations:

> A dead man always belonged to several organizations, such as clubs, and secret orders. And every time one died . . . a big band turned out.
>
> Didn't he ramble, ramble,
>
> Rambled all around, in and out the town,
>
> Oh, didn't he ramble, ramble,
>
> He rambled till the butchers cut him down.
>
> When the band would start. . . they would play different . . . They'd have a second line behind 'em, . . . maybe a couple of blocks long, with broomsticks, baseball bats, and all forms of ammunition, we'd call it, to combat some of their foe when they come . . . to the dividing line . . . The band would get started. They'd hear the drums on the way back, they had boundary lines. The boys had knives, baseball bats, pickaxes, shovel handles, axe handles—everything in the form that they was supposed to try to win a battle. When they got to . . . a dividing line, which was not supposed to be their district, they'd better not cross . . . And sometimes they were beaten up . . . That's the way it always ended in New Orleans. (Morton 1938)

Such a skirmish characterizes the celebratory activities of similar neighborhood organizations throughout the greater Caribbean. Groups in conflict with each other, in fact, are one of the deepest and most important dimensions of black carnival. As in New Orleans, they are at the center of times of passage such as Mardi Gras and St. Joseph's Day as well as at funerals.

Also widely found if not quite so ubiquitous are the legions of warriors who sing of their heroes and who arrange and stage a ritual combat such as the New Orleans' *kalenda* stick-fighting. As the warriors in one local club confront one another under festive conditions, they have a stylized battle, sometimes in song, sometimes in speeches or, as recounted above, with actual chosen combatants. Indeed, in a number of areas, the duels have become so stylized that they achieve their own characteristic styles, as in kalenda, Brazilian *capoeira*, and the Congolese *imbare*.

When skirmishes occur in settings in which the group sings as well as fights, new kinds of combat songs are invented, often separated from the fight itself and held as song or speech competitions. By legend, the leaders were great warriors who danced with a stick or a wooden sword in their hands, while their followers chant the virtues of their chosen leader, their chief and their king. The songs celebrate bravery, social endurance, and personal judiciousness. These are not times of social abandon, but the very opposite—demonstration of a kind of social cohesion that goes beyond merely letting off steam.

The black Indians of New Orleans are among the best examples of how a set of warrior tropes and practices continues to make claims for the members of the club. The chief or king asserts his leadership and his virtue through his history of providing good judgment, as his predecessors in the Congo did. Becoming chief means that an individual has achieved note as a patron of his constituency, and for the moments of his yearly coronation he is endowed with charismatic leadership ability. Moreover, once so elected, he maintains his exalted rank for the rest of his active life.

The Mardi Gras Indians are black working-class groups who trace their origin to eighteenth-century Maroon communities in which Indians and Africans intermarried (Bilby 2005, personal communication, 2006). As do most of the New Orleans maskers, they participate in secret spiritual societies and social clubs. Fifteen or so tribes parade, chanting, singing, and beating percussion instruments. They are costumed in elaborate handmade outfits that they relate to the dress of Native Americans, complete with feathers, ornate beadwork, and enormous headdresses. Like the similar groups of the West Indies and Brazil, known as Wild Indians, they underscore their relations through the use of exquisite costuming. The songs of the Mardi

Gras Indian "gangs" celebrate acts of bravery and defiance ("We won't kneel down") as well as the proud heritage of the Indian nations, as in the signature songs like "Meet the Boys on the Battlefront." In fact, the old battlefield, the very spot where the Louisiana Superdome now sits, was a gathering spot for the Indians, as it was the place where "uptown" and "downtown" tribes encountered each other (Nicholas Spitzer, personal communication, 2006).

Similar clubs have been reported extensively, both in formal histories and by journalists and participants, in most other cities and towns within the black World (Mulvey 1976, 183–203). Moreover, the use of these clubs to achieve a place within a city or in some larger polity emerges in descriptions of New World urban life in cities, smaller towns and, for that matter, in frontier encampments wherever they sprang up. The costumes, songs, and processional movements all maintain Old World symbols and practices when deaths of members occur or during festivities connected to holidays regarded as special to the ethnic group. This is as true of African American organizations as it is of those of Irish, Scottish, German, or Italian Americans.

Such clubs, often operating as secret societies, are best known for their civic involvement, both as mutual benefit groups and as celebrants in civic celebrations. Between these groups and sisterhood organizations in the same vicinity, a putative second government was brought into being around calendared festivals and ritual activities.

Recent historical studies reveal that commercial development extended throughout coastal Africa as well as throughout the West (Kiddy 2005). At times of holiday, secret societies emerged from their lodges, joining others in processions, marking out their turf with festive abandon. While ethnic aid and benefit societies are relatively well known among yeoman workers of Germanic, Celtic, and Romance populations that emigrated from the Old World, the same cannot be said of the African enclaves in the New World. In the black Atlantic world, the existence of secret societies under slavery was thought to be controlled by the joined forces of the plantation and the metropolitan authorities. Thus, the story of African American attraction to the little-advertised secret organizations begins under the veil of their covert practices. Yet the persistence of such mutual aid and celebratory groups in even the poorest black neighborhoods in New World ports-of-call now begins to receive the attention it deserves, as their festive programs and religious practices have been brought to public notice through tourist productions.

These clubs, whether European American or African American, became all the more important as a means of bringing about the social and economic adjustments necessitated by the movement of large numbers of people seeking to better themselves. This was so with merchants and journeymen. Many of these organizations were maintained as burial societies, refugee relief groups, and civic associations intended to celebrate the variety of peoples to be found in commercial centers. They also organize recreation and celebratory events. (In New Orleans, they are called Social Aid and Pleasure Clubs.) Commonly, their public face in the community was developed in civic pageants and parades, events in which such groups could contend with others for what amounts to "best in show" in whatever form they chose to array themselves. However, while such competition is ostensibly open to all such groups in the liberal democracies of the New World, African American organizations are seldom given a place in the main show.

In these commercially driven parades and shows, city governments and chambers of commerce attempt to subordinate ethnic and class divisions within their borders. Yet scratching the surface of daily life in such communities inevitably reveals that class and color distinctions have always been in evidence. Elite organizations celebrate in an aldermanic manner on public holidays. Those who are regarded as socially marginal in the commercial life of the cities are seldom wholeheartedly invited to such celebrations unless through the intervention of local governments that seek to burnish their image to tourists. In New Orleans, as in many other cities that have become tourist centers, class and color distinctions are subordinated, apparently in the attempt to clean up the city's image and make its streets seem safe to outsiders.

Class and color differences have been translated into racial divides, in the past and the present, in the entrepôts to which African American ex-slaves were drawn. Throughout the black Atlantic, especially in the New World ports-of-call, African American voluntary societies arose partly in opposition to the socially exclusive color line, and in festivities these organizations often rehearse and express this opposition in resistance and derision performances. In actuality, even in the most open civic festivities, these groups are encouraged to have their own local celebration.

This division along grounds of class and race is characteristic of festivities throughout the Americas in towns in which there was a major ex-slave population. As Cuban Fernando Ortiz noticed of his native Havana: "This Afro-Cuban festival was the carnival of the negroes, and this should be taken [as] its true meaning. The blacks did not copy or imitate the carnival of the whites. Rather, both blacks and whites, as all peoples, have their own carnival, their loud orgy of festivity, firmly rooted in the popular mind, as rank, religious ritual withstands the action of time" (Ortiz 2001, 27).

Of course, in Havana the event emerges from the local social societies, the *cabildos*, many of which have self-consciously retained their Africanity. This is also true of the informal and voluntary neighborhood organizations of grassroots African Americans in cities as diverse as Buenos Aires and Port au Prince, in the smaller islands in the ex-colonial Caribbean, along the coast of the Gulf of Mexico, and throughout the North American seaboard. Many stylistic rules and different styles of weapon are maintained from the past, including in many places in which enslavement and the moments of emancipation are replayed, generally turned into contemporary events that have kept the social and economic situation in place. In songs and dances, rites of passage, healing ceremonies, and the observation of the holiday year, a felt opposition between African and European styles of enactment is clearly in evidence.

While New Orleans is perhaps the best-known hub of cultural inventions in the United States, there are many similarities between the culture of the Crescent City and other ports-of-call formed as a by-product of the plantation economy as it entered a decline. The urban outposts of the European empires might have sunk into the swamps and the sea, in line with the disappeared cities of Port Royal, Jamaica, and Nelson's Harbor in Nevis, but after emancipation, a good number of these entrepôts became magnet areas for ex-slaves who wanted no more of agriculture. Needless to say, much of the population most affected by the Katrina hurricane and flood in New Orleans were descendants of those retreating from the plantation.

Dan Crowley, who attended carnival in a great many places—and in fact, died while attending one—maintained the continuities among and between them, giving them a sexual, racial, and class reading. Comparing European and African American events, he noted: "Profanation is the specialty of European Carnivals, elements of which are specifically designed to be sacrilegious, as shocking as possible to the conservative and the religious. But in the New World Carnivals, such specific sacrilege is rather rare, and where it occurs it is a specialty of the upper classes who are usually relatively lighter-skinned than their lower-class countrymen, Bahians and African-nationalist Cariocas (natives of Rio)" (1999, 223–28).

* * *

The Creole inventions that have established continuities between the various African American markets and holidays are manifest in the display practices in those cities that began as ports-of-call during plantation years. In these enclaves, slaves came together with Indians, runaways, maritime workers of many origins, and the castoffs of European imperial regimes—privateers, pirates, sailors, and the unlanded and unemployed.

Before emancipation itself, sailor towns and Maroon communities, market higglers and musicians were established worlds apart from the surveillance and control of the agents of empire. These ports-of-call arose as staple crops grown on the plantations needed transshipping to the metropolitan Old World factories where they were refined and transformed into items of trade.

The bit of freedom achieved by slaves in the United States and elsewhere began with their own provision plots and the markets that developed in which market higglers carved out the spot at the crossroads or in town where they sold their surplus provisions and domestic animals. These Sunday markets, once established, were usually beyond the control of the civic authorities, especially when the markets were the point of passage for the plantations' staple crop. Here slave higglers came together with Indian vendors and with runaways who had hidden in the swamps or on the barrier islands. On emancipation, these enclaves grew into the jerry-built communities that provided the launching pad for the development of new public display forms, still based on African principles of aesthetic organization.

Through the elaboration of the former slave holidays, new styles were improvised using the detritus of European commerce. These holidays, observed at the same time as those of the lighter-skinned elites, were regarded as the product of black song, dance, and other musical orientations. The two traditions shared many of the same display techniques, yet the celebrations in the black part of town carried a different spirit as well as a divergent stylistic organization, the distinctions continuing to be driven by the effects of segregation or economic disparities.

In most cases, the colonial agents seem to have persuaded themselves that the slaves were only playing—and they were correct, though this play meant something more to the carousing population. They hoped that the slaves were only letting off the steam arising from the intensity of their labors on and off the plantation. This was the common European approach to the tumultuous doings around carnival, Christmas, or Pentecost, in which the lower strata of the population were given license to make merry by acting in a topsy-turvy and helter-skelter manner. According to Michael Mullen, "Slaves played throughout the era of slavery, sometimes secretly sometimes with the leave of whites, who were never to sure what plays were" (1992, 66). The report of the Jamaican "uprising of 1823–24 reported by Richard Hart suggests strongly that slaves themselves saw in plays a joyous occasion, and one that might go over the edge into a rebellion" (Hart 2002, 230–34). Thompson (1988) notes the African character of this holy practice, paying special attention to the Yoruba *pagbo*: *pa*—to bring things into contact with each other; *agbo*—to "circle" similar patterns of movement and similar guiding values (see also Lohman 1999, 283).

The voluntary associations provided an alternative organization of power and order, in which a senior member of the community was drawn to the center of a moving celebration and elected "governor." When the black population organized their merriment, one of their number, a Great Voice or Big Man, was elevated as a leader of his "warriors"—that is, the organizing metaphor involved a warrior set of norms, including the assembly of bravos who surrounded the elevated personage. In such cases, mock weapons, including silvered wooden swords, were displayed as an important feature of the festivity.

During times of fear of foreign invasion or internal insurrection, the possibility of a slave rebellion came to the fore from the perspective of the civic authorities. This led to an overreaction by those charged with policing the colony, and, as in the Antigua slave revolt of 1736 or the aborted Denmark Vesey "revolt" in South Carolina in 1822, fears of organized resistance boiled over, and the warriors were confronted and routed. Historian John Thornton suggests that a number of slave revolts began with a misunderstanding of the Shield *(ikem)* Ceremony, in which leaders were "ennobled, not because of their ability at war but through their commercial success . . . The symbolism of the shield ceremony was military in nature, but it was not specifically a military event and was acquired by merchants rather than by soldiers" (1991, 1109), suggesting that the source of the slaves was from an area in which enslavement was not regarded as a permanent or binding status. These were a change-oriented people in Africa who asserted their political flexibility by elevating "kings for themselves" rather than ennobling by descent.

In an account from an 1823 eyewitness report from Jamaica by a slave called Montignac, "James Thompson came to drink . . . and said he would be King, Dennis Kerr said he would be governor, but all was meant in fun . . . The negroes so assembled some times made play, with their sticks, and paraded to James Thompson's house, and . . . some of them had wooden swords" (Hart 2002, 23). Hart argues that this fun was a pretense designed as a cover for conspiratorial activity, and he provides evidence of the elaborate plan.

This view is reinforced by Kenneth Roberts (2003) with regard to the Pointe Coupee Rebellion in Louisiana in 1795. He ties the affair specifically to Congo slaves who had been introduced into the Louisiana slave population after the Haitian Revolution. Robert Farris Thompson 1998) points to the similarities in festive practices in Congo-, Yoruba-, and Igbo-speaking areas, suggesting an Old World sub-Saharan attitude toward syncretism among the slave population, whether or not they came from Congolese families). Whether in Europe or in European colonies, the two styles of carnival carried the message of licensed profanity, engendering groups of players who seized the license of the moment, developing display activities in their songs and speeches that overtly made fun of those in authority. When these improvisations focused on individuals and their doings within the colony, the result was openly libelous.

Of course, throughout the black Atlantic such celebrations carried messages that might be perceived as greater threats. One way or the other, whenever these holidays were replayed after emancipation, the message of militant resistance was maintained, now serving as a reminder of the frustrations of enslavement and subsequent liberation. Nothing stirred the fears of colonial civic authorities—and planters and overseers—more than unticketed gatherings of slaves. The many descriptions we have of the slaves' Sunday markets and holidays reflect a deep fear of noisy, unpredictable, and eccentric movement. Noise made by slaves when they gathered to *play* added to the sense of tumult in a world of their own creation. Fashioning a ceremonial identity by drawing on the extended marketplace practices, a scintilla of liberation was developed in the lives of the celebrants.

Criticism of the doings of their enslavers came to be embodied in some of the improvised songs and dances. And so it has remained after emancipation, for these black celebrations are held in full understanding of how they serve the survivors. More than any other regular public activity, the crowded Sunday markets and ceremonial burials came to the notice of visitors. The noise and wild movement at these occasions seemed "arrogant" to those who owned them. It is not surprising to find the shadow of slavery and displacement still hovering within the important expressive events throughout the greater Caribbean. Little motivation was to be found in the hierarchical social structure of these outposts of empire to erase the distinctions between European and African ancestry. These struggles provide a consistent frame of reference still present today throughout the black Atlantic, especially evident in the community rituals of the Atlantic littoral communities, which had been built on the reality of differentiation between enslaved and freed.

In New Orleans, as in Havana, Rio, and the other ports-of-call in which carnival is practiced, whites and blacks continue to celebrate in different styles, often in opposition to each other, in spite of calls for national unity that emanate from all of these states. This discernment of a black Atlantic culture area, then, parallels and complements the Atlantic studies discussion, giving heft and historical depth to the continuation of the voluntary associations, the transatlantic religions and their houses of worship, and the maintenance of a legendary Africa to which the spirits of the dead might return: all comment on the imperial politics of the past and the postcolonial pose of the present global "community."

* * *

In the face of the destruction of many neighborhoods in New Orleans after Hurricane Katrina, the attention of the outside world was drawn to the victimization of such a large portion of the population. Those involved in the subsequent official hearings and negotiations neglected to remember the resilience of African American grassroots organizations, which have provided a source of local pride since the Louisiana Purchase and the introduction of slaves from Haiti who vastly outnumbered those who were already there. Whatever else might ensue, neither Mardi Gras nor the Second Line burials would disappear. A timely example from contemporary New Orleans: little local, much less national, attention has been given to the crowds that gathered in 2007, meeting near Orleans and Claiborne Avenues at the very spot where black Mardi Gras had traditionally assembled. When their neighborhoods were paved over to make a highway, many saw this as the end of the spirit of Place Congo, the area of town in which slaves came together on Sundays and holidays. The various real estate and governmental forces combined to route Interstate 10 through this area, effectively cutting the old neighborhood of Tremé in half. In the seriously emptied spot created by this move—that is, the socially blank space created by this great engineering feat—a capacious underpass was created. That year, in characteristically ironic and quietly resistant fashion, the null underpass space was transformed into a gathering spot for thousands of black players.

In retrospect, no one who knows of the inner life of New Orleans should have been surprised by this counterattack, this reappropriation of streets and parks. Carving out powerful social spaces has been one of the most important elements of black celebrations in the Crescent City from the dance on Congo Square early in the nineteenth century. The clubs, and especially the Mardi Gras Indians, have always presented themselves in martial terms. Songs boasting of the invincibility of both their elected leader and the club he represents "front" the groups as they course the streets and give hilarious battle.

In the legendary jazz funerals, and especially the organization of the group of followers called Second Line, one community after another finds ways of burying its dead, paying appropriate attention to the life passage, celebrating with an exuberant procession the path from the house of the dead person to the cemetery and back. Seizing the coffin, revelers/mourners carry it throughout the neighborhood to the spots in which the deceased had lived, worked, and played, new marks made on top of old ones, reminding the community of life's continuities and of the importance of maintaining the integrity and honor of the neighborhood. The center of gravity of the community moves with the casket, reinscribing the neighborhood with places of importance in the dead man's life, reminding the mourners of the shared ownership of the home ground.

For many New Orleanians, this Second Line characterizes the spirit of the city. Mardi Gras is unthinkable without the brass bands and the eccentric movement of the crowds, operating even apart from the funereal event that gave it name and shape. As with other forms of the ring pattern of movement, the band does not lead the crowds so much as it moves within the assembled mourners—surrounded, in fact, by the singers and dancers, then followed by the expansive Second Line. Perhaps the message and the movement come together, sometimes ecstatically, in the song that has marked the turn from the dirge to the street march in jazz funerals. For some of the funeral party, the body and the casket have lives of their own until buried correctly. The pallbearers create a rambling procession directing the crowd to the places of importance in the life of the dead man: rambling in death as in life, "till the butchers cut him down." These parades are more than a display of honor and respect: they are celebrations of the mourners' own sense of cohesion and their ability to play the dead march appropriately while consigning the body to the appropriate place of rest.

* * *

Like many of the other ports-of-call involved in the transshipping of the staple crops raised on the plantations, New Orleans was built on unstable wetlands, subject to weather-related disasters. New Orleans had come to signify the most powerful operation of the creolizing of cultural forms in the midst of instabilities of all sorts. For outsiders who loved the city for its edginess, and as the social openness of life in the Crescent City seemed to reveal, the hurricanes and their aftermath seemed like the fulfillment of their worst nightmares—but were hardly unexpected.

These clubs and these events they produce are at the heart of what allows us to posit the existence of a black Atlantic world. Ironically, each local festivity is taken to be unique to the city in which it has become the yearly celebration and homecoming. It is not that the various touristic carnivals are in competition with each other for their piece of the action from the paying and playing visitors. To the contrary, they don't even acknowledge each other. Each has a time that erases all other times in a city that has cleared a way for itself to bring everyone together at high pitch. They represent the power implicit in the mutual aid organizations that operate in counterpoint to civic authorities. This style of community building in which Big Men and Big Drums (or some other rallying organization) prevailed is, in fact, one of the major features of carnival and Christmas play, and is attached to many other recurrent seasonal celebrations—not only those of the Mardi Gras Indians, who encounter each other two or three times a year, but also those of the famed Landship players of Barbados, Jonkonnu in Jamaica, the Bahamas, and South Carolina, the Gwo Ka of Haiti and Martinique, the New York Pinkster celebrations, and the Black Governors from New England. Even if these too are costumed events involving masks, the outfits are homemade. They engage the creativity of the needleworkers and ironmongers of the community, and the design and construction of the costumes and floats that travel to the cemetery and back remind each member that the celebration is not just Mardi Gras but the many other Second Lines and reunions that spring up through the year. This is secret stuff only to those unwilling to listen for the drums and brass bands emerging at those other times during the year. Each club, then, manages to renew itself as the members come together to design, sew, paint, eat, and ramble.

Slaves came from many different language groups and warrior nations, bringing with them the cultural resources by which they developed celebrations incorporating elements of playing that ran counter to the planters' efforts to oversee and totally control their chattels. When, following emancipation, those ex-slaves went to one or another metropolis, setting up temporary housing and a jerry-built sense of community, they embroidered on what had been their markets and their holiday celebrations. They created moments in the year in which they could give voice and body to their new status of being free. Contrary to the perspective of European observers, these holiday practices served not only as days of festivity but as ways of recognizing the neighborhood organizations and their continuing vital spirit.

From the slaves' perspective, cultural production had to be carried out following the European church and state calendar, the latter depending on the production cycle of the main crop, how much of the refinement process had to be carried out in situ, and how much could be disposed of through the industrial processes developed in Europe. Sugar demanded a different kind of work calendar than indigo, cotton, or rice. In all cases, however, the production process called for the same kind of intense work and leisure pattern characteristic of all agrarian people. Unlike in European customary practice, those "free times" arising from the calendar of the agricultural year based on the export crop were not in any way related to sugar or tobacco or whatever was the export commodity. In both Europe and Africa, where the workers benefited by their labors, the rites of annual passage celebrated the bounties of natural increase. As slaves did not benefit from these bounties in any way under the plantation regime, the slave holidays that developed celebrated relief from work and the attainment of a modest amount of improvisation. Where they benefited from nature's bounty, as they developed their own garden plots and animal husbandry, they built a system of internal trade as well as play and display moments in which they came to celebrate whatever liberties were granted them.

With emancipation, then, the slaves' markets and holidays provided the basis for the celebration of something else: the moment of emancipation itself, often through the fulfillment of a rebel or runaway element within the slave population. Just as Sundays, Christmas, and Easter had become their holidays, so too the night was remembered as the time in which liberties could be seized. Even today, holidays and ritual ceremonies all over the black Atlantic world underscore that success is judged by lasting all night.

But when discussions of the Atlantic world include the residents of sailor towns beyond the marketers and celebrants, commercial matters take on a different coloration. As historian Stephen Hahn notes: "The Atlantic might usefully be imagined as a large political, as well as cultural 'contact zone', in which Africans and African Americans mingled regularly with each other, and with sailors, soldiers, servants, and other plebeians from Britain, France, Spain, and the Netherlands . . . in which all were simultaneously transmitters and receivers of news and ideas carried through increasingly dense networks of maritime communication" (Hahn 2003, 53).

Thus, the coastal ports in the Old World and the New shared a common human resource bank, with a heavy emphasis on an already dislocated and often enslaved or imprisoned population, the product of the development of one or another kind of removal that occurred because of being conquered by outsiders. Far from representing a previously sedentary population, neither the African nor the European immigrants were landed or proto-national in any way. All of them, if they had ethnic loyalties, came from a clan brotherhood style of organization, and were often themselves the losers in clan warfare. The settled people on both continents were those among the victors who had been elevated to leadership positions by others of their clan. They had undergone rituals of status elevation. Their leaders were lauded as warriors by their bards. The rest were dirt. And it was this population, of course, that made up the great majority of the population of the New World.

Contrary to expectations, the African mercantile system, which conspired with that of the European traders, was never connected to any national enterprise. Rather, as J. Lorand Matory noted of Africa, "nations" were imagined that had trade rather than territory as their unifying characteristic. "The 'Congo' and 'Angola' nations . . . were products of [an] Afro-Atlantic dialogue. They emerged from ongoing historical changes of West-Central African social identities." He continues: "A class of international merchants was able to reshape and indeed invent national identities . . . across multiple territorially imagined communities . . . [of] merchants and travelers on both sides of the Atlantic" (2005, 112).

Significant contemporary ethnographers and historians have established a great number of ways through which such dialogues was carried out in spite of the political control of agents of European nation-states. Obviously not through political negotiation, but rather through the establishment of clientele, religious and health workers created channels of cultural maintenance and innovation that only tangentially touched on transatlantic interactions.

Slave and ex-slave watermen were also central to the development of the ports-of-call out of which these festivities arose: flatboatmen, fishermen, draymen, carters, stevedores, and most notably able-bodied seamen, lived a mobile existence that presented a much less controlled and circumscribed life than that led by the field workers on the plantations. The leaders of the commercial community knew well how these off-plantation activities tore at the heart of white oversight and control. Not only did they call for a kind of personal mobility dramatically in contrast to the lives of most slaves, they brought the slaves into contact with other grassroots workers who represented an international cosmopolitan world of the underclass, the drifters, many of them carrying legally questionable modes of exchange.

The availability of such independent enterprises to slaves differed from one area to another, depending on the legal and religious status of slaves, the number of workers on a given plantation, the population differential between whites and blacks, the distance from storage factories and wharfs, and the presence or absence of other darker people involved in the trade, from usurers and slave auctioneers to retail merchants: all of these factors account for the many differences from one port-of-call to the next within the black Atlantic.

The distance between the colony and the metropolitan center of operations impacted the development of the resistance apparatus to these authorities. And, of course, the differences between the Protestant and Roman Catholic attitudes toward enslavement and conversion to Christianity created considerably diverse developmental patterns among the slave populations. Finally, the nature of the agricultural enterprise must be factored in, for colonies that were primarily made up of yeoman farmers (who might or might not enter into the international trade with their staple crop) would differ considerably from those areas characterized by plantations, from small to , which called for a much larger slave force in comparison to the resident planters and overseers.

In spite of all of these variables, the patterns of performance and of worship that occurred throughout the plantation world indicate that the overlap of expressive practices reflects not only common ways of stylized organization of the senses but a common economic perspective. Periodic markets take on a life of their own because they are generated in good part by slaves exercising their rights to a slave holiday as they came together with maritime workers, outcasts, and traveling folks of all sorts. The ports-of-call seemed to invite internal colonies, trade communities made up of wandering marketers, who set up business on a family basis now in one colony, now another.

From the slaves' perspective, cultural production had to be carried out by following the "buckra" (white master's) calendar, which itself depended on the cycle by which the main crop was produced. The slaves were given, and in most cases took, their "leisure"—that is, settling on an alternative work and play regime—by seizing the European calendared holidays and employing them in dramatic ways that in other situations would appear to lead to acts of resistance, even rebellion. The tone and swagger of these celebrations differed from the fetes being held on the white side of town.

Unlike European customary practice, those "free times" encouraged by the surplus crop were not related to the crop itself. In both Europe and Africa, the rites of passage of the year celebrated the bounties of natural increase. But in the New World, the staple crop agricultural year may have impacted on the plantocrats and the town merchants. But this was the European calendar. Slave holidays were reliant on those of the masters, but were celebrated in entirely different fashion.

These slave holidays celebrated relief from work. The festivities, including the "battles," create a significant festive noise, and the ways in which the battles and the noise are enacted are ubiquitous throughout the Atlantic and Mediterranean basins. Mock elections as well as mock battles are at the center of festivities throughout this world; although almost always done for fun, they call for open demonstrations of military-like organizations. And most of them call for the elevation of a titular leader. But festivities in the black world are played out in the middle ground between serious and playful motives. Fighting by slaves and ex-slaves carries different messages and motives than in European-derived revelries.

Rather than looking for historical figures with cosmopolitan ideas that ask for an essentially pluralistic democratic positioning, I look to the community groups and their celebrations for evidence of a transatlantic African American world, one tied together by customary practices played out in ritual celebrations such as carnival and burial ceremonies. Examining the history—and present practices—of New Orleans Mardi Gras and the contemporary Second Line burial rituals and comparing them with similar displays and cognate organizations, I call attention to the observable continuities found throughout the Caribbean as well as mainland ports-of-call in the United States. In all of these grand marches in the neighborhoods, today as a century and more ago, they ramble till the butcher cuts 'em down.

REFERENCES

Bilby, Kenneth. 2005. *True Born Maroons*. Gainesville: University Press of Florida.

Crowley, Daniel. 1999. "The Sacred and the Profane in African and African-Derived Carnivals." "Studies of Carnival in Memory of Daniel J. Crowley," ed. Peter Tokofsky. Special issue of *Western Folklore* 58 (3/4): 223–28. http://dx.doi.org/10.2307/1500457.

Gilroy, Paul. 1993. *The Black Atlantic: Modernity and Double Consciousness*. Cambridge: Harvard University Press.

Gomez, Michael. 1998. *Exchanging Our Country Marks: The Transformation of African Identities in the Colonial and Antebellum South*. Chapel Hill: University of North Carolina Press.

Hahn, Steven. 2003. *A Nation under Our Feet*. Cambridge, MA: Harvard University Press, 2003.

Hart, Richard. (Original work published 1985) 2002. *Slaves Who Abolished Slavery: Blacks in Rebellion*. Kingston, Jamaica: University of the West Indies Press.

Kiddy, Elizebeth. 2005. *Blacks of the Rosary: Memory and History in Minas Gerais, Brazil*. Harrisburg: Pennsylvania State University Press.

Lohman, Jon. 1999. "It Can't Rain Everyday: The Year-Round Experience of Carnival." In "Studies of Carnival in Memory of Daniel J. Crowley," ed. Peter Tokofsky, Special issue, *Western Folklore* 58:279–98.

Matory, J. Lorand. 2005. *Black Atlantic Religion: Traditions, Transnationalism, and Matriarchy in Afro-Brazilian Candomblé*. Princeton: Princeton University Press.

Morton, Ferdinand Joseph. 1938. "Jelly Roll." Library of Congress Transcriptions of Interviews with Alan Lomax. http://www.loc.gov/exhibits/treasures/tri007.html.

Mullen, Michael. 1992. *Africa in America: Slave Acculturation and Resistance in the American South and the British Caribbean, 1736–1831*. Urbana: University of Illinois Press.

Mulvey, Patricia A. 1976. "The Black Lay Brotherhoods of Colonial Brazil: A History." PhD diss,, City University of New York.

Ortiz, Fernando. 2001. "The Afro-Cuban Festival 'Day of the Kings.'" Trans. Jean Stubbs. In *Cuban Festivals: A Century of Afro-Cuban Culture*, ed. Judith Bettelheim and Fernando Ortiz, 1–40. Princeton, NJ: Markus Weiner.

Roberts, Kevin David. 2003. "Slaves and Slavery in Louisiana: The Evolution of Atlantic World Identities, 1791–1831." PhD diss., University of Texas.
Thompson, Robert Farris. 1988. "Recapturing Heaven's Glamour: Afro Caribbean Festival Arts." In *Caribbean Festival Arts,* ed. John W. Nunley and Judith Bettelheim, 17–29. St. Louis, MO: Washington University Press.
Thornton, John K. 1991. "African Dimensions of the Stono Rebellion." *American Historical Review* 96 (4): 1101–13. http://dx.doi.org/10.2307/2164997.

4

Protesting and Grieving
Ritual, Politics, and the Effects of Scale

Beverly J. Stoeltje

INTERTWINED WITH POLITICS IN ITS MANY GUISES, RITUAL and its related forms enact the cultural preoccupations and political orientations of social groups. The inauguration of presidents, religious services and graduation ceremonies, funerals and weddings, all integrate the ritual and the political through complex strategies. As preoccupations and orientations are always subject to changing conditions, from within and without, ritual and political events both shape and reflect the sociopolitical environment.

Though often unnoticed, ritual behavior frequently develops in response to contradictions, ambiguities, and uncertainties as they reverberate through social groups and societies; at times ritual clarifies ambiguity, as in rites of passage, whereas in other instances ritual embodies ambiguity. Writing of paradox, ritual, and change, A. David Napier argues that an awareness of ambiguity (which informs the simplest transitions) aids in establishing a point of view and "in evaluating phenomena that we may later view quite differently," and therefore that the potential for ambiguity remains fundamental to change. Further, the recognition of illusion is the prerequisite for recognizing contradiction and paradox, "and the recognition of change is, then, possible only with this understanding: that something may appear to be something else" (1986, 3).

If we accept (1) that political activity revolves fundamentally around ideas or individuals related to change (for or against) as it affects public life or status in the public eye, (2) that the performance of politics is saturated with ambiguity, (3) that ritual, a symbolic form, is immersed in and expresses ambiguity, and (4) that ritual enables transformation, we can identify a link through which ritual and politics intertwine. Consequently, the ritual/political domain runs in parallel with and comments on the social and political structures in a society, at times providing for the exploration or contestation of changes and at other times creating space for the rehearsal, experimentation, and implementation of changes (Cohen, Wilk, and Stoeltje 1996; Comaroff 1985; Moore and Myerhoff 1977; Noyes 2003; Turner 1974).

The enactment of ritual represents an interpretation of reality reflecting the ideologies of the group creating it: a hegemonic institution, a secret society, a form of government, a resistance movement, a political protest, a religious body, adherents of holiday traditions and other cultural practices. In other words, groups of all sorts—small and large, hegemonic or resistant, use ritual as a social process. From the perspective of individuals facing challenging but inexplicable situations filled with contradictions and ambiguities, ritual frequently offers a solution. Analyzing ritual responses to contradictions created by modernity in postcolonial Africa, Jean and John Comaroff have explained: "Ritual, as an experimental technology intended to affect the flow of power in the universe, is an especially likely response to contradictions created and (literally) engendered by processes of social, material, and cultural transformation, processes re-presented, rationalized, and authorized in the name of modernity and its various alibis" (Comaroff and Comaroff 1993, xxx).

The ritual/political domain has also proven to be an important resource for groups outside of Africa who attempt to affect the flow of power in the universe (see also Ronald Loewe 2010). As Enrique Lamadrid has commented, Native Americans and mestizo peoples have been able to effectively undermine the authority of modernity and express their experience of struggle through the performance of the ritual genres. "For five centuries, the native and mestizo peoples of the Americas have dramatized their political and cultural struggles in festival and ritual display. Utilizing victory and morality plays, ritual dance, and even contemporary fiesta parades, the Indo-Hispanic peoples contribute to a global conversation about the limits of empire in our own time."[1]

Not only does the example above enable expression of political struggles, the ritual/political domain has also served to define and sustain identity. As an essential feature of ritual, identity has been important for ancient societies, preindustrial ones, and all the more so for contemporary citizens living in a globalized world layered with levels of hierarchy. Returning to Napier once again, he considers the "apprehension of identity" so crucial that the recognition of change hinges on it as well as on the awareness of a potential for paradox (Napier 1986, 3).

In the late twentieth and early twenty-first centuries the phenomena known as globalization, transnationalism, and technology have profoundly affected ritual/political events, expanding them in size and attracting people in the thousands, largely due to the role of social media and the influence of global news systems, enabling instant and widespread communication. These phenomena have drawn scholars to the concept of scale as a means of understanding the ways various forces and institutions expand to meet the next reach and then the next.

An especially productive approach in the social disciplines is E. Summerson Carr and Michael Lempert's premise that scale is process before it is product, leading them to argue for research that explores how, why, and to what ends people and institutions scale their world. Pointing to a key feature of scale they state: "In other words, the scales that seem most natural to us are intensively institutionalized, and that is why collectives readily accept that the leviathan of State or God hovers above landsmen, or that one realm of political or ritual authority encompasses another" (Carr and Lempert 2016, 3–4).

In this essay I am specifically concerned with contemporary ritual/political events, most of which involve vast numbers of participants and global communications. They all involve the public and represent various levels of scale, from the local to the international. The political and the ritual intertwine in all of these performances, especially because they reach deeply into experience, define identities, and travel across continents, shaping the interpretation of acts and developments or the potential of ones to come. Finally, the essay also features a strategy that challenges the balance of the ritual/political: corruption. Like Jack Santino's category of the "ritualesque," these events attempt to affect the world beyond the space and place of their occurrence (2011, 124).

THE POWER OF RITUAL

Participation and transformation are fundamental to the ritual genres (ritual and related forms) in a wide range of forms.[2] That is, the performance of a ritual event will be structured so that some or all of the participants will experience a transformation. A change of status will be effected for those who are the focus of initiation rites, a wedding, or an inauguration, but all of the participants will, nevertheless, experience degrees of transformation by virtue of their presence and their relationship to the initiates. Ritual events directed toward a community produce transformations also, both social and individual. In festivals defined by the calendar, contemporary music concerts, and political protests, participants take on the identity of the experience. Moreover, the status of individuals may change; some might become winners and others losers, leaders will be acknowledged or honored, and romance or divorce initiated. Transformation is part of the ritual structure because it is a time of liminality (ambiguity, illusion, paradox) for all who participate. The potential for change is licensed, including what some scholars have called the "license" to indulge in drinking, eating, dancing, sex, talking to strangers, and other social acts. Even when a ritual is designed to support the status quo in opposition to change, or when the ritual is focused on rites of passage, through the intensification of emotional and symbolic links liminality enables the social action that provides the transformative experience.

Characterized by a specific purpose (though individuals or subgroups often have goals other than the stated purpose), ritual is the performance genre associated with rites of passage, revitalization movements, political processes, religious conversion, resistance activities, and more. Such ritual events can unify a social group, instill loyalty, enact symbolic resistance, enable the emergence of a movement and, especially, affect the emotional and social status of individuals involved. Whatever the scale and the reach, the enduring power of ritual resides in this feature, the capacity to create or effect transformation.

Suzanne Langer writes, "Ritual is a symbolic transformation of experiences that no other medium can adequately express" (1957, 49). She identifies the significance of the symbolic and notes that experience is the subject of transformation in ritual. This power of ritual rests on a framework that relates a specific experience of change to those present and/or participating. Because ritual defines an experience and intensifies emotion, endowing the moment with probity, depth, permanence, and especially authority, it impacts the lives of all levels of participants.

In a wedding, for example, two individuals who have been defined socially as "single" will transition into a new identity. They will become a married couple who have acquired a new social and legal status. Among those present, family members will be transformed into "in-laws" and the audience into witnesses, confirming the transformation. Terence Turner emphasizes that such a transformation consists of a concrete social process and that it is the specific formal nature of the transition, "and not merely its gross character as a change or transition *per se*, that defines it as a 'transformation'" (Turner 1977, 55).

Because the stated purpose of a wedding is to create a married couple, a political agenda may be subordinated. Yet in some cultures marriages are arranged with the purpose in mind to advance the status of the bride or groom or to satisfy the parents' goals.[3] In societies governed by a monarchy and dominated by an elite class, marriages are usually arranged or encouraged in order to maintain the social order by restricting marriage partners among the elite to others of that class. As an exception to the rule, Prince William's marriage to commoner Kate Middleton in England was noted as a significant departure. In some modern social groups individuals who have acquired vast wealth in one or two generations may look upon the wedding of a daughter or a son as an opportunity to display their wealth and thereby increase their status. All of these and a range of other motives can be understood as attempts at political gain submerged beneath the stated purpose of a specific ritual.

In events defined as political the significance of ritual is presumed. Only when some detail goes awry is attention drawn to the ritual itself. Such a situation occurred in President Obama's first inauguration when Supreme Court Justice Roberts misread the text of the oath. The swearing in with the oath had to be repeated after the inaugural event to ensure that it was legitimate.

Whether a political purpose or a ritual goal is primary, events will integrate the two through the ritual framework, the sequence of activity, the placement of key actors, the words spoken and music performed, and especially the social relationships enacted.[4] Rituals need to be done *correctly*, not necessarily "well," that is, aesthetically pleasing (see also Santino 1995).

POWER RELATIONS AND SYMBOLIC ACTION

In a pathbreaking work, Abner Cohen (1974) explored the relationship between ritual and politics, arguing that Political Man is also Symbolist Man. Theorizing the dialectical interdependence between power relationships and symbolic action, he used the term *symbol* to encompass *ritual, myth, customs, values*, and more. He identified power as an aspect of almost all social relationships and defined "politics" as the process involved in the distribution, maintenance, exercise, and struggle for power. Cohen's work emphasized that symbolic formations and power relations (or ritual and politics) occur together in the social life of all human societies, but that they are nevertheless different phenomena—"relatively autonomous orders"—and are not reducible one to the other. Emphasizing that symbolic activities have political consequences, he considered the range of phenomena encompassed by his term *symbols* to be fundamental mechanisms for the development of selfhood and for tackling the perennial problems of human existence (life and death, good and evil, misery and happiness).[5]

In spite of their intimate relationship and an abundance of scholarly studies recognizing it, ritual and politics are lodged in separate domains of knowledge, that is, religion and political science. David Kertzer has identified the source of that separation in the epistemological roots of Western scholarship, specifically a distinction between the rational and irrational: "The call to place politics on a more rational basis has a long history in the West, rising to international prominence with the philosophers of the Enlightenment. In this view, there is little place for ritual in politics, for rites are the products of passion, not reasoned reflection" (1988, 181).

In another separation instituted by modernity, ritual and festival are frequently organized as quite separate events. We can turn to Mikhail Bakhtin (1984) for a historical explanation. In his study of Rabelais's controversial novel *Gargantua and Pantagruel*, Bakhtin identified the transition period from the Middle Ages to modernity when Christianity spread over Europe as a crucial moment for the performance of ritual. He demonstrates that the Christian Church established a distinction between ritual and festival by the sixteenth century, appropriating ritual for worship in the church. Festival and ritual were detached from each other but remained under the control of the church. However, Bakhtin saw a "genetic link" between forms of carnival in the Middle Ages associated with the church and "ancient pagan festivities," agrarian in nature. He argues that Rabelais (1494–1552) (a monk who became a doctor and influential author who was persecuted for his critical portrayal of authorities) drew upon the tradition of popular-festive laughter from the Middle Ages. This led Bakhtin to coin the term *carnivalesque* in reference to the subversion and inversion of official culture represented in Rabelais's novel. Especially significant, Bakhtin perceived the expression of laughter and festivity in a struggle with a new culture of absolute monarchy in which the prevailing concepts emphasized a single meaning of seriousness.

Consistent with the ideology of the Enlightenment, is Bakhtin's description of the period from the seventeenth through the twentieth century as an era when authorities of religious and economic institutions directed social life toward practices consistent with modern ideologies—those considered rational, productive, and singular in meaning, denying humor, mockery, and parody a space. Yet, he reminds us that "popular-festive carnival is indestructible" (Bakhtin 1984, 33–34).

Further, he notes that "One carnival did not coincide with any commemoration of sacred history or of a saint but marked the last days before Lent, and for this reason was called *Mardi gras* or *careme-prenant* in France and *Fastnacht* in Germany (Bakhtin 1984, 8). It is this form (carnival) that retained the potential for the expression of humor, social criticism, or political opposition and has continued to provide the stage for the expression of symbolic resistance in numerous Catholic cultures (Cowley 1996; DaMatta 1991; Gilmore 1998).

The ideologies and practices described above have impacted the organization of ritual and festival in cultures dominated by Christianity, separating the two. Yet community-based fiestas and festivals usually incorporate ritual within festival. Catholicism throughout the world continues to link festival to the celebration of saints and to incorporate a mass in a fiesta. In Protestant culture festival is generally a secular event but will nevertheless often include a ritual independent of any religious affiliation. The contemporary practice of embedding a beauty pageant within a festival represents a secular ritual (Besnier 2011; Cohen, Wilk, and Stoeltje 1996; Haynes 1998).

In Egypt, contemporary Muslim saints-day festivals have also been affected by the expansion of modernity. Having emerged in the late Middle Ages along with Sufism, the festivals create an atmosphere of the extraordinary; however, as Samuli Schielke (2008) has shown, reformers and the state have imposed new boundaries on space and rules of behavior. Critics say the festival should not be an occasion to let go and break the boundaries that guide everyday behavior; instead it should be an occasion to learn and enact proper morals and authoritative knowledge: "they aim to civilize *mulids*, that is, to turn them from moments of disorder . . . that relativize the normal order of things into vehicles for hegemonic power that demonstrate and impose a universalist order of urban space, civic habitus, and morality" (548).

Scholars have been equally affected by the differences described above, leading to the use of multiple terms to describe the ritual genres in societies around the world. Scholarly approaches are to be found in numerous disciplines and utilize a variety of theoretical models. Santino discusses the widely varying literature in considerable detail, noting difficulties and attempted solutions. He states, "As the study of ritual has become increasingly interdisciplinary, the concept of ritual itself has become increasingly polysemic and problematic" (2001, 66).

In spite of the broad scope of the ritual literature and the wide variation in ritual events from weddings to protests, the fundamental structures on which ritual events are built prove to be quite consistent. Most important of these are the form characteristic of ritual and the means of communication. Identifying these features is key to understanding the interaction of ritual and politics; it is useful, then, to turn briefly to a discussion that outlines these features.

THE DYNAMICS OF PERFORMANCE AND THE RITUAL FRAMEWORK: FORM AND COMMUNICATION

Ritual scholars have devoted considerable attention to the form and structure of ritual, the means of communication, and the overall features that constitute the ritual framework, whether the ritual genres are perceived as sacred or secular, political or personal. These features, which converge around a specific message or purpose, are the primary reason why power is intertwined with ritual and thus politics is present, whether or not it is articulated. Due to the spatial and temporal arrangements that permit ritual to be performed within a specified space and time, and the heavy reliance on symbols as the means of communication, the authorities who manage ritual (discussed below) have the power to direct the experience of participants whether or not they physically lead the event. Because symbols carry emotional freight as well as information, participants respond to ritual communication and to the authorities or other leaders performing the genres familiar to the participants. This reliance on fundamental features, which can be quite simple or very elaborate, sacred or secular, ensures that ritual succeeds in accomplishing its purpose. Consequently, when political goals are woven together with the fundamentals of ritual, they are generally accomplished.

The ritual framework requires a shift in the perception of reality from the routines of everyday life to the heightened consciousness of performance and symbolic communication.[6] To create this shift, two cosmological features are manipulated: space and time. A space separate from that of the everyday must be created, or an everyday space such as the town square must be transformed into a ritual space, no longer available for everyday use. Second, a time must be declared outside the usual demarcation of time and its routines. In this space and during this time, experience will be altered because ritual removes restrictions and/or places new ones on the participants.

The designated space and the time-out-of-time take precedence over all other activities for the period of a ritual. The length of time involved might be hours, days, weeks, or uncertain. Though the time set apart for contemporary rituals is generally much shorter than ritual events were in preindustrial societies, exceptions do exist. A development of the late twentieth century is the destination wedding or other event that requires participants to travel to a distant location where the ritual will be enacted, increasing the investment of time and money for all participants. Another counterexample is the funeral as performed in Ghana today among the Asante, which can be held throughout a weekend or for as many as five or six days. Many of those who attend are well educated, employed in modern occupations, and engaged in politics. If it is the funeral of a prestigious person, individuals will attend from the United

Figure 4.1. At the funeral of Nana Abena Frimpoma, the Juasohemaa, QueenMother of Juaso, in 2015 Asante QueenMothers attend to show their respect. Funerals of QueenMothers, Chiefs, and other members of royal families in Ghana may attract thousands of people, as did the funeral of the Juasohemaa. (Photo by author)

States, England, Holland, and other outside locations. Held outdoors, a small funeral will be attended by a hundred people, whereas several thousand people may attend the funeral of a person of high status. All of those who come to the funeral must dress in red or black African dress and formally greet the chief mourners. Drumming and dancing of the funeral dance will be performed at intervals. The tradition requires that the body of the deceased be on display on a brass bed. Moreover, the event also serves as a stage for politicians who are expected to attend funerals, and further, as Beverly Stoeltje (2010) points out, it may prove to have political consequences.

Spaces and structures are often created for the purpose of specific rituals but, like time, ritual space can also be altered to meet changing social and political conditions. William Eastwood has documented a dramatic example that occurred in the Republic of Georgia with the collapse of the Soviet Union. The bishop of the Baptist Church was determined that his congregation should be able to identify with their cultural heritage; therefore, he introduced classic Orthodox icons into the church. This represented a quite remarkable change because the Baptist Church had previously eschewed any visual signs associated with the Orthodox Christian Church. Yet, in an effort to relocate the church from the margins to the mainstream of Georgian society, the bishop has relied heavily on changing the interior space of the church; he has filled it with religious icons, a multivocalic symbol that represents Georgian culture but has previously been identified with the Georgian Orthodox Church (Eastwood 2009, 20–28).

SYMBOLS AND COMMUNICATION

Because symbols are embedded within dynamic cultural systems, they both shed and gather meaning over time, altering in form (Turner 1982, 22). As the means of ritual communication, symbols make it possible for diverse peoples to respond to the same symbol and for a certain efficiency of communication in ritual. Turning to the way that symbols, or signifiers, are organized, we note that when rituals embody social structure and/or gender relations, specifically, and focus on accomplishing a specific purpose that serves an existing system, they can be described as having singular meaning (additional meanings may be threaded around or hidden but are not part of the official symbolic purpose). This description most often fits rites of passage such as installation into political office, initiation rites into organizations or religions (in both modern and preindustrial societies), or weddings, birth rituals, or funerals. It can also apply to those efforts of hegemonic forces to transform events of multiple meanings into ones with singular meanings geared to the criteria of modernity, especially evident when the purpose is political. These have often been described as instrumental rituals.

Distinguished from rituals that concentrate all meanings toward a single purpose (patriotism, religious messages, political rhetoric, etc.) are those recognized as festivals, fiestas, carnival, saints' day celebrations, or feast days; these are often described with Bakhtin's term, the *carnivalesque*. These create through symbolic communication the possibilities of multiple meanings, including parody and humor, expressed in a cacophony of sound and sight. Barbara Babcock argued that the carnivalesque is characterized by a surplus of signifiers and further, that ritual events bracket out ordinary modes of signification in one of two ways: "by literally denying and stripping away or by multiplying to the point of indeterminate nonsense: by fasting or by feasting, by sexual abstinence or sexual license, by nakedness or by costumes of motley, by immobility or excessive movement, by seclusion or public display, by silence or noise" (1978, 297).

Rituals considered ludic or carnivalesque, rituals of reversal and festivals, are generally characterized by a surplus of signifiers, creating a sensory overload that deconstructs or challenges the orderly meanings of specific official systems, while those considered serious are more likely to be enacted with single or few signifiers performed in a sequence one at a time with multiple signifieds. Babcock further argued that the simultaneity and multiplicity of sounds, words, costumes, food, drink, movement and action, persons, and animals (a surplus of signifiers) liberates participants from the usual social rules and customary habits. This surplus of signifiers alters the normal modes of signification, creating a rich environment of possibility, including the emergence of new meanings and transformations of identity and social relationships as well as challenges to the social order and the articulation of alternative political positions.

In contrast, orderly rituals such as graduation ceremonies or religious services will capture a multiplicity of signifieds, or meanings, in one sign, or symbol. Though such rituals make use of multiple genres such as narrative, song, dress, movement, and objects, they occur in a logical sequence, and all attention is focused on one genre at a time that expresses an idea supporting the purpose of the ritual. The entire event is enacted within a hierarchy of authority and knowledge that is always on display, and all action builds toward the goal to be accomplished.

Particularly powerful in ritual are familiar patterns. The rituals of religious institutions, universities, governments, law courts, and ceremonial events will follow a pattern considered its form, and specific genres also follow a form (a campaign speech, a pledge, a song, a prayer, a dance). Festival form has a much looser structure and thus much greater flexibility, but is equally familiar to participants. Kenneth Burke reminds us that form invites participation. The power of the form, as it builds, somewhat like stairs, leads participants to yield to the formal development, preparing for assent to the matter identified with it. The form itself invites participants to follow, to yield to its rhythms, repetitions, and familiarity, and then to accept an attitude of assent that "may then be transferred to the matter which happens to be associated with the form" (Burke 1969, 58). In summary, participants respond to the power of the form and accept the message, embedded in familiar genres, material objects, space, and time (the symbols that carry the message—"the matter associated with the form").

Together these features constitute the ritual framework and account for the power of the symbolic to produce transformation and persuade participants: space and time are essential to define an event as ritual, communication occurs through symbols and symbolic action and, especially important for effectiveness, the form directs participants to arrive at the attitude or position that reflects the purpose of the event. As politics is centrally about power and influence, we can understand why these two domains so frequently join together to achieve a purpose. Of particular advantage for the play of politics within ritual are the boundaries of the ritual genres. However porous or solid they are, boundaries of a ritual event ensure that messages and matters relevant to the ritual purpose will be communicated.

AUTHORITY

Of particular relevance to the dynamic that links ritual and politics is the presence of authority in ritual. Whether a ritual is designed to inspire revolution or religious conversion, it is imbued with authority. In the actual performance of a ritual, authority is embodied in a specific person or persons, though in some instances a space can come to represent authority because of events that have happened there. The person who embodies authority in a ritual may have a role much like a director of a play, who is not visible, or he or she may be the key figure who directs the transformation. An individual often represents the conceptual validating authority of an institution, such as a judge, who embodies the legal system, or a university president, who stands for the university. Quite often ritual enables voices not heard in routine social life unless one is associated with specific institutions.

Often present in rituals are multiple authorities who embody different kinds of authority. One authority may direct an event while another represents the authority that validates the transformation of the ritual. Throughout Africa the ritual genres provide the stage for the performance of genres that not only express authority but reveal political positions and criticism. Kwasi Ampene (2005) has documented a genre of women's songs in Ghana, performed at funerals and other ritual events, that express social and political commentary. Lisa Gilman (2009) found that women's groups in Malawi have been performing with songs and dance for politicians for many decades, and Yoruba women in Nigeria sing praise poetry at ritual events that includes commentary on political figures (Barber 1991).

For the Abrahamic religions, the foundation of authority is a sacred text. Other religions are built on an equally authoritative body of belief, but the knowledge is passed on through individuals rather than in a written text. For secular or nonreligious rituals, authority resides in an ideology, a set of practices, oral or written history, or any body of knowledge that serves to legitimate the ritual. Whatever the specific goal, ritual authority assumes a unity of purpose and directs the participants toward the goal. In a succinct statement Suzanne Langer argues that the ultimate product of ritual is "a disciplined rehearsal of 'right' attitudes" (1957, 153).

These analytical observations point to the means by which rituals assert a profound influence on participants or, from another perspective, comprehending the characteristics of ritual enables us to understand the experience of ritual from the point of view of participants. More important, we gain insight into the intertwining of ritual and politics. Not surprisingly, then, politics and all things institutional, including government (democracies and dictators alike), military, religions, and law, all utilize ritual. It displays and creates authority, makes transformation possible, provides identity with a larger entity distinct from other entities, and orchestrates a rehearsal of "right attitudes" that can then be attached to the content and the goal of the ritual. The experience of ritual enables a participant to become a believer, a follower, or a leader; she or he can be a member or a participant or an authority in religious organizations or gangs, groups that promote peace and those that practice violence.

The form and structure used by ritual, together with the symbolic communication and the recognized authorities, constitute the ritual framework. Most prominent of its features for discussion of contemporary events, however, is the fact that ritual reflects, responds to, and shapes society through its many constituents. Among its most significant benefits to participants is the sense of belonging it creates, producing identification and unification around its purpose.

CONFLICT, RITUAL, POLITICS

As mentioned above ritual events emerge and evolve with the forces of change in society. Not limited to formal occasions established by institutions and directed by recognized authorities, ritual can be used to oppose the domination of oppressive governments or other agents of power; it has proven effective for resistance and contestation, including protests and rebellions.

Characteristic of contemporary societies is the phenomenon familiar to us as globalization, in which ideas, goods, money, natural resources, manufacturing, jobs, and above all weapons circulate around the globe; people, too, are continually in motion, whether as agents, tourists, immigrants, or refugees. Of significance in this process are the developments of technology, none more influential than what has come to be known as social media and the individual object—the cell phone. These developments have enabled new communications, yielding unanticipated consequences in rituals of contestation. Further, new social formations and organizations, some legitimate and others not, have also emerged, creating entanglements of ritual and power that did not exist prior to the late twentieth century.

These twentieth- and twenty-first-century events qualify as emergent rituals (Jack Santino 2011; Raymond Williams 1977), expressions developed in response to specific social and political contexts. Recent decades have been witness to political events of monumental proportions: upheavals, revolutions, oppression, aggression, and violence. Though the examples considered below are quite different from each other, they are nevertheless characterized by their public nature. Not only does the term *public* reference an open invitation to participate with others in a public space, it means that the message of the ritual can go out to the world. Further, it has the *intent* to communicate publicly, perhaps to a government or a political entity. The larger goal is to address anyone who will notice, whether it be one's neighbors, the city, the government, or the world. In most instances the goal is to have an impact on a specific action.

Though these rituals are, for the most part, massive in scale, they are all the more important for their ability to define identity, especially because of the prominence of the political in some cases, or the prominence of the international in others. Several rituals are overt responses to contemporary social and political circumstances while others play out contradictions present in society. In all cases participants have joined with others in an act of commitment to a particular idea or emotion that blends together politics and identity in an emergent ritual. This ritual constitutes a message that relates to power, but through the ritual action the participants are also defining an identity. Using the term *cultural forms*, Dorothy Holland and Jean Lave find enactments to be "the significant media through which identities are evoked in social practice and in intimate dialogue" (Holland and Lave 2001, 12).

In the examples below, the expression of emotion and identity is equally as visible as the political orientation, though this ratio varies from one to another. The examples from Northern Ireland and London are rites of passage involving death, but the influence of the political transforms the ritual into a public event, intensifying identity. In Gezi Park and other examples of resistance, the political is the topic of the communication and a political action is the goal, but the event rests on the ritual framework. Each ritual discussed below is derived from published sources (scholarly journals, popular media, the internet).

Northern Ireland

Violence and death call out for the transformational capacities of ritual. When conflict and violence are rooted in political conditions, ritual is of paramount importance. Northern Ireland was the site of violent conflict between the Protestant British and Irish Catholic residents until the two groups agreed to a ceasefire in 1995. Conflict was focused on the land, the space occupied by both groups—Irish to some, British to others. Jack Santino described the situation as it stood in 1994 as follows: "Challenge and contestation over the right to define the nature of the place occur at all levels. Parade routes are met with organized resistance. Murals are whitewashed or defaced. People's interpretations of symbols are contradicted by counterinterpretations . . . The metanarrative of history is constantly debated at all levels of society. The conflicts are internal to Ulster, but extend to include all of Ireland and Great Britain, and even to Canada and the United States" (2001, 6).

Not only parades, murals, and narratives offered a platform for expressing this conflict, but paramilitary organizations representing the opposing positions engaged in violence and caused deaths, many deaths, especially of young men. In response to a particular attack in a Catholic neighborhood at a betting office named Sean Graham's in which five men, including two seventeen-year-old boys, were killed, a spontaneous ritual developed, initiated by a fourteen-year-old-girl, the daughter of one of those killed (Santino 2001).

The front of Sean Graham's was immediately transformed into a shrine. The daughter who lost a father in the killing posted a note to him on the window shutter, and soon others left notes to the deceased; then newspaper clippings, prayers, distinctive neckties of the schoolboys' uniforms, and rosaries were added; significantly, many bouquets of flowers were stacked in layers on the steps. Those close to the deceased created this shrine, but its presence encouraged everyone in the neighborhood to take notice; indeed, people of all ages stopped to pray, read the notes and clippings, and stand in silence. Flowers were sent from Dublin in great quantity. The shrine was photographed and images were circulated internationally by the British press. Santino commented: "The components of the shrine transcended the local neighborhood, and those living in the neighborhood were aware of this . . . The processes of cleansing and healing are accomplished in part by making known to the world not only what happened at this place, but also by insisting that what happened matters" (2001, 79).

The response that transformed the site of death into a shrine, a sacred but public space, inviting anyone to contribute flowers or notes, also created a ritual, but one that was generated by family. The site itself, of untimely and violent death, constituted the authority, legitimating the ritual acts of people who came to the site, both those from the community and strangers. The spontaneous public ritual served to transform the living to the dead in social space, but it incorporated the knowledge of the violence, the political battle that caused the deaths. Though this spontaneous ritual, and others like it, made no mention of the political conflict, the people of Ireland did not need to be told why this happened or have it explained as a political act.[7]

London

A similar ritual on a monumental scale, not limited to the neighborhood, developed when Princess Diana was killed in a car crash in 2007. The response to the untimely death of an aristocrat known as "the people's princess" belongs to the same genre of spontaneous rituals that emerged from the political violence in Ireland. London was witness to a spontaneous outpouring of grief. Millions of people left bouquets of flowers and notes to Diana for days preceding the funeral (Kear and Steinberg 1999). Though her death was not the consequence of political violence, she was a much-beloved and very public figure whose life was embroiled in the politics of the monarchy. Those politics initially influenced the queen of England to refrain from recognizing Princess Diana as a member of the royal family and therefore deserving of a royal funeral. Persuaded by the grieving public and the politically astute prime minister, the queen relented and agreed to a royal funeral. The international as well as the national press reported around the clock on these events as they developed. Princess Diana's death elicited a spontaneous ritual of enormous scale, an unprecedented expression of grief. Ultimately, the Londoners' display of devotion to "the people's princess" evolved into the royal funeral of a princess. Framed by a public outpouring of grief and a Westminster Abbey funeral, this event was witness to a struggle of power in which ritual succeeded in taming the political.

Liberia

The Ebola epidemic in Liberia has reverberated into the spaces where ritual and politics converge. Decoration Day is a national public holiday when Liberians clean, paint, and decorate the graves of their relatives, a ritual that involves intimate funeral practices. Sadly, in 2015 survivors could not tend the graves of their loved ones because the bodies of those who died had to be cremated. (The order issued by President Ellen Johnson Sirleaf requiring cremation has since been lifted.) As a poor substitute, women and survivors who lost family members in the epidemic were bused to the site of the concrete hut that contained the barrels of ashes of the deceased. There the mourners placed wreaths at the foot of the black iron doors separating them from the hut, and there they wailed and wept. Ten minutes later they were hustled into the bus and taken back to Monrovia.

Not only did the Liberian government take action governing the treatment of the deceased, but international representatives from the United States, including Marines, the United Kingdom, and Doctors without Borders and other NGOs provided care in Liberia, Sierra Leone, and Guinea during this epidemic. However, the politics goes beyond the burial rituals. As frequently noted in news reports, the country was devastated by the civil war in the 1990s, leaving it vulnerable to a disaster, and aid from Western countries was inadequate and difficult to obtain, as President Ellen Sirleaf Johnson noted in the film about her presidency, *Iron Ladies*. Moreover, the World Health Organization reported that it could have responded to the epidemic much earlier if its budget had allowed, but countries were not fulfilling their commitments, leading to limitations on the staff. Consequently, not only was this a massive epidemic, due in large part to the politics of civil war and inadequate international aid, but the living were no longer able to carry out their rituals to honor the dead. One can view this situation as a complete imbalance between ritual and politics. Ritual was defeated, even abolished, by politics.

Istanbul: Gezi Park

Protests are political events that utilize the ritual framework to express resistance. Unlike in rites of passage, which focus on individuals, participants in protests represent a segment of the population or, perhaps, the general public. Though the message of a protest can be aimed at a specific target (government, institution, or individual) or to the culture at large, communication is accomplished publicly for the most part. Resistance and contestation do not represent a political innovation, but technology and social media have made it possible today for a local protest to expand quickly and reach international audiences rapidly. Increasingly in the twenty-first century contestation has proven to be widespread, especially in countries where the population has endured long years of dictators or oppressive governments.

Turkey, a country governed by a democratically elected prime minister and president, was the site of a ritual protest that received global attention in May 2013. Focused on Prime Minister Recep Tayyip Erdogan's decision to transform Istanbul's Gezi Park into a shopping mall that would be architecturally reminiscent of the Ottoman era, the protestors occupied the park; the protest quickly grew into a major ritual contestation and spread to other cities in Turkey, garnering international attention. Gezi Park is located in an upscale neighborhood called Taksim; consequently, the primary slogan of the protest became "Everywhere is Taksim. Everywhere is Resistance!"

Emerging from two decades of increasing authoritarianism imposed by Prime Minister (now President) Erdogan, tens of thousands of people responded to a protest opposing the government's decision. A group of scholars and activists documented the event from multiple perspectives, and Arzu Öztürkmen, professor in the history department at Bogazici University, published an article incorporating its research (2014). The following discussion is based on her work.

The Gezi Park protest was a political movement with no leadership, but the internet offered a massive platform where ideas emerged. Popular music served as a source for language and themes, including music from the Grand Theft Auto game. "This language was the *lingua franca* of the internet—a platform for communication that could not be shut down. The virtual world was where we worked and communicated, encompassing and shaping what we call 'real'" (Öztürkmen 2014, 57). The prime minister recognized the centrality of the internet to the protest and blamed social media for the emerging Gezi language, short phrases which adapted football slogans and old political slogans to the new situation and ones that referenced specific music popular in youth culture. In an effort to block the protestors' communication, the prime minister banned Twitter on March 20, 2014.

Though no one authority organized the protest, a major influence throughout was the football fan club Carsi, fans of the professional team known as Besiktas. They brought their considerable skills in organization and the crafting of slogans to the protest. At one point members of Carsi took possession of a bulldozer and drove toward the police forces, which were throwing tear gas, and at another point Carsi led other fans into the park to join the protestors (who at one point numbered 100,000). In a significant move fan cubs also organized forums as a follow-up to the protest.

Other groups involved in the protest included a collection of leftist oppositional organizations, residents of the Gazi Mahallesi neighborhood (populated by left-wing and marginalized Alevi and Kurdish communities), and anti-capitalist Muslims, motivated by their oppositional stance to the prime minister's political party's consumerist policies. (AKP is the political party of the prime minister, now president.) Especially active participants were a large number of youth who were influenced by video games that challenge the police (e.g., Grand Theft Auto). Others who offered support included residents of the neighborhood who opened their homes and a hotel to the protestors, doctors who gave masks when tear gas was used, and celebrities, performers, and academics.[8]

Performance and creativity characterized this protest throughout. The protest spread beyond the park itself, from graffiti on surrounding buildings (including curses) intended to send a message to the prime minister to pop songs written for the protest to spontaneous theatrical and musical performances. Particularly notable was the international pianist Davide Martello's several-day performance, from June 12 to June 15, when police once again brought in tear gas. His huge piano was set up in Taksim Square (near Gezi Park) and he played for thirteen hours the first day, capturing the attention of the police as well as the thousands of protesters.

The prime minister refused to hear the message of the protestors; he consistently gave orders to the police to use tear gas and water cannons and made declarations of his intent to overpower the opposition. Encounters with the police killed a number of young people, one merely on an errand to buy bread. Bread then became a symbol of the protests, emerging organically from the events. In various stages the encounters and protests continued until June 15, when the occupation of the park was ended, but follow-up activities continued into July, "the era of the forums." At least forty-one forums (organized by the fan clubs) were established in different parks for people to share their experiences and consider the future.

In a remarkable development, the Gezi Park participants merged with the Gay Pride Parade on June 30, making the 2014 Gay Pride Parade the largest in Istanbul's history. Moreover, shifting the protest to the ritual genre of parade, a more orderly enactment of display, made a statement of closure. At the same time, however, a parade exhibits the constituents of a community or society. Parade participants send a message to the general public, the media, and politicians; that message is a declaration of identity and a claim of belonging. The act of parading provided a platform for the Gezi Park participants and their supporters to establish their identity as legitimate, respectable members of society with a voice and a rightful place in public life.

Certainly the Gezi Park protest articulated a we/they opposition, and it did so with an army of signifiers, the thousands of participants who, with multiple performances, challenged the police, armed with tear gas, water cannons, and bulldozers. Öztürkmen described this perspective on the protest as a "new construction of 'we.'" Prime Minister Recep Tayyip Erdogan labeled the protesters "looters" and openly stated that the protestors were not his people, confirming a political divide within the Turkish people (Öztürkmen 2014, 40).

The Gezi Park ritual events used a wide variety of semiotic systems and brought together a very mixed population to express their political position:

resistance to the government. First and most prominent of those semiotic systems was the occupation of the park itself, a contested space; then performances were added, and finally a parade and follow-up forums provided interpretation and solidarity. From the perspective of the ritual framework, the parade and forums provided reintegration of the protestors into everyday life with a new and transformed identity based on their political position, publicly displayed.

The prime minister, subsequently elected president of Turkey, continues to exercise control with authoritarian methods. The ritual protest succeeded in establishing a popular opposition that blocked the planned building of a mall in Gezi Park. Nevertheless, the opposition has concerns that President Erdogan will move ahead with the mall, a temple to his consumerist ideology and a further erasure of Ataturk, the founding father of Turkey as a secular nation.[9]

FAN CLUBS AS ACTIVISTS

As early as 1944 Johan Huizinga recognized the importance of events that integrated play with ritual/festival, including contests (Huizinga 1950). More recently Jeremy MacClancy has argued that the cultural domain of sport can become politicized. Fan clubs, attached to professional teams relatively recently, belong to the cultural domain of sport but are not subject to the control of team owners nor to the government. As autonomous units they can engage in resistance and contestation, as they have in situations of "profound conflict" (MacClancy 1996, 11). While this is not always acknowledged in the media, in some instances in the twenty-first century fan clubs have provided order within the chaos of a massive protest. As mentioned above, the Gezi Park protest in Istanbul involved many thousands of people from different sectors of the city; considering the numbers involved, the protest was remarkably peaceful and orderly except when the police were spraying tear gas or shooting water cannons. Much of the credit for the order as well as the inspiration of the protest and the reorganization after attacks by the police has been laid at the feet of a fan club known as Carsi, supporters of Besiktas, a professional soccer team. As a fan club, members of Carsi had experience organizing large crowds, singing inspirational songs, and providing slogans. They applied these skills to the protest and were repeatedly acknowledged as powerful players in sustaining and organizing it as well as in creating the follow-up forums (Öztürkmen 2014).

In Egypt organized football fans known as "ultras" became a major protest group in the uprisings in Cairo. Though Egypt has six major football clubs, the two most popular and active are Al-Ahly whose fans are known as Ultras Ahlawy, and Zamalek, whose supporters are called the White Knights. The fan clubs first appeared in 2007, and though their allegiance is to their team and not to any particular political party, they are experienced in fighting with security forces and the police. When the protests began, they were among the first to "take to the streets," bringing their intensity, antiauthoritarianism and organizational skills to the revolution. The struggle continued as clashes between police and football supporters occurred in February 2015 in which forty people were killed (*Al-Jazeera* 2015).

Football fans have also played a role in the battles in Ukraine, where soccer ultras became a political power there during the uprisings. Many of them were members of a paramilitary group known as Right Sector, and this group led the crowds against Ianukovich's corrupt police in the initial period of the conflict. Later the Right Sector became the first military unit to fight against the pro-Russian separatists (Ulan Bigozhin, personal communication).

These examples point to fan clubs as significant actors in political rebellions from Ukraine to Egypt; they are autonomous organizations that have bridged the space between the ritual event (the game) and the political movement, shifting their weight to the political in conflicts with the state.

SPORT AS RESOURCE FOR DOMINATION

Commenting on the significance of futbol/soccer in an account that qualifies the game as ritual, recognizing its potential for transformation and its position in the political landscape, *Al-Jazeera* stated: "The game can be an engine of conflict or a force for change, transcending borders and cultural backgrounds and forging new affiliations and identities" (2012). In contrast to resistance, we turn in the following example to domination, a view of the game as an engine of conflict that transcended national borders and engaged multiple cultures. Lest we forget the attraction sports have for dictators, Jeremy MacClancy reminds us of the role of sport in creating identity at the level of the nation-state, especially for subject countries within imperial regimes and newly independent states: "Sport may be used as a resource by which the powerful attempt to dominate others," citing the Soviet state and the Sandinista government of Nicaragua as examples (1996, 13). Perhaps the prime example was the 1936 Olympics in Berlin. In Alessandro Falassi's words, "A dazzling dimension of spectacle was applied to the whole production in such a way that the participants and international public were thrust into the role of spectators at the celebration of Nazi Germany's greatness" (1987, 118).

In the Africa Cup of Nations tournament, African nation-states send their representative team to the host country where they will compete for the opportunity to participate in the FIFA Confederate Cup (a prelude to the World Cup). The 2015 tournament exposed major contradictions and challenges to this significant ritual event. Centering around the question of what country would host the Africa Cup of Nations, the fissure emerged from the crisis caused by Ebola. Morocco was designated the host for the tournament in 2015, but concerns about Ebola caused it to cancel, leaving a vacuum. The president of the small country of Equatorial Guinea, Teodoro Obiang Nguema, offered his country as the host, grabbing an opportunity to improve his nation's standing. Juan Tomas Avila Laurel (2015) argued that the Africa Cup of Nations shouldn't be supported "because Obiang is . . . Africa's longest serving dictator, having been in power for 34 years. He oversees a regime that oppresses its own people, refusing to allow any political opposition and regularly cracking down on critics. A wealthy country that protects the interests of a tiny elite while the majority live in severe poverty." Laurel also noted that the president bought tickets for the tournament and forced government ministers and private companies to do so in order to ensure full stadiums. The author also claimed that more than one Equatorial Guinean has died at the hand of foreign police or in the crush of stampeding hordes during games.

Although Equatorial Guinea had been disqualified from entering the Africa Cup because of fielding players from outside the country, a violation of the rules, once the country offered to host the Cup, it was allowed to participate. Equatorial Guinea made it to the semifinals and played against Ghana, who won by 3-0. An ugly scene followed the game as Equatorial Guinea fans attempted to attack the Ghanaian team, throwing objects at them. Laurel's response to the violence was: "Given the state the country is in, it was always ridiculous to think that herding young and adult Equatorial Guineans like sheep to the stadium to support the team would not expose the inevitable cracks and contradictions" (Laurel 2015).

A commenter on Laurel's article in the *Guardian* identified as "thesmallerhalf" responded with insight into the process by which politics and sports are sometimes entwined: "But you are missing the point, politicians will shamelessly exploit sporting events to affirm their position, increase their prestige or divert their people from the real issues. It is a time honoured, if not particularly honourable, political ploy. And the more dictatorial the politician the more blatant is the exploitation. Try as you might, separating politics from sport is a futile exercise" (February 8, 2015).

Expanding its reach, this small country, excluded from the Africa Cup of Nations, exploited the situation created by the international epidemic and increased its status and the scale of its involvement, thereby contravening the regulation that had disqualified the Equatorial Guinea team from participating. As Laurel emphasizes, however, the violence directed against the Ghanaian team reveals frustrations, contradictions, and a suppressed violence in the population, a violent fissure in the ritual that points to the dismal political conditions in the country.

CONCLUSIONS

The preoccupations and political orientations of twenty-first-century people around the globe continue to be generated by the ambiguities, contradictions, and uncertainties encountered in everyday life, exaggerated in recent decades by neoliberal economic policies imposed internationally. Responding to these with rituals intended to affect the flow of power in the universe, social groups have found expression in the enduring partnership of ritual and politics.

As modernity, technology, mobility, and globalization have introduced, imposed, and implemented changes in social and political life, the ability of persons to create events embodying the ritual/political domain has expanded in scale proportionate to the conditions faced. In this essay I have examined protests, public grieving, and sport as ritual action. These responses employ a full range of contemporary media, facilitating the expansion of scale. In addition to the cell phone and social media linking individuals, the global news and commentary directed to the world at large defined these events as ones that matter, ones imbued with significance.

Another twenty-first-century innovation has been the influential role of fan clubs in organizing protests. Familiar with organizing groups and experienced in challenging security forces, fan clubs have been the unsung heroes in numerous massive protests. Noting their crucial role reminds us that in almost all of these instances people have participated in face-to-face interactions; they have been co-present with others, confirming that technology is an addition to social action, not a substitute for it.

The spontaneous rituals of grief in Northern Ireland and in London have demonstrated that while institutionalized authorities or agents of violence retain power, when persons are moved by identification, they will express their feelings through public ritual and the accompanying communications. The public's expression of grief to honor Princess Diana reached an unprecedented scale, sending a message to the monarchy to acknowledge her with a royal funeral. In contrast, Liberian survivors of the Ebola epidemic were not able to express their grief over the loss of their family members through a public ritual. Instead, the failure of the political, nationally and internationally, left the citizens vulnerable to Ebola and denied survivors the ritual of transformation that would recognize the loss of the specific deceased individual and her or his relationship to the living.

Resistance to authoritative government also employed the ritual framework to express political opposition. In Gezi Park the ritual and the political were performed in a range of genres, all directed toward a government decision. In Istanbul, as in London, the numbers who joined the protest were on the scale of immense, the forms of expression were spontaneous and unique, and the international communication through the global news was continuous.

The role of soccer fan clubs appears prominently in Istanbul and proves to have been even more influential in other protests. Throughout the world futbol/soccer fan clubs enable identity formation as they are attached to teams that are affiliated with specific cities or neighborhoods, providing a link between the local and the national or international. As Matthew Guschwan (2011) has shown, each team is characterized by a package of symbols, including the names of players that become indices of their teams or nation states.

The sport known as *futbol* in Europe, Latin America, and Africa, and *soccer* in the United States, is one that plays out the contradictions of competition on the ritual site of the playing field in contemporary societies. It also generates identity around the world with its rotating us-and-them opposition and through the ubiquitous fan clubs attached to specific teams. Nevertheless, professional teams are owned by billionaires, and professional players are paid in million-dollar salaries, creating a political situation of enormous disparity between the intensely rich and the ordinary people who follow the game. The fan clubs, however, are an organized, vernacular response to these corporate sports giants, autonomous enough to apply their skills, including knowledge of ritual and symbol, to political protests. As a ritual form defined by its symbols, however, soccer can also be used by authoritarian governments to increase their power, and indeed the dictator of Equatorial Guinea proved to be successful in manipulating international sports to his advantage.

These distinctive and dramatic circumstances from around the globe invoked the ritual/political response at multiple degrees of scale. They embody a full range of outcomes, revealing the political and ritual forces in a struggle for dominance. Whether balance and a transformation were achieved or not, each ritual event, located in a specific local site, evolved through social media and global communications to become the subject of international news.

As the wide range of dramatic situations presented above demonstrates, events characterized by the intertwining of ritual and politics have taken on new significance in the twenty-first century, running in parallel with the expanded scale of social and political activity. As the construction of identity has become more complex in our mobile, transnational world, and as contradictions, competition, ambiguities, and uncertainties threaten daily life with increasing frequency, persons feel a greater and greater need for transformation that will clarify and resolve. While the intertwining of ritual and politics cannot promise transformations that will resolve conflict, the ritual framework provides an opportunity for the symbolic expression of contradictions, the ambiguous, and the unexplainable, and facilitates the attempt to influence the forces of politics on any scale.

NOTES

1. Professor Enrique Lamadrid's statement served to announce a lecture he was to deliver at the School of Advanced Research, Santa Fe, New Mexico, March 25, 2015.
2. See Stoeltje 1993 for a discussion of this term and power in the various genres.
3. In contemporary India, for example, newspapers include several pages of ads for brides, organized according to caste, religion, and ethnicity, and in May 2015, a mother advertised for a husband for her son.
4. See Moore and Myerhoff 1977 (introduction) for a discussion of the importance of the enactment of social relationships in secular rituals in particular.
5. Exemplifying his approach, Cohen published a study of London's Notting Hill Carnival, which transformed from a revived traditional English fair into a fiercely contested event, a carnival exclusively West Indian in arts, music, and leadership. In *Masquerade Politics*, he refers to politics as articulated in terms of nonpolitical, cultural forms such as religion, kinship, and the arts (Cohen 1993, ix–3).
6. See Bauman 1992 on performance; see Turner 1974 on symbolic communication.
7. Though such shrines were very personal and included notes that expressed a longing for peace (referencing the conflict), the practice of designating the exact place where an individual has died an untimely death does occur in the United States. as well. It is not uncommon to see a cross and artificial flowers alongside a highway, especially in heavily Catholic areas of the country such as the Southwest.
8. The Divan Hotel, owned by the industrialist Koc family, became a refuge for gassed and hosed people; the lobby was the site of the first piano recital of the Gezi events, given by Bugra Temel, a young protestor. The Lycee Notre Dame de Sion was also an important refuge site for gassed people.
9. Following the attempted coup in July 2016 the state imposed authoritarian draconian methods on the population, the political definitively abolishing the ritual.

REFERENCES

Al-Jazeera. 2012. "Empire: Scoring Big: The Global World of Football." December 29.
Al-Jazeera. 2015. "Ultras." February 12.
Ampene, Kwasi. 2005. *Female Song Tradition and the Akan of Ghana: The Process in Nnuwonkoro*. Burlington, VT: Ashgate.
Babcock, Barbara A. 1978. "Too Many, Too Few: Ritual Modes of Signification." *Semiotica* 23 (3/4): 291–302. http://dx.doi.org/10.1515/semi.1978.23.3-4.291.
Bakhtin, Mikhail. 1984 (1965). *Rabelais and His World*. Bloomington: Indiana University Press.
Barber, Karin. 1991. *I Could Speak until Tomorrow: Oriki, Women and the Past in a Yoruba Town*. Washington, DC: Smithsonian Institution Press.
Bauman, Richard, ed. 1992. "Performance." In *Folklore, Cultural Performances, and Popular Entertainments*, 41–49. Oxford: Oxford University Press.
Besnier, Niko. 2011. *On the Edge of the Global: Modern Anxieties in a Pacific Island Nation*. Palo Alto: Stanford University Press.
Burke, Kenneth. 1969. *A Rhetoric of Moves*. Berkeley: University of California Press.
Carr, E. Summerson, and Michael Lempert, eds. 2016. *Scale: Discourse and Dimensions of Social Life*. Berkeley: University of California Press.
Cohen, Abner. 1974. *Two Dimensional Man: An Essay on the Anthropology of Power and Symbolism in Complex Society*. Berkeley: University of California Press.
Cohen, Abner. 1993. *Masquerade Politics: Explorations in the Structure of Urban Cultural Movements*. Berkeley: University of California Press.
Cohen, Colleen B., Richard Wilk, and Beverly Stoeltje. 1996. *Beauty Queens on the Global Stage*. New York: Routledge.
Comaroff, Jean. 1985. *Body of Power, Spirit of Resistance: The Culture and History of a South African People*. Chicago: University of Chicago Press.
Comaroff, Jean, and John Comaroff. 1993. *Modernity and Its Malcontents: Ritual and Power in Postcolonial Africa*. Chicago: University of Chicago Press.
Cowley, John. 1996. *Carnival, Canboulay and Calypso: Traditions in the Making*. Cambridge: Cambridge University Press.
DaMatta, Roberto. 1991. *Carnivals, Rogues, and Heroes: An Interpretation of the Brazilian Dilemma*. Notre Dame: University of Notre Dame Press.
Eastwood, William. 2009. "Processions in the Street: Georgian Orthodox Privilege and Religious Minorities' Response to Invisibility." *Anthropology of East Europe Review* 27 (1): 20–28.
Falassi, Alessandro, ed. 1987. *Time out of Time: Essays on the Festival*. Albuquerque: University of New Mexico Press.
Gilmore, David D. 1998. *Carnival & Culture: Sex, Symbol & Status in Spain*. New Haven: Yale University Press.
Gilman, Lisa. 2009. *The Dance of Politics: Gender, Performance, and Democratization in Malawi*. Philadelphia: Temple University Press.
Guschwan, Matthew. 2011. "Fans, Romans, Countrymen: Soccer Fandom and Civic Identity in Contemporary Rome." *International Journal of Communications* 5: 1190–2013.
Haynes, Michaele Thurgood. 1998. *Dressing Up Debutantes: Pageantry and Glitz in Texas*. Oxford: Berg. http://dx.doi.org/10.2752/9780857854063.
Holland, Dorothy, and Jean Lave. 2001. *History in Person: Enduring Struggles, Contentious Practice, Intimate Identities*. Santa Fe: School for Advanced Research Press.
Huizinga, Johan. 1950. *Homo Ludens: A Study of the Play Element in Culture*. Boston: Beacon.
Kear, Adrian, and Deborah Lynn Steinberg, eds. 1999. *Mourning Diana: Nation, Culture and the Performance of Grief*. London: Routledge.
Kertzer, David. 1988. *Ritual, Politics, and Power*. New Haven: Yale University Press.

Langer, Suzanne. 1957 (1942). *Philosophy in a New Key: A Study in the Symbolism of Reason, Rite and Art.* Cambridge: Harvard University Press.
Laurel, Juan Tomas Avila. 2015. "Why We Shouldn't Support the Africa Cup of Nations." *Guardian*, February 8.
Loewe, Ronald. 2010. *Maya or Mestizo? Nationalism, Modernity, and its Discontents.* Toronto: University of Toronto Press.
MacClancy, Jeremy, ed. 1996. *Sport, Identity, and Ethnicity.* Oxford: Berg.
Moore, Sally F., and Barbara G. Myerhoff, eds. 1977. *Secular Ritual.* Assen, Netherlands: Van Gorcum.
Napier, A. David. 1986. *Masks, Transformation, and Paradox.* Berkeley: University of California Press.
Noyes, Dorothy. 2003. *Fire in the Placa: Catalan Festival Politics After Franco.* Philadelphia: University of Pennsylvania Press. http://dx.doi.org/10.9783/9780812202991.
Öztürkmen, Arzu. 2014. "The Park, the Penguin, and the Gas: Performance in Progress in Gezi Park." *Drama Review* 58 (3): 39–68. http://dx.doi.org/10.1162/DRAM_a_00372.
Santino, Jack. 1995. *All Around the Year: Holidays and Celebration in American Life.* Champaign: University of Illinois Press.
Santino, Jack. 2001. *Signs of War and Peace: Social Conflict and the Use of Public Symbols in Northern Ireland.* New York: Palgrave. http://dx.doi.org/10.1007/978-1-4039-8233-9.
Santino, Jack. 2011. "The Carnivalesque and the Ritualesque." *Journal of American Folklore* 124 (491): 61–73. http://dx.doi.org/10.5406/jamerfolk.124.491.0061.
Schielke, Samuli. 2008. "Policing Ambiguity: Muslim Saints-Day Festivals and the Moral Geography of Public Space in Egypt." *American Ethnologist* 35 (4): 539–52. http://dx.doi.org/10.1111/j.1548-1425.2008.00097.x.
Stoeltje, Beverly J. 1993. "Power and the Ritual Genres: American Rodeo." *Western Folklore* 52 (2/4): 135–56. http://dx.doi.org/10.2307/1500083.
Stoeltje, Beverly. 2010. "Custom and Politics in Ghanaian Popular Culture." In *Facts, Fiction, and African Creative Imaginations*, ed. Toyin Falola and Fallou Ngom, 60–74. London: Routledge.
Turner, Terence. 1977. "Transformation, Hierarchy and Transcendence: A Reformulation of Van Gennep's Model of the Structure of Rites de Passage." In *Secular Ritual*, ed. Sally F. Moore and Barbara G. Myerhoff, 53–70. Amsterdam: Van Gorcum.
Turner, Victor. 1974. *Dramas, Fields, and Metaphors: Symbolic Action in Human Society.* Ithaca: Cornell University Press.
Turner, Victor. 1982. "Liminal to Liminoid, in Play Flow, and Ritual: An Essay in Comparative Symbology." In *From Ritual to Theatre: The Human Seriousness of Play*, 20–60. New York: PAJ Publications.
Williams, Raymond. 1977. *Marxism and Literature.* Oxford: Oxford University Press.

5

Political Percussions
Cork Brass Bands and the Irish Revolution, 1914–1922

John Borgonovo

JACK SANTINO AND OTHER SCHOLARS HAVE investigated Northern Ireland's rich political procession culture of Ulster Unionism, including the prominent role played by marching bands (Santino 2001; Bell 1987; Bryan 2000; Cairns 2000). Despite the work of historians Maura Cronin, Fintan Lane, and Jack McGrath, much less is known about an earlier band tradition in other parts of Ireland during the nineteenth and early twentieth century (Cronin 1994, 146, 151–53, 167, 195; Lane 1999; McGrath 2010, 13–16). This chapter will explore the political brass band culture in the city of Cork during that time frame, with special focus on its manifestations during the the Irish revolutionary period (1914–1923). It will conceptualize the Cork bands within Irish nationalist popular politics, explain the use of processions by Irish separatists, and highlight revolutionary tensions between different political groupings as expressed by affiliated brass bands.

SOCIAL AND POLITICAL BANDS IN NINETEENTH-CENTURY IRELAND

Modern Irish nationalism offers compelling material for scholars interested in processions and contested public space. Starting in the early nineteenth century, nationalists led by Daniel O'Connell pioneered civil disobedience tactics to challenge the British administration of Ireland. In the 1820s and 1830s, imaginative mass mobilizations of the Catholic peasantry helped secure Catholic access to political office and end onerous tithe tax payments to the Anglican Church. During the early 1840s, the campaign to repeal the Act of Union (which placed Ireland within the United Kingdom) produced some of the most sophisticated political theater seen in Europe up to that point (Owens 1994, 1998, 1999). Daniel O'Connell and his Repeal Movement held a series of "monster meetings" that attracted hundreds of thousands of peasant supporters. These nationalist festivals culminated in elaborate processions of tens of thousands that deliberately echoed British judicial, regal, and military parades of the period. Participants implicitly threatened physical resistance to continued British rule of Ireland by incorporating military symbols into the processions such as uniforms, mock weapons, and cavalry units. Brass bands added to the militaristic atmosphere by playing marching airs on drums, fifes, and pipes. Village bands typically led spectators to and from their homeland, sometimes covering distances of over fifty miles. O'Connell preferred to use temperance bands in these monster meetings, as their sobriety and orderly behavior advertised Ireland's capacity for productive self-government (Malcolm 1986, 132–33).

O'Connell's monster meetings coincided with the explosion of the Irish temperance movement in the early 1840s (Malcolm 1986, 101–50). Led by the Catholic Capuchin monk Father Theobald Mathew of Cork City, temperance briefly swept Ireland. At one point, nearly half of all Irish adults had pledged total abstention from alcohol. Father Mathew encouraged the formation of temperance brass bands at the local level to gather crowds for pledge meetings and to offer nonalcoholic entertainment to peasants and the urban working classes. Band practice kept men out of the public house, while Sunday band processions and concerts served as wholesome nonalcoholic family events that spread the temperance message. At the movement's height, the city of Cork maintained thirty-three temperance bands, with uniforms and instruments financed by Father Mathew (Cooke 1992; Malcolm 1986, 132; Birmingham 1996). The brass bands were one element of a broader popularization of Irish politics that linked nationalism to notions of working-class respectability and self-improvement. Brass bands often developed alongside reading rooms (many provided by Father Matthew's temperance campaign), which provided the working classes with opportunities for social mobility (Townsend 2003.)

Irish brass bands were part of an international "brass band movement" that found particular success in the United States and Great Britain during the second half of the twentieth century (Newsom 1979; Russell 1983, 1997). The popularity of brass bands can be attributed to social changes brought about by the Industrial Revolution, especially urbanization and the development of leisure time. Technical innovations and mass production made numerous band instruments available and affordable to working-class musicians, while widespread literacy and media-disseminated brass band arrangements, sheet music, and technical instruction proliferated. Band contests became a form of popular entertainment in Britain, sometimes drawing as many as 80,000 spectators. Much of the British brass band activity was found in England's industrial north, with bands organized in working places such as factories and mines (O'Neill 1987; Bythell 1994; Newsom 1979; Herbert 1990; Herbert 2000). However, Irish brass bands were more frequently formed around geographic locales of towns, villages, and urban neighborhoods. Band contests were less popular in Ireland, though the bands found alternative outlets in the popular politics of Irish nationalism (Borgonovo 2016). This was particularly true in the city of Cork.

As Maura Cronin has convincingly argued, Cork bands were "noted, from the 1840s onwards, for their close identification with popular nationalism, when they became an essential feature of all local nationalist demonstrations of both the constitutional and militant traditions" (1994, 152). A major impetus was provided by the Irish National Land League, which mobilized peasant tenant farmers during the 1880s. Ireland's "Land War" saw a sustained campaign to secure tenant rights and redistribute massive land estates owned by Ireland's small gentry. Land League meetings echoed the popular pageantry of O'Connell's earlier movements, and were ritualized events that strengthened nationalist communities' political identity (Kane 2011, 26, 39, 69, 73, 80). According to historian T. W. Moody, "Bands playing patriotic tunes were an essential element" of these gatherings. Brass bands led large processions of horsemen, decorated marchers, and tenant farmers carrying signs with messages such as "The land for the people" and "Down with the land robbers" (1982, 348). The Land League also deployed bands during major civil disobedience actions, including protests at public auctions of goods seized from tenant farmer rent strikers; the harvesting of crops of imprisoned Land League activists; and disruptions of fox hunting, a sport closely associated with the Irish gentry (Borgonovo 2016; Laird 2005, 18–19, 74–75).

"THE BAND MENACE" AND OTHER MUSICAL RIVALRIES

By the late nineteenth century, brass bands enjoyed great popularity among Cork City's working classes. A port city and commercial center, Cork held a population of 70,000, with high rates of severe poverty. Band members were often made up of men from the "respectable" working class (those with steady employment, usually artisans), though drum and fife bands (classified in this chapter as "brass bands") might attract lower-status laborer musicians, owing to the affordability of instruments.

Geographically, Cork City was dense and built into hillsides that created numerous small but distinct neighborhoods. Intense rivalries between neighborhoods often spilled into politics and sports (O'Brien 1993, 717). Small rented band rooms provided the groups with headquarters for rehearsals, meetings, and instrument storage. Throughout the late nineteenth and early twentieth century, Cork's brass bands expressed fierce neighborhood pride and identity; they offered members excitement and entertainment; and participation was affordable. Cork bands also utilized the city's large former British soldier population, which offered musical expertise learned in the rich British Army regimental band tradition. Having long given up the temperance pledge, brass bands continued their Sunday parades in Cork, often with hundreds of followers. Before the introduction of organized sports, these processional outings provided an outlet for male youths; they also allowed for unsupervised interaction with the opposite sex in a socially conservative society. The band parades could be rowdy and drunken, and this produced friction between followers from rival neighborhoods.

In the late 1870s, clashes between parading bands became a serious problem in Cork, which the city authorities dubbed the "Band Menace" (Lane 1999). Historian Fintan Lane has explored these extraordinary events, which might be described as musically scored faction fights. During the Sunday parades, marching bands "invaded" rival bands' urban territory, resulting in mass brawls that sometimes caused scores of casualties. Musicians often raided their rivals' band rooms to smash instruments, which generated more violence. The band riots continued for two years, until mounted police and strong clerical intervention finally ended the trouble.

During this period, the city's brass bands expressed allegiance to politicians advocating Irish legislative autonomy (known as home rule) to be secured by nonviolent constitutional means. Constitutional nationalism enjoyed a strong majority of public opinion in the south of Ireland, with a much smaller minority believing that Irish independence could only be achieved by physical resistance to Britain. (These latter physical force adherents became known as "republicans.") Both constitutional and republican activists engaged in elaborate processions, marches, and demonstrations. At a time of strict government controls over political speech and public processions (including the banning of party banners and certain "party tunes"), bands often expressed seditious ideas through music (Maddox 2004). Playlists included tunes that celebrated Irish resistance to British rule, from ancient times up to the present. Songs also leveraged Ireland's strong street ballad culture. The new lyrics added to old airs often championed local martyrs and political prisoners, or abused unpopular landlords, magistrates, and police officers. The Cork bands during this period added color to political receptions and parades. Their music also played a more subversive role. Periodically, Cork bands (and local bands across nationalist Ireland) appeared at evictions, in support of protesting tenant farmers; they processed political prisoners to and from their place of incarceration; and they played concerts near jails to raise the morale of prisoners, or outside courthouses to disrupt the proceedings inside (Borgonovo 2016). Similar activity could be found among brass bands across southern Ireland, though Cork and Limerick City seemed to have developed an especially rich political music milieu.

In the first decade of the twentieth century, Cork bands aligned themselves with two main constitutional political parties: John Redmond's Irish Party and William O'Brien's All-for-Ireland League (*Evening Echo*, April 10, 1978).[1] The two parties held similar stands on most issues, including the securing of Irish home rule, yet they still waged a bitter war for dominance in the city. The Cork writer Frank O'Connor described the rivalry in his short story "The Coronet Player Who Betrayed Ireland":

> Our great national leader, William O'Brien, once referred to us as "The Old Guard." Myself and other kids of the Old Guard used to parade the street with tin cans and toy trumpets, singing, "We'll hang Johnnie Redmond on a sour apple tree" . . . Unfortunately, our neighborhood was bounded to the south by a long ugly street leading uphill to the Cathedral, and the lanes off it were infested with the most wretched specimens of humanity who took the Redmondite side for whatever could be got from it in the way of drink . . . It always saddened me, coming through this street on my way home from school, and seeing the poor, misguided children, barefoot singing, "We'll hang William O'Brien on a sour apple tree." It left me with little hope for Ireland. (1981, 118)

During the Redmond/O'Brien feud, politically affiliated marching bands served as shock troops, spearheading mob assaults on rival party crowds (Birmingham 1996, 11; *Southern Star*, January 8, 15, May 28, September 24 1910). Musicians used their instruments as weapons; and bands often marched into rival party meetings to drown out speakers, which usually provoked a brawl. About eight of the city's bands were routinely engaged in this political faction fighting from 1908 to 1914 (*Cork Constitution*, January 20, 1914; *Cork Examiner*, January 17, November 30, 1914; *Southern Star*, December 17, 1910). Mirroring the band riots of the 1870s, members also raided rival band rooms to smash instruments (*Cork Examiner*, May 23,

1908, November 30, 1910; *Southern Star*, October 29, 1910). Expensive bass drums seemed to be special targets. They carried the band name on the drumhead, and seemed to have been perceived as the symbolic heart of the band. In Cork, bass drums were sometimes hidden in supporters' homes, covertly carried into safe houses like hunted fugitives.[2] These lyrics testify to the situation:

> Creedy, Reidy, Dessy, and Snell
> Not judging their souls, they're already in hell
> The night of the battle we'll show them some fun
> We'll hang up the ruffian that stole our big drum
>   (O'Connor 1981, 6–7)

A 1910 newspaper report illustrates the feud's intensity:

> When Mr O'Brien and his supporters returned to Cork on Monday night there were some exciting scenes. In a scrimmage outside the [train] station the drum of the Quarry Lane Band was smashed, an opponent putting his foot through it. It is stated that an attempt was also made to break the drum of the Blackpool Band but this was prevented. As some of the Irish Party followers were passing down the Lower Road a man named Horgan was seriously injured and had to be removed to the infirmary. Several other scrimmages occurred in King Street but the police prevented any serious outburst. (*Southern Star*, September 24)

(The injured man, Horgan, testified in court that as four men beat him with sticks and kicked him unconscious, one warned that he would "never beat a drum again.")

Violence became endemic during election campaigns, as rival bands led nightly torch-lit processions through Cork streets (*Cork Examiner*, October 24, November 14–15, 19, 25–26, 28, 30, December 1, 3, 5, 1910).[3] Routine clashes between supporters taxed police authorities. Following the chaotic December 1910 general election, the local police inspector demanded written guarantees from the two political parties that they would refrain from public meetings in the next election.[4] Cork satirist Susanne Day described the 1910 general election with only some overstatement: "The number of voters who subsequently went to the polls without bandage or sticking-plaster adjoining their heads was small. The public houses ran out of porter, the hospitals ran out of lint and bandages, the streets were impassable for nights altogether, the big drum of the Cork Exchange Band was smashed to fragments, and the Gallows Green trombone was in bed for three weeks" (1916, 30–31).

WARTIME ALLEGIANCES AND DEMONSTRATIONS

The outbreak of the First World War suspended the Redmond/O'Brien political conflict. Despite traditional Irish nationalist opposition to service in the British Army, the war effort initially attracted public support by both constitutional parties in Cork. Thousands of working-class residents enlisted in the British forces, with some recruits accompanied to the train station by marching bands. Four Cork brass bands joined the British Army en masse: the Barrack Street Band, the Cork Workingmen's Drum and Fife Band, the Blackpool Drum and Fife Band, and the Fair Lane Drum and Fife Band (Prendergast 2010). Their enlistment reflected bands' tight social cohesion, which created peer pressure among members. Scholars of First World War military recruiting have noted the same construct in mass enlistments by similar social units and peer groups (Fitzpatrick 1995). Beyond the neighborhood bands, British Army regimental bands also mobilized support for the war, frequently playing at recruiting meetings and other pro-war public events (Dooley 1991; *Cork Constitution*, December 4, 1915, December 11, 1916, May 18, 1917; *Cork Examiner*, April 10, 1915, August 18, 1916).

Ireland's failure to secure home rule prior to and during the war, an international movement for self-determination, and political destabilization during the First World War created the conditions for revolution. Following a failed separatist rebellion in 1916 (known as the Easter Rising), Ireland underwent a dramatic political transformation (Borgonovo 2013). A mass independence movement took shape under the auspices of the Sinn Féin political party and its military wing, the Irish Volunteers (later known as the Irish Republican Army, or IRA).

Cork brass bands experienced turbulence during this switch of allegiance from pro-war constitutional parties to the antiwar, revolutionary Sinn Féin movement. In 1915, conductor James Delaney led the Greenmount Industrial School Band at concerts used to promote British Army recruitment meetings. However, in 1918, Delaney appealed to the government for a new job outside of Cork because he found himself "completely ostracized" for his earlier recruitment concerts (Borgonovo 2013, 210). Prior to the war, the Fair Hill Band supported John Redmond and engaged in violent altercations with political rivals. In 1915, members enlisted as a body in the British Army and stored their drums in Hannah Cronin's home for safekeeping. When the Fair Hills reformed the band after the war, they asked Cronin to return their drums. But Hannah Cronin had switched her political allegiance to Sinn Féin and refused to hand the drums over, telling members, "Those who fought for King George should go to King George now and get a band from him." They never recovered their drums, though they did return to the political mix (*Cork Examiner*, July 30, 1919).

In the Cork suburbs, musicians in the Raffeen Lodge of the Ancient Order of Hibernians, a fraternal order affiliated with John Redmond's Irish Party, also found themselves swept away by the revolutionary tide. A number of Raffeen Lodge members were expelled for switching their political loyalty to Sinn Féin, though they were allowed to remain in the lodge band because of their musical talents. This proved a fatal mistake, as the dissidents soon convinced the rest of the band to defect to Sinn Féin with their instruments, much to the consternation of the Hibernian leadership.[5]

Overall, about half the city's marching bands supported Sinn Féin outright, a couple maintained Irish Party allegiances, and the others stayed essentially apolitical. However, particularly coercive government policies or repressive actions occasionally drew all the city bands into the streets to express civic and national solidarity. The most notable occasion occurred when the government attempted to introduce military conscription to Ireland in 1918, causing the city to erupt into demonstrations and a general strike. All the city bands participated in these anticonscription rallies, processing their neighborhood residents to mass meetings and playing at protests themselves (*Cork Constitution*, April 24, 1918; *Cork Examiner*, April 16, 24, 1918).

Two new Cork bands emerged during the political turmoil of 1918. Recently returned wounded and discharged soldiers in Cork organized themselves to lobby for government assistance for wounded and unemployed ex-servicemen. Illustrating Cork's popular correlation of politics with brass bands, members formed a band at the very first meeting of the Cork branch of the National Federation of Discharged and Demobilized Soldiers and Sailors (NFDDSS) (*Cork Constitution*, December 24, 1917). Composed primarily of ex-soldier amputees, the NFDDSS band played at rallies, paraded through towns to recruit new members, and led war commemorations (*Cork Constitution*, August 16, 30, November 12, 1918; Borgonovo 2010).

A very different political band also sprung up in 1918, as the radical Irish Transport and General Workers Union experienced dramatic membership growth in Cork's unstable wartime economy. The syndicalist union promptly organized a drum and fife band named after James Connolly, the socialist union leader executed after the 1916 Easter Rising. In 1919, the James Connolly Drum and Fife Band led Cork's first recognized May Day celebration, as thousands of workers marched with red flags through city streets (*Cork Examiner*, May 2, 1919). The James Connolly Band appeared at nearly every Sinn Féin event during the next three years, as well as at meetings and demonstrations associated with the cause of labor. It gave a visibility to Irish trade unionism during a period of expansion and militancy (*Cork Examiner*, November 26, 1917, January 22, March 6, April 16, 1918; *Watchword of Labour*, December 15, 1917).

PIPE BANDS AND CIVIL DISOBEDIENCE

Among the city's most visible bands were two bagpipe bands, both closely associated with the independence movement. The Brian Boru Pipe Band first appeared during the Irish cultural revival in the early years of the twentieth century, taking its name from a medieval Irish nationalist hero. Members played Irish war pipes (bagpipes), and claimed to be the first Irish band to wear kilts (Mitchell-Ingoldsby 1998). By self-proclaiming a distinctly Irish cultural identity, the Brian Boru pipers attracted Irish separatists, including a number of teenagers from the republican boy scout organization, Na Fianna Éireann.[6] In 1914, they were joined by another pipe band, the Irish Volunteer Band, the musical arm of the paramilitary Irish Volunteers, later known as the Irish Republican Army (*Evening Echo*, April 17, 1975). The Irish Volunteer Band also wore kilts and played war pipes, providing an Irish parallel to the British military bands of the period. Like the Brian Boru pipers, the Irish Volunteer Band drew musicians involved in the republican movement, and both bands were associated with the republican leader Tomás MacCurtain. The two pipe bands played prominent roles during two phases of the Irish Revolution in Cork. The first occurred during the mass popular mobilization and civil disobedience campaigns from 1917 to 1919; the second took place during the violent guerrilla conflict of 1920–1921 as republicans sought to express and legitimize their campaign.

In the first year of the revolution, Sinn Féin possessed little civic power. Political opponents enjoyed a monopoly on municipal government, and a coercive British administration used special wartime legislation to limit antigovernment expression. Two musical examples illustrate the repressive environment in Cork: during 1917 police arrested one youth for singing the republican anthem, "Who fears to speak of Easter week?" and jailed a printer for producing song sheets of traditional rebel ballads (Borgonovo 2013, 53, 55–56). Given this challenging environment, republicans expressed their subversive message through music and processions in public space. For example, when Sinn Féin won a series of parliamentary by-elections against the Irish Party in 1917, each victory sparked a band-led procession through Cork's streets, usually with torches (*Cork Constitution*, May 11, 1917; *Cork Examiner*, July 12, 1917). Pipe bands also greeted visiting separatist dignitaries arriving at the Cork railway station and political prisoners released from jail (*Cork Examiner*, June 25, September 24, November 23, December 10, 1917). Such receptions often followed established public meeting liturgies, which had established protocols for national anthems, speaking platform attendance, introductory speeches, and motions of support passed by acclamation. In doing so, the republicans expropriated the political symbols and modes of public expression used by respected nationalist campaigns during the previous century.

In 1917, the Brian Boru Pipe Band and its followers earned a reputation for rowdy antigovernment behavior, which included violent clashes with police (Borgonovo 2013, 71). The pipers frequently drew crowds to the Cork Men's Prison, where they played for political prisoners. On at least two occasions, armed police threatened to fire into the band and its stone-throwing supporters. Police patience with the band finally wore out in November 1917, after the pipe band paraded around the Cork city center with a recently released political prisoner. Outside their band rooms, Brian Boru followers stoned police constables and two passing British Army officers and their female companion. Police quelled the riot only after two hours of repeated bayonet and baton charges. Later that night, the police decided to pay the pipers. A party of constabulary led by senior officers broke into the band rooms, wrecked the interior, and smashed all the band instruments. They then proceeded upstairs and delivered a savage beating to Irish language students who had the misfortune of sharing the premises with the band. (Three of the students had to be hospitalized for a month.) The republicans used this attack as a propaganda device, issuing pamphlets describing the assault (details of which the government censored from Irish newspapers) and conducting concerts to raise funds to purchase new instruments (Borgonovo 2013, 71–72).

During this period, the kilted Irish Volunteer Band played martial music and flew the republican banner. Throughout 1917, the IRA drilled publicly and conducted marches to recruit new members, usually led by the Irish Volunteer Band. Appearances were often planned to take place outside Catholic churches immediately following Sunday services, or at public fairs, outdoor entertainment events, or on market days. In response, British authorities prohibited all paramilitary processions and drilling. The Cork IRA answered with a campaign of direct defiance, undertaking mass marches through the city and countryside over three successive Sundays. The Irish Volunteer Band led all the marches, which usually lasted eight hours and gathered up to 2,000 IRA members. At the start and conclusion of the marches, the IRA conducted military marching drills in the city streets in direct contravention of government regulations, before thousands of startled onlookers. The band typically played before and during the drilling to help draw spectators. Because of the large numbers of IRA volunteers involved, the police were helpless to stop these processions; the IRA called them off only after winning a major propaganda victory (Borgonovo 2013, 91–93).

The two republican pipe bands led further civil disobedience against government suppression. At the height of Ireland's anticonscription campaign in 1918, the government banned all public assemblies without a police permit, including sporting and cultural events. The Gaelic Athletic Association (GAA) was closely associated with the independence movement. As a result, police and military broke up GAA hurling, Irish football, and women's camogie (a form of hurling) matches. In Cork, police likewise dispersed promenades and concerts by republican-affiliated bands as well as Gaelic League picnics (*Cork Constitution*, July 13, 17, 1918). These latter cultural gatherings, usually held in the city suburbs, featured Irish dancing and singing contests, recitations, sports matches, and concerts. Typically one or two of the city bands played at each event. After armed police and soldiers broke up the Gaelic League picnics, republican organizers responded by publicly announcing meetings in certain venues but then secretly moving them to another location a few miles away. They advertised the false meetings and even built decoy venues, complete with stages, flags, and bunting, which the Crown forces duly occupied. Meanwhile, by word of mouth organizers notified thousands of residents of the real location of the meeting, which was usually carried off without discovery. Ultimately, this elaborate civil disobedience charade made an absurdity of the ban, which was rescinded after a few weeks (Borgonovo 2013, 203–9).

In the final stage of the First World War, the British Army opened a new recruiting campaign in Cork. The two republican pipe bands helped disrupt the recruitment meetings held in October 1918. When a British Army regimental band struck up martial airs on a street corner to attract crowds to one event, the pipe bands set up across from them. Patriotic military tunes were drowned out by Irish anthems celebrating rebellion and military resistance to British rule (*Cork Constitution*, October 21, 1918). Political lines were clearly drawn in this battle of the bands.

Bands also featured in a conflict over the annual Manchester Martyrs' Commemoration, a popular annual civic procession honoring three Irish separatists hanged in 1867. The government banned the 1918 march in Cork, posting armed soldiers around the Manchester Martyrs' monument in the city center and setting up machine guns at nearby street corners.

Republican organizers used brass bands to outflank the British troops. Two bands led half the participants to open space on the north side of the city, while two other bands marched supporters to a venue on the south side, thereby confusing the military. Meetings then proceeded in defiance of the prohibition until soldiers located the gatherings and threatened to fire on participants. The bands once again processed the residents back into the city. For the rest of the evening they performed rebel tunes around the city centre, playing a game of hide and seek with police and troops trying to disperse them (*Cork Constitution*, November 25, 1918).

BANDS AND REPUBLICAN FUNERAL SPECTACLES

At the end of the First World War, Sinn Féin swept the parliamentary elections and formed its own parliament called Dáil Éireann, which immediately declared Ireland's independence from Britain. As the IRA prepared to launch an armed campaign against the British administration, processions and demonstrations increasingly took a back seat to paramilitary operations. In Cork City, the IRA promoted the Irish Volunteer Band leader to the rank of captain for "having made a complete success of a difficult job." In recognition, the IRA leadership promised, "We are considering the matter of a set of pipes, and should our finances improve, I have no doubt but these will be provided."[7] Other IRA leaders, however, viewed brass bands as a distraction.

Operating in a rural area in the northeast corner of County Cork, IRA leader Seán Moylan objected to local IRA units "spending money on flags and fifes and drums and paraffin for torches" and organizing band practice rather than military training (2004, 32). He later complained, "There seemed to be one in every townland, the organization extended to the accompaniment of drumbeats ... if the vibration of the drums could have disintegrated an Empire, imperialism as a political theory would now be defunct" (33). In the village of Kiskeam, Moylan described a particular band "with a long and chequered career and a fighting tradition." Evolving from a temperance band to a Land League band in the 1880s, the Kiskeam musicians reformed as an IRA band, Moylan explained: "Now and again through the years it disappeared but in time of public turmoil or rejoicing it sprang forth again." While marching with IRA volunteers to attract recruits, Kiskeam band members were attacked by police and soldiers who smashed their instruments. Moylan was secretly pleased because the attack "tended to accentuate the dislike for British authority in the district." The Kiskeam band would eventually taste sweet revenge (35–38; Ó Ríordáin 1985, 15–21).

By early 1920, Irish separatists in Europe and the United States attempted to secure international recognition of the self-declared Irish Republic, while in Ireland the IRA demanded that citizens acknowledge its position as the country's rightful army. Republicans faced British propaganda that portrayed the IRA as criminals holding the Irish public hostage. The government repressed the underground republican countergovernment (Dáil Éireann), while Irish jails frequently experienced disturbances over the criminal status subscribed to IRA prisoners. In this struggle for legitimacy, republican funerals became a powerful propaganda device.

Paramilitary funerals and burials, frequently held in violation of the law, served as elaborate republican propaganda exercises. They also allowed popular expressions of support for the independence movement. These funeral spectacles began prior to the outbreak of guerrilla warfare and continued a long separatist tradition of using funerals for political subversion (Bisceglia 1979; Morgan 1998). In Cork, the first paramilitary funerals were held in 1917 and 1918 for members of the IRA or republican boy scouts who died of natural causes (*Cork Examiner*, May 18, 1917, March 6, July 24, November 18, 1918). For example, in 1918 an Irish Volunteer who died of pneumonia received an elaborate military-style funeral. The Irish Volunteer Band led uniformed units of the IRA, echoing the British Army regimental band tradition and thus emphasizing the IRA's claim to be a legitimate military force. They were followed by other uniformed republican organizations, including Cumann na mBan (a women's counterpart to the IRA) and groups of republican boy and girl scouts. The cortege wound its way through the main city boulevards, following a traditional procession route (*Cork Examiner*, March 5–6, 1918).

These precedents were expanded in 1920 and 1921 when IRA volunteers began to die in action against the Crown forces (*Cork Examiner*, July 22, September 11, 13, 1920). As IRA casualties mounted in Cork, the IRA pipe band led corteges that appropriated British Army funeral traditions (*Cork Constitution*, 22, 1919, November 22, 1920). IRA members typically dressed the corpse in the illegal IRA uniform, draped the coffin in the illegal Irish tricolor flag, and marched in illegal military processional order.[8] The cortege usually made a point of marching past the Cork Men's Prison, where it stopped and allowed the leading band to play to political prisoners inside while inmates paid their respects to their fallen comrade (*Cork Constitution*, October 22, 30, November 1, 1920). At the graveside, a uniformed IRA color guard (armed with illegal weapons) fired a volley over the coffin, while pipers led the mourners back through the city. Such elaborate public displays mirrored state mourning rituals for fallen members of the Crown forces that continued throughout the conflict. These typically contained marching bodies of police and military, a British Army band playing mourning tunes (usually Handel's "Death March"), and a flag-draped coffin carried on a horse-drawn artillery gun carriage (*Cork Examiner*, May 5, 15, July 21, October 13, December 3, 1920). The procession always followed a similar route through the center of the city. When the burial would take place outside of Ireland (for British soldiers and police), the procession would end at the Cork docks, where the coffin would be lowered ceremonially onto a waiting naval vessel and taken to Britain. The burial rituals expressed state power and legitimacy to the public, and thus proved attractive to the republican movement trying to claim the loyalty of Irish citizens.

The most spectacular paramilitary funeral followed the police assassination of Lord Mayor Tomás MacCurtain, who also commanded the IRA in Cork. The republicans mobilized all elements of Cork civic society for the procession, including the various marching bands representing different political loyalties. Special note was made of the appearance of the Cork ex-servicemen's NFDDSS Band, which participated even though MacCurtain had actively opposed recruitment into the British Army and Irish involvement in the First World War. MacCurtain's funeral cortege was led by members of the Catholic clergy but immediately followed by the kilted Irish Volunteer Band. Uniformed IRA officers accompanied the hearse, while neighborhood bands were interspaced among assemblages of various civic public officials, commercial associations, trade unions, student bodies, and cultural groups. Overall the procession included 10,000 participants, took ninety minutes to pass, and attracted a crowd of 100,000, in a city with a population of 75,000 (Borgonovo 2007, 79).

To end these propaganda spectacles, the British authorities banned marching in funeral processions and limited corteges to 100 mourners (*Cork Constitution*, September 23, 1920). The first implementation of this rule occurred after IRA prisoner Michael Fitzgerald died on hunger strike in Cork Men's Prison. During Fitzgerald's funeral service, a military officer entered the church with armed soldiers and announced that his troops would open fire on the cortege if it exceeded the stated limit (*Cork Constitution*, October 20, 1920). MacCurtain's successor as lord mayor of Cork and IRA commander Terence MacSwiney died on hunger strike days after Michael Fitzgerald. The military authorities laid out very specific regulations that prohibited marching in step, the wearing of uniforms, and all republican flags, except one permitted for the coffin (*Irish Independent*, October 30, 1920). The restrictions essentially excluded the marching bands from the procession. In response, republican organizers stationed each of the city marching bands along the procession route so that mourners could hear music throughout their two-mile walk to the cemetery. One British newspaper correspondent wrote of being moved by the NFDDSS Band, made up of amputee war veteran musicians, playing "Ardeste fidelis" (*London Daily Herald*, November 1, 1920). Though the British troops accompanied the funeral procession to the cemetery to prevent any paramilitary displays, the republicans waited them out. Shortly after soldiers left the cemetery, an IRA honor guard emerged from hiding and promptly fired a volley over the grave before dispersing (*Cork Examiner*, October 28, 1920). The republicans had given MacSwiney a military funeral befitting an officer of the Irish Republic, thus maintaining the legitimacy of the republican cause. In the months to come, IRA funeral processions were typically followed by armed British troops in lorries and armored cars, threatening to fire against anyone participating in paramilitary displays (*Cork Constitution*, October 28, November 13, 27, 1920; *Cork Examiner*, November 22, 26, December 15, 1920).

By late 1920, the British government responded to the IRA insurgency by banning all elements of the independence movement. From mid-1920, the city was also placed under a dusk-to-dawn curfew, and public meetings and processions were prohibited. In July 1920, British troops fired into civilian crowds during antigovernment street clashes, killing two and wounding about twenty others (Borgonovo 2007, 82). Numerous other civilians were shot dead on the city streets during late 1920 and early 1921, usually in episodes relating to the enforcement of the city curfew. Scores of other civilians died at the hands of the IRA, either killed accidentally as bystanders during guerrilla attacks on the police and military, or deliberately executed by the IRA as suspected collaborators. Life on the streets of Cork had become remarkably dangerous in a relatively short period of time.

During the government crackdown, city bands perceived as supporting the republican movement received special attention from the British forces. In early 1920, armed police evicted the Irish Volunteer Band from its headquarters (*Cork Examiner*, February 5, 1920). Later in the year, the Brian Boru Pipers had their band rooms wrecked; police burned down the entire structure a few weeks later, resulting in the destruction of the band instruments (*Cork Examiner*, November 4, 25, 1920). In January 1921, the Butter Exchange Band rooms were raided, while the James Connolly Fife and Drum Band had its instruments smashed by rampaging police (*Cork Examiner*, January 19, 25, 1921). City bands essentially put their instruments away for safekeeping until the British Army and IRA agreed to a truce in July 1921.

BRITISH EVACUATION AND CIVIL WAR

The truce announcement was greeted across urban Ireland with bonfires and other popular celebrations, including nocturnal processions by local brass bands (*Freeman's Journal*, July 12–13, 1921; *Irish Independent*, July 12, 19, 1921; *Southern Star*, July 16, 1921). But in Cork, city officials worried about possible clashes between civilians and the Crown forces. They specifically requested that brass bands refrain from processing through the city, lest they trigger a dangerous antigovernment riot (*Freeman's Journal*, July 12, 1921). In Kiskeam, the truce also signaled retribution to the Kiskeam Irish Volunteer Band which, as previously mentioned, had had its instruments smashed by the Crown forces three years before. According to a republican narrative, armed musicians tracked the local police district inspector to a club restaurant in Cork City. They barred the club doors and presented the inspector with a detailed list of their smashed instruments and replacement costs. Refusing to accept a check, they forced the inspector to borrow cash from fellow diners. New instruments were purchased, and the next week the Kiskeam Irish Volunteer Band celebrated by triumphantly parading around the village police station (Moylan 2004, 38; Ó Ríordáin 1985, 20–21).

The truce between the British government and the IRA took effect at the height of summer, when the Irish public took advantage of warm weather by attending sporting contests, outdoor picnics, and other forms of public entertainments. In Cork, most of the popular venues for such events were in small towns outside the city, which were accessible by train and bicycle. Throughout the summer, Cork brass bands appeared at events outside of Cork but seemed reluctant to play within the city limits (*Cork Examiner*, August 10, September 6, 24, October 3, 1921).[9] This was understandable in the immediate aftermath of the War of Independence, when navigating Cork's streets could be lethal. Despite the lull in hostilities, many bands sensed the potential danger of gathering a crowd and drawing the attention of either the IRA or the Crown forces.

At the end of 1921, Britain and Ireland signed the Anglo-Irish Treaty, which partitioned the island of Ireland and created a self-governing Irish Free State within the British Empire. Divisions over the Anglo-Irish Treaty eventually led to a civil war in mid-1922 between moderate nationalists and republican separatists in the south of Ireland. During the run-up to the outbreak of civil war, the Cork IRA strongly opposed the treaty and governed Cork City through an IRA police force. As in previous political cleavages, Cork marching bands aligned themselves with both pro- and antitreaty factions. Among the bands favoring the treaty was the Fair Hill Band, comprised of former British soldiers. In March 1922, pro-treaty politicians held a massive rally that drew 50,000 supporters into Cork (*Cork Examiner*, March 13, 1922; *Irish Independent*, March 14, 1922). To join the proceedings the Fair Hill Band had to cross a bridge into the city center. However, it was stopped by armed members of the antitreaty IRA who threw the Fair Hill bass drum into the river and forced the musicians back to their neighborhood at gunpoint (*Irish Independent*, March 13, 23, 1922).

A few days later, on the night before St Patrick's Day, the Fair Hill Band paraded with its followers across the city. This "Patrick's Eve" procession had been a band tradition before the First World War, but this was the first to be held since 1914. In the city center after midnight, a small IRA police patrol ordered the band and up to 100 followers to disperse, owing to the late hour. Probably because of the recent bass drum incident, tensions rose rapidly and a physical altercation broke out. The Fair Hill Band group attacked the four-man IRA patrol with stones and sticks; the IRA responded by firing revolver shots over the heads of the crowd. This in turn attracted another IRA police patrol, which fired directly into the crowd. Band members may have returned gunfire, though the details are sketchy (the initial warning shots could have been misconstrued as an attack by the second IRA police group). When the smoke cleared, one bandsman was dead, thirty-one-year-old ex-soldier Patrick Hogan, while another band member and one of the IRA police were wounded (*Cork Constitution*, March 18, 1922; *Irish Independent* March 18, 23, 1922). In this case, the particularities of Irish revolutionary politics created a strange parallel to the repressed political processions of 1917 and 1918, with former rebels taking on the role of police and former soldiers acting as subversive dissidents. It also echoed the band disturbances so common to late nineteenth- and early twentieth-century Cork.

Throughout the revolutionary period, Cork brass bands acted as audible and visible symbols of Ireland's turbulent popular politics. The bands' internal divisions, participation in or abstention from different types of street processions, and clashes with various authorities can be used to construct a parallel narrative to the struggle for Irish independence. For the Cork bands, political identity and musical expressions were practically interchangeable, while the contestation of public space in Cork City fell among many divisions within Irish society during the disruptive years of 1914 to 1922.

In early 1922, the British withdrew from their bases across southern Ireland. Ritualized changing-over ceremonies at barracks aroused public curiosity and celebration. The last major base evacuated was Victoria Barracks in the city of Cork during May 1922 (*Cork Examiner*, May 19, 1922; *Irish Independent*, May 19, 1922). On a sunny afternoon, British Army officers handed over the installation's front gate keys to representative of the new Free State government. The military's last act was to lower the Union Jack and then cut down the flagpole, lest it fly the republican flag before soldiers had completely exited the barracks. Hundreds of troops marched behind their regimental band from Victoria Barracks through the city streets to the docks, where they boarded waiting ships. Thousands of residents cheered their replacements, an IRA detachment that processed across the city and into the base. These IRA volunteers carried rifles and wore civilian clothes, flat caps, and ammunition bandoleers. Observers noted the neat military bearing of their pipe band, which led the parade. Thus ended the 300-year military occupation of Cork City by forces of the British Crown. On this occasion, at least, the drone of bagpipes was drowned out by delirious cheers from the people of Cork.

Throughout this chapter we have seen the ways parades, processions, public rituals, and other forms of public performance have been active agents in situations of social conflict. Far from being mere reflections of culture, these dynamic processes helped to shape modern Irish history, and the people of Ireland fully understood, and exploited, this potential.

NOTES

1. From this article and contemporary newspaper reports, it would appear that the O'Brien bands included the Butter Exchange, Blackpool, and Quarry Lane bands; while Redmondite bands included the Fair Lane and Barrack Street bands.

2. For additional examples of band-related political violence and activism around County Cork, see the *Southern Star*, November 28, 1908, January 30, February 27, March 27, May 1, June 10, July 31, September 4, November 6, 1909, February 5, April 23, July 16, August 13, August 20, December 17, 1910.

3. See also the Royal Irish Constabulary (RIC) County Inspector's (CI) Monthly Report for Cork City and East Riding, November 1910 and December 1910, CO 904/82, *British in Ireland Series* (microfilm), Boole Library, University College Cork.

4. RIC CI Report for Cork City and East Riding, January 1910, CO 904/83, *British in Ireland Series*.

5. Report of the Ancient Order of Hibernians County Cork Convention, January 15, 1922, U389a/25, Cork City and County Archives.

6. Bureau of Military History Witness Statement 1628, James Busby, National Archives of Ireland, Dublin.

7. Cork No. 1 Brigade Adjutant to Captain Sean Courtney, Irish Volunteer Band, February 12, 1919, MS 31,181, National Library of Ireland, Dublin.

8. For the symbolism and uses of the Irish tricolor flag in the revolutionary period, see Morris 2005, 26–37.

9. For newspaper comments on the lack of band entertainment in the city, see the *Cork Examiner*, August 1, 3, 1921.

REFERENCES

Bell, Desmond. 1987. "Acts of Union: Youth Subculture and Ethnic Identity amongst Protestants in Northern Ireland." *British Journal of Sociology* 38 (2): 158–83. http://dx.doi.org/10.2307/590530.

Birmingham, Cathy. 1996. *Living Tradition*. Vol. A. The Cork Butter Exchange. Cork: Cork Arts Committee.

Bisceglia, Louise. 1979. "The Fenian Funeral of Terence Bellew MacManus." *Eire-Ireland* 14:45–64.

Bythell, Duncan. 1994. "Class, Community, and Culture: The Case of the Brass Band in Newcastle." *Labour History* 67 (November): 144–55. http://dx.doi.org/10.2307/27509281.

Borgonovo, John. 2007. *Spies, Informers, and the Anti–Sinn Fein Society: The Intelligence War in Cork City, 1920–1921*. Dublin: Irish Academic Press.

Borgonovo, John. 2010. "'Justice They Would Have': The Cork Branch of the Demobilised and Discharged Soldiers and Sailors Federation, 1919–1921." In *A Great Sacrifice: Cork Servicemen Who Died in the Great War*, ed. Gerry White and Brendan O'Shea, 575–83. Cork: Evening Echo.

Borgonovo, John. 2013. *The Dynamics of War and Revolution: Cork City, 1916–1918*. Cork: Cork University Press.

Borgonovo, John. 2016. "Politics as Leisure: Cork Brass Bands, 1845–1914." In *Leisure and the Irish in the Nineteenth Century*, ed. Leeann Lane and William Murphy, 23–40. Liverpool: Liverpool University Press.

Bryan, Dominic. 2000. *Orange Parades: The Politics of Ritual, Tradition, and Control*. London: Pluto.

Cairns, David. 2000. "The Object of Sectarianism: The Material Reality of Sectarianism in Ulster Loyalism." *Journal of the Royal Anthropological Institute* 6 (3): 437–52. http://dx.doi.org/10.1111/1467-9655.00025.

Cooke, Richard T. 1992. *Cork's Barrack Street Silver and Reed Band, Ireland's Oldest Amateur Musical Institution*. Cork: Seamus Curtin.

Cronin, Maura. 1994. *Country, Class, or Craft? The Politicisation of the Skilled Artisan in Nineteenth-Century Cork*. Cork: Cork University Press.

Day, Susanne. 1916. *The Amazing Philanthropists*. London: Sidgwick & Jackson.

Dooley, Thomas. 1991. "Politics, Bands, and Marketing: Army Recruiting in Waterford City, 1914–1915." *Irish Sword* 28:206–19.

Fitzpatrick, David. 1995. "The Logic of Collective Sacrifice: Ireland and the British Army, 1914–1918." *Historical Journal (Cambridge, England)* 38 (4): 1017–30. http://dx.doi.org/10.1017/S0018246X00020550.

Herbert, Trevor. 1990. "The Repertory of a Victorian Provincial Brass Band." *Popular Music* 9 (1): 117–32. http://dx.doi.org/10.1017/S0261143000003779.

Herbert, Trevor, ed. 2000. *Musical and Social History*. Vol. A. The British Brass. Oxford: Oxford University Press.

Kane, Anne. 2011. *Constructing Irish National Identity: Discourse and Ritual during the Land War, 1879–1882*. New York: Palgrave MacMillan. http://dx.doi.org/10.1057/9781137001160.

Laird, Heather. 2005. *Subversive Law in Ireland, 1879–1920*. Dublin: Four Courts.

Lane, Fintan. 1999. "Music and Violence in Working Class Cork: The 'Band Nuisance.' 1879–1882." *Saothar* 24:17–31.

Maddox, Neil P. 2004. "'A Melancholy Record': The Story of the Nineteenth Century Irish Party Processions Acts." *Irish Jurist* 39:243–74.

Malcolm, Elizabeth. 1986. *"Ireland Sober, Ireland Free": Drink and Temperance in Nineteenth Century Ireland*. Dublin: Gill & MacMillan.

McGrath, Jack. 2010. *St Mary's Prize Band, Celebrating 125 Years, 1885–2010.* Limerick: St Mary's Prize Band.
Mitchell-Ingoldsby, Mary. 1998. "History of The Cork Pipers Club 1898–1980." In *The Cork Pipers Club—A Hundred Years of Piping 1898–1998*, ed. John Mitchell, Pat Moynihan, 6–12. Cork: Cork Pipers Club.
Moody, T. W. 1982. *Davitt and the Irish Revolution, 1846–82.* Oxford: Clarendon.
Morgan, Jack. 1998. "The Dust of Maynooth: Fenian Funeral as Political Theatre: St. Louis, 1865." *New Hibernia Review / Iris Éireannach Nua* 2 (4): 24–37.
Morris, Ewan. 2005. *Our Own Devices: National Symbols and Political Conflict in Twentieth-Century Ireland.* Dublin: Irish Academic Press.
Moylan, Seán. 2004. *Seán Moylan, in His Own Words.* Cork: Aubane Historical Society.
Newsom, Jon. 1979. "The American Brass Band Movement." *Quarterly Journal: Library of Congress* 36 (2): 114–39.
O'Brien, John B. 1993. "Population, Politics, and Society in Cork, 1780–1900." In *Cork: History and Society; Interdisciplinary Essays on the History of an Irish County*, ed. Patrick O'Flanagan and Cornelius Buttimer, 699–720. Dublin: Geography Publications.
O'Connor, Frank. 1981. *The Coronet Player Who Betrayed Ireland.* Dublin: Poolbeg.
O'Neill, Julie. 1987. "Village Bands." *Oral History Journal* 15 (1): 50–53.
Ó Ríordáin, J. J. 1985. *Kiskeam versus the Empire.* Tralee: Kerryman.
Owens, Gary. 1994. "Hedge School of Politics: O'Connell's Monster Meetings." *History Ireland* 2 (1): 35–40.
Owens, Gary. 1998. "Nationalism without Words: Spectacle and Ritual in the Repeal 'Monster Meetings' of 1843–45." In *Irish Popular Culture, 1650–1850*, ed. James S Donnelly and Kerby Miller, 242–69. Dublin: Irish Academic Press.
Owens, Gary. 1999. "Constructing the Image of Daniel O'Connell." *History Ireland* 7 (1): 32–36.
Prendergast, Jean. 2010. "Cork Bands and the Great War." In *A Great Sacrifice: Cork Servicemen Who Died in the Great War*, ed. Gerry White and Brendan O'Shea, 155–64. Cork: Evening Echo.
Russell, Dave. 1983. "Popular Musical Culture and Popular Politics in the Yorkshire Textile Districts, 1880–1914." In *Leisure in Britain, 1780–1939*, ed. John K Walton and James Walvin, 99–116. Manchester: Manchester University Press.
Russell, Dave. 1997. *Popular Music in England, 1840–1914: A Social History.* Manchester: Manchester University Press.
Santino, Jack. 2001. *Signs of War and Peace: Social Conflict and the Use of Public Symbols in Northern Ireland.* New York: Palgrave. http://dx.doi.org/10.1007/978-1-4039-8233-9.
Townsend, Paul. 2003. "'Academics of Nationality,' The Reading Room and Irish National Political Movements, 1828–1905." In *Reading Irish Histories: Texts, Contexts, and Memory in Modern Ireland*, ed. Lawrence McBride, 19–39. Dublin: Four Courts.

6

¡*Que Bonita Bandera!*
Place, Space, and Identity as Expressed with the Puerto Rican Flag

Elena Martínez

> *¡Que bonita bandera, que bonita bandera!*
> *¡Que bonita bandera, es la bandera puertorriqueña!*
> *¡Que bonita bandera, la bandera puertorriqueña!*
> *Quisiera verla flotando sobre mi Borinquen bella.*
>
> What a pretty flag, what a pretty flag!
> What a pretty flag is the Puerto Rican flag!
> What a pretty flag, the Puerto Rican flag!
> I would like to see it waving over my beautiful Puerto Rico.
>
> —*Florencio Morales Ramos (Ramito),*
> *set to a traditional Puerto Rican* plena *tune*

WHEN I RETURNED TO NEW YORK IN 1997 I was amazed to see Puerto Rican flags everywhere I looked—on cars, windows, and bodies. I had just spent a few years in Oregon and had never seen any flag or symbol employed in such a manner. So I started documenting the flags, which eventually led to an exhibit. In the summer of 2013, after over a decade of attending, documenting, and researching the history of the Puerto Rican parade and flag, at last I formally participated in the pinnacle of flag-waving glory, the National Puerto Rican Day Parade, down Fifth Avenue in Manhattan. A friend invited me to take part in a group that would represent Camaradas, a bar/restaurant located in East Harlem, that is a central spot for the local young traditional Puerto Rican and Dominican musicians involved in the roots music scene. The theme for our contingent depicted important political and cultural figures in Puerto Rican history. Instead of flags, we all held up painted images of historical Puerto Rican personages and walked behind a group of musicians playing traditional Puerto Rican *plena* (as opposed to the loud, amplified music of salsa and reggaetón roaring from the parade's floats). Two large flags were at the head of the contingent: one was the official Puerto Rican flag but with a light blue triangle (as opposed to the dark blue field more common in the mass-produced flags), and the other was the historical Lares flag (more on this later). Instead of wearing the red, white, and blue of the Puerto Rican flag, we were all asked to wear black and white, these being the colors of the island's Nationalist Party flag.

All these decisions about particular colors and specific flags were not intended to make *la bandera monoestrellada* (single-star flag) invisible or downplay its significance; they were responses to the way the flag, and the culture it represents, is commodified in the parade and elsewhere. That year the parade also included another controversy. The parade has sparked past incidents—fictionalized and actual—including the notorious 1998 *Seinfeld* episode that featured Kramer stomping on a burning Puerto Rican flag while attending the parade, which led to protests in front of the NBC office; and the 2000 criminal incident called a "wilding" by the media when young women were groped and assaulted at the parade. The community outcry this time concerned a representation of the flag placed on beer cans by Coors, one of the parade's endorsers, which was seen as particularly egregious since the theme of the parade that year was health and the community (the offending beer can was later withdrawn). So when activists such as the group we marched with in the parade use other historical flags and different colors to represent and honor Puerto Rican culture, they are conscious acts meant to subvert the flag's commodification as well as to honor the flag's legacy.

THE PUERTO RICAN FLAG ON DISPLAY

The display of *la bandera puertorriqueña* is pretty common all year long throughout the five boroughs of New York City—waving from car antennas, painted on wall murals, and draped from windows, fire escapes, and car hoods—but from the end of May until the middle of June, prior to and during the National Puerto Rican Day Parade in Manhattan (always the second Sunday in June), it reaches its peak. It is hard to walk anywhere in the city without seeing the image proudly displayed or worn. Any item or apparel imaginable is adorned or decorated with the image: umbrellas, shorts, ties, fingernails, hats, jewelry, sunglasses. This was especially true from the late 1990s through the early 2000s. It appears that the custom may have peaked a few years ago, and during the last few years the flag seems to be less visible in the time period leading up to the parade. Whether this latest trend has to do with grassroots and official campaigns intended to make sure the flag is used only in a respectful manner or just represents declining interest remains to be seen.

The Puerto Rican flag, like all flags, is obviously a political symbol representing the government and political entity of a specific country or nation-state (except in Puerto Rico's case, without sovereignty). However, for Puerto Ricans on the island and the diaspora communities elsewhere, the island's colonial history and current ambiguous status endows the flag with an added significance—that of representing the culture and the essence of *puertorriqueñidad* (Puerto Rican-ness). Since Puerto Rico's colonial status makes the recognition of national identity as belonging to a discrete geographical entity difficult, it is *culture* with which the community identifies (one can live in San Juan or New York and still be a Puerto Rican).[1] Every ethnic group or nationality attaches importance to the flag representing the country of its origin. Attend any one of the multitude of New York City's ethnic parades and you will see flags incorporated into the processions and floats. Yet Puerto Ricans and their flag obsession have transformed this cultural expression into an art form.

THE PUERTO RICAN FLAG AS FOLK ART

Innovations in folk art genres have included the flag's image created and embedded in traditional art such as *mundillo* (bobbin lace) and painted on the masks of the carnival *vejigantes*. However, during the Puerto Rican Day Parade, one sees not only T-shirts and bandanas emblazoned with the flag but whole arrangements of flags that transform people, cars, bicycles, and baby strollers into mobile works of art. In fact, the Puerto Rican flag when used in this manner can best be understood as folk art arising from a community signifying shared values or aesthetics and confirming group beliefs. It is not the object itself that connotes "folk" but its meaning and practice within the community. Folklorist Elliott Oring explains the changing nature of folk arts: "As reliance on craft processes in the twentieth century diminishes, forms increasingly arise that stress arrangement. As the economy comes to stress consumption of ready-made items, the folk response is to alter and arrange such items into new, unofficial forms . . . The arranger is exerting control and emulating the making of objects by creating a new appearance and use from pre-fabricated materials . . .[and] commercially manufactured materials to create folk environments which make personal and collective statements" (1986, 216).

Figure 6.1. The vejigante, a masked figure from carnival celebrations in Ponce, Puerto Rico, taking part in the Puerto Rican Day Parade, June 2000. The vejigante is decorated in the colors and symbols of the flag. (Photograph by Martha Cooper/City Lore)

The image of the flag also works as a folk motif, a motif being the smallest content element existing within a genre or tradition. These arrangements Oring refers to are similar to the "folk *assemblages*" Jack Santino describes in his work documenting Halloween decorations: "the combining of a variety of symbolic elements within a single frame, and the creation of a single aesthetic entity by grouping together disparate things" (1986, 159). These ideas have their precedents in the work of anthropologist Claude Lévi-Strauss, who discussed in *The Savage Mind* the concept of *bricolage*, the idea of implementing systems that "are capable of infinite extension because basic elements can be used in a variety of improvised combinations to generate new meanings within them" (Hebdige 1979, 104). Scholars of semiotics would later use the concept of bricolage to discuss subcultural styles that also inform the flag and the flag assemblages as political symbols within the Puerto Rican community. J. Clarke states: "Together, object and meaning constitute a sign, and within any one culture, such signs are assembled, repeatedly, into characteristic forms of discourse. However, when the bricoleur re-locates the significant object in a different position within that discourse, using the same overall repertoire of signs, or when that object is placed within a different total ensemble a new discourse is constituted, a different message is conveyed" (Hebdige 1979, 104).

Participants at the Puerto Rican Day Parade and other events celebrating or focusing on Puerto Rican culture take commercially manufactured items, such as flags, T-shirts, and bandannas (most likely manufactured halfway across the world), and arrange them in unique ways to adorn their bodies, cars, homes. These arrangements at times subvert the historical meaning and intended uses of the flag, especially in light of the flag's unsettled past.

THE HISTORY OF THE PUERTO RICAN FLAG

What explains this attachment to the flag? Why has it become such a powerful symbol of Puerto Rican cultural identity and cultural nationalism that Puerto Ricans of any political persuasion, race, or class proudly honor it? The reasons for its significance can be explained by the political history of the island and the flag itself.

The first flag representing Puerto Rico arose out of the first significant attempt to end Spain's rule over Puerto Rico. This event, El Grito de Lares, occurred on September 23, 1868.[2] Prior to this time, while in exile many of the island's intellectual leaders had fled to the Dominican Republic, where rebels there were also struggling to depose the regime. Therefore, the Lares flag looks very similar to the Dominican flag to honor the anticolonial forces there and to recognize an Antillean Confederacy: four squares, of which two are red and two are blue, with a white star in the top left corner. This flag was designed by Dr. Ramón Emeterio Betances and sewn by a member of the uprising, Mariana Bracetti (for which she spent time in jail).

Most Puerto Ricans display la bandera monoestrellada, but the Lares flag has come to signify *independentista* supporters today and can also be seen at events, especially those of a political nature.

What is now commonly known as the Puerto Rican flag came into being in 1895 at a meeting in New York City for the Puerto Rican branch of the Cuban Revolutionary Party. This assembly was composed of political exiles and patriots from Puerto Rico who joined with Cuban exiles to fight for independence from Spain for both islands. The most commonly accepted narrative records that on December 22 at Chimney Hall at 57 W. Twenty-Fifth Street, a meeting was held to try to close the schism between the section's intellectual and working-class members. It was here that the idea for la bandera monoestrellada was conceived.[3] The proposed flag was similar to the Cuban flag (the colors of the two are inverted) to show their solidarity and allegiance in the struggle to break free of colonial rule. The idea of inverting the colors of the Cuban flag supposedly was suggested by Manuel Besosa, who then had his daughter Maria Manuela Besosa sew it (she became, like Bracetti, a Puerto Rican Betsy Ross). This flag was raised during a second revolt against Spain in 1897 known as the Intentona de Yauco.[4]

With the end of the Spanish-Cuban-American War in 1898, the United States occupied Puerto Rico and claimed it as a colony, making the Stars and Stripes the official flag of the island. Soon the Puerto Rican flag became associated only with left-leaning politicians or those favoring independence for the island. In 1917 legislation made Puerto Ricans U.S. citizens without a change in the colonial relationship. Four years later, in 1921, the flag became a subversive political symbol after the appointment of E. Montgomery Reilly (a Texas/Missouri politician) as governor of the island. During Reilly's term, the importance of the Puerto Rican flag to the people grew in proportion to his opposition to it; his administration maintained the attitude that only the U.S. flag should be displayed in Puerto Rico, while the Puerto Rican flag was seen as the "enemy flag." The governor was concerned about the Unionists, a political party that favored independence and held meetings where "they have spoken under one star flags and have indicated that Puerto Rico should control its own affairs" (Fernández 1996, 90). Reilly later sparked public outrage when during a parade that displayed more Puerto Rican flags than U.S. flags, he commented that the local flag was *un trapo desgastado* (a worn-out rag) (Rosario Natal 1980, 60). While a public apology was later issued, the damage had been done, and the display of the flag became a clarion call for those who demanded an end to the island's colonial status.

The Nationalist Party was formed in 1922 and in 1924 Pedro Albizu Campos became its vice president. Though he had gone to school at Harvard, his political ideology was resolutely against U.S. policies. He began his political career as a member of the Unionist Party but left when that party dropped the island's independence from the its platform. In 1930 he made the Puerto Rican flag the symbol of the Nationalist Party. In 1932 the Puerto Rican legislature passed a law making the flag the official emblem of the island, possibly in an attempt to render the flag less controversial. Albizu Campos, outraged that the flag would become the symbol of a colony and not a free nation, led a procession to the capitol building in protest.

The flag, since it was so connected to Nationalist Party identity, was indirectly affected in 1948 by Public Law 53, *la ley de la mordaza* (muzzle or gag law). La mordaza stated that "it was a grave felony, punishable by a maximum of 10 years in jail or a maximum fine of $10,000 to encourage, plead, advise, or preach the necessity, desirability, or suitability of overthrowing, paralyzing, or destroying the insular government, or any political subdivision of this by means of violence." It was also a felony to "print, publish, edit, circulate, sell, distribute, or publicly exhibit any writing or publication which encourages, pleads, advises, or preaches the necessity, desirability, or suitability of overthrowing the insular government" (Fernández 1996, 178). Therefore, any outward expressions of anticolonialist sentiments, including singing the national anthem "La Borinqueña" or displaying a Puerto Rican flag—no matter how minor—were outlawed. This was soon followed by a series of incidents that gave a voice to the opposition to U.S. colonial rule, which included the Jayuya Uprising in 1950 and the attack on Congress in 1954 where four Nationalists carried the flag as they entered its chambers. For non–Puerto Ricans who are surprised by how ubiquitous the flag is in Puerto Rican communities, these past incidents may shed some light on the obsession with it, bordering on fetishism. Scholar Juan Flores notes, "Today many remember being arrested and harassed for exhibiting a flag on their cars or shirts. What is new isn't the intense nationalistic feeling but its open expression" (1999, 2).

On July 25 1952, the anniversary of the 1898 invasion of U.S. Marines at Guanica Bay, the U.S. Congress approved a referendum that declared Puerto Rico a commonwealth or *estado libre asociado* (free associated state) of the United States. Some of the more excessive restrictions of Public Law 53 were relaxed by Luis Muñoz Marín, who was the first elected governor. The flag from 1895 was officially adopted, though with slight adjustments: the blue was matched to that of the U.S. flag (Denis 2015, 301n34). No longer a subversive or partisan symbol of the struggle for independence, the flag was now the official symbol of the island.

THE PUERTO RICAN FLAG AS ICON

Four centuries of Spanish colonial rule made Puerto Rico a Spanish-speaking country that shares many aspects of culture with other Latin American and Caribbean nations, yet it is separated from most of Latin America by a century of U.S. colonial presence. The estado libre asociado status and U.S. citizenship, however, do not benefit Puerto Ricans politically (except insofar as they can move freely between the United States and Puerto Rico) since they do not have representation in Congress. After the 1952 referendum, one of the most popular newspapers on the island, *El Mundo*, wrote:

> From now on there will be no fear of raising the single-star flag as Puerto Rico's official flag. In the future our athletes abroad will not have to face the incomprehension of other peoples when our country's representatives attend competitions with fellow countries. Tomorrow Puerto Ricans who excel in all walks of life will be able to attend meetings and conventions with satisfaction and their hearts overflowing with pride under the same flag that unofficially was accepted by all Puerto Ricans and by all the countries of the world as the Puerto Rican flag. . . The entire Puerto Rican people would never have forgiven the adoption of a national symbol other than the one that has been recognized since that historic December 22nd of the year 1895. (Morris 1995, 51)

Today, in official situations, the flag is allowed to be openly displayed, but only if accompanied by the U.S. flag (note the inference implied in the lyrics given as an epigraph to this chapter). This political ambiguity has placed focus on the flag not so much as a symbol of an independent nation, which Puerto Rico is not, but as emblematic of a Puerto Rican national culture and identity. So while the history of the flag was as a contested political symbol, political nationalism has given way to a politicized cultural nationalism. Puerto Ricans can't identify with their homeland as a sovereign nation from a political perspective, so it is *la cultura* that is honored and celebrated. Even for those not born on the island, and regardless of whether one is pro-statehood, wishes to maintain the status quo, or is an independentista in favor of the island's independence, the island itself and its traditional culture, as symbolized by the flag, are revered. Even pro-statehood Puerto Rican politicians have said that should the island become the fifty-first state, it would be an *estadidad jíbara* (*jíbaro* statehood) and would not lose its cultural distinctiveness.[5]

Nonetheless, the flag has not completely lost its political significance. In the past decade, events have featured Puerto Rican flags on display everywhere, whether on the island or in New York, such as rallies held for the former Puerto Rican political prisoners, opposition to the presence of the U.S. Marines on Vieques (a small island off the coast of Puerto Rico), or protests against the Via Verde *gasoducto* (pipeline to supply natural gas to part of the island). It is at events such as these that participants tend to wave the Puerto Rican flag that has the lighter blue triangle. The official U.S.-sanctioned flag uses a dark blue triangle, but originally it was a turquoise blue. This change occurred after 1952 as Puerto Rico's association with the United States led to a merging with the colors of the U.S. flag. At political events the Lares flag is also seen among the other flags on display. But it is as a symbol of cultural nationalism and cultural pride that the Puerto Rican flag takes its most varied forms. And this flag obsession seemed to reach its peak in the 1990s when the flag assemblages were seen everywhere and "when flag mania reached all social sectors" (Negrón Muntaner 2004, 169).

THE FLAG DEMARCATES PLACE

What are members of the Puerto Rican community in New York City today saying with these flag assemblages? The flag is highly visible in the parade, but under everyday circumstances the flag has a continued presence in Puerto Rican communities. The image is seen in countless murals (community as well as graffiti murals) throughout neighborhoods as well as waving in the community gardens alongside *casitas* (little houses). The murals and casitas, as well as the flags themselves, literally "plant a flag" or claim ownership—they define and demarcate a tangible place for the Puerto Rican community. They are physical manifestations created by individuals to appropriate a place and establish the connection between that place and the people residing there. For a community that feels ignored politically and left out economically from the mainstream, the murals, the casitas, and the flags transform the geography and cry out, "We are here and we will remain here!"

According to research by the Bronx Council of the Arts Casita project in 1987, there were sixty-five casitas in New York City, most of them located in Manhattan's Lower East Side, El Barrio (East Harlem). and the South Bronx, with a few in Brooklyn (Garfinkel 2014). These casitas are based on vernacular housing from Puerto Rico's countryside—the balloon-frame shanty houses constructed in the 1920s and 1930s when many were forced off their lands by the large sugar companies that were set up after the U.S. takeover of the island in 1898. These houses tended to be constructed of scrap material and were easily put up and taken down. This colonial history is reflected in the casitas that dot the vacant lots throughout New York. Originally they were not funded by any organization or institution but consisted of whatever material the community member could afford or find. The transitory nature of the structures echoed their ephemeral quality, since many had been abandoned or relocated to make way for development. The casitas emerged in New York City at the same time as the community gardens, in neighborhoods where local institutions had broken down and experienced extreme neglect and the brunt of the economic and social crises of the 1970s. For community members, these structures provided a refuge and evoked the Puerto Rican landscape. In his study of casitas Luis Aponte-Parés writes that by constructing them people choose "to take an active role in reshaping landscapes of despair into landscapes of hope . . . The key to this attachment is the ability to take possession of the environment simultaneously thorough physical orientation and a more profound identification" (2000, 98). The lots upon which they are built and the structures themselves are symbolic: "The *casita*, like the ubiquitous Puerto Rican flag, becomes a vehicle through which its builders articulate and define their national identity and their imagined community" (Aponte-Parés 1994–1995); and so too the assemblages of Puerto Rican symbols at the casitas—flags, musical instruments, the structures themselves—"transform this place into a space of cultural production and resistance" (Enck-Wanzer 2011, 345). Or as Juan Flores states: "The combination of being 'from elsewhere' and being socially disadvantaged in the new setting conspires to challenge the hegemonies engendered by these asymmetries, and to devise alternative lines of communication and community as forms of conscious and unconscious resistance" (2009, 19).

New York City's landscape is also dotted with murals of various types. Some are commercial murals, some are public art murals created by students, others are graffiti-style murals, which serve as memorial walls. These murals are created by artists from diverse ethnic backgrounds, but murals by Puerto Rican artists in Puerto Rican neighborhoods usually have a few things in common. They become assemblages since they include the flag as one motif among many that are used to represent Puerto Rican culture, a vocabulary that includes the *coquí* (a small frog only found in Puerto Rico and Hawaii), roosters, *pavas* (straw hats worn by jíbaros), the machete used by sugarcane cutters, and a watchtower from El Morro (the colonial fortress in San Juan). They are "a pastiche of images relevant to nationalist memory and identity" (Cashman 2008, 3729) that work because they are identifiable and can be decoded by the community. James de la Vega, an artist from East Harlem who created various public artworks in El Barrio, many of which utilize the image of the Puerto Rican flag, described the flag as a "dictionary" of Puerto Rican culture, with other symbols like the jíbaro as components of that dictionary. He believes that in our everyday, complex lives, the flag is a simple symbol with a direct message—by displaying it on the streets or on walls and mailboxes, people feel a sense of ownership and connection to the community—the flag reminds them that this is a Puerto Rican community (personal communication 1999). By adorning the environment with a symbol that holds so much resonance to the community, the display becomes an appropriation of space in a landscape inclined to ignore the community. The flag may also work as a better folk symbol than the jíbaro because although the jíbaro doesn't imply the negative race and class connotations it once did, the flag serves as an all-inclusive representation for Puerto Ricans, including Nuyoricans (those of Puerto Rican descent born or raised in New York City).

Whether a part of the decorations on casitas or in murals, where many of the symbols are from the island's countryside, the easily identifiable symbol of the flag acts as a bridge between the rural symbols of the island and the urban environment of New York City. Since the casitas are usually situated in lots that also contain community gardens where roosters may amble among the plantings, the rural nature of the lots give the flag an additional subversive meaning. This agricultural element is in opposition to the dominant consumer culture—"gardening translates as a component of a resistive ethnic identity, where Puerto Rican-ness is defined in opposition to American society" (Martínez 2010, 48). And the temporal nature of murals and casitas gives them a quality of being in the moment. The painting of murals and the audiences attracted by this action, as well as the musical performances that take place at the casitas, give the community a constant sense of interaction with these places affirming a cultural identity (Cresswell 2004; Miller 2007).

CREATING A PUERTO RICAN SPACE AND IDENTITY: THE PUERTO RICAN DAY PARADE

As mentioned earlier, in New York City the visibility of the flag reaches its peak every June prior to the Puerto Rican Day Parade. Women paint their fingernails with the flag image, people of all ages can be seen wearing the flag as a cape, and even more cars than usual are decorated with the flag, often stretched across the hood. And what better metaphor for the Puerto Rican community, known as a "commuter nation" due to the heavy migration back and forth between the island and the mainland, than a symbol

Figure 6.2. The official Puerto Rican flag and the Lares flag with light blue colors at a gasoducto protest in lower Manhattan, winter 2012

of mobile identity? Migration to the mainland reached its peak after World War II and the implementation of the industrialization and economic plan known as Operation Bootstrap, and the 1970s saw a rise in reverse migration back to the island. Now with the current serious economic situation on the island, there is an outward flow from the island once again (though mainly by the professional and middle classes and to new regions on the mainland).

The parade, the pivotal event to demonstrate cultural pride, started out as a modest procession of over seventy hometown associations. The clubs helped maintain cultural ties to the island and provide services for the new migrants, such as housing and employment. These groups were organized under an umbrella group called El Congreso de Pueblo (Council of Hometown Clubs) that was instrumental in starting the first Puerto Rican Day parade in April 1958 (Estades 1980). There had been a *Desfile Hispano* (Hispanic Parade) that originated in 1956 to represent all Latinos in New York, but since Puerto Ricans were the largest group to take part in the parade, they finally seceded to form their own a few years later.

Even though there are Puerto Rican parades in other boroughs, the June parade on Fifth Avenue in Manhattan is the central event that brings Puerto Ricans from all over the northeast and the island together to celebrate their culture—80,000 marchers and 2 million spectators (Hu 2013)—and the flag plays a central role in this celebration. A view down Fifth Avenue on this day presents a blur of thousands of waving flags. In fact, the idea of the flag literally "taking up" space began quite early. In 1963, when activist Gilberto Gerena Valentín was president of the Puerto Rican Day Parade, a friend who owned a textile factory invited him to take a look at the flag his workers, many of whom were Puerto Rican, had created—a flag with a sky-blue triangle measuring fifty by thirty-five feet. Gerena Valentín writes how thousands of Puerto Ricans at the parade that year cried with emotion to see that huge flag being walked through a main thoroughfare of the city. Many even broke through the police cordons to touch the flag, "From here forward, the presence of the flag in the Puerto Rican Parade was inevitable" (Gerena Valentín 2013, 126–27).

COMMODIFICATION OF THE FLAG

However, does this display of cultural nationalism have any benefits to the Puerto Rican community in terms of social or economic justice? After the parade is over and the flags have been waved, the Puerto Rican community continues to experience high rates of unemployment, discrimination, low wages, and poor education. For those within the Puerto Rican community, it may be a symptom of *síndrome de la bandera* (flag syndrome), whereby "Latinos become fervent defenders of the homeland" (Améstica 1999, n.p.) for a day or a week only. And the parade itself, although a highlight of Puerto Rican culture in New York City, does have its critics. One of its biggest controversies remains the issue of corporate sponsorship and the commercialization of the parade. Commenting upon this, Angelo Falcón, the senior policy executive of the Puerto Rican Legal Defense Fund, noted that the community rarely comes out in large numbers. The community can mobilize itself and the parade is the prime example of this; but there were no large gatherings of that proportion marking noteworthy events such as the centennial of the Puerto Rican invasion by the United States. Unfortunately, the community is only mobilizing itself for corporations like Goya and Budweiser during the parade.[6] And this was brought to light again in 2013 with the controversy concerning the Coors Light beer cans that featured a likeness of the Puerto Rican flag (a red and blue apple with a star, a border reading, "National Puerto Rican Day Parade Inc." wrapped around the bottom of the can). Many local politicians and local activists called out MillerCoors and the parade's organizers, commenting that the ad's image was wrong for many reasons, and quite ironic as well, particularly in light of the parade's theme that year—which was *Salud*, Celebrating our Health— and that Puerto Ricans have the highest rate of alcohol dependence among

Figure 6.3. This sign at the 2013 parade protesting the misuse of the flag includes an image of Nationalist Party leader Pedro Albizu Campos.

Latinos, according to the National Institute of Health (National Institute for Latino Policy Network 2013).

The sale of flags and various mementos with the flag's image borders on crass commercialism. One can see flags printed with images such as roosters and conga drums among the many being waved or worn. The various displays of the flag during the parade are not conscious acts of disrespect; for the majority of Puerto Ricans the flags are expressions of cultural pride and statements of cultural identity that sometimes carry a political message. Nonetheless, respect for the flag means it should not be worn or have symbols printed on it. The official regulations for how the flag should be handled and displayed are quite specific. According to the Rules for the Use of the Flag, it should not be displayed on the hood or trunk of a car or other vehicle (article IX), used for commercial purposes, or marked with any inscriptions or design (article XXXII), among others directives (*Los símbolos oficiales de Puerto Rico*, n.d.). In 2000 Jaran Manzanet, president of the Salinas Hometown Club, organized to get consumers to be more respectful by not wearing flags or purchasing flags with other symbols on them, such as the coquí or roosters. Manzanet made a commitment that when he saw a flag with those symbols on it he would replace it with an unadorned one (Maria Román, cofounder and former chair and honorary member of the National Puerto Rican Day Parade, Inc., personal communication). The organizers of the parade actively supported Manzanet, and through a board-approved resolution have also adopted this campaign. The Coors controversy bought out protestors against the profaning of the flag once again.

THE FLAG AND CIVIC DUTY

But can we look at the parade-goers' actions in another light? The assemblages demonstrate that the community's members are more than just passive consumers; they are actively creating new material expressions. The flag is seen as something that belongs to the entire community, to everyone. Individuals do have an active role in their use, whether in the parade or when the flags become part of the landscape: "The flags are erected and flown because people feel an affinity for them and value their role both as a means of defining their identity and asserting a right to place . . . In practice this means that they are not fetishized as objects, but rather quite the opposite. They will be left to decay and when the time is right they will be replaced with new ones. The logic and rationale of the consumer society which is heavily ritualized and full of symbolism bas been extended to include elements of the ritual and symbolic culture" (Jarman 2007, 100).

While it is true that the parade organizers could find alternative sponsorship for the parade and parade-goers could purchase historically correct flags, the parade remains an important part of the community because it provides the release that festivals and other carnival-like events do, making this celebration more than just entertainment. The dual quality of the

Puerto Rican Day Parade (and other parades, protests, and public events attended by large contingents of the Puerto Rican community) is best described using Santino's classification of the "carnivalesque" and the "ritualesque, the former describing the festivity aspect of the event and the latter the "performative use of symbols—images, music, movement—to effect social change" (2011, 62). Santino discusses how the festivity aspect is usually emphasized at the expense of the ritualesque, but it is the latter that, in the case of the Puerto Rican Day Parade, will continue to have an effect on the community outside the space of the parade. Sociologist José Ramón Sánchez calls it a "coming-out party" addressed to the city's public officials; and as a way to become involved in New York's civic tradition of ethnic parades, the parade allows the Puerto Rican community "to proclaim its distinctive, separate existence. But it is also true that a parade makes this proclamation through a benevolent, even entertaining medium. Ultimately, parades assert not separation but integration into the wider society (Sánchez 1994, 115–16). In terms of creating a space for the performance of culture, the act of flag waving itself is part of a "collective ritual . . . to inscribe the presence of the Puerto Rican subject in the U.S public space and to institutionalize our visibility" (Aparicio 2007, 165), and this performance depends on the recognition of specific symbols—like flags; and in some cases the resistance occurs even when the symbol is deconstructed.[7] Pineda and Sowards discuss the use of flags in immigrant protests: "Flag waving is a visual argument through which immigrants and their supporters express cultural citizenship, civic virtue and democratic participation. The flags represent pride and remembrance, unity, and participatory civic virtue . . . Immigrants and their supporters seek not to subvert the system by opposing it but, rather, to practice the democratic principles of expression that are celebrated and protected in the United States" (2007, 167).[8]

And while social and economic problems still plague the Puerto Rican community, cultural nationalism should not be disregarded, as it plays a strong role in promoting group unity. Puerto Ricans' identity vis-à-vis nationalist perspectives has been discussed thoroughly (Duany 2002; Gonzalez 2000), and the parade historically has been a means of promoting a political identity as well. In fact, the emergence of the Puerto Rican Day Parade was an important expression of solidarity within the Puerto Rican community as it was growing and beginning to assert itself and express its social and political needs and interests in the 1950s. For the organizations originally involved in sponsoring this event, it "secured a visible foothold in the affairs of the City and proudly unfurled the full vitality and potential power of the community" (Sánchez Korrol 1983, 226).

Cultural nationalism also remains a powerful force because the United States has not resolved the island's political status (or allowed its population to do so); this "further reinforces cultural nationalism and the perceived distinctions between 'Puerto Ricans' and 'Americans'" (Aranda 2007, 21). Yet cultural nationalism, which sees the "nation" as a community sharing a history and traditions—what Anderson has called an "imagined community" (Anderson 2006)—starts from small grassroots movements, thus making it accessible to a wider range of people, many of whom will never meet, and the flag becomes a narrative that brings all them together regardless of political beliefs. It is cultural nationalism that has led Puerto Ricans in the diaspora to return to their roots—whether it is performing the island's traditional music, such as *bomba*, *plena*, and *la música jíbara*, or the celebration of its literary and historical figures, as the Camaradas parade contingent continues to do each year in the parade—as a source of community building (Rivera 2007, 217).

Expressions of Puerto Ricans identity are closely associated with the historical and political situation of Puerto Rico and its relationship to the United States. Many of the Puerto Ricans who display la bandera proudly throughout the year may not be aware of its history, but in the acts of wearing the flag, painting it on murals, and draping it on buildings and cars, there is an appropriation of space and validation of community identity. The flag, as a symbol all Puerto Ricans can relate to, connects disparate members of the community.

CONCLUSION

The flag has had different meanings over time—symbol of the Nationalist Party, symbol of the Commonwealth, at times subversive, and always controversial. Folklorist Barre Toelken discusses how the cultural and artistic codes of a particular community can be expressed in a variety of different artistic and material representations: "The real tradition is not the artifact itself, for it is a particularized statement of traditional premises and assumptions. The tradition is that dynamic process by which these premises are shared, performed, understood, and transmitted through time and space among members of a close group" (1996, 293). In the case of the Puerto Rican flag, we can take these codes to include the nationalistic sentiments of the community. So whether one is singing a plena about la bandera, creating its lace image in mundillo, or wearing a costume made entirely of commercially made flags, one is proudly and clearly declaring one's participation within the community.

NOTES

1. Puerto Rico is by decree a commonwealth or territory of the United States called a free associated state). Puerto Ricans became citizens of the United States through the Jones-Shafroth Act on March 2, 1917.
2. The Cry of Lares; Lares is a town in the Puerto Rican countryside.
3. Another narrative says that in 1891 Antonio Vélez Alvarado, a close friend of José Martí's and a founding member of Club Borinquen, came up with the idea of inverting the Cuban flag colors while at his office at 219 Twenty-Third Street. He designed this new flag and gave it to his daughter Micaela Dalmau to sew.
4. Attempted Coup of Yauco; Yauco is a town near the southwest coast of the island.
5. Jíbaros are the rural farmers of the island and are sometimes idealized as embodying the spirit of puertorriqueñidad.
6. Panel discussion, "The Evolution of Latino Communities," October 24, 1999, at the Museum of the City of New York.
7. Members of the Filipino delegation at the Smithsonian Folklife Festival had to use clever means to incorporate the Philippine flag when they were told that national flags weren't allowed on the Mall; they used its colors only in their display at the festival. For them "the absence of the flag as unthinkable . . . How can we celebrate without the flag?" (Trimillos 2008, 68).
8. Puerto Ricans, of course, are not immigrants, in that U.S. citizenship was imposed on them by the Jones-Shafroth Act of 1917, but their experiences are often similar.

REFERENCES

Alméstica, Miguel. 1999. "Bomba y Plena Forever." *Guiro y maraca* 3, no. 3. Jersey City: Segunda Quimbamba Folkloric Center.

Anderson, Benedict. 2006. *Imagined Communities*. London: Verso.

Aparicio, Frances. 2007. "Exposed Bodies: Media and U.S. Puerto Ricans in Public Space." In *None of the Above: Puerto Ricans in the Global Era*, ed. Frances Negrón-Muntaner, 165–79. New York: Palgrave Macmillan. http://dx.doi.org/10.1057/9780230 604360_13.

Aponte-Parés, Luis. 1994–1995. "What's Yellow and White and Has Land All Around It? Appropriating Place in Puerto Rican Barrios." *Centro* 7 (1): 8–19.

Aponte-Parés, Luis. 2000. "Appropriating Space in Puerto Rican Barrios: Preserving Contemporary Urban Landscapes." In *Preserving Cultural Landscapes in America*, ed. Arnold R. Alanen and Robert Z. Melnick, 94–111. Baltimore: Johns Hopkins University Press.

Aranda, Elizabeth. 2007. *Emotional Bridges to Puerto Rico: Migration, Return Migration and the Struggles of Incorporation*. London: Rowman & Littlefield.

Cashman, Ray. 2008. "Visions of Irish Nationalism." *Journal of Folklore Research* 45 (3): 361–81. http://dx.doi.org/10.2979/JFR.2008.45.3.361.

Cresswell, Tim. 2004. *Place: A Short Introduction*. Malden, MA: Blackwell.

Denis, Nelson A. 2015. *War against All Puerto Ricans: Revolution and Terror in America's Colony*. New York: Norton Books.

Duany, Jorge. 2002. *The Puerto Rican Nation on the Move*. Chapel Hill: University of North Carolina Press.

Enck-Wanzer, Darell. 2011. "Tropicalizing East Harlem: Rhetorical Agency, Cultural Citizenship, and Nuyorican Cultural Production." *Communication Theory* 21 (4): 344–67. http://dx.doi.org/10.1111/j.1468-2885.2011.01390.x.

Estades, Rosa. 1980. "Symbolic Unity: The Puerto Rican Day Parade." In *Historical Perspectives on Puerto Rican Survival in the United States*, ed. Clara E. Rodríguez and Virginia Sánchez Korral, 97–106. Princeton, NJ: Markus Wiener.
Fernández, Ronald. 1996. *Island of Disenchantment: Puerto Rico and the United States in the Twentieth Century*. New York: Praeger.
Flores, Juan. 1999. "El colonialismo lite: Diversiones de un discurso puertorriqueño." *Revista de ciencias sociales* 7 (June): 1–32.
Flores, Juan. 2009. *The Diaspora Strikes Back: Caribeño Tales of Learning and Turning*. New York: Routledge.
Garfinkel, Molly. 2014. "Preserving a Hometown Corner for Posterity: Rincón Crillo as a Traditional Cultural Property." *CultureWork: A Digital Broadside for Arts & Culture Workers* 18 (1). http://culturework.uoregon.edu/2014/01/29/january-2014-vol-18-no-1-preserving-a-hometown-corner-for-posterity-casita-rincon-criollo-as-a-traditional-cultural-property-molly-garfinkel/.
Gerena Valentín, Gilberto. 2013. *Soy Gilberto Gerena Valentín: Memorias de un puertorriqueño en Nueva York*, ed. Carlos Rodríguez Fraticelli. New York: Center for Puerto Rican Studies.
Gonzalez, Juan. 2000. *Harvest of Empire*. London: Penguin.
Hebdige, Dick. 1979. *Subculture: The Meaning of Style*. London: Routledge.
Hu, Winnie. 2013. "For Puerto Ricans, a Parade of Questions." *New York Times*, June 7. http://www.nytimes.com/2013/06/08/nyregion/as-puerto-rican-parade-grows-so-do-complaints.html?_r=0.
Jarman, Neil. 2007. "Pride and Possession, Display and Destruction." In *Flag, Nation and Symbol in Europe and America*, ed. Thomas Hylland Erikson and Richard Jenkins, 88–101. London: Routledge.
Martínez, Miranda J. 2010. *Power at the Roots: Gentrification, Community Gardens, and the Puerto Ricans of the Lower East Side*. Lanham, MD: Lexington Books.
Miller, Rosina. 2007. "Sharing Property: Critical Regionalism and Place-Based Social Change." *Western Folklore* 66 (3/4): 354–81.
Morris, Nancy. 1995. *Puerto Rico: Culture, Politics and Identity*. Westpoint, CT: Praeger.
National Institute for Latino Policy Network on Latino Issues Listserve. 2013. "Here They Go Again! Coors and the Puerto Rican Parade." May 25.
Negrón-Muntaner, Francis. 2004. *Boricua Pop: Puerto Ricans and the Latinizatin of American Culture*. New York: New York University Press.
Oring, Elliott. 1986. *Folk Groups and Folklore Genres: An Introduction*. Logan: Utah State University Press.
Pineda, Richard D., and Stacey K. Sowards. 2007. "Flag Waving as Visual Argument: 2006 Immigration Demonstrations and Cultural Citizenship." *Argumentation and Advocacy* 43:164–74.
Rivera, Raquel Z. 2007. "Will the 'Real' Puerto Rican Culture Please Stand Up? Thoughts on Cultural Nationalism." In *None of the Above: Puerto Ricans in the Global Era*, ed. Frances Negrón-Mutaner, 217–31. New York: Palgrave Macmillan. http://dx.doi.org/10.1057/9780230604360_17.
Rosario Natal, Carmelo. 1980. *Escudo, himno, y bandera: Origen e historia de los símbolos de Puerto Rico*. Rio Piedras, Puerto Rico: Editorial Edil.
Sánchez, José Ramón. 1994. "Puerto Ricans and the Door of Participation in U.S. Politics." In *Handbook of Hispanic Cultures in the United States: Sociology*, ed. Felix M. Padilla, 111–18. Houston: Arte Público.
Sánchez Korrol, Virginia Sánchez. 1983. *From Colonia to Community: The History of Puerto Ricans in New York City*. Berkeley: University of California Press.

Santino, Jack. 1986. "The Folk Assemblage of Autumn: Tradition and Creativity in Halloween Folk Art." In *Folk Art and Folk Worlds*, ed. John Michael Vlach and Simon J. Bronner, 151–69. Logan: Utah State University Press.
Santino, Jack. 2011. "The Carnivalesque and the Ritualesque." *Journal of American Folklore* 124 (491): 61–73. http://dx.doi.org/10.5406/jamerfolk.124.491.0061.
Los símbolos oficiales de Puerto Rico. n.d. San Juan, Puerto Rico: Editorial Cordillera.
Toelken, Barre. 1996. *The Dynamics of Folklore*. Boston: Houghton Mifflin.
Trimillos, Richard D. 2008. "Histories, Resistances, and Reconciliations in a Decolonizable Space: The Philippine Delegation to the 1998 Smithsonian Folklife Festival." *Journal of American Folklore* 121 (479): 60–79. http://dx.doi.org/10.1353/jaf.2008.0002.

7

The Lives of Processions in Bali and Lombok, Indonesia

David Harnish

PROCESSIONS SERVE MYRIAD PURPOSES IN INDONESIA and beyond and may stand alone or be one public part of a larger event, such as a festival (see Peterson 2007 and Harnish 2006 for examples). Most processions can be considered a moving theater as actors, ritual attendants, clowns, musicians, and others traverse through selected space (Dibia 1985), often wearing varied and colorful costumes and working to promote or to subvert the social order. The sound element—marching or other loud processional music to activate political or spiritual indices—moves groups forward, defines their missions, and announces their significance; in fact, a general rule is that the more instruments and ensembles and the louder the music, the more important the procession. The visual element may represent status (e.g., royal processions), martial power (military processions), orientation, and historic narratives or be juxtaposed to express parody, humor, or religious or political positions.

Processions may be public displays of religiosity or pageants and carnivalesque as a community tells "a story *about* itself and *for* itself" (Gunkel 2003, 7; see also Geertz 1973) and members "perform an elaborate public display of faith, ethnic affiliation and neighborhood" (Gunkel 2003, 7). Some societies have had processional "seasons" carved out of a year, with specific music to specify purpose (Page 1999)—with many instruments manufactured solely for this use (Roos 1979)—and clearly some cultures (such as Bali) organize many more processions than others. Subcultural or countercultural processions may arise to counter dominant ritual expressions, and migrant or diasporic groups may organize processions to celebrate their ethnic survival and to orient the group to today's world. Gender is always represented, particularly shades of masculinity. In Indonesia, however, overt sexuality is rare, partially because of religious sensibilities (most Indonesians are Muslims) and norms about public displays of bodies (either straight or gay) and desire.[1]

Motion and movement are central to processions, both for the participants and whatever implements, often symbolically charged, they carry. Items not normally seen or available to the community—sacred objects or relics, for instance—may be publicly paraded for the benefit of either one party or class or for everyone. More rarely, processions based on ethnicity or those reenacting battle victories are meant to restate a group's dominance and intimidate nonmembers, for example, those carried out by the Orange Order in Ireland (Bryan 2000); immigrants may preserve or modify these homeland practices in their new environment (Seales 2008). Processions representing a plurality may work to unify diverse constituencies within a culture (Komlosy 2004); on the other hand, in hierarchical societies processions have been a medium to bring ruler and subjects together in order to affirm control and showcase symbols of power, glory, and rank.

City-states and countries tend to use processions and parades to memorialize and celebrate shared histories, and newly wealthy middle-class, religious, or fraternal organizations are sometimes patrons for "journeys of state," "welcoming dignitaries," or "honoring sovereign" pageants that constitute status-enhancing "corporate gifts" (Bowles 1961, 147, 151). These events are also often held to address catastrophes, such as the rain processions in early twentieth-century China enacted to deal with severe drought or famine (Jones 1999, 38). Patrons may organize processions—and participants may be engaged—because of vows and promises to the divine (see Hagedorn 2002 for a *promesa* [promise] example in Cuba). Processions may take advantage of cultural or religious tourism, intended to "create tradition" (Bowman 2004, 274). In all circumstances, processions make things happen, mark the importance of the occasion, and allow special behavior to occur.

In Bali and Lombok, these active ritualized events break the normal flow of time, are always temporally marked, and can be characterized as religious and/or temple- or mosque-sponsored or secular and state-sponsored (Harnish 2016). Those events considered "religious" or spiritual always have political overtones and secular implications, while those held as secular uphold or resort to metaphysics to gain solemnity and sanction (Falassi 1987). I've observed many processions in Indonesia that conflate nation-state, rulership, or central authority along with modern religiosity and citizenship; indeed, some processions seem meant to show Indonesians how to be modern citizens and may feature sanitized or aestheticized music to promote regional identity and government agendas of proper behavior, dress, and such values as tolerance (Harnish 2011). Processions and parades in Indonesia are glossed by the Indonesian word *pawe* (also spelled *pawai*), but these events are normally defined by terms of the insider language (e.g., Balinese or Javanese languages) and many are attached to institutions, such as temple festivals, with an assortment of distinct terms and purposes.

This chapter discusses processions generally on Bali, then explores one specific, mostly religious, series of processions at one festival on Lombok. The actors under discussion in Bali are Hindu Balinese; those in Lombok are migrant Hindu Balinese and Muslim Sasak (the indigenous and majority inhabitants). Underlying the social dynamic of events that conjoin both religious/ethnic groups in Lombok is the fact that Hindu Balinese ruled over Lombok and the Sasak for 200 years, while Islam became the inspiration for Sasak resistance, and both Hindu and Islamic reform movements have been forces for change in processions and all other ritual events. Processions in Indonesia, both political and spiritual, are public barometers for measuring socioreligious and political change.

THE ORDER OF BALINESE PROCESSIONS

Processions are a core element of Hindu Balinese religion, which is perhaps manifest most publicly at temple festivals. With circa 25,000 temples in Bali celebrating a festival generally every 210 days, there are many hundreds of such events happening throughout the year, and the majority of these festivals include one or multiple processions. The Balinese and national governments also use processions to celebrate themselves or to memorialize historic events (e.g., independence, the sacrifice of Balinese heroes), and to announce developments and progress.

Processions are also crucial in cremation ceremonies, when a corpse in a tower is accompanied by a sarcophagus, family and community members, dozens and sometimes up to 100 young men to carry the tower and sarcophagus, attendants carrying offerings, ritual specialists, and gamelan (percussion ensembles) musicians proceeding to the cremation grounds. The procession marks the final journey of a soul's travel through life; additional death ceremonies, sometimes involving new processions, may occur in following years, largely determined by the social caste of the deceased and the resources of the family. The event also traces a line from the home compound of the deceased to the cremation grounds and the village "temple of death" (*pura dalem*) and stimulates a specific array of normally celebratory behavior (mourning takes place earlier within the home compound). Generally the body and tower are spun around three times at a crossroads to prevent the soul from knowing the path back to the home (a different interpretation is to confuse bad spirits and keep them from the deceased). The culminating rite, after purifications, is the burning of the tower and sarcophagus (where the body is inserted after arriving at the grounds), along with many of the deceased's earthly belongings. Many guests then depart for home, while others may picnic and young people might flirt. Family members collect the remains of the deceased, some of which may be stored for a second cremation or for processing to the sea (or a river to the sea) to be ritually dispensed.

No two cremations or their processions can ever be precisely the same, and cremations for commoners sharply differ from those for royalty or higher-caste members. Caste and wealth are immediately apparent at any cremation. A ceremony for a member of royalty or a wealthy commoner might include numerous gamelan ensembles, dance, theater, and/or shadow play performances, food to feed hundreds of neighboring villagers and guests, giant tower and sarcophagus (often in the form of a giant bull), hundreds of community volunteers to carry the tower and sarcophagus and various offerings and paraphernalia, and officiating by high priests (*padanda*) with a number of ritual assistants. A commoner cremation may include a brief procession, a common priest (*pamangku*), and simply the use of bamboo poles to suspend the corpse over a burning pit. Since the cost of a cremation is high, commoners often hold off on the ceremony, awaiting the death of a wealthy or royal villager, then join with that family and many others in the community for a mass cremation largely underwritten by that royal or wealthy family or *banjar* (ward). Bodies of people of caste are generally burned by the third day after death, while commoners are buried in the cemetery grounds until the opportunity arises; sometimes so many years have passed that bones are all that remain to be cremated. The fact that such mass cremations have greatly increased over recent decades indicates the spiraling costs of holding cremations and the financial burden experienced by a great many commoner or poor families. While caste disparities have declined since national independence around 1950, they have not disappeared, and income disparity between the elite (the remaining nobility and wealthy commoners and expatriated foreigners, including Westerners and Chinese) and the common classes is as wide as ever. The constitution of the procession reveals the status and orientation of the deceased and his or her family.

Processions at temple festivals differ in meaning and social structure; since festivals are communal and not family rituals (excepting those at family and clan temples), they may mask or downplay caste and wealth disparities and are meant to benefit whole communities. These processions often connect sacred sites of importance that are tied to a common point in history; figurines, if used, represent deities or divinities and are brought to a sacred spring or river for bathing or purification. Participants and/or officials carry a myriad of ritual implements and offerings, including clothing and toiletries for deities, water bottles or vessels, and symbolic poles or woven plaits in addition to numerous ornate family offerings of rice flour and food (mostly fruit, often stacked high and carried on women's heads). Processions in the context of festivals are part of reenactments of the founding of a temple. The procession route highlights a chosen and privileged path, and sacred objects, which may be connected to the establishment of the temple, are publicly exhibited or danced. The processional music, generally performed by the gamelan *balaganjur*, makes both cosmological and martial statements. While the music is often thought to clear the path of malevolent forces, the musicians represent "walking warriors" (Bakan 1999) who protect the procession, its main offerings and implements, and its participants as everyone traverses through potentially dangerous space. This type of festival procession thus proceeds from the temple out into profane space before arriving at another sacred space; the return to the first temple may constitute a second procession. Purifications or sacrifices are necessary to generate or maintain spiritual cleanliness at sacred spaces and to help safeguard the mission.

Another kind of festival procession circumambulates temple altars or structures. These processions may set in motion the life of a festival and serve to activate the temple items, such as sacred implements and offerings. Generally a procession circumambulates in a clockwise motion (sometimes called *Purwedaksina*, east-south) at the beginning of a festival and then in a counterclockwise motion at the conclusion. Priests I've spoken with concur that the clockwise procession invites and accompanies deities down from the heavens or mountain peaks into the temple and the counterclockwise procession accompanies or sends them home.

These two types of festival processions—journeys through the appointed path to connecting sacred sites (often involving water) and circumambulations around temple altars or structures—are found at the annual Lingsar temple festival in Lombok. The Lingsar temple has particular importance to Balinese migrants: it was the source that, according to Balinese legend, helped convince nobles to come to Lombok, conquer Sasak kingdoms, and restore righteousness; the Balinese mission was led to Lombok by butterflies, which had transformed from leaves to guide the platoon (Agung 1991; see Harnish 2006 for explication). For the Sasak, Lingsar represents a central point in early Islam; credited by many as initiating Sasak culture, it was the place of a culture hero's pact with God and his divine sacrifice, which preserves the fecundity of the region. The temple grounds are also the site of the major water spring irrigating most of west and central Lombok, offering some of the best rice yields in Lombok, and thus represent the center of fertility. The temple, its festival, and its processions were historically a demonstration of the power of the Balinese kings and thus represented noble power and the promise of fertility (Gerdin 1982; Harnish 2001, 2006).

FESTIVALS AND PROCESSIONS AT LINGSAR

The festival, called Pujawali, is held around the full moon in December and lasts five days, though only three days have set, active programs (the other days are "empty" to allow hundreds of people who are unavailable on other days to come to pray).[2] Up to 20,000 people visit the temple and participate in the dozens of rites at the festival.

The temple and festival bring migrant Hindu Balinese and Muslim Sasak together, and thus the festival and its processions are equally shared. Each group has its own legend of the temple's founding. Not surprisingly, each group's legend privileges its own ancestors as the pioneers. Balinese kings and nobility controlled the temple, its festival, the neighboring rice collectives, and the rice harvests on temple lands here for hundreds of years until the Dutch battled and defeated Balinese forces in Lombok in 1894. The process of conducting the festival, still controlled by the Balinese temple organization Krama Pura, was not widely challenged until the 1960s and 1970s; until that time Balinese dominated the public meanings of the festival. The reasons for modifications in the later twentieth century arise primarily from socioreligious changes among the Sasak.

The festival cannot be considered "Islamic," although Sasak authorities and officials, called *pamangku*, have been working to Islamize the founding of the temple, asserting that an early evangelist claimed the area with the help of Allah and established the festival traditions. Until the 1960s, the Sasak participants at Lingsar were called Wetu Telu, nominal Muslims who uphold only the first of the five pillars of the Arkān, the Shahadah or confession of faith. The Wetu Telu were obliterated during the 1960s in vigilante and state violence against those appearing to be "communist"; largely farmers, Wetu Telu had supported land reform and as a result were slaughtered by the thousands (Pepplinkhuizen 1991). Many remaining members started following Muslim religious leaders called *Tuan Guru* in the late 1960s

Figure 7.1. Flag-bearers with Indonesian flags (representing the union of Balinese and Sasak) lead the Mendak Tirta procession, immediately followed by a Sasak gamelan tambur and a host of Balinese participants, priests, and gamelans.

to protect themselves, and nearly all renounced the traditionalist practices of the Wetu Telu, registering themselves with the government as Muslim. It was widely thought—and the government wanted it that way—that anyone not following an established world religion (*agama*, consisting of Hinduism, Buddhism, Islam, Protestantism, and Catholicism) might be a communist, and the Wetu Telu faith was not a world religion.

In the late 1960s, a regional government leader refused to allow the Sasak pamangku to officiate at the festival on the grounds that the festival is Hindu and the pamangku is Muslim, and the acts at Lingsar are not endorsed by the Qur'an or Hadith. Balinese political leaders prevailed in pleading their case that the pamangku was needed to officiate, but the government official only consented on the basis that the participation was "cultural" and not "religious," thereby creating a wedge between these two dimensions that has been restated over and over again for nearly five decades. The tensions between Balinese and Sasak—whether the festival is Hindu or Muslim, Balinese or Sasak, who discovered the water springs first, which camp really leads the event—and intraethnic Sasak tensions—reformist Muslims versus "tradition," disagreements about the origins of

Figure 7.2. Balinese participants, offerings, decor (parasols, *penyor* poles), and gamelan musicians (in tan jackets) in Mendak Tirta

Islam in Lombok, whether any Lingsar rites can be considered "Islamic," friction over the importance of ancestors—are played out at the festival each year. The substance for each position is found within processions.

The opening day of the festival—Penaek Gawe (Begin Ceremony) for Sasak, Pengadagang or Pemendak (Greet or Begin) for Balinese—begins with an initial procession called Mendak Tirta (Greet Holy Water), and is led by a Sasak gamelan ensemble called *tambur*, preceded only by two Indonesian flags representing unity.

The gamelan tambur—consisting solely of a gong and drum—is associated with the earliest ancestors at Lingsar, publicly displays Lingsar's spiritual power (the instruments themselves are sacred), and provides a Sasak claim to origins.[3] The participants, however, are overwhelmingly Balinese, who add at least three more processional gamelans.

This procession goes eastward to a temple with a sacred water spring; another procession proceeds west with little fanfare to a different water spring and temple. Each procession collects water in two vessels with specific colors representing the two high deities of both Bali (the western spring) and Lombok (the eastern spring). Then these two processions converge on the three-way intersection outside the entrance to the Lingsar

Figure 7.3. Telek dancers perform in the procession.

temple. Led by Balinese common priests, the waters and deities are "married" through ritual, thus unifying Bali and Lombok under Balinese control and confirming the Balinese legend. Long ago many Sasak participated in this procession; today, however, the only Sasak are the gamelan musicians, some dancers for a related performance (see figure 7.3), and a few officials because Sasak do not want to be seen supporting the Balinese claim over Lingsar. Much of the ritual life has become politicized over recent decades.

The next procession, called Mendak Kebon Odeq (Greet Little Garden) begins at the Sasak pamangku's home compound. The two main festival offerings, a male/female pair called *kebon odeq* (little garden), consist of fruits, Chinese coins, flowers, and seeds. These offerings are processed in a large, nearly entirely Sasak entourage to the *kemaliq*, the second courtyard of the temple shared by Sasak and Balinese. The kemaliq encloses a pond with sacred spring water guarded by large eels. The shrine beside the pond consists of many dressed stones, and the Sasak pamangku leads worship at that site each day of the festival. This procession morphs into Ngilahang Kebon Odeq, a thrice circumambulating procession that concludes with the kebon odeq being positioned in the shrine and a prayer session. A variety of processional performing artists, including two or more Sasak gamelans and a group of martial dancers in Dutch military outfits escorting three to

Figure 7.4. Martial dancers lead the telek dancers in procession around the sacred pond in the kemaliq. Balinese participants follow.

five female cross-dressed dancers who abstractly perform a narrative dance (*telek* or *batek*), envelop the participants.

Also featured in this procession are the *pesaji*, covered food offerings, which are supposed to be made in any increment of nine (nine, eighteen, twenty-seven, etc.). Many Sasak state that the festival "really" begins once the kebon odeq are in position. One other item carried in this and other Sasak processions is *momot*, a bottle that is sealed while empty and placed in the shrine. The level of water that mysteriously appears in the bottle by the end of the festival is considered equivalent to the produce of the coming harvest.

Soon afterward, a large procession consisting of Balinese and Sasak, an extended range of offerings and ritual implements, dancers, and four to five processional ensembles accompany a water buffalo, and all circumambulate the entire temple structure three times in a clockwise direction, representing the descent of deities. The water buffalo, a sacrifice for the residing deity, is ritually slaughtered the following morning; the head and right foreleg are then positioned in a tree within the kemaliq, representing the buffalo's ascent into the heavens. (A second buffalo is also sacrificed and the meat of both is divided between Sasak and Balinese for feasts.) This procession is meant to unify the Balinese and Sasak camps around ritual action and a central sacrifice.

Figure 7.5. Momot (*in front*) and the two kebon odeq circumambulated during the Ngilahang Kebon Odeq procession in the kemaliq

Following the procession, which takes around an hour due to the sheer numbers of participants and gamelans, two other processions take place: one with only Balinese circumambulating the inner altars of the *gaduh*, the exclusive Balinese courtyard at Lingsar, three times, and the other with mostly Sasak encircling the inner structures of the kemaliq three times. The number three is not arbitrary; it is charged with cosmological/numerological significance. The processions conclude with prayer periods in both courtyards. After these processions, the inherent qualities of the offerings are believed to be activated and alive, and the deities are believed to be present in the courtyards.

This ends the opening day of events, although there may be evening performances that are considered recreational. Six processions—which initiate the festival, unify Balinese and Sasak (and Bali and Lombok), introduce and activate the kebon odeq, usher in the deities in the gaduh and kemaliq, offer the water buffalo, and bring the courtyards and offerings to life—are held on this first day.

The second day is the main day (Rainan Karya for the Balinese and Perang Topat for the Sasak), which falls on the full moon and brings out many thousands of participants. Due to the importance of the event and the sheer numbers, politicians want to be involved and seen as endorsing (and claiming credit for) the festival. With the exception of the current governor, who is also a reformist religious figure, governors have attended and generally spoken at every Lingsar festival since 1988.

Many more offerings (*pesaji* by the Sasak, *banten* by the Balinese) are made on the main day, and most of them will be processed in later events. A procession called Mendak Pesaji originating from the Sasak pamangku's home proceeds to the kemaliq in the afternoon (much like Mendak Kebon Odeq on the opening day), with full entourage of gamelan ensembles and dancers; this is again an overwhelmingly Sasak event. Both groups engage in separate feasts as music floods the temple grounds from Sasak and Balinese gamelans. A number of sacred or semisacred dances occur in the Balinese gaduh followed by the unison chanting of the sacred Trisandya text and the major prayers called Mabakti (To Do Prayer) or Panca Sembah (Pray Five Times), while in the kemaliq begins the Ngilahang Pesaji, the three-time circumambulation around the shrine and pond, accompanied again by gamelans and dancers.

For this occasion, many Balinese farmers participate in the kemaliq rather than the gaduh, demonstrating their history and commitment to that space; originally Balinese farmers (all of them low caste) were not allowed in the gaduh. They instead worshipped in the kemaliq with the Sasak, who also consisted largely of farmers. With the end of feudalism (1894) and independence/democratization (1945/1950), Balinese commoners increasingly attended rites in both temple courtyards. The gamelan musicians and dancers in the kemaliq, however, are Sasak; the dance, telek, features three to five women cross-dressed as Sasak male culture heroes. The dancers dance while in procession and usually perform again when congregants sit before the shrine. While the Balinese position a high priest (padanda) and a women's group of *kidung* (poetry-honoring deities) praise singers in the kemaliq, the Sasak pamangku leads the worship around the shrine. Following Ngilahang Pesaji is the worship period known as Ngaturang Pesaji; Balinese outnumber Sasak in this prayer period in the kemaliq shrine area led by the Sasak pamangku.[4] Meanwhile, Balinese prayers continue in the gaduh. The official conclusion of the day is the Perang Topat, the ritual of participants throwing *topat* rice squares cooked in palm leaves at each other outside the gaduh and kemaliq (the Balinese tend to be outside the gaduh, the Sasak outside the kemaliq for fifteen to twenty minutes). This act is fun and often rowdy (it draws some participants, particularly among the Sasak, who are not involved in any other festival rites), but it signifies abundance. Afterward, farmers collect the topat and place them in trees or rice fields, as they are considered blessed. For many, this is the culminating rite at the festival.

The final day—Penglemek (Fertile Soil) in Balinese and Beteteh (Discard) in Sasak—features more offerings, particularly pesaji by the Sasak and frequent Balinese and Sasak gamelan performances. The new pesaji are again processed to the kemaliq in another Mendak Pesaji procession accompanied by dancers and gamelans, and another slow Ngilahang Pesaji circumambulation of the shrine and pond follows. Balinese conduct more prayers in the gaduh and gamelans continue almost unceasingly. A concluding worship Ngaturang Pesaji rite is held in front of the kemaliq shrine; it is sometimes called Nunas Pamit (Request to Leave), while the Balinese hold a procession of circumambulation around altars within the gaduh.

Then the largest procession of all (sometimes called Melukar [To Send Back] by the Balinese) begins to organize. It is led by the Sasak gamelan tambur once again, followed by Balinese gamelan, priest, and congregants from a separate Lingsar temple (the "head" temple, which thus needs to go first), followed by the Balinese gamelan, priest, and congregants in the gaduh, and then by the (mostly) Sasak group of gamelans, dancers, pamangku, and congregants in the kemaliq. Another group of Balinese—gamelan, priest, and congregation—from a shrine area just outside the temple is the last group in the procession.

There are perhaps 5,000 participants in total and the procession stretches over nearly a mile. The destination is the temple to the west, where the small Balinese procession arrived during the morning of the opening day. The unified participants of Balinese and Sasak walk two by two in their respective groups, disrupting traffic for hours as they march to the sounds of five or six gamelans. Several Balinese men also play ceremonial music on a wooden oboe as they walk, sometimes because they have made a personal vow.[5] All participants wear ceremonial dress; hundreds carry parasols or implements and thousands carry offerings. Priests are intermixed throughout, carrying offerings and incense bowls. Interestingly, during many of these final processions the leaders of the Balinese Krama Pura and Sasak temple organization hold hands as they walk in procession—usually with the kemaliq group—signifying the renewed union between them and, by extension, Balinese and Sasak as a whole, as a result of the festival and this particular procession. This unity represents male/female and thus fertility.

When all arrive to the grounds, most Balinese enter the temple—which had been the site to invite and now to send back the high deities of Bali—and pray, while the kemaliq group goes to a nearby river, conducts a final rite (often including dance), and ritually discards the kebon odeq offerings.

Later the momot, the bottle sealed while empty at the festival's beginning, is ceremonially opened. In all the years that I attended save one, this bottle was opened to reveal it was about 30 percent full of water, considered sacred and bestowed by the deity. The water is dispersed in portions to the encircled participants—mostly farmers and a mixture of Sasak and Balinese—who drink some of it and ritually sprinkle more around parts of their heads. Most will store the remaining water, believed to have purifying and healing powers, in vessels at home for their families.

INTERPRETATIONS OF PROCESSION AT LINGSAR

Ritual protocol signals spiritual/political hierarchy (Hefner 1985, 73). The political order and its inherent tensions, the arrangement of the divine, the elements of legends, and the icons of harmony and balance—necessary to enact or restore interethnic relations (a primary festival outcome)—are all public in the processions. The Sasak pamangku and the Balinese pamangku and religious officials are clearly the leaders. Offerings come from Sasak and Balinese ritual officials—these have publicly acknowledged symbolic elements and are placed in efficacious spots in the processions—as well as from thousands of individuals, particularly Balinese.

Not all processions, however, have a balance of Balinese and Sasak participants. The first festival procession consists only of Balinese walking westward to collect holy water; the immediate second procession, officially Mendak Tirta, is led by gamelan tambur and musicians but consists, again, almost entirely of Balinese. Here the Balinese supplant the Sasak as "local" by appropriating the sacred ancestral booty of the gamelan tambur, the land (initiated by connecting the sacred water points around Lingsar), and even the deities (bringing forth the high deities of early Sasak Wetu Telu faith and marrying them to Balinese counterparts where they are nearly equal but "younger").[6] This creates a pact between Bali and Lombok, though it does so under the auspices of the Balinese, hence marking the temple and festival as under Balinese hegemony. The former colonizing of the Balinese over Lombok was at least partially centered on and rationalized by the Lingsar temple, its festival, and the resulting rainwater and fertility. This is the main reason why fewer and fewer Sasak participate in these processional rites.

The following event—the processing of the kebon odeq with its male and female symbolism from the Sasak pamangku's compound to the kemaliq—features almost entirely Sasak and provides a counternarrative to the Balinese processions described above. I believe this procession has become a statement of Sasak ethnicity and history at Lingsar, a history that does not include the Balinese. Balinese farmers were often attracted to the kebon odeq—representing the fertility of the area—and also the momot, which is considered sacred and bestowed by the deity. Kebon odeq and momot are processed to the kemaliq, but Balinese are no longer encouraged to participate in that opening Sasak procession. The ethnic divide—acknowledged distinctive religions and legends and contestation over ownership—has dissolved some of the unity and led to fewer joint participations. Interestingly, it is ethnic unity (and by extension the harmony of male and female as embodied also within kebon odeq) that leads to fertility, and unity is a primary, if not *the* primary, goal of the festival. Processions today both negate that unity due to increasing ethnic exclusivity in some rites and also generate interethnic unity in the shared rites.

During the opening day, the main day, and the closing day, the kebon odeq are processed by men and women around the temple and around the shrines in the kemaliq. Formerly, Balinese were given the opportunity the carry the offerings as well; transporting the kebon odeq is a high honor and touching them provides access to the power of the festival and the unification of male/female and the generation of fertility. But one time, in 1988, some Balinese were denied access to these crucial offerings. The Balinese leader of the time, Anak Agung Biarsah, confronted the Sasak pamangku, Sanusi, and demanded to know why this was happening (I was interviewing Sanusi at the time). Sanusi immediately relented and said, "Of course Balinese can carry the kebon odeq. Just like always." There has been an effort by the Sasak to restrict those rites considered "Sasak" only to Sasak, despite the shared history of access—leaders have crafted the idea that gaduh and kemaliq are separate and represent respective temples for Balinese and Sasak—and the interaction between Anak Agung Biarsah and Sanusi brought the issue to the fore.[7] Separation from the Hindu Balinese is important; if there is too much sharing (particularly regarding anything considered "religious"), it could create problems for Sasak leadership and bring reformist groups to bear pressure on the Sasak. Access to the kebon odeq in processions remains a high-tension issue between Balinese and Sasak. These offerings allow leaders to state that the Sasak are the true leaders of the festival.

CONCLUDING THOUGHTS

I have been researching the Lingsar festival and its processions for thirty-three years. Although leaders and participants consistently state every year that the festival hasn't changed, I have noticed some significant alterations

(Harnish 2005). Most changes have to do with Balinese and Sasak reorienting their culture (and actions/rites at the festival) to contemporary sociopolitical developments in Indonesia. In 1983, the first year I attended, reformist forces, both Hindu and Islamic, had just begun to flex their muscles in governing ritual actions but had little influence at Lingsar. Changes became evident within a decade, however, in ritual protocol, processional music, and ethnic makeup, and the pressure from reformists has increased since then. While many modifications took place within the gaduh and kemaliq, the true barometer of change is indicated by the many processions because it is the processions that make all public statements—moving out from temple spaces into the streets and environs—about who the Balinese and Sasak are and what they believe.

The grandiose processions are often filled with power and tension and other times are effective vehicles for creating and maintaining unity and harmony. What they represent has evolved from simply unifying Bali and Lombok (via Mendak Tirta on the opening day) and collectively returning the deities while embracing the union that has stimulated divine boons via prayer and momot (through the final procession and actions); they have become major ethnic theaters defining both the separate Balinese and Sasak communities (via respective Balinese and especially Sasak processions) and the union that emerges by the final procession. The cosmological narratives the music imposes upon the environment and the many processions moving together in tandem nurture the transformation from postures of respective ethnic borders to a collapse of those borders into the oneness that leads to fertility and abundance, and this spiritual union has always been the goal of the festival.

NOTES

1. This does not mean that sexuality is always publicly suppressed. On the contrary, such semipublic events as weddings or harvest festivals and the popular style known as *dangdut* (or *joget nakal* in Bali and *aleh-aleh* in Lombok) frequently feature women (or very occasionally male transvestites) dancing erotically with men. Religious boards often seek to ban these performances but generally fail. See Weintraub 2010 for more on dangdut.

2. The date is determined by the sixth full moon of the Balinese *sasih* lunar-solar calendar and the seventh full moon of the Sasak *wariga* calendar. The date can range from late November to early January.

3. Some Balinese believe that rajas gave the ensemble to Sasak as a way to stimulate more local participation. Other instruments that make up the ritual gamelan *baris* may be carried and occasionally played by other musicians.

4. The reason there are fewer Sasak is that this prayer period is clearly not Islamic. Long ago, no one scrutinized Sasak when they participated in worship with Balinese. Today,

however, those praying are recognized as Wetu Telu and that identity can lead to embarrassment or even violence. Fewer and fewer Sasak participate in worship today.

5. The piece they play is "Turun Daun," a Sasak poem of praise that has been performed at the festival for generations. Two Sasak oboe (*preret*) players used to play this piece, too, but that tradition is associated with Wetu Telu and thus ceased as the Sasak at Lingsar began to Islamize.

6. For the Sasak, the deities are Batara Gede Rinjani of the main volcano and Batara Gede Lingsar of the Lingsar area; for the Balinese, they are Batara Gunung Agung of the main volcano on Bali and Batara Alit Sakti, a deity born a noble human who sacrificed himself and directed Balinese to Lombok.

7. The reason that Sanusi quickly submitted to Anak Agung Biarsah is that Biarsah was the grandson of the last king of Lombok and Sanusi had officiated for decades under a political climate that had always favored Balinese.

REFERENCES

Agung, Anak Agung Ktut. 1991. *Kupu Kupu Kuning yg Terbang di Selat Lombok* [Yellow Butterflies That Flew across the Lombok Strait]. Denpasar, Bali: Upada Sastra.

Bakan, Michael B. 1999. *Music of Death and New Creation: Experiences in the World of Gamelan Beleganjur*. Chicago: University of Chicago Press.

Bowles, Edmund. 1961. "Musical Instruments in Civic Processions during the Middle Ages." *Acta Musicologica* 33 (2/4): 147–61. http://dx.doi.org/10.2307/931868.

Bowman, Marion. 2004. "Procession and Possession in Glastonbury: Continuity, Change and the Manipulation of Tradition." *Folklore* 115 (3): 273–85. http://dx.doi.org/10.1080/0015587042000284266.

Bryan, Dominic. 2000. *Orange Parades: The Politics of Ritual, Tradition and Control*. London: Pluto.

Dibia, I. Wayan. 1985. "*Odalan* of Hindu Bali: A Religious Festival, a Social Occasion, and a Theatrical Event." *Asian Theatre Journal* 2 (1): 61–65. http://dx.doi.org/10.2307/1124507.

Falassi, Alessandro. 1987. "Festival: Definition and Morphology." In *Time out of Time: Essays on the Festival*, ed. Alessandro Falassi, 1–10. Albuquerque: University of New Mexico Press.

Geertz, Clifford. 1973. *The Interpretation of Cultures*. New York: Basic Books.

Gerdin, Ingela. 1982. *The Unknown Balinese: Land, Labour, and Inequality in Lombok*. Goteburg: Universitatis Gothoburgensis.

Gunkel, Ann Hetzel. 2003. "The Sacred in the City: Polonian Street Processions as Countercultural Practice." *Polish American Studies* 60 (2): 7–23.

Hagedorn, Katherine. 2002. "Long Day's Journey to Rincón: From Suffering to Resistance in the Procession of San Lázaro/Babalú Ayé." *British Journal of Ethnomusicology* 11 (1): 43–69. http://dx.doi.org/10.1080/09681220208567328.

Harnish, David. 2001. "Like King and Queen, Like Balinese and Sasak: Musical Narratives at the Lingsar Temple Festival in Lombok, Indonesia." *Ethnologies (Québec)* 23 (1): 63–88.

Harnish, David. 2005. "New Lines, Shifting Identities: Interpreting Change at the Lingsar Festival in Lombok, Indonesia." *Ethnomusicology* 49 (1): 1–24. http://dx.doi.org/10.2307/20174351.

Harnish, David D. 2006. *Bridges to the Ancestors: Music, Myth, and Cultural Politics at an Indonesian Festival*. Honolulu: University of Hawaii Press.

Harnish, David. 2011. "Tensions between Adat (Custom) and Agama (Religion) in the Music of Lombok." In *Divine Inspirations: Music and Islam in Indonesia*, ed. David Harnish and Anne Rasmussen, 80–108. New York: Oxford University Press. http://dx.doi.org/10.1093/acprof:oso/9780195385410.003.0003.

Harnish, David. 2016. "Religious Processions, Cultural Identities, and Politics on Bali and Lombok, Indonesia," *Yale Journal of Religion and Music* 2(2): 52–74.

Hefner, Robert W. 1985. *Hindu Javanese: Tengger Tradition and Islam*. Princeton: Princeton University Press.

Jones, Stephen. 1999. "Chinese Ritual Music under Mao and Deng." *British Journal of Ethnomusicology* 8 (1): 27–66. http://dx.doi.org/10.1080/09681229908567280.

Komlosy, Anouska. 2004. "Procession and Water Splashing: Expressions of Locality and Nationality during Dai New Year in Xishuangbanna." *Journal of the Royal Anthropological Institute* 10 (2): 351–73. http://dx.doi.org/10.1111/j.1467-9655.2004.00193.x.

Page, Janet. 1999. "Music and the Royal Procession in Maria Theresia's Vienna." *Early Music* 27 (1): 96–118. http://dx.doi.org/10.1093/em/27.1.96.

Pepplinkhuizen, Coen. 1991. "Religion: Visions of Duality and Balance." In *East of Bali: From Lombok to Timor*, ed. Kal Muller, 36–42. Berkeley-Singapore: Periplus Editions.

Peterson, William. 2007. "Holy Week in the 'Heart of the Philippines': Spirituality, Theatre, and Community in Marinduque's Moriones Festival." *Asian Theatre Journal* 24 (2): 309–37. http://dx.doi.org/10.1353/atj.2007.0039.

Roos, Wilhem. 1979. "The Musical Instrument Collection at Meran." *Galpin Society Journal* 32:10–23. http://dx.doi.org/10.2307/841533.

Seales, Chad. 2008. "Parades and Processions: Protestant and Catholic Ritual Performances in a Nuevo New South Town." *Numen* 55 (1): 44–67. http://dx.doi.org/10.1163/156852708X271297.

Weintraub, Andrew. 2010. *Dangdut Stories: A Social and Music History of Indonesia's Most Popular Music*. New York: Oxford University Press. http://dx.doi.org/10.1093/acprof:oso/9780195395662.001.0001.

8

The Anthropology of Festivals
Changes in Theory and Practice

Laurent Sébastien Fournier

IN THIS CHAPTER I WOULD LIKE TO PRESENT some theoretical aspects of the problems I face when studying the ritualesque and the carnivalesque in social anthropology. To this end, I will build on Jack Santino's (2011) analysis of the notions of ritualesque and carnivalesque, adapting these ideas to the French calendrical festivals I've been investigating for about ten years. I will show how folklorists in the past generally looked at these festivals as universal patterns connected with the agrarian cosmology, whereas social anthropologists today are less universalist, insisting on the importance of the audiences, the political meanings, and/or the economy of the festivals. This shift in anthropological theories dramatically changes perceptions within academia, especially at a time when the UNESCO 2003 Convention for the Safeguarding of Intangible Cultural Heritage begins to consider ritualesque and carnivalesque practices as valuable cultural features. Fieldwork helps to identify the changes that have occurred in the anthropological study of festivals both in theory and in practice.

First, I will focus on festivals and the carnivalesque. Second, I will insist on the importance of ritual and the ritualesque. Last, I will present some final thoughts concerning changes in the academic perception of both the ritualesque and the carnivalesque. In my analysis I will mainly use a series of French theoretical references in order to contribute to a more general understanding of contemporary public performances.

FESTIVALS AND THE CARNIVALESQUE
Festivals, Excess, and the Carnival Model

According to many classical theoretical works within the field of social sciences, festivals are quite far from what is usually implied by the word *culture*. The two notions can even easily be considered as antithetic, especially if "culture" remains synonymous with the fine arts. Very early in the history of the social sciences, festivals were described by sociologists as an inversion of everyday life (Durkheim 1991) and by psychologists as a moment for transgression when cultural standards get loose (Freud 1976). Moreover, festivals have often been considered through the archetypes of carnival and reversal. In this respect they oppose everyday life and dominant cultural standards; they feature a dangerous place from which the usual laws of economy are rejected and banished.

According to these theories, festivals are means of "catharsis" (Caillois 1988). They are often compared to stages of periodic chaos that display mythical times and oppose everyday life in the same way as nature opposes culture. Festivals mark a cyclical renewal of the cosmos during which ancestors are embodied in masks, time is stopped, ghosts appear, initiation or fertility rituals are performed. Thus festivals are interpreted as a renewing excess, a moment when the usual moral rules grow lax and when social life follows the logic of inversion. Excess and periodic corruption have in this respect a strong social function: they are symbolically used to heal the weakening of the social order. Festivals, then, are conceived as paroxysms in the social life: both excessive and purgative, they're a place for dangers and risks, a moment when a community deliberately calls for chaos and wilderness to become stronger.

Recent research in social science in France still neatly opposes festivals and culture. Very often it focuses on the more excessive aspects of festivals. Among French historians and anthropologists, leading scholars in festival studies have insisted on the relations between masks and wilderness (Fabre 1992), on festivals' subversive or political meanings (Le Roy Ladurie 1979), on the noise they make, on the physical insensitivity of the people participating in them, on the waste, on the excitement, and on the suppression of taboos (Fribourg 1985). Other researchers have described the violence in festivals and have distinguished different types of dangers connected with them (Bercé 1994).

All these theories connect festivals with the sacred or with utopia. For Girard (1972) festivals are synonymous with sacrifice, and for Bataille (1967) they exemplify consumption. As places for excess and disorder, festivals figure the inverse of the rational Cartesian modern society. As festivals are opposed both to the rationality of culture and to the rationality of economy, they are often separated from leisure or tourist studies, which are more connected with employment issues and better known by economists.

Festivals, Culture, and the Heritage Model

Despite this strong theoretical difference between festivals and culture in social sciences, the promoters of contemporary local festivals paradoxically often enhance festivals as genuine cultural and economic resources. Obviously, such a perspective on festivals is not new: it was legitimized first by folklorists and romantic avant-gardes in France and elsewhere in Europe as early as the nineteenth century. In Provence, as in other places, traditional festivals began to be revitalized at the beginning of the nineteenth century, when the new railways opened the area to the global world (Vovelle 1976). At the same time, as has been clearly shown for Greece (Herzfeld 1986), Romania (Karnoouh 1990), Germany (Chiva and Jeggle 1987), and France (Thiesse 1997), nationalist and regionalist movements focused on costumes and local dialects and enhanced festivals as new cultural expressions. Festivals, from then on, had to be codified and quiet in order to obey the laws of the new modern nation-states. At the same time as folklore and popular traditions became areas of study, festivals became more and more standardized. At the same time as the different regions in Europe were increasingly connected with one another and the outside world, festivals were ideologically perceived as a cultural element. During the eighteenth and nineteenth centuries, then, festivals were at once perceived as places where collective cultural identities could be valorized, and frowned upon as times when individual freedom could lead to the most excessive behaviors and disorders.

Unlike social scientists, folklorists argued that festivals were a privileged place where traditional popular cultures could develop. As periodic collective celebrations, they revealed local beliefs and values and played a part in political and cultural legitimization processes. As such, they were acknowledged as cultural resources that needed protection. But folklore is not the only factor that has strengthened the connections between festivals and culture. After World War II, festivals became a part of the cultural industries in modern global societies, which were according increasing importance to leisure (Dumazedier 1962). From then on festivals addressed consumers, joined the entertainment sector, and had to bring in money. In contemporary festivals, merchants or showmen become richer, nonprofit organizations are subsidized for the spectacles they organize, town councils collect taxes. As the financial aspects are now very important in festivals, festivals have little by little become a new means for local development and tourism. They are transformed into holidays or spectacles and play a part in cultural and economic development strategies.

In small communities that fear to lose their local cultural identities, the image of festivals as sites of excess is progressively withdrawn. As festivals become new heritage features, they find a place in cultural institutions such as museums, which see festivals as genuine cultural phenomena. Masks, emblems, disguises, or material culture in festivals are acknowledged as cultural goods. With the UNESCO concept of "intangible heritage," festivals get closer to cultural industries: they both represent a valuable cultural heritage and have important economic implications.

At a regional scale, in Provence, for instance, as in other famous touristic places in the Mediterranean, festivals get closer and closer to cultural heritage (Fournier 2005). On a local scale, festivals have become evident cultural symptoms that have led to a significant increase of the number of festivals in each village for about thirty years. Today, as Provence has become extremely attractive to tourists, many books mention the "typical" or "authentic" elements in local festivals (Bec 1994). Moreover, many tourist guides devote chapters to festivals. Some of the festivals are hidden while others are pushed forward. The criteria used to select which ones to highlight answer to the media's requirements and are supposed to be connected with the tourists' tastes: success, exoticism, originality, authenticity, references to the classical excessive image of festivals in general, and so on. Festivals therefore become useful opportunities to show off local roots and cultural identity.

Thus, festivals are built up as new cultural resources in Mediterranean France. Even the excessive part of the festivals, often mentioned in nineteenth-century descriptions, is now enhanced as a synonym for exoticism. In Provence, this showcasing of festivals goes with the accentuating of the stereotypical Provençal person, who is supposed to love joking and celebrating. Festivals are thus conceived as an organic part of the Provençal culture; they become a local resource, a cultural symbol, and a means to fix the Provençal identity and to propose it to tourists.

Fieldwork in Provençal Festivals: Investigating a Paradox

Once the theoretical shift between the carnival model and the heritage model in the analysis of festivals has been examined, it is especially important to see what happens at a local scale when considering empirical data. How to grasp the shift between excess and cultural heritage in practice? Anthropological analyses devoted to the identity of Provence in general or to the local Provençal festivals in particular (Fournier 2005) have shown that the display of Provençal festivals as cultural features was especially important in this regard. Ethnographical fieldwork enables us to be more precise in order to understand the very nature of this heritage-making process.

To learn more about the paradoxical building up of regional festivals as cultural heritage, I have set up a general comparative survey of about 200 contemporary local festivals in about thirty villages in the area of Arles, in the Bouches-du-Rhône district, and I have carried out intensive fieldwork in two different villages as well (Fournier 2005). The methods I used were the accepted ones in the field of social anthropology, including an extensive comparative study of the festivals' origins, dates, length, sites, organizations involved, specific elements and structures, and audiences. A collection of discourses thickened the analysis of the "cultural heritage" value of the different festivals. I have conducted more than eighty interviews since 1998 and compared them with the written archives of two specialized local journals advertising the different festivals in the area. Every year since 1998 I have witnessed the different festivals as a "participant observer," especially in the two little villages of Mollégès and Mouriès, where my most intensive fieldwork was done, but also in other places in the same region.

The combination of the different methods clearly shows how new festivals today are superimposed on old ones, changing the whole regional cultural landscape and widely opening it to issues of economic development. In fact, the changes have been so strong that in the most touristic areas in the region some villages welcome several new annual festivals. In the Alpilles hills near Avignon, for instance, there are three to five times more local festivals today than thirty years ago, which induces a diversification in the styles of the celebrations

Repeated Festivals versus Invented Festivals

Fieldwork shows that festivals in Mediterranean France form a very complex field and obey both cultural and economic logics. This is why the new festivals, unlike the old ones in which the programs were ritually repeated from one edition to another, add new elements to their programs each year. Festivals therefore enable us to observe how a local culture is created by adding new elements to older ones, in a way that strongly determines the local development processes.

New festivals tend to combine more varied elements than the old ones, in order to enable anybody to participate. Whereas the old festivals were centered on a corporation, a congregation, or a parish, and thus were addressing a restricted social group, the new festivals choose explicit themes—local "terroir" products, traditional know-how, farm animals, and so on—that can address outsiders as well as locals. Unlike the old festivals, in which organizers used to build up a single ritual around the most homogeneous program possible, the new festivals favor multilevel programs in which different activities take place at the same time in different places to allow a more diversified audience to participate. This change in the structure of the programs is connected with the changes in the audience's tastes. Thanks to this new structure, people can take part in the festivals whatever their social or cultural origins. According to their tastes, the audience members can choose, at any time, the program that fits best.

Regarding their structures and their programs, festivals in touristic places provide more freedom for individuals than the old ones, in which everybody had to follow specific customary behaviors in order to respect the collective standards. Because they want to attract people from outside the village, the new festivals use common elements that are found in almost every festival and are often inspired by modern mass culture. Thus they answer to new requirements in order to suit a new society based on leisure and the tourism economy. According to the Dutch anthropologist Boissevain (1992), this revitalization of local festivals follows different patterns: invention, innovation, renewal, revivification, reanimation, restoration, resurrection, retraditionalization, folklorization, and the like.

Local festivals are eventually built up to answer new social needs. They quit the field of symbolism and customary rituals to enter the field of cultural economy. They are more and more imaginative in order to compete with other new festivals created in the same areas. They use the most up-to-date media and therefore play a new part in local development and the economy of leisure.

RITUALS AND THE RITUALESQUE

My second point is to address the evolution of the concept of *rite de passage*, developed by the famous French folklorist Arnold Van Gennep more than a century ago. According to Jack Santino: "Rites of passage . . . focus primarily on the life-cycle transitions and only secondarily on seasonal festivals and other community-wide celebrations" (2011, 64). However, I would like to suggest that this concept is flexible enough to be adapted to very different sort of rituals. Moreover, I will assess its usefulness for folkloric and anthropological theories on the one hand and for the ethnography of ritual practices on the other.

Why "Rites de Passage"?

Arnold Van Gennep pioneered the rite de passage concept (1981). An important congress held in Grenoble, France, in October 2008 explored Van Gennep's legacy and the importance of his findings for contemporary social sciences. Interestingly, this congress was entitled "From Homeric Greece to Our 21st Century." Some of the papers were devoted to the study of marginal spaces in ancient Greece; others focused on marginal situations in fairy tales. Some social anthropologists presented papers on the margins in which contemporary refugees live. Festivals and spectacles—from traditional public ceremonies to contemporary theater or cinema—were also examined through the rite de passage lens. One of the final sections in the congress focused on age groups and initiations from the cradle to the grave. Interestingly, this congress was subtitled "Hommage à Arnold Van Gennep et Pierre Vidal-Naquet," the latter a famous French historian of ancient Greece well known for his publications on Greek mythology. Such a program gives an idea of the way Van Gennep is understood today. At the same time, it indicates how broad the topic of rites de passage is: it runs through history from antiquity to modern times and concerns various academic disciplines from sociology to literature and from folkloristics to anthropology.

In this context, it is important, first of all, to look at the different ways in which the concept of rite de passage has been used during the twentieth century. To begin with I will remind the reader of Van Gennep's theory itself, his presentation of rite de passage as a functional scheme to describe rituals in three stages corresponding to the phases of separation (preliminal), transition (liminal), and incorporation (postliminal). According to this scheme, many rituals may be classified as rites de passage. Accordingly, Van Gennep's book is devoted to providing a description of these rituals, dividing them into the eight following classes: territorial passages, rituals concerning the individual and the group, pregnancy and confinement, birth and childhood, initiation, marriage, funerals, and "other rituals." In his later works, especially in the huge *Manuel de folklore français contemporain* (1998), which he considered as his best achievement, Van Gennep again used these categories. However, as he wasn't acknowledged for his work and as he didn't earn any stable academic position, his books suffered from an uneven reception among scholars before World War II.

It was only after the 1960s that the rite de passage concept became a standard in cultural analysis. In 1966 Victor W. Turner worked out his famous distinction between "structure" and "communitas" and focused on liminal behaviors in different contexts (Turner 1966). Turner assumed that culture is strongly embedded in liminal or marginal situations. His work played a great part in reviving the idea of rite de passage at an international and at a multidisciplinary level. A few years later, Van Gennep was rediscovered in France thanks to Nicole Belmont (1974), who published a book on the history of folklore in which she emphasized the role of the great folklorist.

Since then, rites de passage have become key in folklore and cultural studies. Rather than pointing out all the different existing theories, I will simply concentrate on three different ways of using the rite de passage perspective in French anthropology today. This will enable me to show what kind of debates are going on around the rite de passage concept and how these debates can be useful to ritual studies in general. The anthropologist Claude Rivière developed the notion of "profane rituals" in order to understand the rituals of our own time (1995). He uses this expression for political parades, rave parties or concerts, hazing initiations in high schools, neosatanism in hard-rock music, or extreme sports like parachuting. All these examples enable him to show how the rite de passage pattern can be adapted to postmodernity.

In a similar way, French sociologist and psychologist David Le Breton began in the 1990s to speak of "individual rites de passage" (Le Breton 2007). Studying suicidal tendencies among teenagers today, he assumes that the quest for danger is something necessary to fully becoming an adult. His studies focus on alcohol and drug abuse as well as tattooing and high-speed driving, interpreting such behavior as initiatory transgressions that enable the participants to reach a higher status. "Under our very eyes," he writes, "new 'rites de passage' appear, specific to contemporary occidental societies" (239, translation by the author from French). These new rites are no longer based on custom, communities, and peer solidarities but on the individual, and they are connected with the pain of not finding any significance in modern life. They are therefore a means of replacing all the old social rituals that have been abandoned in modern times. Such an analysis is interesting because it encourages the study of rituals and rites de passage in the frame of modernity, which inevitably leads to a focus on the social changes in old rituals or on the appearance of new ones.

Besides these theoretical attempts to change the very notion of rites de passage, other scholars have tried to apply it to new topics: for instance, the French Society for the Sociology of Religion has recently focused on the idea of "ritual modernity" (Dianteill, Hervieu-Léger, and Saint-Martin 2004). This has led to research into public mourning for politicians in modern democracies, religious rituals among Muslim migrants in Europe, new funeral rituals, or rituals connected with diseases such as AIDS. Such examples show that the rite de passage concept is still an active one, both in a theoretical perspective and for new case studies.

Using the Notion of Rites de Passage Tomorrow: How Useful Is It?

These examples show that the rite de passage concept is a tool versatile enough to be of use in comparative studies at a global level and on a descriptive as well as a structural basis. In a way, the rite de passage idea enables us to dissect any folkloric fact or social event into distinct sequences and therefore to distinguish the significant cycles that frame local cultures. In this context, it keeps a theoretical ambition and at the same time appears as a useful multidimensional tool for the descriptive and structural analysis of cultural events. The passages are at once physical (or territorial, i.e., the places the ritual passes through), individual (or psychological, i.e., the important moments in the lives of people performing the ritual), collective (or social, i.e., moments when social and political standards are asserted), and symbolical (when the rites exemplify mental representations, e.g., are connected with the passage of time or the relationship between nature and culture).

In spite of its theoretical complexity, however, it is not easy to say if the rite de passage concept can be adapted to describe modern rituals in a changing world. There are some problems with applying the rite de passage notion to contemporary rituals, but it nevertheless remains potentially interesting, and as I will argue, it can be successfully adapted to suit modern and postmodern rituals.

The first problem with applying the rite de passage in today's world is that the notions of liminality, latency, and margins have considerably evolved, to the extent that some central places have become liminal and vice versa. In the last century, moreover, sociologists have observed a shift from a society in which local communities were central to a society centered on the individual. Such changes have led to confusion in the definition of what is marginal and what is central. Wilderness, for instance, which once inspired terror in the majority of people, has now been transformed into a dream place for adventurers. In a situation where the values connected with centrality and marginality have definitely shifted, it is difficult to spot where and when the different ritual sequences begin and end.

In such a context, the "prestructuralist" value of the rite de passage pattern becomes rather problematic. According to postmodern theories, our world's best characterization would be "fluidity" (Bauman 2000). Other specialists of contemporary social changes have emphasized the role of "nonplaces" in postmodernity: places such as airports, supermarkets, and the like would be liminal places where no structured ritual is possible (Augé

1992). Regarding such theories, the rite de passage pattern would be too rigid to describe individual freedom and tastes in our contemporary world.

Likewise, one can ask if the rite de passage notion is still relevant in a secularized society. Arnold Van Gennep himself insisted on the fact that the rite de passage represented above all the moment when the sacred and the profane could communicate. In traditional societies where individuals are completely governed by the sacred, life itself could be understood as the major rite de passage, a wavering moment between the underworld and the afterworld. But what if life is considered as profane? If the sacred no longer exists, the rite de passage notion may easily become void.

These remarks show how difficult it can be to use a concept conceived a hundred years ago in the context of contemporary social sciences. However, this doesn't mean that the idea itself must be withdrawn from academic researches. On the contrary, I would advocate the use of the concept in at least two cases: first, when dealing with any historical material that presents a clear relationship with the sacred; second, when studying the transformations of rituality and/or the sacred in the present. The main problem that arises with the rite de passage concept is that it needs to be connected with empirical data, not to be used in general. In this respect, the rite de passage concept remains a tool for field ethnographers rather than for theoretical anthropologists, a tool for the study of practices more than a tool for theoreticians.

CHANGES IN THE ACADEMIC PERCEPTION OF THE RITUALESQUE AND THE CARNIVALESQUE

In the first section I have shown how community festivals have progressively been disconnected from the carnival model and connected with culture and with the economy. This shift has changed the ways we see the festivals, both in theory and in practice. In theory, for instance, the festivals are less and less considered as universal patterns connected with the agrarian cosmology or with psychology. In turn, they are more and more connected with political meanings and/or with the economy. In practice they are less and less ritually repeated and more and more constructed, marketed, and built up to attract tourists and an outside audience.

In the second section I have focused on the rite de passage concept and on the ways it has been adapted in contemporary societies. Here it is obvious that the extension of the concept to "profane rituals" possibly leads to a massive use of the ritualesque. Rituals escape the field of religious studies and are adapted to various concerns, including health and security problems.

In both cases, notions such as the carnivalesque (for festivals) and the ritualesque (for rituals) appear as powerful analytic tools to understand the ways the traditional sense of the "sacred" has been transferred to "profane" aspects of everyday life. Such an extension of the notions of carnival and ritual might, however, be criticized, if one considers that the extension can lead to confusion. In order not to use these notions as metaphors only, it is important to keep in mind that they should mainly be used as "descriptive" terms (Santino 2011, 62).

On a practical level, likewise, the frame of globalization deeply changes the stakes of local festivals and rituals, which increasingly use the same elements from one place to another. There is a paradox here: on the one hand, festival organizers compete in order to attract audiences and therefore diversify the local rituals, and on the other hand, the media give a limited number of models that are adapted everywhere as transposable "festive kits." This is true for different community festivals as well as for carnivals. As Dorothy Noyes (2016) has shown in Berlin, most contemporary European carnivals adapt the Brazilian model because it answers the requirement of the participants and the media imaginary. But at the same time, some other carnivals try to maintain their cultural specificity.

The main problem for anthropologists, then, is to keep an eye both on the unification of different rituals and on the inventions and diversification of their programs. Case studies are needed in this field because each region or each town uses different elements within the stock of existent elements. In the different festivals and rituals, elements of various origins can agglutinate or be hybridized. Notions such as the "carnivalesque" or the "ritualesque" are interesting because they help to escape positivism: they clearly show that in our postmodern world nothing is a carnival or a ritual by itself. On the contrary, a subjective feeling of carnivalesque or ritualesque can appear outside the world of festivals, yet not all the traditional festivals keep their carnivalesque or ritualesque features.

In such a context, the different features may be pointed out in a structuralist way. In my opinion the carnivalesque and the ritualesque can be understood as original languages with their own sentences, words, and even grammar. I would then plead for a comprehensive study of the carnivalesque and the ritualesque through the different elements they encompass. In this respect, the field of the carnivalesque and the ritualesque has first to take into account elements such as dances, games, spectacles, and other performative behaviors. But it also needs to be connected with specific times and places: which holidays, which celebrations, which occasions of public display are the more open to the ritualesque and the carnivalesque? A mapping is possible here with the help of ethnographical fieldwork. Again following Jack Santino's suggestions concerning the carnivalesque, I would try "not to restrict this term to a single category of events but to suggest it as a quality, which might be present in a great many commemorations, celebrations and gatherings, that has remained unacknowledged" (2011, 71).

All the changes in the theory and the practice of festivals are especially relevant in light of the UNESCO 2003 Convention for the Safeguarding of Intangible Cultural Heritage and its consideration of traditional festive events, rituals, and carnivals as valuable cultural features. In France, carnival parades were acknowledged by UNESCO in 2005 as such intangible cultural heritage. Over ten years later, fieldwork shows an influence of the new label on the ways the carnival parades are performed. This is a fantastic opportunity for the humanities and social sciences because the institutional changes that have occurred enable reflection at several levels, concerning as they do the practices themselves, the local cultural policies and the tourism industry, and the influence of institutions and experts on the practices.

REFERENCES

Augé, Marc. 1992. *Non-lieux: Introduction à une anthropologie de la surmodernité*. Paris: Seuil.
Bataille, Georges. (Original work published 1949) 1967. *La part maudite*. Paris: Editions de Minuit.
Bauman, Zygmunt. 2000. *Liquid Modernity*. Cambridge: Polity.
Bec, Serge. 1994. *Fêtes de Provence*. Aix-en-Provence: Edisud.
Belmont, Nicole. 1974. *Arnold Van Gennep: Créateur de l'ethnographie française*. Paris: Payot.
Bercé, Yves-Marie. (Original work published 1976) 1994. *Fête et révolte*. Paris: Hachette.
Boissevain, Jeremy, ed. 1992. *Revitalizing European Rituals*. London: Routledge.
Caillois, Roger. (Original work published 1939) 1988. *L'homme et le sacré*. Paris: Gallimard.
Chiva, Isaac, and Utz Jeggle, eds. 1987. *Ethnologies en miroir*. Paris: Maison des Sciences de l'Homme. http://dx.doi.org/10.4000/books.editionsmsh.2332.
Dianteill, Erwann, Danièle Hervieu-Léger, and Isabelle Saint-Martin, eds. 2004. *La modernité rituelle: Rites politiques et religieux de sociétés modernes*. Paris: L'Harmattan.
Dumazedier, Joffre. 1962. *Vers une civilisation du loisir*. Paris: Seuil.
Durkheim, Emile. (Original work published 1912) 1991. *Les formes élémentaires de la vie religieuse*. Paris: Le Livre de Poche.
Fabre, Daniel. 1992. *Carnaval; ou, La fête à l'envers*. Paris: Découvertes Gallimard.
Fournier, Laurent Sébastien. 2005. *La fête en héritage: Enjeux patrimoniaux de la sociabilité provençale*. Aix-en-Provence: Publications de l'Université de Provence. http://dx.doi.org/10.4000/books.pup.1573.
Freud, Sigmund. (Original work published 1913) 1976. *Totem et tabou*. Paris: Petite Bibliothèque Payot.
Fribourg, Jeannine. 1985. "La fête patronale en Espagne: Substitut de carnaval?" In *Le carnaval, la fête et la communication*, 41–53. Nice: Ed. Serres.
Girard, René. 1972. *La violence et le sacré*. Paris: Grasset.
Herzfeld, Mickael. 1986. *Ours Once More: Folklore, Ideology and the Making of Modern Greece*. New York: Pella.

Karnoouh, Claude. 1990. *L'invention du peuple: Chroniques de Roumanie*. Paris: Arcantère.
Le Breton, David. 2007. "Conduites à risque des jeunes générations." In *Peurs et risques au cœur de la fête*, ed. Jocelyne Bonnet-Carbonell and Laurent Sébastien Fournier, 227–44. Paris: L'Harmattan.
Le Roy Ladurie, Emmanuel. 1979. *Le carnaval de Romans*. Paris: Gallimard.
Noyes, Dorothy. 2016. "Cultural Warming? Brazil in Berlin." In *Humble Theory: Folklore's Grasp on Social Life*, 276–96. Bloomington: Indiana University Press.
Rivière, Claude. 1995. *Les rites profanes*. Paris: PUF.
Santino, Jack. 2011. "The Carnivalesque and the Ritualesque." *Journal of American Folklore* 124 (491): 61–73. http://dx.doi.org/10.5406/jamerfolk.124.491.0061.
Thiesse, Anne-Marie. 1997. *Ils apprenaient la France*. Paris: Maison des Sciences de l'Homme. http://dx.doi.org/10.4000/books.editionsmsh.2475.
Turner, Victor W. 1966. *The Ritual Process. Structure and Anti-structure*. Chicago: Aldine.
Van Gennep, Arnold. (Original work published 1909) 1981. *Les rites de passage*. Paris: Picard.
Van Gennep, Arnold. (Original work published 1938–1958) 1998. *Manuel de folklore français contemporain*. 4 vols. Paris: Robert Lafont.
Vovelle, Michel. 1976. *Les métamorphoses de la fête en Provence de 1750 à 1820*. Poitiers: Aubier-Flammarion.

9

The Politics of Cultural Promotion
The Umthetho Festival of Malawi's Northern Ngoni

Lisa Gilman

> *We, sons and daughters of M'mbelwa in Mzimba District, in the Republic of Malawi, having recognized the importance of our heritage in the cultures of our forefathers, being concerned about our lost traditions, our forgotten language and our weakening sense of unity, and seeking to revive and preserve the said cultural heritage and promote the general welfare and development of our district, do hereby and on this day of . . . in the year . . . form an Organization called the Mzimba Heritage Association (MZIHA).*
>
> —Preamble to the Constitution of the Registered Trustees of
> the Mzimba Heritage Association, December 11, 2002

THE MZIMBA HERITAGE ASSOCIATION (MZIHA) was formed in 2002 by people from the Mzimba District of Malawi to promote and preserve the languages and cultural practices of residents of the district. Soon after its inception, it began organizing an annual cultural festival called Umthetho at Mt. Hora in Mzimba District to showcase and honor local culture, especially dance, music, and material culture. The formation of this association and its festival are welcome developments in a country that has a long history of limited attention and resources devoted to cultural promotion. The festival provides important opportunities for cultural performances, significant for keeping them vital, and it honors local cultural identities in a context where postcolonial political realities and globalization have resulted in widespread undervaluing of indigenous cultural practices. The festival is also intertwined with local and national political machinations that inevitably contribute to ethnic tensions locally and political power plays at the national level.

Beverly Stoeltje (1993) provides a productive model for analyzing the intertwining of power within rituals and festivals. In addition to examining what happens in a festival itself, she rightly contends that it is necessary to consider other dimensions associated with the festival where power manifests, namely, the evolution of the form, the organization of its production, and the discourses that surrounds it. Attending to these dimensions is especially useful for analyzing the relatively recent emergence of the Umthetho Festival and its relationship to a complex web of cultural and national politics. Examining the political dimensions in the nascent years of the festival highlights relationships between politics and festivals but also sheds light on ways in which labels of culture as innocent celebrations can mask potentially dangerous political dynamics. This essay contributes to the scholarship on relationships between festival and institutions of power in its argument that inasmuch as the liminoid dimensions of festival can provide opportunities for participants to contest the status quo, they can just as much be used by the status quo to reinforce power hierarchies; or, as in the case of the Umthetho, festivals can be used by organizers to establish or reestablish new hierarchies intended to contribute to the exertion of social and political power outside of the festival arena.

CONTEXT: EFFORTS AT CULTURAL PROMOTION

As in many African countries, tensions exist in contemporary Malawi over cultural identity. Ongoing interactions and intermarriage between people from different ethnic groupings, the widespread adoption of Christianity and to a lesser extent Islam, the long-term consequences of the history of British colonization, the politicization of cultural identity, the omnipresence of foreign cultural practices, and economic and cultural globalization result in cultural complexities. Though all cultural practices in contemporary Malawi are inherently dynamic and hybrid, many Malawians discursively reify a dichotomy of African versus European/Western, local versus foreign, and traditional versus modern. Within this perceived duality, a spectrum of perspectives exist: at one extreme are those eschewing "traditional indigenous" culture because it is pejoratively deemed backward and *zakhale* (of the past) in favor of *zatsopano*, translated literally from the Chichewa language as "of now" or "new." This position posits that adoption of Western cultural practices or cosmopolitan hybrids are the way of the present that will lead to a more prosperous and healthy future at individual, community, and national levels. On the other end of this spectrum are those who express concern that too many Malawians are undervaluing and discarding local cultural practices, which they feel are critical for cultural identity and social well-being. This position perceives social problems that exist as a result of this rejection and fears the short- and long-term repercussions of cultural loss.

These competing discourses comprise the backdrop for current efforts to safeguard, preserve, and promote indigenous cultural practices in contemporary Malawi. The government has a Department of Culture whose mission is to promote local culture and that oversees such things as the National Dance Troupe, the country's museums, and the orchestration of occasional festivals. The Department of Culture has always been severely underfunded, and its activities have been limited. The first government after Malawi's independence from British colonial rule was led by Dr. Hastings Kamuzu Banda, who ruled the single-party authoritarian regime from 1964 to 1994. Banda's government co-opted Malawi's cultural institutions and many of the cultural practices of Malawians across the country to further its own authoritarian goals (Chirwa 1998; Gilman 2004, 2009a; Lwanda 1993; Mkamanga 2000). The few institutions dedicated to promoting culture were used largely to further political interests rather than to productively attend to the cultural sector. This inattention to culture created a legacy that continued through the transition to a multiparty system of government that took place in 1994 and into the time of writing. Up until the 2000s, few cultural initiatives existed in the country.

A shift started to happen in the early 2000s as efforts to promote indigenous cultural practices and identities began to emerge, inspired by a combination of local concerns about cultural degradation, power plays by the political elite, and Malawi's ratification of the 2003 UNESCO Convention for the Safeguarding of Intangible Cultural Heritage (ICH), which mandated that the government increase strategies for cultural preservation. Though those working in the cultural sector whom I have interviewed deemed these initiatives to be relatively few, and most at the grassroots level were not aware of them, nor did they perceive much benefit, these efforts were a substantial increase from what was happening prior to the ratification of the convention (Gilman 2015). The 2000s also saw the emergence of ethnic heritage associations for many of the country's ethnic groups. The motivations and contexts in which these organizations were formed were different for each. Though the mission that was explicitly articulated in each of their constitutions was to celebrate cultural identity and preserve and promote the cultural activities and languages of the ethnic group, each has also been variously intertwined with local and national politics.

THE MZIMBA NGONI: A BRIEF HISTORY

Malawi, a small country of 46,000 square miles (slightly smaller than the U.S. state of Pennsylvania), is home to around twenty ethnic groups, some much more numerous than others. The more numerically dominant ethnic groups—Chewa, Lhomwe, Ngonde, Ngoni, Nyanja, Sena, Tonga, Tumbuka, and Yao—are the ones most often listed in descriptions of the country. Numerous others exist that are less numerically dominant, especially in the northern districts of Karonga and Chitipa. Many of the ethnic groups in Malawi exist across the national boundaries with neighboring Mozambique, Zambia, and Tanzania.

The northern Ngoni, the group at the center of the Umthetho Festival, is an especially complicated example for considering ethnic identity in the region. As with most African countries, colonial boundaries for the former British colony Nyasaland, renamed Malawi after independence, were arbitrarily set by colonial representatives in Europe at the Berlin Conference (1884–1885); these boundaries did not take into account the existing cultural and political structures in the region. The political boundaries imposed arbitrary fissures that divided existing cultural groups politically at the same time that they brought together diverse ethnic groups into a single political entity. Each colony comprised multiple ethnic groups, each with its own individual historical trajectory and relationships with other nearby groups. Many single ethnic or political entities were divided, part being located in one colony and other parts in neighboring ones. This complete lack of respect for the existing political and cultural structures by the colonial administrators continues to plague the contemporary politics and cultures in formerly colonized states on the African continent, which for the most part continue to honor the national boundaries set during the colonial era (Young 1994).

The Ngoni in Mzimba District are descendants of the Ngoni who left the coastal regions of what is now South Africa in the nineteenth century, fleeing the Zulu chief Shaka Zulu after having been defeated by his army. To oversimplify a complicated history, after battling and losing to Shaka, at least one female and a number of male leaders fled what is now South Africa with their armies and followers. As they migrated, they raided, warred, conquered, captured people as slaves, took wives, had babies, and eventually settled in different parts of southern and eastern Africa (Phiri 1982). The outcome is that there are settlements of people in the countries of Malawi, Mozambique, Zambia, Tanzania, and others in the region who call themselves Ngoni or another closely related name (e.g., Nguni) and who trace their ancestry to a particular leader within the broader Ngoni identification. Though each of these groups identify as Ngoni, different settlements bear allegiance to a difference leadership lineage. The paramount chief (*inkosi makosi*) of each of these groups is for the most part a direct descendent of the original leader who settled the group in a particular geographic location.

In Malawi, there are two main groups of Ngoni: the Mzimba Ngoni in the northern region, the topic of this essay, whose allegiance is to Paramount Chief Inkosi ya Makosi M'mbelwa, a descendent of the Nguni Zwangendaba, one of the leaders who fled Shaka, and the Maseko Ngoni in the central region whose allegiance is to Paramount Chief Inkosi ya Makosi Gomani, a descendant of another leader, Ngwana Maseko (Phiri 1982). To complicate things further, Ngoni people residing in the Mchinji District of Malawi along the border with Zambia bear their allegiance to Inkosi ya Makosi Mpezeni, another descendent of Zwangendaba, who lives across the border in eastern Zambia. This group of Ngoni exemplifies the arbitrary division by the colonialists: though these Ngoni are part of the group that bears allegiance to Mpezeni, the border between Malawi and Zambia cuts through their territory. The Ngoni in Malawi are therefore not unified politically, but they do constitute an ethnic group with shared cultural identifiers and practices and interrelated histories; however, the different groups of Ngoni in Malawi are distinct and have limited interaction with one another and have not historically been political allies.[1]

THE MZIMBA HERITAGE ASSOCIATION

The Mzimba Heritage Association was one of the first ethnic associations formed in the country and was officially registered with the government on December 11, 2002. The Mzimba District is located in the northern region of Malawi and is the home district of the northern Ngoni under Paramount Chief M'mbelwa. (Note that M'mbelwa is an honorific title that anyone who ascends to the position of paramount chief receives.) According to Aupson Thole, one of the organization's founders and its general secretary at the time of our interview on February 20, 2013, the association began in 2000 as the Alingoni Association. Its mission was to revive the Ngoni language, which largely died out in the 1930s and is spoken only in a few remote areas in the district. The organization later shifted to the broader designation of Mzimba Heritage Association when it was officially registered with the government in 2002. As the Mzimba Heritage Association, it was intended to represent *all* people in the Mzimba District rather than focus only on those of Ngoni heritage. This is significant because other ethnic groups also reside in the district. Members of the Executive Committee whom I interviewed claimed that the focus of the association was to strengthen the cultural identity of those from Mzimba with a heavy emphasis on a shared Ngoni identity, despite the cultural diversity within the district.

Before the arrival of the Ngoni, Mzimba District was home to the Tumbuka people. When the Ngoni, who by then were multicultural, having integrated and intermarried with people they conquered along the way, settled in what is now Mzimba District under Paramount Chief M'mbelwa, they dominated the existing Tumbuka population. They took over Tumbuka lands and imposed their political power. As they did everywhere they passed, they subsequently intermarried with Tumbuka women and borrowed extensively from the Tumbuka, culturally and linguistically (Phiri 1982). Currently, the district includes people who are direct descendants of the Ngoni warriors; descendants of people they conquered prior to arriving in this location but brought with them; descendants of people who were already in the locale, primarily from the Tumbuka ethnic group; many people who are descendants of some combination of the above; and plenty of people from other ethnic groups in the country who either have lived in the district for generations or moved there more recently for work or other reasons. Intermarriage between people of diverse backgrounds has been common. The heritage of many present-day people in Mzimba District is therefore diverse and culturally hybrid. To complicate things more, many people identify as Ngoni even if they trace their own ancestry to those the Ngoni conquered from other areas or to multiple different ethnic groups. The two most active members of the MZIHA's Executive Committee at the time of my research, Boston Soko and Aupson Thole, identify in this way. They often present themselves as and celebrate their Ngoni identity, though when asked about the specifics of their heritage, they explained that they are descendants of people who had been conquered along the way before the Ngoni settled in what is now Mzimba District. Though many people in the district do identity as Ngoni, many others do not, especially those who identify as Tumbuka.

When the Ngoni warriors moved through the area conquering and taking on wives and eventually settling, the pattern was that they often relied on their non-Ngoni wives to establish homes and raise the children. Much of what Ngoni people do today is therefore based on the cultures of the people they conquered. Thus, the Ngoni language in Mzimba District is spoken only in a few remote locales; Ngoni people in the region by and large speak the language of the Tumbuka people, Chitumbuka. Many of the cultural practices in Ngoni day-to-day life, such as foodways, housing structures, and gardening practices, are rooted in the culture of the Tumbuka people, while other dimensions are more identifiably Ngoni, such as the emphasis on cattle rearing, the strong patriarchal structure and, very relevant to this essay, the dance *ingoma* and its associated costume elements, for example, the beading and animal skin costumes, all of which are strongly associated with the Ngoni across southern Africa and other Zulu-related ethnic groups.

THE INVENTION OF TRADITION: THE UMTHETHO FESTIVAL AND THE NGONIFICATION OF THE DISTRICT

Prior to the emergence of the Mzimba Heritage Association, the people living in the Mzimba District who identified with different ethnic groupings did not bond together under an umbrella identity of Mzimba; rather, people belonged to specific families, villages, areas, ethnic groups, and so on, all of which were contained within the artificial boundaries of the official district. The cultural activities in the district revolved around usually village-based activities, such as installations of chiefs, dance competitions, wedding celebrations, funerals, healing rituals, or political rallies. No district-wide cultural activities existed that were explicitly conceptualized as events to promote culture across the district.

As David Kertzer (1988) explains, organizations are abstractions. In order for people to identify with an organization, they must somehow be able to experience and participate in it in meaningful ways. When a handful of people from Mzimba, many of them social and political elites, in collaboration with the Ngoni Paramount Chief M'mbelwa IV and his advisors, decided to start MZIHA, it was not known to most people in the district, nor did it hold any particular meaning for those who were aware of it. The MZIHA organizers have thus been in the process of developing the association by creating a leadership and membership structure intended to provide opportunities for people in the district to participate and by extension to perform Ngoniness, an intensification of an ethnic identity (cf. Toelken 1991). Though its objectives have been focused on Ngoni cultural promotion, the MZIHA leadership created itself and continues to present itself under the auspices that it is not culturally specific: the association is not for Ngoni people, but rather exists to promote the cultures (note the plural) of the district. However, the structure, as stipulated in the association's constitution, is significant because it puts at the helm the Ngoni paramount chief, who was given the title "Life Patron" of the association. This title echoes that of the former authoritarian President Hastings Kamuzu Banda, who was the "Life President" of the Malawi Congress Party—which, in a single-party state, implicitly implied also the Life President of the country. Under

M'mbelwa are the "Ex-Officio Members," M'mbelwa's subchiefs within the Ngoni chieftaincy structure. Under them are the "Ordinary Members: Malawi citizens originating from Mzimba District living in Malawi or abroad." Note that at the top of the association are Ngoni power leaders; only lower in the hierarchy are those not explicitly associated with the Ngoni leadership structure. Running the day-to-day activities of the association is an Executive Committee, and there is no stipulation about ethnic affiliation for those serving on this committee.

The mission of the association as expressed in the preamble to its constitution quoted at the beginning of the essay is "to revive and preserve the . . . cultural heritage and promote the general welfare and development of our district." As a strategy to "revise and preserve" cultural heritage in a context of cultural diversity where there were no preexisting district-wide activities, the founders of the association started a process of inventing traditions (Hobsbawm and Ranger 1983) for the district, which has included creating an annual secular festival rooted in Ngoni history and customs that they hope will serve as a cultural nexus for the association and for people from and living in the Mzimba District. Unlike some festivals, the Umthetho is not a festival characterized by liminality and abandon in which participants enjoy the license to break social codes and transgress norms. Rather, the Umthetho Festival is intended to be a tidy, well-organized event coordinated and controlled by festival organizers. It occurs in a set location, and activities are choreographed spatially and temporally, giving the organizers a certain amount of control over who participates and the nature of participation, though what happens before and after and on the periphery is outside organizers' control. At the time of writing, the festival is in its nascent stages; organizers are still in the process of building its traditions, popularity, and—importantly—its legitimacy as a culturally significant event for district residents. Despite the history of cultural mixing and to some degree appropriation, the cultural forms emphasized at the Umthetho Festival, especially during framed performances, are those that are explicitly Ngoni. Thus, though it is presented as a festival for the district, the annual Umthetho Festival serves as a mechanism for the Ngonification of the association and by extension the district.

Because the district is diverse and Ngoni heritage is to a great degree hybrid, attempts to establish a strong Ngoni identity necessitates a strategy to codify what it means to be Ngoni. People in the district, whether or not they identify as Ngoni, are well aware of the diversity within their own and others' heritage and are also aware that their cultural and linguistic practices are not strictly Ngoni. Efforts to solidify a sense of what it means to be

Ngoni therefore require a concerted effort to draw from existing cultural practices and add some new ones, either originals or those borrowed from other Ngoni groups, to establish a set of rituals, historical mythologizing, symbolic practices, dress, dance, and so on that will come to be identified as Ngoni and through which people can perform their Ngoniness.

One strategy that leaders of the association have used is to travel to Ngoni settlements within the region to research other Ngoni groups' cultural practices and festivals as Mzimba develops its own. Unlike in Malawi, where ethnic associations and festivals have been rare, the practice is well developed in neighboring Zambia. Since independence, multiple Zambian ethnic groups have orchestrated elaborate annual festivals that foster cultural identity and create local and broader economic possibilities (Guhrs 2008; Cancel 2006; Simbao 2006; Flint 2006). Aware that the Ngoni in neighboring Zambia under Paramount Chief Mpezeni hold an extremely popular and successful annual harvest festival called Nc'wala, Mzimba Association's Executive Committee are using it as a model as they develop the traditions associated with their own festival. The Nc'wala Festival takes place in February and attracts thousands of people across Zambia in addition to Ngoni people in neighboring countries for several days of intensive ritual, ceremony, dancing, and merrymaking.

The Umthetho Festival, first held in 2008, is intended to occur annually in the month of July, though for a variety of reasons, it has been held only a few times thus far. The 2013 festival was canceled due to the death of M'mbelwa IV in February 2013, which precipitated a year of grieving. The 2014 festival was postponed. In 2015, the festival took place on August 8. The festival celebrates the leadership of the Paramount Chief M'mbelwa of the Ngoni people, who is honored and celebrated throughout. Dancers of ingoma, the iconic Ngoni dance form, from across the district come to perform for an audience that has been gradually growing, comprising mostly people from not too far from the festival ground, affluent Ngonis living in other parts of the district or country who can afford to travel, and important regional and national dignitaries invited to be honored guests. Ingoma dance groups from Ngoni settlements in other parts of Malawi and southern Africa are also invited to participate, contributing to the performance of a broader Ngoni identification across chieftaincies and national borders. According to the current association chair, Boston Soko, in 2008 only 300–400 people attended, but at the most recent festival the attendance was in the "thousands."

People at the Umthetho Festival might speak Chitumbuka and serve food that is not associated specifically with the Ngoni; however, the staged

The Politics of Cultural Promotion 173

Figure 9.1. Ngoni dancers in a Nc'wala festival, 2013 (Photograph by author)

events and other activities explicitly framed as "cultural" are mostly those easily recognized by Malawians to be Ngoni. Though there are many dances associated with the Tumbuka people performed in the district, such as *malipenga*, *chiwoda*, and *vimbuza*, none of these are featured at the festival, which showcases only ingoma, a very distinctive dance of the Ngoni, a clear articulation of the mono-cultural focus of the festival. Groups of men and women from different locales within the district form ingoma dance troupes and come to the festival to perform, one group at a time. Male dancers wear animal skins and rags tied around their waists as skirts, often don head rings made out of animal skins, and drape themselves with strings of beads, all connected to the historical Ngoni economic base of cattle herding and hunting, and the strong identity of Ngoni men as warriors. The ingoma dance itself is often said to be a warrior dance and includes rhythmic stomping, war cries, and threatening gestures with knobkerries, wooden clubs. The women play a more supportive role, often standing or sitting to the sides clapping and singing, also wearing costumes of animal skins and beads, though a few women do occasionally dance in the "warrior" stance alongside men.

Jack Santino offers the term *folk assemblage* to describe such bringing together of "visual images that communicate larger, somewhat more complex social and political messages" (2001, 50, see also Santino 1986, 1992). Alessandro Falassi writes that "rites of conspicuous display permit the most important symbolic elements of the community to be seen, touched, adored, or worshipped" (1987, 4). Through their visual displays of symbolically Ngoni dress, movement, musical instruments, and physical placement, organizers and participants bring together an assemblage that contributes to the intensification of the individual symbols and symbolic quality of the festival as a whole, giving all who are present the opportunity to see, wear, and display Ngoniness. These symbolically laden Ngoni communicative elements occur in juxtaposition to others that are clearly not Ngoni, for example, the pervasive Western clothing items or Tumbuka language; yet, these non-Ngoni elements are not highlighted as being salient or symbolic at the event, so they blur into the generic district's sociocultural context and are not what is intended to draw attention at the festival as being significant.

The focus on Ngoni elements is especially explicit in the central position played by the paramount chief of the Mzimba Ngoni. He plays an important ceremonial role, performed in wearing accouterments associated with a Ngoni chief, leading the procession of his Amakosi, or council of chiefs, to his special seating area, receiving guests in the Ngoni ceremonial hut, and occasionally joining the ingoma dancers, symbolically as the leader of all his warriors. The politics of his centrality is complex. He is the traditional leader of all the Ngoni in the district. In addition, in the national government chieftaincy structure, which is rooted in the British indirect-rule style of colonial administration, M'mbelwa is the head chief over both Ngoni and non-Ngoni chiefs under his jurisdiction within the Mzimba District. This system is complicated in that the paramount chief can only be a direct descendent from the royal family and thus is restricted only to Ngonis and specifically to those in the Jere clan. His subchiefs do not have to be Ngoni.

The manifestation of this hierarchy at the festival occurs within ritualized presentations of leadership that are explicitly cloaked within Ngoni symbols and cultural practices: the dress worn, the presence of the paramount chief's advisors wearing very symbolically Ngoni animal skins, the escorting of the inkosi ya makosi by men dancing ingoma, the prominence of Ngoni markers of power made from animal skins, wooden walking sticks, and so on (cf. Simbao 2006). His subchiefs, whether they are or not themselves Ngoni, participate in the performance symbolically in a hierarchy that explicitly places the Ngoni paramount chief as the leader of all. That this ceremony occurs largely within a symbolic cultural framework recognized by all to be Ngoni further reifies the cultural and political prominence of the Ngoni ethnic group in the district. Thus, by implication in this festival where the cultural practices are so Ngoni, those non-Ngoni chiefs under him are nevertheless participating a Ngonified ceremony, which is inherently political in that it positions one ethnic group in the district as more powerful than the others, even if only in the context of a festival billed as cultural celebration.

MZIHA, UMTHETHO, REGIONALISM, AND ETHNIC POLITICS

In recent years, ethnic tension has not been a significant issue in the country, mostly because regional rather than ethnic divisions tend to be the bigger concern in politics. Malawi has been fortunate in that, unlike in some countries in the region, tribalism, tension between people of different ethnic groups, though it exists, has not been the basis for postcolonial political struggles. Instead, though it has changed significantly in the past few years, regionalism has tended to be the basis for political party formation and affiliation. The country is divided into three regions: southern, central, and northern; an additional eastern region has recently been designated. In the years following the country's transition to a multiparty system of government in 1994, the main political parties were affiliated with one of these three regions, and people tended to vote for politicians who came from their region. Relatedly, politicians have tended to favor their home regions, providing more resources and initiating more development in their region at the expense of others, fueling tension between people from different regions (Chirwa 1994, 1998). Though the political arena has become more messy and complex, the prominence of regional identity continues to be significant.

Ethnic identity is tied to regionalism in that certain ethnic groups are located within particular regions and thus have historically been associated with the political parties and figures of their home regions. For the Ngoni, this has meant that Mzimba Ngoni in the northern region have tended to support northern politicians while the Maseko Ngoni in the central region have been more likely to support those from the center. Though this regionalism has dominated politics, ethnic tensions have always simmered in the background, rooted in pre-colonial relationships between the ethnic groups and tethered to political developments during the colonial period, the independence movement, and postindependence political realities (Vail and White 1991).

Tumbuka and Mzimba Ngoni people are all from the northern region and thus have tended to be political allies, and ethnic divisions have not been a significant source of tension, especially in the contemporary political arena. The emphasis on Ngoni culture in the MZIHA and at the Umthetho Festival raises concerns because some see it as replicating the domination of the Ngoni during the period immediately preceding British colonization, and in some ways, the organization reinforces Ngoni dominance in the district on cultural, economic, and political fronts, something that has not been an issue since before British colonization. I should emphasize that since independence, the Ngoni have not dominated the Tumbuka; rather, many Tumbuka people have been very successful educationally and professionally because some of the earliest Christian mission stations were established in Tumbuka areas. The Tumbuka are the numerically dominant ethnic group in the neighboring Rumphi District. By my interpretation, the association and festival are thus fueling historical hierarchical relations that have long been dormant.

MZIHA, UMTHETHO, AND NATIONAL POLITICS

In addition to the complicated cultural politics of the district, from the time of its inception, the MZIHA has also been wound up with national politics. According to Thole, when its founders first tried to register the association with the national government, they were blocked from doing so because of assumptions that since the association was named for the district rather than an ethnic group, its goal was for the district to eventually secede from the country to form an independent state. The association's leadership had to convince the powers that be by inviting Khumbo Kachali, a Ngoni from the Mzimba District who was a powerful politician, to a meeting of the association's board so that board members could convince Kachali that the association's mission was strictly cultural promotion.[2] Kachali was convinced, and the organization's application was accepted. Though they overcame this misunderstanding early on, more recently, members of the association spearheaded an initiative to convert the district into a Ngoni kingdom; they submitted a petition in April 2014 to then President Joyce Banda to transform the district into the Mombera Kingdom, inspired by the Kingdom of Swaziland. This structure would give the kingdom a great deal of autonomy under Paramount Chief M'mbelwa who would serve as its king, while maintaining parts of its relationship with the country of Malawi. Discussion about this potentiality precipitated a great deal of opposition and controversy both within the Mzimba District and across the country.[3] Note that this proposed development would be structured as a *Ngoni* kingdom, with the most powerful leadership positions restricted to men of the Jere clan, relegating those from other ethnic groups—and, significantly, Ngoni women—to less powerful political positions. The patriarchal structure of the Ngoni leadership structure contrasts with the gender equity built into the country's democratic system of government. Women have access to all positions within the official government structure, but they are restricted from serving in the highest positions of power within the Ngoni leadership structure.

The association has also been intertwined with party politics in potentially problematic ways. The state is the dominant governing institution of Malawi. Yet, it coexists with traditional leadership structures operating throughout the country. Thus a particular territory is governed by a hierarchy of traditional chiefs *and* by local and national government officials. The traditional leaders, such as M'mbelwa, are not supposed to participate in political parties or actively promote any political figure. They can vote as individuals; however, as representatives of their communities, they are supposed to remain politically neutral and encourage people to support whichever politician they choose, a central tenet of the relatively new democratic system of government (1994 through present). Despite this policy, some traditional leaders do participate in politics and have been used by politicians to try to increase their support base.

The late Ngoni Paramount Chief Inkosi ya Makosi M'mbelwa IV was enthroned in 1984 and served in the capacity of paramount chief under Presidents Kamuzu Banda, Bakili Muluzi, Bingu wa Mutharika, and Joyce Banda, all of the presidents since Malawi's independence who served prior to his death. M'mbelwa IV's critics contended that he strategically formed alliances with whichever political party was in power in order to further his own interests. He was known to court each of the presidents and their associated ruling parties and to actively promote the candidates in his district from whichever party was in government at the time. This strategic shifting of political affiliations has been very characteristic of Malawi's political culture, and many political figures have come to be dubbed "chameleons" (Dzimbiri 1998; Englund 2002). In exchange for supporting a ruling party, M'mbelwa IV is said to have received financial and other material remuneration, and his district was favored for various government initiatives. His willingness to shift his allegiance to different parties and politicians based on who was in power at any given time and thus actively serving the ruling party—for example, influencing his constituents to vote for ruling party candidates—made him a controversial figure.

The Umthetho Festival provided an arena for this political maneuvering; time will tell whether it will continue to do so under the leadership of M'mbelwa's son, Inkosi ya Makosi M'mbelwa V, who was enthroned on October 4, 2014. Though the festival is intended to be a cultural event showcasing the culture(s) of the Mzimba District, because the representatives of the ruling party have always been invited and given a prominent role, it has become one more opportunity for the ruling party to promote itself and display its political legitimacy and power. This is particularly striking in the Mzimba District because in the regionalism that has dominated party politics, many in the north feel that their region has been consistently undermined and neglected by politicians. Furthermore, no one from the north has been elected president, nor have most northerners been supporters of the ruling party. The politicization of the festival therefore has not been congruous with the political affiliation of most participants.

This chameleon allegiance of the late M'mbelwa to the ruling party has been part of the symbolic displays in the festival. Alongside the presentations of the M'mbelwa chieftaincy and all the Ngoni symbols and cultural performances have been parallel demonstrations of the ruling political party and politicians. At past festivals, the president and other ruling party politicians arrived at the event in a motorcade replete with security, and the politicians and their supporters were sometimes clad in the colors of their political party.[4] The presence of the president has contributed to the legitimacy and status of the event at the same time that it has provided one more opportunity for the ruling party to promote itself and make itself a powerful presence in relatively remote rural locations (cf. Cancel 2006). At the Umthetho Festival attended by politicians, women from the district wearing colorful fabric in the ruling party's color adorned with the president's face have sometimes awaited politicians' arrivals and welcomed them with dancing and political praise singing that promoted the party and its politicians, much as they would at a political rally or government function. The president and his or her entourage have been escorted to visually prominent seating areas, where their power was displayed through their having the best seating, physically

Figure 9.2. Women in People's Party fabric at M'mbelwa IV funeral (Photograph by author)

removed from the rest of the audience. Speakers at the event acknowledged politicians' presence at the beginning of each speech, and the highest-ranking politician present—the president, if available—gave a speech at the event (Gilman 2009a, 2009b). The lines were further blurred between festival as cultural event versus political rally when the focus of much public discourse and news coverage of these festivals has been on the president and his or her speech rather than the cultural performances that took place.

Because M'mbelwa IV changed his allegiance with each administration, this politicization of the festival resulted in significant shifts in the symbolic displays at different festivals. In its first year, when Bingu wa Mutharika was Malawi's president, turquoise, the color of the then ruling party, the Democratic Progressive Party (DPP), and images of President Mutharika's political party cloth worn by some of his supporters, added to the visual imagery of the event. In 2012, images of President Joyce Banda and the bright orange party paraphernalia of her People's Party, dominated; in both cases, the colors and fabric symbolically represented party politics generally while the specific colors, images, and people represented parties and politicians in opposition to one another (Gilman 2009b).

In addition to politicians displaying their party symbols at the festival, the event also provides opportunities for political leaders to symbolically perform affinity for the district and region when they put aside their own party paraphernalia in exchange for that associated with the region or Ngoni. When President Joyce Banda attended the 2012 festival, for example, rather than don an elaborate outfit made out of orange fabric, as was often her attire at public events, she wore an outfit that covered her from head to toe in clothing commemorating the festival, royal blue fabric adorned with Ngoni shields and other symbols. Though she is not Ngoni, her choice of dress performed respect for the Ngoni people, the festival, and the paramount chief, and on this day, symbolically aligned the president with the local population—they corporally and performatively shared a Ngoni identity. Given the criticism that this and all previous presidents generally neglected the north, her performance of shared identity with people of this northern district—which was projected in newspapers and television news coverage across the country—was a strategic demonstration, albeit symbolic, that the president was committed to the north, surely an attempt to gain more supporters from the district and region (Gilman 2009a, 2009b, forthcoming).

When M'mbelwa IV died in February 2013, President Joyce Banda attended his funeral, again to much controversy because presidents do not typically attend the funerals of traditional leaders, and many felt that her attendance was not only a waste of government time and funds but that it could be interpreted as the problematic favoring of some ethnic groups over others by the government. President Banda arrived at the funeral with her usual entourage, including lots of bright orange vehicles and folks clad in orange, thus drawing attention to the marketing of her political party rather than to the grieving for the long-term Ngoni leader. The funeral, a large public event, shared some of the features of the Umthetho Festival, including ingoma dancers and people clad in bits and pieces of Ngoni paraphernalia, such as head rings, beads, and animal skins. As at the festival, the ruling party's orange intertwined with these Ngoni symbols, complicating the symbolic displays. Competing for prominence were the Ngoni ruler, whose death was being honored with a traditional ceremony, and the very alive president of the state, who performed her political prominence at this local event as the national leader.

This relationship between the festival and the national government has diminished the power of the MZIHA. When asked about challenges that the association faces, its chair at the time of research in 2013, Professor Soko, explained that members have been unable to set a fixed date for the festival, which would greatly facilitate its organization and promotion. Each year, they cannot set a date until the government approves a day when they can send representatives, ideally the president. When the president's schedule changes, as it often does, they have sometimes had to reschedule the festival. I should note that my conversations with Soko and Thole indicate that the association wants the presence of the president because it brings the event legitimacy and attention as well as resources. For example, prior to the 2012 festival, recognizing how terrible the roads were to the festival site at Mt. Hora, the government expended resources to temporarily improve the road from the highway to Mt. Hora so that the president's ride would be more comfortable. An improved road was welcomed by everyone. Unfortunately, by the time I took the same route in 2013, the improvements were already deteriorating. The government did not put forth the resources to meet the long-term infrastructural needs of the community.

Though the MZIHA courts the ruling party in its festival organizing, other festivals that have emerged since the early 2000s explicitly avoid political participation, evidence that festivals do not have to be one more arena for party politics. For example, the Kungoni Annual Cultural Festival, organized by the Canadian priest and anthropologist Claude Boucher Chisale at the Kungoni Cultural Center at Mua Mission in Dedza District, is scheduled independently from the availability of political figures. In an interview in July 2013, Father Boucher explained to me that he works hard to keep the festival and other activities of the Kungoni Cultural Center separate from politicians. He does not invite politicians to the festival and does not create performance opportunities for those who attend to promote their parties. In the festival I attended in July 2013, though there were some politicians representing the constituency where the mission is located, none wore political regalia and they were not given special attention or opportunities to speak.

CONTESTATIONS OF TRADITIONAL AND GOVERNMENT POWER

At the same time that the festival has showcased the president's legitimacy as the ruler of the country, the association has also used the festival to promote M'mbelwa's legitimacy as the local ruler, and the festival has provided opportunities for power negotiations between the traditional and national leadership systems. For example, a ritual of the festival is that M'mbelwa receives guests in a ceremonial hut. Guests enter the hut kneeling to greet and sometimes briefly chat with the paramount chief. Common etiquette in Malawi generally and among the Ngoni specifically is that the person of lower status must kneel and be physically lower than the one of higher status during greetings. In previous festivals, Presidents Mutharika and Banda ritually entered the hut to greet the leader. Like his other guests, the presidents knelt before the seated chief, symbolically enacting reverence to the chief and accepting his higher status at the event and in the locale. Furthermore, the hut was very small, and M'mbelwa IV was very large; when the president entered, in addition to kneeling, he or she had limited space, squeezed between M'mbelwa's large frame and the walls, and thus the state president was physically positioned in the margins. This ceremonial greeting symbolically constituted a subversion of the power structures in the country, whereby the president is the most central and powerful leader over all the people. In the enactment of this ritual, M'mbelwa reigns supreme even in relationship to his own president.

At the Nc'wala celebration I attended in Zambia with the MZIHA chair Soko in February 2013, this interplay between displays of national and ethnic leadership was even more pronounced. On the main day of the festival, Paramount Chief Mpezeni was escorted to the festival grounds with his male advisors, all clad in ceremonial Ngoni warrior garb, singing and dancing in the ingoma style. Draped over Mpezeni's shoulders was a full lion skin complete with head, a very striking visual symbol in the region where not only is killing a lion symbolic of the ultimate warrior, but most lions have been killed off and are no longer ever seen except on wildlife preserves (not to mention that it is illegal to hunt them). His special seating area was set off from everyone else other than his entourage and featured a stuffed full-size lion, also symbolically provocative. The country's president was supposed to attend the event, but did not. The political figure who came to represent the government instead sat in special VIP seating, but was not accorded anything close to the visual or symbolic prominence of Inkosi ya Makosi Mpezeni, who presided. Soko, impressed with this dimension, explained that it was important at this event that it be recognized that the traditional authority of Mpezeni was more significant than that of the political official, suggesting that might also be Soko's goal in the future for the Umthetho Festival.

MZIMBA HERITAGE AND THE FESTIVALS OF OTHER ETHNIC ASSOCIATIONS

Since the formation of the MZIHA and the Chewa Heritage Foundation, an organization for Chewa people that crosses national boundaries and was formed around the same time as the MZIHA, other ethnic groups have followed suit, using the MZIHA as their model, at least according to the association's leadership. The most politically salient example is the formation of the Mulhako wa Alhomwe, an ethnic association for the Lhomwe people created at the initiative of Malawi's former president Bingu wa Mutharika. The mission of this organization was purportedly to promote the culture of his own ethnic group, in itself problematic because he was funneling government resources for cultural initiatives only for his ethnic group at the expense of others. Even more troublesome was that it was widely accepted in Malawi that Mutharika used the association as a tribalistic mechanism for identifying people from the Lhomwe ethnic group. According to many people with whom I discussed this issue, the association registered members as a way to create a database of Lhomwe people whom the government could then reward with jobs and political positions. Not surprisingly, the organization's leaders, whom I interviewed in July 2013, denied this claim. The Mulhako wa Alhomwe created the annual Lhomwe festival, which takes place in October. Though I have not had the opportunity to attend this festival, reports of the event in the media during Bingu wa Mutharika's presidency were replete with images of the president and his entourage symbolically performing their cultural identity and displaying their political power. Bingu wa Mutharika's brother Peter Mutharika was elected Malawi's fifth president in May 2014. He presided over the Lhomwe festival in October 2014 and November 2015.

When President Bingu wa Mutharika died very suddenly of a heart attack in April 2012, his vice president—who by then was also his political opponent—Joyce Banda rose to the presidency. Soon after becoming president, Banda announced that her ethnic group, the Yao, should have a cultural association as do other ethnic groups, emphasizing the cultural rather than the political. Her announcement and the efforts to form the Chiwanja cha Ayao that followed evoked much criticism, given the actions of her predecessor. Critics stated that ethnic associations should be initiated and formed by members of ethnic groups, not by state presidents. Moreover, if state presidents were interested in forming associations and instigating annual festivals, they should do so for all ethnic groups, not just their own. Media coverage of efforts to form this association were full of concerns that Banda and her party would use the association for political objectives, as did her predecessor. One of the organizers whom I interviewed in July 2013 was adamant that the then president was not involved in the organization and that it was completely divorced from the political arena, though plenty of evidence suggested otherwise. For example, several news articles indicated that the president had been asked to be the association's patron, just as Bingu wa Mutharika had been the patron of the Mulhako wa Alhomwe. Though I have not been back to Malawi since Banda lost the 2014 presidential election, media coverage suggests that Yao leaders are continuing to form the Chiwanja cha Ayao independent of her leadership. In an article in the online newspaper *Malawi Voice* on April 2, 2015, Dr. Allan Chilimba is said to be the association chair, and the report states that "the group has made it clear that Chiwanja cha Ayao is non-political as it observes individual rights to freely belong to, participate or support any political party and ideologies" (Mauluka 2015). Time will tell how this association emerges in relationship to national politics. The examples of the Mulhako wa Alhomwe and the Chiwanja cha Ayao are worthy of their own studies. For the purpose of this essay, I refer to them in order to emphasize that the proliferation of ethnic heritage associations and the festivals that help to reify them have been intricately linked to politics.

CONCLUSION

In many ways, the formation and activities of the Mzimba Heritage Association, including the annual Umthetho Festival, evidence a very positive shift. For a long time, government structures did little for the cultural sector, allocating only limited funds. People outside government concerned about their own culture, interested in cultural promotion, or working in the cultural sector as civil servants complained about this lack of attention but did little to mobilize existing resources or identify other sources to develop initiatives outside the government's Department of Culture. These new associations, at least the ones not initiated by a president, are a welcome change to this pattern because cultural leaders are taking it upon themselves to establish organizations valuable to them and initiate activities to promote their own cultures rather than waiting for the government to do so.

The initiatives of MZIHA, such as the Umthetho Festival, efforts at language preservation, and attempts to revitalize some traditional arts, are very valuable to Ngoni people because they help forge a stronger cultural identity, especially within the context of globalization and the overvaluing of all that is Western. The MZIHA also hopes that its efforts will have economic benefits. Already, the annual Umthetho Festival brings people to Mt. Hora once a year. These visitors pay for transport, purchase food and drink, and buy handicrafts. The vision of the association leaders is to build a hotel, museum, and historical tour at the site, which they hope will become a tourist destination year-round, bringing much-needed income to local businesses and potential revenue to support the association's activities. The economic potential of such initiatives could be significant. At the Nc'wala Festival I attended, thousands of people from across Zambia and neighboring countries attended and hundreds of vendors sold a variety of goods at the festival site, a real economic boon for the area.

On the other hand, the Umthetho Festival contributes to the reification of ethnic identities in a country where ethnicity has been important culturally but usually not politically divisive. The linking of ethnic identity to political entities and the emphasizing of ethnic divisions have the potential for fueling tribalism, a dynamic that has led to great strife in other countries in the region, most notably the genocides in Rwanda and Burundi. That cultural identification is always simultaneously tied to cultural differentiation (Bauman 1971) needs to be critically recognized so that the scale can be tipped toward productive ethnic pride rather than destructive tribalism.

In an entry titled "Confusedly tribal" on August 14, 2012, blogger Khumbo Soko, a young man originally from Mzimba District, contemplates the significance of the Ngoni festival as it relates to his own cultural identity. Following are some excerpts from his entry:

> You see I am not as enthusiastic about these *tribal things*. I would hardly muster enough excitement within myself, for instance, to travel all the way to Hora Mzimba to attend some cultural function such as *Umthetho*...
>
> If I heard my paternal grandfather well, his ancestors were Karangas from Zimbabwe. They were uprooted from there by their Nguni conquerors and forced to trek to Tanganyika before finally finding themselves in northern Malawi... Am not sure about the ethnicity of the women that my paternal great-grandfathers married, though am sure they were from diverse ethnic backgrounds...
>
> Like I have said, if what I was told is correct, my father could only have laid claim to have been a ngoni by association save perhaps to the extent that some of his maternal ancestors could have been ngonis? What however is the ethnicity of a progeny of an inter-ethnic marriage?
>
> Take the *Umthetho* festival, for instance. Didn't you find it curious that a ngoni function was celebrated in *tumbuka* language?...
>
> So really, we don't have pure ethnic groups in Malawi. And certainly no untainted cultures... Why then do we find it so necessary to exaggerate our ethnic distinctiveness when we are anything but such in reality?... Stay with me... my thoughts are still evolving.[5]

This blog entry addresses several of the issues that are commonly brought up about the festival as it relates to the complexities of individuals' cultural heritage, and suggests concern with people's efforts to "exaggerate our ethnic distinctiveness when we are anything but such in reality."

The emergence of these associations and their activities, including festivals, though mired in controversy, also seem to be generally accepted by most in the country as relatively benign. Yet, one does not have to look too closely to notice that entanglement with local cultural politics and party politics at the district, regional, and national levels, which is fraught with clientelism and corruption, raises some critical issues about the role these associations can play in what has become a devastating political arena where most politicians are doing little to benefit the country, focusing instead on their own political and material aggrandizement. My analysis highlighting some of the political ramifications sheds light on the more insidious side of things in order to make a plea for more attention to the political implications of the intertwining of cultural promotion with local and national politics. Recognition of these potential pitfalls could motivate participants, some of whom are academic and public sector culture workers, to redirect their activities to better ensure that they meet the missions of the organization rather than contribute to ethnic and political tensions.

NOTES

Preliminary research was funded by the University of Oregon's Center for the Study of Women in Society and the University of Oregon's Office of Research. Subsequent research was funded by a Fulbright Scholar Fellowship in 2013 with support from Mzuzu University.

1. See Fleming 1972; Phiri 2002; and Thompson 1981 for a history of Ngoni migration and settlement in northern Malawi.
2. Khumbo Kachali subsequently served as Malawi's vice president under Joyce Banda from April 2012 to May 2014.
3. A flurry of responses followed the news of the petition, many of which were critical. For example, see the online comments for the article announcing the petition: "Mzimba Heritage Association Petitions JB on Mombela Kingdom" in the *Malawi Voice,* April 28, 2014, http://www.malawivoice.com/2014/04/28/mzimba-heritage-association-petition-jb-on-mombela-kingdom/, accessed September 10, 2014.
4. In such a poor country, the expenses associated with transporting politicians and supporters to remote locations to attend festivals is significant, and some feel the money would be better allocated to other needs in the country, such as poverty alleviation.
5. Khumbo Soko's blog entry can be found at http://kbsoko.blogspot.com/2012/08/confusedly-tribal.html, accessed September 11, 2014.

REFERENCES

Bauman, Richard. 1971. "Differential Identity and the Social Base of Folklore." *Journal of American Folklore* 84 (331): 31–41. http://dx.doi.org/10.2307/539731.

Cancel, Robert. 2006. "Asserting/Inventing Traditions in the Luapula: The Lunda Mutomboko Festival." *African Arts* 39 (3): 12–93. http://dx.doi.org/10.1162/afar.2006.39.3.12.

Chirwa, W. C. 1994. "Elections in Malawi: The Perils of Regionalism." *Southern Africa Report* 10 (2): 17–20.

Chirwa, W. C. 1998. "Democracy, Ethnicity, and Regionalism: The Malawian Experience, 1992–1996." In *Democratisation in Malawi: A Stocktaking*, ed. Kings M. Phiri and Kenneth R. Ross, 52–69. Blantyre, Malawi: Christian Literature Association in Malawi (CLAIM).

Dzimbiri, Lewis B. 1998. "Competitive Politics and Chameleon-like Leaders." In *Democratisation in Malawi: A Stocktaking*, ed. Kings M. Phiri and Kenneth R. Ross, 87–101. Blantyre, Malawi: Christian Literature Association in Malawi (CLAIM).
Englund, Harri. 2002. "Introduction: The Culture of Chameleon Politics." In *A Democracy of Chameleons: Politics and Culture in the New Malawi*, ed. Harri Englund. Stockholm: Elanders Gotab.
Falassi, Alessandro. 1987. "Festival: Definition and Morphology." In *Time out of Time: Essays on the Festival*, ed. Alessandro Falassi, 1–10. Albuquerque: University of New Mexico Press.
Fleming, C. J. W. 1972. "The Zwangendaba Succession." *Society of Malawi Journal* 25 (2): 38–48.
Flint, Lawrence. 2006. "Contradictions and Challenges in Representing the Past: The Kuomboka Festival of Western Zambia." *Journal of Southern African Studies* 32 (4): 701–17. http://dx.doi.org/10.1080/03057070600995483.
Gilman, Lisa. 2004. "The Traditionalization of Women's Dancing, Hegemony, and Politics in Malawi." *Journal of Folklore Research* 41 (1): 33–60. http://dx.doi.org/10.2979/JFR.2004.41.1.33.
Gilman, Lisa. 2009a. *The Dance of Politics: Gender, Performance and Democratization in Malawi*. Philadelphia: Temple University Press.
Gilman, Lisa. 2009b. "Genre, Agency, and Meaning in the Analysis of Complex Performances: The Case of a Malawian Political Rally." *Journal of American Folklore* 122 (485): 335–62. http://dx.doi.org/10.1353/jaf.0.0095.
Gilman, Lisa. 2015. "Demonic or Cultural Treasure: Local Perspectives on Vimbuza, Intangible Cultural Heritage, and UNESCO in Malawi." In *UNESCO on the Ground: Local Perspectives on Intangible Cultural Heritage*, ed. Michael Dylan Foster and Lisa Gilman, 59–76. Bloomington: Indiana University Press.
Gilman, Lisa. Forthcoming. "Performance, Maternalism, and Joyce Banda's Brief Presidency in Malawi." *Africa Today*.
Guhrs, Tamara (coordinating author). 2008. *Ceremony! Celebrating Zambia's Cultural Heritage*. Lusaka: Celtel Zambia PLC and Seka.
Hobsbawm, Eric, and Terence Ranger, eds. 1983. *The Invention of Tradition*. Cambridge: Cambridge University Press.
Kertzer, David I. 1988. *Ritual, Politics, and Power*. New Haven: Yale University Press.
Lwanda, John Lloyd Chipembere. 1993. *Kamuzu Banda of Malawi: A Study in Promise, Power and Paralysis; Malawi under Dr. Banda (1961 to 1993)*. Glasgow: Dudu Nsomba.
Mauluka, Edwin. 2015. "Yao Ethnic Group Registers 'Chiwanja Cha a Yao.'" *Malawi Voice*, April 2. Accessed July 13, 2015. http://malawivoice.com/2015/04/02/yao-ethnic-group-registers-chiwanja-cha-a-yao/.
Mkamanga, Emily. 2000. *Suffering in Silence: Malawi Women's 30 Year Dance with Dr. Banda*. Glasgow: Dudu Nsomba.
Phiri, Desmond D. 1982. *From Nguni to Ngoni: A History of the Ngoni Exodus from Zululand and Swaziland to Malawi, Tanzania, and Zambia*. Lilongwe, Malawi: Likuni.
Phiri, Desmond D. 2002. "Some Notes on the Ngoni Clans of Malawi and the Ngoni Celebrations at Mabili of September, 2002." *Society of Malawi Journal* 55 (2): 65–71.
Santino, Jack. 1986. "The Folk Assemblage of Autumn: Tradition and Creativity in Halloween Folk Art." In *Folk Art and Art Worlds*, ed. John Michael Vlach and Simon Bronner, 151–69. Ann Arbor, MI: UMI Research Press.
Santino, Jack. 1992. "Yellow Ribbons and Seasonal Flags: The Folk Assemblage of War." *Journal of American Folklore* 105 (415): 19–33. http://dx.doi.org/10.2307/541997.
Santino, Jack. 2001. *Signs of War and Peace: Social Conflict and the Use of Public Symbols in Northern Ireland*. New York: Palgrave. http://dx.doi.org/10.1007/978-1-4039-8233-9.

Simbao, Ruth Kerkham. 2006. "Crown on the Move: Stylistic Integration of the Luba-Lunda Complex in Lunda-Kazembe Performance." *African Arts* 39 (3): 26–41, 93–96. http://dx.doi.org/10.1162/afar.2006.39.3.26.
Stoeltje, Beverly. 1993. "Power and the Ritual Genres: American Rodeo." *Western Folklore* 52 (2/4): 135–56. http://dx.doi.org/10.2307/1500083.
Thompson, T. J. 1981. "The Origins, Migration and Settlement of the Northern Ngoni." *Society of Malawi Journal* 34 (1): 6–35.
Toelken, Barre. 1991. "Ethnic Selection and Intensification in the Native American Pow-wow." In *Creative Ethnicity: Symbols and Strategies of Contemporary Ethnic Life*, ed. Stephen Stern and John Allan Cicala, 137–56. Logan: Utah State University Press.
Vail, Leroy, and Landeg White. 1991. "Tribalism in the Political History of Malawi." In *The Creation of Tribalism in Southern Africa*, ed. Leroy Vail, 151–92. Berkeley: University of California Press.
Young, Crawford. 1994. "The Colonial Construction of African Nations." In *Nationalism*, ed. John Hutchinson and Anthony D. Smith, 225–31. New York: Oxford University Press.

10

Music as Activist Spectacle
AIDS, Breast Cancer, and LGBT Choral Singing

Pamela Moro

And since noise is the source of power,
power has always listened to it with fascination.
—Jacques Attali

IN THE UNITED STATES AND BEYOND, CAUSE-ORIENTED public events such as awareness runs and fund-raising fitness walks have become a familiar part of each year's calendar. These events range in size and degree of institutionalization, from professionally coordinated—and commercialized—events like the Avon Walk for Breast Cancer and urban LGBT Pride parades to small, highly local events, perhaps for a specific cause such as a child suffering from leukemia. Such mass participatory forms of activism and awareness raising are spectacular in nature. They are big, they are performative, they are dynamic (MacAloon 1984, 243–45), and they're something you can't help but look at. A related phenomenon is musical performance for activist purposes. Here too the scale ranges from celebrity concerts that make international headlines as they raise funds for global debt relief or AIDS (see Behrman 2004, 270–77 on Bono of the band U2) to lower-profile community music making as a form of awareness raising or fund-raising.

This chapter identifies spectacular features of mass-participatory embodied activist events, be they fitness walks or choral concerts. Such events are distinct from genuine protest (investigation of which involves different questions and requires a different theoretical tool kit) and also distinct from music and theater that are intended to function as public education or propaganda. Why have spectacular forms of "awareness raising" become prominent or even superseded more radical actions? In particular, I am

DOI: 10.7330/9781607326359.c010   189

interested in public music making that produces meaning in part through the techniques of spectacle. How do spectacular features contribute to music making for activist purposes? Thus this essay pursues two lines: the role of the spectacular in activist awareness events, and the specific characteristics, and potential, of musical performance and the aural within such events. As an example, this investigation will focus upon a single concert, featuring compositions about AIDS and breast cancer, as performed by an international group of gay-identified choruses in New York City in February 2006. An examination from the perspective of singing participants reveals a complex picture, in which meaning is constructed in multiple and unpredictable directions.

ACTIVIST SPECTACLE AND THE AFFECT OF MUSIC

Mass activist events share several features and draw upon forms of communication that include the visual and the aural. They are *embodied* in multiple ways. They involve walking, running, performance, the human voice, and frequently respond to problems of a medical or other physical nature, such as domestic violence, child abuse, or hunger. Embodiment perspectives emphasize that individual bodies are active agents (Csordas 1990; Farnell 1999). Diseases are symbolically well suited for embodied responses: we walk/run to assert that we can—if we are ill or in recovery, completion of a lengthy event can be a goal to work toward—or because we can physically exert ourselves on behalf of those who cannot. We physically suffer (a little) because others physically suffer (a lot)—which stirs empathy. William H. McNeill considers "muscular bonding" through dance and song a human universal, traceable through human evolution: "Moving our muscles rhythmically and giving voice consolidate group solidarity by altering human feelings" (1995, viii; see also Ehrenreich 2007 on embodied participation in the production of ecstatic joy).

These events are intended to prompt a *predictable emotional experience* of solidarity and bonding, or communitas (E. Turner 2012). Victor Turner's subcategory of "ideological communitas," with its ability to at least superficially unite groups of people despite their differences and to suggest ways for living, is an apt label. Such communitas is based on "explicitly formulated views on how men may best live together in comradely harmony" (V. Turner 1995, 134). These emotions are uplifting, a metaphor consistent with the stated goal, "to raise awareness."

These mass participatory events are *performative*, in the simple sense that they require performance on the part of participants, and they assume an audience that witnesses and whose awareness is raised. The audience may not be literal or stationary or physically present, but rather what Jack Santino has described as "a fluid and unpredictable spectatorship" (Santino 2006). The term "to raise awareness" is shorthand for a complex set of motivations, responses, and assertion of identity—in the sense of quiet identity statements ("I am the sort of person who cares about domestic violence or heart disease or . . .") that in some way will be witnessed by others. The possibility that awareness raising has replaced the earlier "consciousness raising" will be taken up later.

Extending John MacAloon's 1984 work on spectacle (which used the Olympics as a grand example), I call these events *activist spectacles* because much of their intended or perceived effect comes from their spectacular nature. Even relatively small-scale events of this nature are massive in that they amass groups of people for a singular purpose. They occur in public spaces and may involve the disruption or temporary conversion of public spaces for unorthodox use, and they are intended to be seen. More is better: the more participation, the more awareness raised, the more funds generated. Participants are likely to wear something or mark themselves in a visually striking way—T-shirts, ribbons, placards. Regardless of their actual pragmatic or material benefits, their stated intent is activist. Their purpose is to bring about change, whether in the lives of individuals, in public policy, or in scientific knowledge made possible by fund-raising. In the United States, spectacular activism is usually intended to raise money and to raise awareness. Elsewhere in the world, the mass media, music, and other forms of performance are often used to induce changes in behavior at the level of the individual. Communications scholars Arvind Singhal and Everett Rogers use the term "entertainment-education strategy" to describe performances and mass media programs intended to bring about social change (Singhal and Rogers 1999, 2003), especially efforts in developing countries to spread messages about AIDS, birth control, and spousal abuse (see also Bourgault 2003). Such activities are fundamentally different from the activist spectacle.

As argued so persuasively by MacAloon, the spectacle as a genre—somewhat akin to ritual, somewhat akin to festival—emphasizes the visual, as reflected in both the etymology and idiomatic uses of the word *spectacle* itself. It has been argued persuasively that the visual, and the sense of sight, is primary in contemporary culture (see Mulvey's 1975 gaze theory; Dundes's 1972 "seeing is believing") and indeed, this is how MacAloon explains the prominence of spectacle in the twentieth century. Spectacle fits our emphasis upon the visual, our concern with the relationship between image and reality (1984, 270.) We can think as well as Walter Benjamin (2008) and our age of mechanical, now digital, reproduction. With the distractions of information overload and competition for media attention, the spectacle may in fact be necessary as an instrument for change, the only way to get attention. It is not surprising, then, that scholarly attention has emphasized the visual in massive public events, perhaps to the point that we have overdetermined the role of sight in the spectacular.

More recently, some have begun to theorize hearing and the aural in burgeoning areas of scholarship known as sound studies or acoustemology—often as subspecialties within the disciplines of anthropology and history (Bull and Back 2003; Bendix 2000; Drobnick 2004; Erlmann 2004; Feld and Brenneis 2004; Smith 2004; Sterne 2012; many of these are prefigured by Attali 1985). Is there room for the sense of hearing in our consideration of the spectacular? What is the aural nature of spectacle? English vocabulary fails us here, as there simply is no hearing-oriented word equivalent to *spectacle*. Yet surely the communicative capacity of music accounts for much of the impact of mass activist events. "Music is directly physical. Listeners experience music with their bodies as sound waves. This physicality allows musicians to turn their moods and emotions into sounds that listeners directly share, without recourse to language, in a way that produces immediate quality of experience. Such sharing can occur at both large-scale events and more intimate settings . . . In short, while the lyrical content of music more clearly communicates ideas, the physical and affective dimensions lend it potency as a form of communication" (Mattern 1998, 17–18).

The aurally spectacular is not limited to activist events. Audiences have long been compelled by loud noise in music (cannons firing in Tchaikovsky's 1812 Overture) and aural power (gigantic audio speakers at arena concerts, reed instruments in Asian festival processions). Other examples suggest a fascination with big sounds from very large groups of people. An oft-viewed video clip posted multiple times on YouTube and circulated through social media features the final movement of Beethoven's Ninth Symphony, performed in Japan with an exceptionally large choir, purportedly 10,000 vocalists (titled *Beethoven—Symphony No. 9 [10000 Japanese]*).[1] Composer and producer Eric Whitacre's "Virtual Choir" projects have drawn together thousands of participants worldwide, through individual submission of video recordings compiled to form mass e-choruses. On Whitacre's website, one participant opined, "Do you remember that song they used for the Coca Cola ad 'I'd like to teach the world to sing in perfect harmony'—now we have!"[2]

COMMUNITY BUILDING AND ACTIVISM IN THE LGBT CHORAL MOVEMENT

The possibilities for musical sound to contribute to activist spectacle can be highlighted through an ethnographic example. For several years, beginning in 2004, I was involved with Confluence: The Mixed GALA Chorus of the Willamette Valley, which was founded in 2000. Since its inception, the ensemble has been directed by Ray Elliot, a native of Oregon, and has rehearsed at a Unitarian-Universalist church in Oregon's capital, Salem. As a mixed LGBT chorus, the ensemble includes women, men, and transgendered people of any sexual orientation, but is explicitly welcoming to the LGBT community. The term *GALA* means that the chorus is a member of the Gay and Lesbian Association of Choruses, an association founded in 1983 that unites lesbian and gay choruses, primarily in North America (see www.galachoruses.org).

Like other GALA choruses, Confluence has a strong dedication to social justice and LGBT awareness, and also has a lively, and proudly proclaimed, commitment to fun. Members of the nonauditioned chorus aspire to build supportive, family-like bonds with one another. Some of the members have also sung with earlier-established GALA choruses in Portland, Oregon, and elsewhere in the United States. I initially got to know the chorus as a researcher, but over time my role and relationship with the group changed, as is typical for many who do long-term fieldwork close to home (Amit 2000). Chorus members rarely think of me now as a researcher but consider me a friend, emergency rehearsal accompanist, audience member, and spouse of a one-time chorus board member. Since the time of my research with the group, at least two of my undergraduate students have conducted fieldwork with the ensemble, including one from Japan who sang with the chorus for a year. In the extended example discussed below, I sang in the alto section and contributed my home for some rehearsals.

GALA choruses in general hold three main goals, which they articulate in their own words in their mission statements, websites, and concert programs, although—as is evident if you talk to chorus members—they are valued somewhat differentially among participants. But most chorus members would agree that they are all important. These goals are:

1. musical excellence and love of music making;
2. community and solidarity building within the chorus and within the queer community and its allies;
3. social change: usually phrased as social harmony, tolerance, or concern for justice, enacted through outreach and education.

The choruses use electronic media to convey their goals as well as to publicize concerts, sells tickets, and communicate with both singers and audience members. Through their websites and Wikipedia, choruses share their histories. Some, for example, the Twin Cities Gay Men's Chorus of Minneapolis/St. Paul, post selected biographies or personal testimonials from members (see "Our Amazing Stories" on tcgmc.org). Choruses typically have concise mission statements, shared online and on concert programs, for example: "The San Francisco Gay Men's Chorus creates extraordinary musical experiences that inspire community, activism, and compassion "(http://www.sfgmc.org/about-sfgmc/?gclid=CMzA97rA99 MCFVGTfgodCW0A-w) and "The Portland Gay Men's Chorus aspires to expand, redefine, and perfect the choral art through eclectic performances that honor and uplift the gay community and affirm the worth of all people" (www.pdxgmc.org/about/).

In addition, LGBT choruses perform repertory reflecting the three main goals identified here. The eclectic repertory varies by chorus, but often includes music arranged for high school or college choirs, gospel, justice-oriented anthems, music used in liberal religious congregations, women's music, pop music (sometimes with lyrics subversively altered), Broadway show tunes, and occasionally classical. An original body of works has also emerged, mostly commissioned by the larger urban choruses, with texts exploring themes and experiences relevant to chorus members. A number of those compositions were studied by Robert Mensel, long-term artistic director of the Portland Gay Men's chorus, in his 2007 doctoral dissertation at the University of Oregon. Mensel describes such works as "affinity compositions" because of their specific focus on LGBT community concerns. Of the two works highlighted in the discussion below, the first might be considered an example of affinity composition because of its close association, in inception and performance, with a gay men's chorus.

In its social activist goals, the gay choral movement joins a venerable tradition of cause-oriented singing in the United States, from the nineteenth-century abolition movement, early ethnic community choruses, and the 1930s–1940s workers' movement to the civil rights movement and the 1980s antinuclear movement.[3] In their earliest days—in the late 1970s and early 1980s—gay-identified choruses were part of a lively urban gay subculture, celebratory in nature and part of the radical solidarity-building ethos of the time. Elder members of the Portland Gay Men's Chorus have described to me the bawdy songs ("very, very bawdy," as one put it, with a smile) chorus members used to perform at the time, sometimes in nightclub venues. Since then, the ensembles have grown to become major arts organizations with mission-oriented roles of community leadership (see especially Strachan 2006.) The 1980s–1990s AIDS epidemic in urban gay men's communities profoundly influenced gay choral singing and composition—shaping experiences of men in the choruses, who watched fellow chorus members die—and this is echoed in a more recent attention to breast cancer. During performances, members of Confluence wear awareness ribbons constructed from two pieces of grosgrain ribbon—one red for AIDS, one pink for breast cancer—fastened with a small safety pin representing safe sex practices.[4] Despite generational changes in chorus membership over the years, concern for AIDS and breast cancer was very strong during the most active period of my research (2004–2006). Choral activism has shifted somewhat post–2010 toward the movements for equal marriage rights and for empowerment of queer youth. Many GALA-type choruses, as community organizations, have contributed to the It Gets Better Project (Savage and Miller 2011) and performances of the Laramie Project (Kaufman 2010), both of which highlight youth.

SINGING AWARENESS AT CARNEGIE HALL

In February 2006, some members of Confluence took part in a mass choral performance intended to raise awareness about AIDS and breast cancer and to bring GALA choruses into the very visible and legitimate site of Carnegie Hall. There is a long story behind the experience. When the invitation to take part came in late 2004, there was heart-wrenching wrangling about fund-raising, concerns about the potential divisiveness of participation (because not everyone could go), extra rehearsals to prepare the music—nothing surprising to anyone who has been involved in a small organization such as a youth sports team, a church or synagogue, or any local voluntary association.

The event was initiated by Timothy Seelig, who is something of a celebrity among choral directors in the GALA movement, and who leads the Turtle Creek Chorale (which is primarily a gay men's chorus) and related ensembles in Dallas, Texas. None of the ensembles for which Seelig is the director use the words *lesbian* or *gay* in their names, which leads to some gentle criticism within the scene, mixed with genuine respect for the groups' tremendous public visibility and accomplishments. The Turtle Creek Chorale has been the subject of two documentary films (*After Goodbye: An AIDS Story*, 1994, and *The Power of Harmony*, 2005). Seelig's reputation extends beyond GALA choruses as he is on the music faculty at Southern Methodist University and is nationally known among choral directors in general.

Arrangements for the concert were handled by MidAmerica Productions, which since 1984 has organized visits by all the community and scholastic groups that perform at Carnegie Hall, and provides the house orchestra, billed as the New England Symphonic Ensemble. If a church or high school music group near you has performed at Carnegie, chances are great that its visit was organized by MidAmerica, which offers a package deal for hotel rooms, shuttle buses, rehearsal space, and some entertainment in the city. A new version of the familiar joke sums it up: "How do you get to Carnegie Hall? Pay, pay, pay." This is how grassroots musicians get access to the famed stage that, through more than a century of performance by the greatest musicians in the world, has been elevated to a sacred status.

In the end, the concert combined twenty-two choruses from the GALA movement, from four countries and three continents, in a performance of two song cycles for chorus, soloists, narrators, and orchestra. The sound was big, though not always big enough to avoid being drowned out by the orchestra, which included prominent brass and percussion. (GALA choruses perform in standard choral style; there is generally nothing subversive about their vocal style.) The first half of the concert featured a work devoted to the grief and the loss of a loved one entitled *When We No Longer Touch*. The work was composed in 1991 by Kris Anthony, at the time the assistant conductor of the Turtle Creek Chorale in Dallas, who died of AIDS not long thereafter. (The 1994 PBS documentary featuring the chorale focused on his work and death.) Lyrics were by Peter McWilliams, known to many at the time as one of the authors of a mass-marketed self-help/therapy text entitled *How to Survive the Loss of a Love* (McWilliams, Cosgrove, and Bloomfield 1991), which drew heavily upon the stages of grief outlined by Elisabeth Kübler-Ross (1969).[5] Both the lyrics and the musical style align with the accessible aura of popular psychology and popular media. The composition's lyrics are not specifically about AIDS, but about grief and loss in general. However, because the work was initially performed by a gay men's chorus, a chorus that—due to its size and longevity—as of 2006 had lost more than 140 members to AIDS, it is unmistakably perceived as, first and foremost, about grief related to AIDS.

The second half of the concert is when Confluence members took part, and featured *Sing for the Cure*, copyrighted in 2000 and, like *When We No Longer Touch*, connected in its inception to the Turtle Creek Chorale. Nancy Brinker, the founder of the Susan G. Komen Breast Cancer Foundation, approached Timothy Seelig and asked for a piece of music similar to *When We No Longer Touch* based on the stories of breast cancer patients and their friends and families. An Austin, Texas, lyricist, Pamela Martin, interviewed men and women from around the United States, and on the basis of their accounts, wrote the lyrics for the ten-movement work and for the narrated segments that precede each movement. The work weaves together emotional portraits of a cancer patient's experience as well as perspectives from people in different relationships to her, such as child, partner, sister. Each musical movement is written by a different composer, and hence the work intentionally includes a wide range of musical styles. The composers are mostly from Texas and the South, and are not identified with gay choruses. The work was originally performed and recorded by Timothy Seelig's ensembles in Dallas and narrated by Maya Angelou. In the GALA choruses performance at Carnegie Hall, the narrators all had personal experiences with breast cancer, either as survivors or loved ones.[6]

The Susan G. Komen Foundation, which initiated the work, is perhaps best known to the public through its sponsorship of Race for the Cure events. The organization was founded in 1982; tens of thousands of volunteers form a network of local affiliates to raise funds for research grants and to do community outreach about breast cancer. At the time of the Carnegie concert in 2006, Race for the Cure events were "the largest series of 5K runs/fitness walks in the world," with 1 million participants expected that year (www.komen.org). Also in 2006, the foundation's website included instructions for how to produce "Sing for the Cure" events, but these instructions have since been removed; it is possible that the choral and orchestral musical composition did not succeed as an easily reproducible spur for community activism or fund-raising.

It came as a late slight surprise to Oregon's Confluence chorus members that the concert did not include fund-raising. A MidAmerica employee spoke to the assembled singers prior to the concert, telling us, "Someone asked, where do the proceeds go? This isn't about the proceeds, this is about raising awareness." Nonetheless, the unquestionable goodness of bringing attention to AIDS and breast cancer was a soft but insistent undertone to Confluence's participation in New York. Concern for life-altering illnesses and mortality provided an emotional and moral dimension that bubbled up throughout the experience, sometimes gently, sometimes intrusively. By the time participants had learned their scores, absorbed the words, and read about the inception of the musical works, they had developed considerable familiarity with textual content that is, quite simply, rarely put into musical form.

Singers in the GALA choral movement are not strangers to such unusual, and deeply affecting, musical material. They frequently sing inspirational anthems and works with cause-oriented lyrics, and numerous choruses include ASL interpreters in their concerts, representing a commitment to outreach, access, and equality. Nonetheless, the immediacy of emotions stirred by life-threatening disease made these contemporary musical works particularly moving. Within Confluence, members spoke about the difficulty of singing some of the sadder, interior movements of the *Sing for the Cure*. They played mental games to avoid choking up while singing. One singer blogged that during those emotionally challenging moments of performance, she distracted herself by thinking about eating burritos. The chorus had lost a member to breast cancer in 2004, and some felt that participation in the concert was a memorial to her. The highly emotional lyrics were cathartic; they invited us to read in our own stories and memories, and to cry as release. Some singers quietly carried out acts of remembrance, putting photographs of deceased loved ones or of partners undergoing chemotherapy into their music folders. During Confluence's rehearsals of the music, members shared personal experience narratives about illness, death, and grief, facilitated on one occasion by a chorus member who is a professional counseling therapist.

Nonetheless, once in New York—and, in fact, even during the final rehearsals in Oregon—concern with breast cancer receded. The Oregonians were swept away by the thrill of seeing Times Square, of attending a Broadway show, of selecting a museum to visit, of negotiating cramped hotel room space with multiple roommates and, of course, of singing at Carnegie Hall on that very famous stage. Moments before going onstage, middle-aged Elaine made a phone call from a crowded green room: "Mom, all those choir rehearsals at St. John's when I was a kid finally paid off!"

ANALYSIS

These experiences were meaningful and memorable, but to return to our concern with spectacle, activism, and musical performance, what really happened? What was the role of the spectacular? And how does the mass choral event in New York fit into the bigger picture of LGBT outreach and activism?

The concert was big in look, sound, and length, with palpable constitutive energy from the assembled participants. Voices and bodies from different geographic locations were united. Onstage, the chorus made a visually compelling image of massed bodies, uniformly dressed, wearing red and pink AIDS/breast cancer ribbons. In the musical work *Sing for the Cure*, varying voices and perspectives were presented through text, with musical contributions from multiple composers. The event was an embodied, mass-participatory, highly emotional performance in a sacred space. The music was intended to make one cry and to produce a strong, uniform emotional response that could potentially change lives. The metaphor of voices joined together becomes literal in such performance, befitting the goal of solidarity.

For the small group of participants from Oregon, participating in *Sing for the Cure* produced two affecting experiences. There was at one and the same time the thrill of being in New York *and* the deepening of introspective, tearful, emotional bonds with one another, intensified by sharing stories of grief and loss over the months of preparation. But what of the audience who actually listened to the concert? In truth, the audience in Carnegie Hall the evening of the performance was not large. Participants onstage looked out at a hall with many empty seats. Friends and family of the chorus accounted for many in attendance, and of course on any given evening, visitors to New York attend whatever musical event happens to be occurring in Carnegie, just for the sake of visiting the site. Our attention to this concert as activist spectacle must emphasize the experience of performers, not audience.

Thus, while our example provides a focus for interpretation, we should not overstate the aurally and visually spectacular aspects of the Carnegie concert. Context on all levels points to additional reasons for the impact of the performance: the history of the gay rights movement in the United States and its gradual mainstreaming, the small public—in the sociopolitical sense—of the LGBT choral movement, the prestige value and history of each musical composition, the personal motivations of individual participants and their own relationships to breast cancer and AIDS. Yet by considering this single concert, it may be clearer why the spectacular is appropriate for awareness raising. Through the human body, it makes visible the unseen, and gives voice to the silent. It is all about coming out. This is why GALA-type choruses, whose members are experienced in one way or another with coming out, may be well positioned to sing loudly about challenging issues.

The engagement of LGBT choruses with social justice and political issues has been persuasively documented (Balén 2017; Hayes 2007; Moro 2005; Sparks 2005; Stachan 2006). Such involvement takes place adjacent to, or overlapping with, participation in gay and lesbian Pride activities, which have been theorized as carnivalesque festival, a form of both resistance and subcultural consumption, and a way to negotiate cultural legitimacy for queer people (Johnston 2005, 2007; Kates 2002, 2003; Kates and Belk 2001).[7] Pride activities have changed considerably over several decades' time, but the twin goals of celebration and solidarity have persisted; over time they have expanded through a widening social and commercial pool of participants.[8] Like Pride, LGBT choral performances are a way to build solidarity in the public sphere, within and beyond the affinity group. However, choral singing is by and large mainstream in nature; it is rarely carnivalesque, and only minimally a form of consumption.[9] The ways in which LGBT choruses simultaneously enact resistance and establish normativeness is somewhat different from the strategy of Pride. However, like Pride, choral singing may be a way to promote what has been called "perceived deservingness" among the majority, a strategy that Ratcliff, Miller, and Krolikowski (2013) identify in Pride activities. Music does not always produce feelings of affinity, subcultural or otherwise, and some kinds of political or identity-related music are in fact intended to do just the opposite, to voice opposition (Mattern 1998). Yet through the very mainstream aspect of choral performance, and drawing upon the potential for music to unite people through shared emotional experiences, over the course of several decades LGBT choruses have surely contributed to such promotion.

The immediacy of the ethnographic perspective, however, introduces counterpoint. From a certain vantage, singing awareness through a mass chorus might be understood as a minority seeking acceptance, a minority contributing in noisy, public ways to concerns shared by all, such as AIDS and breast cancer. Up close to a small group of participants from Oregon, however, the sound is more complicated. Confluence members indeed sang to raise awareness, but through singing constructed their own understandings, resonant with memories and new meanings. Their participation cannot be reduced to the goals of seeking acceptance or promoting a cause, but comes from a range of motivations, including doing it very much for themselves.

CONSCIOUSNESS VERSUS AWARENESS

Examination of vocabulary related to the goals of activism and education leads us to consider the rise of activist spectacles in a slightly different political context. To conclude on a side note, I return to a point raised in passing much earlier. This is the notion of "awareness raising," which may have replaced "consciousness raising" in public discourse. The *Oxford English Dictionary* documents "consciousness raising" (in the sense of understanding women's rights or racial inequality) arising in the late 1960s through the early 1980s. The *OED* does not provide a similar history of usage for "awareness," though it does currently include "to raise public awareness" as part of the word's definition: "concern about and well-informed interest in a particular situation or development" (oxforddictionaries.com/definition/english/awareness, accessed July 9, 2013.) A related concept is "support" in the sense of emotional help and mental comfort. This word has had consistent use in English since the sixteenth century ("victims' support"), but the most current usage seems to emphasize solidarity, a position or stance alongside someone or some issue. A well-founded hunch is that the shift away from consciousness toward awareness and support began around the time that the Susan G. Komen Foundation for Breast Cancer was founded, which was 1982. By 2017, the concepts of "alliance" and "ally," to indicate a supportive position from individuals outside an identity group, have grown rapidly, another semantic shift.

The early 1980s time period provides clues that can help us explain the prominence of activist spectacle. The 1980s saw the beginning of the AIDS epidemic, but also a turn to the right in U.S. political leadership and public religious expression. *Awareness* is a gentler term than *consciousness*, suggesting education—of information being made available—rather than enlightenment and knowledge that one might come to grasp correctly. It is less radical, and more amenable to commodification. Mass events like runs, walks, and concerts that seek so gentle a goal as "awareness" befit an era when many fear causing offense or discomfort in public discussions, and public expression takes forms that conform rather than protrude (stickers on cars, ribbons on lapels, wristbands). Such phenomena are to be looked at and listened to, and treat change not as something to be demanded but as something that individuals can achieve, through their own bodily efforts or by raising money.

A broader political perspective leaves us with new questions. In community action, who can afford to take risks to achieve desired goals? Why do different constituencies, or groups with different relationships to power and the normative, pursue resistance in different ways? Under what circumstances are activist spectacles and affinity-group music making attractive courses for communities seeking justice?

NOTES

An early, shorter version of this paper was presented at the 10th Annual Conference on Ritual, Holidays, and Festivals, hosted by Willamette University in Salem, Oregon, June 2–4, 2006. Funding for research was provided by the Lilly Project and Willamette University's Atkinson Grant program.

1. http://www.youtube.com/watch?v=X6s6YKlTpfw, accessed August 7, 2013, but posted elsewhere as well.
2. http://ericwhitacre.com/blog/virtual-choir-4-broke-all-the-records, accessed August 9, 2013.
3. See Eyerman and Jamison 1998 on music and twentieth-century social movements.

4. The linking of these two "his and hers" diseases, and their metaphors, is provocative and worthy of exploration.

5. Peter McWilliams was also publicly visible as an advocate for medical marijuana use by AIDS patients.

6. Recordings and video clips of both *Sing for the Cure* and *When We No Longer Touch* are available through popular online media such as YouTube.

7. Many chorus members are active in other kinds of community action as well, through political parties, promotion of ballot measures and legislation, and religious and educational institutions.

8. The mainstreaming of the gay community, with possible loss of a distinctive subculture, has not been without criticism. Fiction author Bret Easton Ellis, a gay man, attracted attention in 2013 with an article slamming gay public figures, especially celebrities, for their eagerness to earn acceptance through do-good achievements.

9. Arguably, carnivalesque performance is sometimes a part of a concert, a separate concert within a season (such as a designated cabaret night), or particular events at the quadrennial gatherings of all GALA member choruses. Such performances may include drag or other campy play.

REFERENCES

After Goodbye: An AIDS Story. 1994. Produced/directed by Ginny Martin. KERA-TV Production, PBS, North Texas.

Amit, Vered. 2000. *Constructing the Field: Ethnographic Fieldwork in the Contemporary World*. London: Routledge. http://dx.doi.org/10.4324/9780203450789.

Attali, Jacques. (Original work published 1977) 1985. *Noise: The Political Economy of Music*. Translated by Brian Massumi. Theory and History of Literature 16. Minneapolis: University of Minnesota Press.

Balén, Julia. 2017. *A Queerly Joyful Noise: Choral Musicking for Social Justice*. New Brunswick, NJ: Rutgers University Press.

Behrman, Greg. 2004. *The Invisible People: How the U.S. Has Slept through the Global AIDS Pandemic, the Greatest Humanitarian Catastrophe of Our Time*. New York: Free Press.

Bendix, Regina. 2000. "The Pleasure of the Ear: Toward an Ethnography of Listening." *Cultural Analysis* 1:33–50.

Benjamin, Walter. (Original work published 1936) 2008. *The Work of Art in the Age of Mechanical Reproduction*. London: Penguin UK.

Bourgault, Louise M. 2003. *Playing for Life: Performance in Africa in the Age of AIDS*. Durham, NC: Carolina Academic Press.

Bull, Michael, and Les Back, eds. 2003. *The Auditory Culture Reader*. Oxford: Berg.

Csordas, Thomas. 1990. "Embodiment as a Paradigm for Anthropology." *Ethos (Berkeley, Calif.)* 18 (1): 5–47. http://dx.doi.org/10.1525/eth.1990.18.1.02a00010.

Drobnick, Jim, ed. 2004. *Aural Cultures*. Banff: YYZ Books.

Dundes, Alan. 1972. "Seeing Is Believing." *Natural History* 81 (5): 8, 10–12, 86–87.

Ehrenreich, Barbara. 2007. *Dancing in the Streets: A History of Collective Joy*. New York: Metropolitan Books.

Ellis, Bret Easton. 2013. "In the Reign of the Gay Magical Elves." *Out*, May 13. http://www.out.com/news-opinion/2013/05/13/bret-easton-ellis-gay-men-magical-elves.

Erlmann, Veit, ed. 2004. *Hearing Cultures: Essays on Sound, Listening, and Modernity*. Oxford: Berg.

Eyerman, Ron, and Andrew Jamison. 1998. *Music and Social Movements: Mobilizing Tradition in the Twentieth Century.* Cambridge: Cambridge University Press. http://dx.doi.org/10.1017/CBO9780511628139.

Farnell, Brenda. 1999. "Moving Bodies, Acting Selves." *Annual Review of Anthropology* 28 (1): 341–73. http://dx.doi.org/10.1146/annurev.anthro.28.1.341.

Feld, Steven, and Donald Brenneis. 2004. "Doing Anthropology in Sound." *American Ethnologist* 31 (4): 461–74. http://dx.doi.org/10.1525/ae.2004.31.4.461.

Hayes, Casey J. 2007. "Community Music and the GLBT Chorus." *International Journal of Community Music* 1 (1): 63–67. http://dx.doi.org/10.1386/ijcm.1.1.63_0.

Johnston, Lynda. 2005. *Queering Tourism: Paradoxical Performances of Gay Pride Parades.* New York: Routledge.

Johnston, Lynda. 2007. "Mobilizing Pride/Shame: Lesbians, Tourism, and Parades." *Social & Cultural Geography* 8 (1): 29–45. http://dx.doi.org/10.1080/14649360701251528.

Kates, Steven M. 2002. "The Protean Quality of Subcultural Consumption: An Ethnographic Account of Gay Consumers." *Journal of Consumer Research* 29 (3): 383–99. http://dx.doi.org/10.1086/344427.

Kates, Steven M. 2003. "Producing and Consuming Gendered Representations: An Interpretation of the Sydney Gay and Lesbian Mardi Gras." *Consumption Markets & Culture* 6 (1): 5–22. http://dx.doi.org/10.1080/10253860302699.

Kates, Steven M., and Russel W. Belk. 2001. "The Meaning of Lesbian and Gay Pride Day Resistance through Consumption and Resistance to Consumption." *Journal of Contemporary Ethnography* 30 (4): 392–429. http://dx.doi.org/10.1177/089124101030004003.

Kaufman, Moisés. 2010. *The Laramie Project.* New York: Random House Digital.

Kübler-Ross, Elisabeth. 1969. *On Death and Dying.* New York: Macmillan.

MacAloon, John J. 1984. "Olympic Games and the Theory of Spectacle in Modern Societies." In *Rite, Drama, Festival, Spectacle*, ed. John J. MacAloon, 241–80. Philadelphia: Institute for the Study of Human Issues.

Mattern, Mark. 1998. *Acting in Concert: Music, Community, and Political Action.* New Brunswick: Rutgers University Press.

McNeill, William H. 1995. *Keeping Together in Time: Dance and Drill in Human History.* Cambridge: Harvard University Press.

McWilliams, Peter, with Melba Cosgrove and Harold Bloomfield. 1991. *How to Survive the Loss of a Love.* Los Angeles: Prelude.

Mensel, Robert. 2007. "A Music of Their Own: The Impact of Affinity Compositions on the Singers, Composers, and Conductors of Selected Gay, Lesbian, and Feminist Choruses." Ph.D. diss., School of Music and Dance, University of Oregon.

Moro, Pamela. 2005. "Our Voices Win Freedom: Meaningful Music-making in Gay and Lesbian Choruses." Paper presented at the Society for American Music conference, University of Oregon, Eugene, February 16–20, 2005.

Mulvey, Laura. 1975. "Visual Pleasure and Narrative Cinema." *Screen* 16 (3): 6–18. http://dx.doi.org/10.1093/screen/16.3.6.

The Power of Harmony. 2005. Produced/directed by Ginny Martin. AMS Production Group.

Ratcliff, Jennifer J., Audrey K. Miller, and Alex M. Krolikowski. 2013. "Why Pride Displays Elicit Support from Majority Group Members: The Mediational Role of Perceived Deservingness." *Group Processes & Intergroup Relations* 16 (4): 462–75. http://dx.doi.org/10.1177/1368430212453630.

Santino, Jack. 2006. Keynote address at the 10th Annual Conference on Holidays, Rituals, Festival, Celebration, and Public Display, Willamette University, Salem, OR, June 2–4.

Savage, Dan, and Terry Miller, eds. 2011. *It Gets Better: Coming Out, Overcoming Bullying, and Creating a Life Worth Living.* New York: Penguin.

Singhal, Arvind, and Everett Rogers. 1999. *Education-Entertainment: A Communication Strategy for Social Change*. Mahwah, NJ: L. Erlbaum Associates.
Singhal, Arvind M., and Everett M. Rogers. 2003. *Combating AIDS: Communication Strategies in Action*. Mahwah, NJ: L. Erlbaum Associates.
Smith, Mark Michael, ed. 2004. *Hearing History: A Reader*. Athens: University of Georgia Press.
Sparks, John D. 2005. "Gay and Lesbian Choruses–Then and Now." *Voice* 28 (4): 27–44.
Sterne, Jonathan. 2012. *The Sound Studies Reader*. New York: Routledge.
Strachan, Jill. 2006. "The Voice Empowered: Harmonic Convergence of Music and Politics in the GLBT Choral Movement." In *Chorus and Community*, ed. Karen Ahlquist, 248–64. Urbana: University of Illinois Press.
Turner, Edith. 2012. *Communitas: The Anthropology of Collective Joy*. New York: Palgrave Macmillan. http://dx.doi.org/10.1057/9781137016423.
Turner, Victor. (Original work published 1969) 1995. *The Ritual Process: Structure and Antistructure*. Piscataway, NJ: Transaction.

11

The "Days of Scanzano"
The Carnivalesque and the Ritualesque in an Antinuclear Protest

Dorothy L. Zinn

THIS CHAPTER CONSIDERS AN EVENT OF SOCIAL-ENVIRONMENTAL protest in light of Santino's (2011) elaboration of the carnivalesque and the ritualesque. Santino justly points out the need to consider those "earnest" and transformative aspects of public events he aligns with a notion of the "ritualesque," aspects that often coexist with carnivalesque forms. Even so, a rigid distinction between the two modalities, as Santino concedes, is not feasible; this is in part due to the hoary question of the definition of ritual, but also because the carnivalesque itself may be expressed in ritualesque forms. Indeed, as Bakhtin himself defined it, "[Carnival] is a *syncretic pageantry* of a ritualistic sort (1984, 122, original emphasis). In order to favor a distinction that may yield some heuristic purchase, I suggest that it may be useful to turn to Bakhtin's ideas regarding genre and hybridization. In doing so, it is important to consider how and where the carnivalesque and ritualesque appear in a protest event. By teasing out the relations between the carnivalesque and the ritualesque in the expressive genres making up a protest, it may be possible to gain a nonreifying view of how and why "people invest these actions with transformative and symbolic power" (Santino 2011, 65). In order to do this, I examine the Scanzano antinuclear protest of November 2003, which took place in the southern Italian region of Basilicata.

Over the last two decades, several disciplines have contributed to a proliferation of social science literature that analyses social protest and social movements. Sociologists have been among the most prominent scholars looking at collective social movements of various sorts; much of this literature, however, has tended to neglect the role of the cultural in social protest (Johnston and Klandermans 1995; Reed 2005). A more recent focus on performative aspects has led researchers to consider culture in a more dynamic and productive manner (Johnston 2009), and even draw on performance studies theorizing to analyze social movements (Blee and McDowell 2012). As fruitful as their analyses have been on many counts, however, sociologists have tended in general to compartmentalize the cultural as an epiphenomenal category of the idealistic/mental that can eventually spur protest action on—for example, as "frames"—but the actual materiality of cultural performance is not usually taken into account in such studies. Ritual in particular, when it is considered at all, may be described as one feature within social movements.

Anthropologists, folklorists, and social historians—notably, scholars from the *Annales* tradition, but also those associated with the area of cultural studies, such as E. P. Thompson—have instead been more sensitive to cultural forms that make up social protest, especially in rituals of carnival. In this sense, carnival presents a special case of challenging social hierarchies and established orders through inversion, parody, and protest, allowing the subaltern to envision and depict alternative order, though, as many scholars have argued, it may actually reinforce the dominant order in the long term by serving as a safety valve. In recent years, anthropological studies have paid increasing attention to the study of so-called new social movements (Edelman 2001), though much of this work has focused on social-structural aspects, engaging the sociological literature that has dominated the field of collective movements. Though Kurzman (2008) asserts that there has been a "cultural turn" in the interdisciplinary area of social movement studies, I would suggest that this new attention to culture has generally not, however, dealt very directly with culture in its expressive forms.[1] Particularly relevant to the present discussion, a few works have looked to Handelman's (1990) concept of the "public event" to analyze how movements and protests themselves constitute rituals (e.g., Juris 2008; Peake 2010).

In two previous analyses of aspects of the Scanzano revolt (Zinn 2007a, 2007b), I myself placed relatively little attention on the expressive forms deployed by the participants. Drawing from the work of Kertzer (1988, 1996), I invoked instances of folklore as key symbols around which a common resistant southern Italian identity could coalesce. Moreover, following Lombardi Satriani's (1966) Gramscian-inspired vision, I cited local folklore as an instrument of subaltern contestation. I would now suggest, however, that in this instance it may be productive to more carefully follow Gramsci's injunction to take folklore seriously. Rethinking folkloric elements in the cultural performance of the Scanzano protest, I find it useful to apply Santino's (2011) elaboration of the dual concepts of "the carnivalesque" and "the ritualesque." In doing so, I am seeking to address this aspect of the protest in a more organic fashion. Here, the carnivalesque and the ritualesque are not simply quaint ornaments, nor do they simply "reflect" features of the encompassing social order: instead, they reveal a capacity to effect ontological change (see Kapferer 2005). In this sense, the Scanzano revolt may be seen, in Handelman's (1990, 49) terms, as a public event that "re-presents the lived-in world." In addition to this, I take inspiration from Appadurai's discussion of ritual and social change: "Ritual here should not be taken in its colloquial sense, as the meaningless repetition of set patterns and actions, but rather as a flexible formula of performances through which social effects are produced and new states of feeling and connection are created, not just reflected or commemorated. This creative, productive, generative quality of ritual is crucial to consensus building in popular movements, and it is a quintessential window into why culture matters for development" (2013, 192).

I suggest that by looking at the carnivalesque and ritualesque as expressive genres employed in Scanzano, we can see how the actors-spectators not only instrumentally forwarded the explicit aims of the protest but also forged and enacted a new relationship to their collectivity, its identity, and its cultural heritage.

Unscripted and spontaneous as the protest was in its inception, the Fifteen Days of Scanzano (as the event would later be enshrined in public memory) drew upon a wide variety of existing genres of cultural performance in the local society. The drawing together of such genres may be described as their effective *hybridization* (Bakhtin 1981), which Kapchan has defined as "an aesthetic process which allows for the simultaneous coexistence (or combination) of forms and voices, but also for their mutual blending and transmutation" (1993, 304). After briefly outlining the events of the Days of Scanzano, I will argue that this hybridization of genres on the one hand enforced the authoritativeness of the protestors, and on the other created spaces for a Turnerian communitas that cut across virtually all lines of social difference within the group (age, gender, social class, localism, political orientation). This diffuse hybridization not only maximized participation in the struggle and increased its moral authority with respect to achieving its overt goal—that of reversing an unwanted action on the part of the central government— but it also acted upon the populace itself an affirmation/appropriation of collective identity, for upon the antinuclear focus of the protest was grafted a response to perceived antisouthern injustice.[2]

THE PROTEST

The region of Basilicata (also known as Lucania) in southern Italy is one of the least densely populated areas of the country, a territory of some 600,000 with a weak regional identity, known in the social sciences as the setting for Carlo Levi's (1990) *Christ Stopped at Eboli* and for Edward Banfield's (1958) *The Moral Basis of a Backward Society*. The latter work, in fact, attempted to analyze the social and economic conditions in "Montegrano" village, which appeared underdeveloped by U.S. standards. In this context, Banfield developed the concept of "amoral familism" to explain the chronic inability of the villagers to work together collaboratively for the public good above and beyond the short-term interests of their nuclear families. Amoral familism subsequently became an epithet for Basilicata and the south as a whole, not only in the social sciences but also in nonacademic discourses. In the third millennium, Basilicata is still a laggard in terms of numerous economic indicators, though since Levi's and Banfield's time the region has achieved significant modernization. The economy features relatively successful agricultural and tourism sectors, an acclaimed Fiat automobile factory in Melfi, and the exploitation of abundant resources of water and oil.

On November 13, 2003, news broke that the government had issued a decree that provided for the creation of a consolidated national nuclear waste storage facility in the Lucanian coastal town of Scanzano Jonico. With the rationale of "urgency" and "national security," the facility was to be implemented as a militarized initiative. News of the decree precipitated a Turnerian social drama: first among the people of Scanzano and the surrounding towns, then throughout the rest of the region and adjacent regions, a series of actions was carried out to thwart implementation of the decree and to have it repealed. The city hall of Scanzano was the site of a permanent public assembly; four committees formed spontaneously to coordinate protest action; people set up an encampment on the designated site for the waste dump, which became the protest's headquarters, known as the Campo Base (Base Camp); strategic roadblocks were created along the state road leading to Scanzano. In subsequent days, roads were blocked elsewhere in the region and the train station in Metaponto was blocked with citizens occupying its tracks. The road and train blocks united people of all ages and backgrounds, in the daytime with special lessons for schoolchildren and the public, and at night with music and storytelling around the bonfire. Everyday life in the region was suspended: in the coastal towns, schools and shops remained closed, rallies were held almost daily in the main square of the provincial capital, Matera; antinuclear graffiti and banners dotted the regional landscape, and the population was focused on how to combat the decree. Elsewhere I have described the initiatives the Lucanians took on a political level, but these are less relevant to the present discussion (Zinn 2007a, 2007b). At first the central government was taken by surprise by the concerted reaction, but it dismissed the protestors as a few NIMBYs and did not make any concessions. With the hardening of the government's position, the Scanzano protest as a cultural performance culminated in what was later to become known as the March of 100,000, which took place on November 23. This demonstration featured a march along eight kilometers of the state road to Scanzano and saw a participation equivalent to one-sixth of the region's population. Side by side with official delegations of city and regional governments, trade unions, environmentalist organizations, and farmers' associations, a seemingly endless flow of citizens from Basilicata and the neighboring regions marched in an atmosphere of gaiety, chanting, music, banners, and costumes. Four days later, the government struck Scanzano from the decree, to the joyous celebration of the Lucanians.

A REFLEXIVE RECONTEXTUALIZATION

As should be evident from the description above, the revolt of Scanzano was not a single public event, but actually a composite that contained within its framework numerous events, ranging from the simpler (e.g., a single piece of graffiti or a decal decrying the nuclear waste) to the very complex (such as the March of 100,000). We might thus think of it as a sort of meta-event. Yet the expressive forms and genres deployed did not arise from a tabula rasa: unscripted as it was, at the most superficial level Scanzano took a cue from several public event genres already present in contemporary Italian society: antiglobalization protest, student protest, labor union protest, political rallies, and farmers' protest. Both ritualesque and carnivalesque forms simultaneously suffused the single and encompassing events alike. I find Bakhtin's analysis to be of use in considering how the overall protest meta-event comprised a genre embracing still other genres. In Bakhtin's (1986) terms, contemporary social protest is a complex secondary sociopolitical genre that features many subsidiary primary genres. Indeed, one might suggest that this very heterogeneity makes social protest as a genre comparable to carnivalized literature, with its rejection of stylistic unity (Bakhtin 1984, 108). Yet the primary genres do not maintain their original integrity as they are recast within the secondary genre: as Bakhtin observed, "These primary genres are altered and assume a special character when they enter into complex ones" (1986, 62). Once they enter into the secondary genre, the primary genres necessarily make reference to a different realm of experience.

The Scanzano protest served as a frame that invested various expressive forms with new purpose and meaning: for genres of the everyday and the folkloric profane, some were inverted in social value, some solemnized, some ritualized. Other genres drawn from Catholic ritual instead remained fairly stable but lent themselves to the wider protest. In the analysis that follows, I will examine how the Scanzano protest centripetally integrated and hybridized various genres of cultural performance and what this meant in terms of collective participation and the external evaluation of the protest.

The participants' reflexive engagement on various levels was a crucial aspect of this performance and was transformative both of everyday practices and of the folkloric forms deployed. As Kapchan (1993) has emphasized, reflexivity is inherent in the hybrid because of the awareness of "other" within the "self." On one level, a form of hybridization was effected through the shift of context offered by the overarching frame of the revolt. In this sense, carnivalesque and ritualesque actions effected a process of *ritualization* (Bell 1992, 1997) of many everyday or unmarked elements and genres by recontextualizing them within the encompassing protest. Bauman and Briggs have pointed out that entextualization in performance is highly reflexive; texts can become marked through the conscious use of "means available to participants in performance situations to render stretches of discourse discontinuous with their discursive surround, thus making them into coherent, effective and memorable texts" (1990, 73–74). It is through this reflexive ritualization that participants were able to recontextualize and mark many otherwise undistinguished features of the protest, endowing them with transformative potency.

First, the uses of space blended ritualesque and carnivalesque forms, which worked both to sacralize the spaces of the protest (Kertzer 1996, 25) and to inhabit them with a festive communitas. The physical delimitation, occupation, and embellishment of the road and train blockades, and especially the Base Camp, worked to sacralize ordinary spaces that otherwise had no marked significance. Base Camp in particular was "domesticated": this previously abandoned stretch of land was plowed over and weeded; protestors installed tents, campers, an electrical generator, and portable toilets. Thus refounded, it became a hybrid of a sacred space, a domestic space, and a military encampment. Base Camp was not simply occupied and inhabited; it was adorned with numerous colorful banners. It was further sacralized by a ritualesque planting of olive and orange trees (in a very ceremonial fashion by Nobel Peace Prize winner Betty Williams).

These occupations of the roadblocks and Base Camp were militarist, but at the same time they also constituted spaces of leisure and the carnivalesque, free interaction among the very heterogeneous participants (see Juris 2008 for comparable examples of mixing the militarist and carnivalesque in social protest). For Bakhtin, "Carnival is a place for working out, in a concretely sensuous half-real and half-play-acted form, *a new mode of interrelationship between individuals*, counterposed to the all-powerful sociohierarchical relationships of noncarnival life" (1984, 123). The protest's sites of encampment brought various ordinary activities into a shared public setting: eating, sleeping, conversation, storytelling, music making, gathering around the bonfire; the recontextualization of these genres within the frame of the protest hybridized them, imbuing them with a communitas that extended much more widely than their everyday uses would feature. Indeed, if the carnivalesque allows the threatening to be presented without threatening (Santino 2011, 62), this was exemplified as much by the incongruous presence of mothers nursing their infants on the tracks of the Metaponto train station as by a cow grazing, tied onto those same tracks. The frame of the protest therefore turned otherwise mundane activities, but also festive activities, into acts of protest.

The sacralization of these various sites, together with carnivalesque forms that marked the territory, such as graffiti and ironic banners, produced public spaces that, like the public square, allowed for "manifest protest" (Low 2000), in which the experience of the democratic agora prevailed.[3] Especially given the paucity of mass media attention to the protest, the very mundane activity of "hanging out" in towns' main squares or in these new spaces, reinscribed within the protest frame, became a means of participating in the revolt, informing oneself and others, or being a part of the latest rally. The experience of the democratic agora during the Days of Scanzano was a particularly strong evocation of communitas. Even the genre of school lessons was recontextualized by instituting *lezioni in blocco* (roadblock lessons) at Base Camp, at the roadblocks, and in the provincial capital's main square. Teachers, university professors, and scientists held public lectures and conducted workshops regarding themes related to the protest: school and university lessons were thus not cordoned off within their lecture halls, but transposed to open spaces and shared by the wider community.[4]

As mentioned above, the reflexive stance also invested the many expressive forms in the protest that we could define as "folkloric." The protest participants drew on local dialects, traditional foodways, folk Catholicism, traditional music, and various and sundry symbols of southern peasant culture, as I will illustrate below with some specific examples. First, in order to contextualize the protestors' reflexive relationship to these forms, it is important to understand the status of folk culture in Lucanian society.

Until relatively recently (approximately the 1980s), Lucanian folk culture—described, for example in Levi's classic work but also in numerous ethnographies—was, in Alberto M. Cirese's (2006) expression, cast in terms of a *horizontal* opposition between subaltern and dominant classes.[5] With the processes of modernization over the last several decades, nonelite segments of local society experienced first a self-consciousness regarding folk culture that for many of the upwardly mobile translated into its refusal, viewing it as a source of embarrassment and a signifier of "backwardness." Since the 1990s, however, there has been a very gradual reevaluation of folk culture as it has entered into heritage-making processes, making much of it available for commodification. In 2003 these processes were less advanced than at the time of this writing, and with the exception of some artistic and intellectual vanguards, we may note that folkloric forms were characterized by a self-conscious ambivalence on the part of all but the more subaltern strata of the population. In the Scanzano protest, a reflexive stance vis-à-vis folk culture allowed those who would normally distance themselves from it to self-consciously draw upon and participate in it for powerful scripts and symbols: for example, folk Catholicism, peasant foods, dialect, and the southern brigand as folk hero. One slogan read, for example, "+ cicorie, – scorie": more chicory (*cicorie*)—a traditional peasant foodstuff, difficult to find in restaurants until the mid-1990s—and less nuclear waste (*scorie*). The performance of the revolt, in this light, enacted a new relationship to cultural heritage and local identity. The previous negative social value that folklore held for many was transformed into a source of pride and resistance in the face of the government's imperiousness. Using Cirese's scheme, we may say that the revolt shifted the previous horizontal opposition that characterized the social relations of folklore into a *vertical* opposition that pitted the local "ethnos" against the encompassing national society. For this reason, too, the reflexive recontextualization of folk culture within the protest did not necessarily entail competence in or adoption of such forms on the part of the entire population. On the contrary, in this regard there were many internal differences related to social positionality: the protest cut across multifarious differences in socioeconomic class, gender, locality, age, and political affiliation (Zinn 2007a, 2007b). Even so, it was possible to create what Kertzer (1988) has called "solidarity without consensus." Kertzer speaks of how ritual can serve political organization, producing bonds of solidarity without requiring uniformity of belief (67), to which I would also add uniformity of generic repertory and practice. Moreover, these items of folklore were reified as shared pan-regional culture, when in point of fact there are many local varieties and peculiarities. Despite the many lines of difference among the populace, all of the protest participants could potentially invest in performing the revolt according to their respective positionalities (from the Catholic devout to the antiglobalization radical Left, from the consolidated bourgeoisie to the peasant, and including participants from other southern regions), with each contribution being appreciated as part of the overall effort.

BENDING CATHOLIC RITUAL

In my previous analyses of the Scanzano protest, I mentioned the influence of the Catholic Church. However, through the consideration of the carnivalesque and the ritualesque that I am elaborating here, I would like to reevaluate the role of Catholicism as part of the cultural performance of protest in Scanzano. Again, taking such forms seriously suggests that the church as an institution played more than a minor role in sustaining and legitimizing the popular protest, and that Catholic ritual was anything but noninstrumental (see Santino 2011, 63).

Although Roman Catholicism has no longer been Italy's state religion since the 1984 reform of the Lateran Pacts, it continues to wield substantial influence in the Italian public sphere. At the level of public events, the church often blends its voice with that of the Italian state, as for example when a prelate blesses a new public building or public work at an inauguration or ribbon-cutting ceremony. Masses are often held within the framework of state ceremonies, as for example in state funerals or various sorts of commemorations. During the events of Scanzano, however, the church took a solid position in favor of the Lucanians and against the government's decree. In several instances, Catholic ritual forms were bent to the ends of the protest, though deployed in earnest and not in the parodic or subversive manner of the carnivalesque.

Don Filippo Lombardi, a parish priest of Scanzano, emerged as a charismatic figure who crucially represented the church in this meta-event. Early on in the revolt, he opened a local church to host one of the antiwaste action committees that had formed, but his influence was felt more directly by the populace as the protest mounted. In one of the most dramatic episodes of the fifteen days, on November 17 the train station of Metaponto was occupied in order to block any incoming trains from the north that might bring radioactive waste. As news of the occupation spread, people gradually joined in; the occupation eventually involved an estimated 1,000 men, women, and children. The prefect telephoned the organizers from Matera, urging them to remove the blockade, and when his request was refused, police showed up in antiriot gear for a dramatic showdown that seriously risked degenerating into violence. Don Filippo played a fundamental role in calming the tensions; as one leftist trade union leader described it, "He warned against accepting the provocations, almost as if he were saying Mass or holy songs. He maintained peace and tranquility in that moment" (Montemurro 2004, 89, author's trans.). Don Filippo actually did lead a rosary and people prayed in a scene in which, as he later recalled, the train tracks were "like an outdoor church" (Soave 2006, 83). In this way, Catholic ritual not only sacralized the space of the protest in its own fashion, but also lent the church's moral authority to the citizens protesting. As I argued in an earlier analysis (Zinn 2007a), one of the key struggles of the Lucanians was to affirm the struggle as an alternative "moral economy," and contest the depiction of their claims as particularist "NIMBY" demands.[6]

On November 18, the day after the Metaponto blockade was instituted, a Via Crucis procession was held in Scanzano: a life-size cross used in a parish church for Good Friday was borne in a slow, ritually halting procession, and was subsequently planted at the turnoff for Terzo Cavone, where the nuclear waste storage facility was to be located. The timing of the Via Crucis was not at all coincidental: November 18 was the day of national mourning for the nineteen carabinieri who perished in a suicide attack at Nassirya, Iraq, on November 12. The Lucanians, in fact, accused the government of taking advantage of the national shock over Nassirya to slyly pass the nuclear waste decree the very night of November 12, although it was not on the official agenda of the Council of Ministers. By performing a Catholic ritual, again, the protestors were able to assert the moral authority of their position, with the Via Crucis honoring the carabinieri's sacrifice and attest to the people's patriotism while also serving as a metaphor for the people's agony over what they perceived to be a nuclear threat.

We may see the role of folk Catholicism in the protest in yet another instance: the procession of a statue of the Madonna of Loreto, which took place on November 21. The statue had stopped in Potenza on a tour and its next scheduled stop was Matera, but given the situation of the protest its itinerary was changed: the statue made a stop in Metaponto and then led a candlelight procession to Terzo Cavone in Scanzano, site of the planned waste storage facility, arriving at 1 a.m. Over 2,000 "anti–nuclear waste" rosaries, financed by a local donor and blessed by Don Filippo, were distributed among the people who prayed to the Madonna. Hailed as fortuitous, the visit of the Madonna—a black Madonna, herself strongly symbolic of the land and part of a long history of pre-Catholic worship in an agrarian society—was celebrated with a ritual of popular devotion.

We should therefore consider the role that Catholicism played in the protest as, again, not mere ornament to what took place in Scanzano. Nor were folk Catholic forms some quaint, picturesque touch to the protest, as was suggested in some subtly ironic journalistic accounts that "othered" the protestors. These genres were incorporated into the overall protest but maintained much of their original boundedness and thus avoided a carnivalesque hybridization. We may instead observe that through the active support of the clergy, Catholic ritual practices were "bent" through their recontextualization, as executed by the people who partook in them: reinscribing biblical citations with a view to defending the Lucanians; sacralizing the cause and its physical space through the habitus of prayer and procession; advocating peaceful "civic" protest befitting loyal citizens of the Italian state.

FIGHTING THE GOOD FIGHT: THE OFFICIAL AND THE CARNIVALESQUE

A civic protest befitting loyal citizens of the Italian state: this was what even pro-government critics of the Scanzano revolt had to concede when all was said and done and the decree was modified. And yet, in the heat of the protest, this outcome was anything but to be taken for granted: the government, its allies, and many commentators in the northern regions cast aspersions on the protestors as NIMBYs who were unwilling to accept their role for the national good. Many feared that the protest would get out of hand, become another Reggio (a reference to four days of violent tumult in Reggio Calabria in 1972). Indeed, the protestors themselves were in a constant state of tension over the threat of violence, either on the part of the state or by hotheads within the movement.

These tensions were carefully negotiated by the mixing of ritualesque and carnivalesque genres within the cultural performance of the Scanzano revolt as a meta-event. For the two weeks of the protest's duration, time took on a strongly liminal quality, in which the day-to-day routine was suspended as the population's actions gradually mounted and people awaited developments with baited breath. Liminality did not mean anarchy, however: the protest featured a self-organized military design and practice. The carnivalesque injected the atmosphere with gaiety that helped allay the real anxiety and fear felt by the population, and it also advanced the protestors' position through a skillful use of irony and parody. At the same time, just as Catholic ritual added authority to the cause, ritualesque forms—including those put forward by local institutions—added civic gravitas to the revolt.

Official representatives of local and regional governments effected their own sacralization of the space of Scanzano by declaring it the symbolic capital of the region. The ritualesque forms of conducting business of provincial and regional council meetings were also "bent" to the protest by being held in Scanzano. During many of these public gatherings and demonstrations, the Italian national anthem was struck up. Unlike the more impervious Catholic ritual, however, within the liminal context of the protest, the carnivalesque sometimes invaded these official spaces, as when a mock funeral was performed by students who carried a coffin bearing a doll into the Scanzano town hall, but also more generally through an anomalous (in Italian, *irrituale*) public participation in official meetings. Perhaps such ambiguities of genre between the official domain and the carnivalesque were at least in part tied to ambivalences and suspicions widely held among the people regarding the real role of some local politicians in the affair.[7]

Alongside the actions taken by local politicians in official arenas, the Lucanian resistance found its guiding military metaphor in the figure of the *brigante* (brigand), which was invoked in numerous carnivalesque slogans and banners: this was a reference to nineteenth-century post-Unification brigands who fought the new Piedmontese state, constituting a form of revolt throughout southern Italy that lasted for several years before being violently repressed by the central government. I have explored elsewhere the figure of the brigand in a new, revisionist history of southern Italy (Zinn 2007b); suffice it here to say that the appreciation of the brigand as a folk hero in southern society is a relatively new phenomenon. The brigand as symbol of the Scanzano protest was present in a multivocal capacity: it voiced the earnestness of the people's will to self-defense—with all of the military tactics and practice that this implied. Even so, this defense was somehow more spontaneous and "scrappy" in comparison with the government's militarism, led by the Piedmontese military strategist General Carlo Jean, the designated nuclear waste commissioner. Inverting a negative stereotype of the south, the multivocal symbol of the brigand allowed for an investment on the part of multiple positionalities: for leftists in particular, its guerrilla connotation favored comparisons to the Zapatistas of Chiapas, with whom a twinning was formed subsequently; for others, it echoed a pro-southern pride in the face of perceived northern injustice; the brigand also voiced some people's faith in cunning (*furbizia*)—valued in local culture—that would hoodwink the government's more powerful, organized forces.[8]

In the end, the tensions within the movement remained quiescent, and the expression of protest reached its apogee in the March of 100,000 on

November 23. The event—itself a complex hybrid drawing together of simpler genres—was an imposing parade stretching over several kilometers of the state road to Scanzano that featured compact official delegations of local governments (mayors in their ceremonial *tricolore* sash, local police, standard-bearers), trade unions, political parties, and various other associations carrying their own flags and banners. Some towns were also represented by their marching bands.[9] Side by side and interspersed with these "ritualesque" actors, ordinary citizens marched, chanted, and conversed in the brilliant sunshine of an autumn day, as did others who gave a more "carnivalesque" spin to their participation by donning grotesque costumes of imagined "nuclear" monsters, or by carrying rainbow peace flags or colorful, ironic banners (often in dialect). These activities found a musical accompaniment in the rough music that pounded out of mobile sound systems, but local folk music elements like the *campanaccio* and *zampogna* were also deployed as rough music in the recontextualization of the protest.[10] In the final stretch of the march, protestors adopted an improvised form of rough music by tapping on the road's guardrail. Tractors, trucks, and other vehicles were also decked out with banners and flags and mobilized in the march.

The March of 100,000 was carnivalesque in its imposing, kaleidoscopic multifariousness, a collective bricolage that constituted the highest moment of the protest's communitas, cutting across the many lines of difference present in this fractious community. The Lucanians themselves were surprised by this group effort, which buoyed them for a few more days until the government finally surrendered. Drawing together such different forms of cultural performance, both carnivalesque and ritualesque, the march demonstrated a determined yet civic front that was able to make its "moral economy" hold sway.

CONCLUSION

For the Lucanians, the events of the Days of Scanzano marked a before and an after. The protest itself has been ritualized, celebrated annually in commemorative ceremonies and invoked in later protests. Certainly, the communitas produced in the course of the struggle has proved difficult to sustain subsequently. In his analysis of antiglobalization protest, Jeffrey Juris (2008) effectively demonstrates how what he calls "affective solidarity" becomes heightened through ritual forms in social protest. Juris posits an inverse relationship between the intensity of this Durkheimian affective solidarity and its ability to be sustained over the longer term, and indeed, Scanzano would seem to fit this pattern.

I have attempted here to play with the notions of the carnivalesque and ritualesque in Scanzano, because this seems a potentially fruitful means of offering a new contribution above and beyond a widely proposed hermeneutic model in which such "cultural material" (Benford and Snow 2000) affects the "collective action frames" that construct reality, or a linear model in which three aspects follow suit: ritual, emotion, mobilization. Hart's (1996) discussion of culture in social movement stakes out a similarly mentalist approach, proposing the consideration of rituals among things provided by "cultural forms" in movements, but does not consider how rituals may actually *act* upon participants and the social setting. Certainly ritual can play a role in evoking emotions that stir movement activists (Taylor and Whittier 1995; Juris 2008). Though this observation at times seems to depict ritual as inducing emotions as a Pavlovian response, I think that at least with regard to Scanzano, a process that Handelman describes as *autopoiesis* may be initiated: "One may argue . . . that a ritual produces the persons that will produce the ritual as that ritual produces them" (Handelman 2005, 11). In this sense, it is possible that the forging of a collectivity in the protest, which invoked a wider southern Italian collectivity, was a real by-product of the main goal of the protest's action to defeat the decree, thereby "reontologizing" participants (Kapferer 2005).

I wish to conclude with one last thought on the Scanzano protest: we must consider the power of ritual as efficacious in the eyes of the participants. Reflecting back on the events, clerical protagonist Don Filippo Lombardi said: "What did I do after the victory? I got in my car and I left the crowd. I went to Loreto to thank the Madonna" (Soave 2006, 84, author's trans.).

NOTES

1. However, there have been some works that are exceptions to the overall tendency: Reed 2005; Holland, Fox, and Daro 2008; Hufford 2010.

2. A third transformative aspect of the protest (which, however, cannot be explored here) might be the personal transformation of many unemployed youths and women who were individually empowered through their participation in the protest.

3. Low draws a direct connection between public space and the possibilities for democratic politics. Bakhtin (1984, 128–30), too, speaks of the public square in carnival.

4. The *lezione in piazza* (lesson in the square) is a stock element of many student protests in Italy.

5. See, for example, Ernesto de Martino's studies of magic (1959) and funeral lament (1958) in Basilicata.

6. The accusation of NIMBYism is akin to what Holland, Fox, and Daro 2008 have termed an "alter version" of movement identity on the part of outsiders.

7. For details regarding the controversies surrounding the local politicians, especially Scanzano mayor Mario Altieri, see Zinn 2007a; Minicuci 2012.
8. On *furbizia*, see Zinn 2001.
9. As a genre, the marching band performance is itself rather complex: associated with a local territory, such bands most often perform during the celebrations of patron saint festivals.
10. The *campanaccio* is a large cowbell, but the term also refers to the traditional festival of the Lucanian villages of San Mauro Forte (see Scaldaferri 2005). The *campanaccio* takes place in the period of Saint Anthony Abbot (January 17) and inaugurates the carnival season; during the event, squads of people march crisscross through the village, ringing their synchronized bells in a loud, steady rhythm, while festival participants enjoy wine and sausages. *Campanaccio* also play a role in rituals held in the same period in the village of Tricarico, with participants masquerading as cows and bulls. The *zampogna* is an Italian bagpipe, and there is a strong tradition of *zampogna* crafting and music in the Pollino mountain area of western Basilicata.

REFERENCES

Appadurai, Arjun. 2013. *The Future as Cultural Fact: Essays on the Global Condition*. London: Verso.
Bakhtin, M. M. 1981. *The Dialogic Imagination: Four Essays*. Edited by Michael Holquist. Translated by Caryl Emerson and Michael Holquist. Austin: University of Texas Press.
Bakhtin, Mikhail. 1984. *Problems of Dostoevsky's Poetics*. Minneapolis: University of Minnesota Press.
Bakhtin, Mikhail. 1986. *Speech Genres and Other Late Essays*. Austin: University of Texas Press.
Banfield, Edward. 1958. *The Moral Basis of a Backward Society*. Glencoe, IL: Free Press.
Bauman, Richard, and Charles Briggs. 1990. "Poetics and Performance as Critical Perspective on Language and Social Life." *Annual Review of Anthropology* 19 (1): 59–88. http://dx.doi.org/10.1146/annurev.an.19.100190.000423.
Bell, Catherine. 1992. *Ritual Theory, Ritual Practice*. Oxford: Oxford University Press.
Bell, Catherine. 1997. *Ritual: Perspectives and Dimensions*. Oxford: Oxford University Press.
Benford, Robert D., and David A. Snow. 2000. "Framing Processes and Social Movements: An Overview and Assessment." *Annual Review of Sociology* 26 (1): 611–39. http://dx.doi.org/10.1146/annurev.soc.26.1.611.
Blee, Kathleen, and Amy McDowell. 2012. "Social Movement Audiences." *Sociological Forum* 27 (1): 1–20. http://dx.doi.org/10.1111/j.1573-7861.2011.01299.x.
Cirese, Alberto M. (Original work published 1971) 2006. *Cultura egemonica e culture subalterne*. Palermo: Palumbo.
de Martino, Ernesto. 1958. *Morte e pianto rituale nel mondo antico*. Turin: Bollati Boringhieri.
de Martino, Ernesto. 1959. *Sud e magia*. Milan: Feltrinelli.
Edelman, Marc. 2001. "Social Movements: Changing Paradigms and Forms of Politics." *Annual Review of Anthropology* 30 (1): 285–317. http://dx.doi.org/10.1146/annurev.anthro.30.1.285.
Handelman, Don. 1990. *Models and Mirrors: Towards an Anthropology of Public Events*. Oxford: Berghahn Books.
Handelman, Don. 2005. "Introduction: Why Ritual in Its Own Right? How So?" In *Ritual in Its Own Right: Exploring the Dynamics of Transformation*, ed. Don Handelman and Galina Lindquist, 1–32. Oxford: Berghahn Books.

Hart, Stephen. 1996. "The Cultural Dimension of Social Movements: A Theoretical Reassessment and Literature Review." *Sociology of Religion* 57 (1): 87–100. http://dx.doi.org/10.2307/3712006.
Holland, Dorothy, Gretchen Fox, and Vinci Daro. 2008. "Social Movements and Collective Identity: A Decentered, Dialogic View." *Anthropological Quarterly* 81 (1): 95–126. http://dx.doi.org/10.1353/anq.2008.0001.
Hufford, Mary. 2010. "Carnival Time in the Kingdom of Coal." *Social Identities* 16 (4): 559–81. http://dx.doi.org/10.1080/13504630.2010.498255.
Johnston, Hank. 2009. "Protest Cultures: Performance, Artifacts and Ideations." In *Culture, Social Movements and Protest*, ed. Hank Johnston, 3–32. Burlington, VT: Ashgate.
Johnston, Hank, and Bert Klandermans, eds. 1995. *Social Movements and Culture*. Minneapolis: University of Minnesota Press.
Juris, Jeffrey S. 2008. "Performing Politics: Image, Embodiment and Affective Solidarity during Anti-corporate Globalization Protests." *Ethnography* 9 (1): 61–97. http://dx.doi.org/10.1177/1466138108088949.
Kapchan, Deborah A. 1993. "Hybridization and the Marketplace: Emerging Paradigms in Folkloristics." *Western Folklore* 52 (2/4): 303–26. http://dx.doi.org/10.2307/1500092.
Kapferer, Bruce. 2005. "Ritual Dynamics and Virtual Practice: Beyond Representation and Meaning." In *Ritual in Its Own Right: Exploring the Dynamics of Transformation*, ed. Don Handelman and Galina Lindquist, 35–54. Oxford: Berghahn Books.
Kertzer, David I. 1988. *Ritual, Politics and Power*. New Haven: Yale University Press.
Kertzer, David I. 1996. *Politics and Symbols: The Italian Communist Party and the Fall of Communism*. New Haven: Yale University Press.
Kurzman, Charles. 2008. "Introduction: Meaning-making in Social Movements." *Anthropological Quarterly* 81 (1): 5–15. http://dx.doi.org/10.1353/anq.2008.0003.
Levi, Carlo. (Original work published 1945) 1990. *Christ Stopped at Eboli*. New York: Penguin Classics.
Lombardi Satriani, Luigi M. 1966. *Il folklore come cultura di contestazione*. Messina: Peloritana.
Low, Setha. 2000. *On the Plaza: The Politics of Public Space and Culture*. Austin: University of Texas Press.
Minicuci, Maria. 2012. *Politica e politiche: Etnografia di un paese di riforma; Scanzano Jonico*. Rome: CISU—Centro d'Informazione e Stampa Universitaria.
Montemurro, Rossella. 2004. *I giorni di Scanzano: Cronaca di un accidente nucleare*. Rome: Ediesse.
Peake, Bryce. 2010. "He Is Dead, and He Is Continuing to Die: A Feminist Psycho-Semiotic Reflection on Men's Embodiment of Metaphor in a Toronto Zombie Walk." *Journal of Contemporary Anthropology* 1 (1): 49–70.
Reed, T. V. 2005. *The Art of Protest: Culture and Activism from the Civil Rights Movement to the Streets of Seattle*. Minneapolis: University of Minnesota Press.
Santino, Jack. 2011. "The Carnivalesque and the Ritualesque." *Journal of American Folklore* 124 (491): 61–73. http://dx.doi.org/10.5406/jamerfolk.124.491.0061.
Scaldaferri, Nicola, ed. 2005. *Santi, animali e suoni: Feste dei Campanacci a Tricarico e San Mauro Forte*. Udine: Nota/GEOS CD Book.
Soave, Edmondo. 2006. *Dopo Scanzano: Storia di scorie*. Venosa: Osanna.
Taylor, Verta, and Nancy Whittier. 1995. "Analytical Approaches to Social Movement Culture: The Culture of the Women's Movement." In *Social Movements and Culture*, ed. Hank Johnson and Bert Klandermans, 163–87. Minneapolis: University of Minnesota Press.
Zinn, Dorothy L. 2001. *La raccomandazione: Clientelismo vecchio e nuovo*. Rome: Donzelli.
Zinn, Dorothy L. 2007a. "Il caso di Scanzano: La ragione di stato e le ragioni di una ribellione." *Quaderni di Sociologia* 51 (44): 151–74. http://dx.doi.org/10.4000/qds.933.

Zinn, Dorothy. 2007b. "I Quindici Giorni di Scanzano: Identity and Social Protest in the New South." *Journal of Modern Italian Studies* 12 (2): 189–206. http://dx.doi.org/10.1080/13545710701298233.

12

"Some Are Born Green, Some Achieve Greenness"
Protest Theater and Environmental Activism

Scott Magelssen

Oɴᴇ ꜰɪɴᴇ ʟᴀᴛᴇ Sᴇᴘᴛᴇᴍʙᴇʀ Sᴀᴛᴜʀᴅᴀʏ ᴇᴠᴇɴɪɴɢ in Stratford-upon-Avon in 2012, audiences gathered to see the Royal Shakespeare Company's production of William Shakespeare's *Twelfth Night*. As the spectators found their seats in the three-quarters in-the-round auditorium, a small band of actors mounted the stage and began delivering broad and somewhat familiar dialogue in iambic pentameter. A fop in yellow cross-gartered stockings and an enormous yellow and green Elizabethan ruff collar (looking distinctly like the British Petroleum logo had been wrapped around the actor's neck) led off:

> If oil be the fuel for us, drill on;
> Give us excess of it, that, surfeiting,
> The planet may sicken, and so die.
> Let's drill again! And cast a dying pall,
> O'er the tar sands of sweet Canada,
> The Arctic and the Gulf of Mexico,
> Stealing and screwing over.

The lines, a playful take on Duke Orsino's first lines of *Twelfth Night*, were here delivered by a representation of BP, the oil multinational that served as a major sponsor for the Royal Shakespeare Company's World Shakespeare Festival in 2012, as well as for the Tate Galleries, the British Museum, and London's Olympic Games (Cooper 2012)—and the company responsible for the worst oil spill–related ecological disaster in human history with the Deepwater Horizon catastrophe of 2010, which devastated ecosystems in the Gulf of Mexico and continues to impact human health in the area's coastal communities. Although the actors occupied only the dim and moody splash of the preshow lighting, they had the full attention of the audience, drawing applause, appreciative laughter, and playful boos at the mention of the oil company. A Royal Shakespeare Company stage manager demanded in a no-nonsense tone from the foot of the thrust stage that they cease this unscheduled work of guerrilla theater, but the actors continued with their parody, not stopping until they had delivered a full two and a half minutes of eco-protest. Enter Feste, with the biting voice of reason reserved for Shakespeare's fools, who called the Royal Shakespeare Company out on its complicity with corporate greed and the plundering of the Earth's fossil fuels:

> Alas, poor RSC, how hath BP baffled thee?
> Thou hast made contract of eternal bond
> With a notable pirate, a deepwater thief!
> Art thou mad, to profit from such a dissembler?
> For some are born green, some achieve greenness,
> And some purchase a semblance of greenness by sponsoring cultural events.

The brief prologue culminated with the allegorical character named RSC convinced of her mistake: "I would I were well rid of this knavery. Out, damned logo!" she cried, ceremoniously tearing the BP logo from the RSC program clutched in her upstage hand. The audience responded with generous laughter and applause. "You have seen a performance of the Reclaim Shakespeare Company," announced the actor playing Feste. "If you share our concern about BP's sponsorship of the arts, please join us in ripping out the logo of the program."

To the Reclaim Shakespeare Company, the *other* RSC, BP was using the imprimatur of corporate sponsorship of the arts as an abominable act of dishonest impression management, a "greenwashing" that performatively absolved the global corporate giant from its crimes against nature and human health. This was one of several infiltrations of Royal Shakespeare Company productions that summer (the "summer of our discontent"), always in the half preshow light, always soliciting laughter and applause, even supportive whoops. The players circulated outside the venue at intermission and after the performances they came around with buckets to collect the torn-out logos as a kind of yardstick to gauge the success of their campaign.

In November of that year, after BP admitted guilt in the Deepwater Horizon disaster and faced fourteen criminal charges (and agreed to pay $4.5 billion in fines, the largest set of corporate legal damages in global history), the Royal Shakespeare Company purportedly ended its brief relationship with the company, indicating in a statement to the *Independent*, "We have no further sponsorship [with BP] confirmed" (Climate Radio 2012). Reclaim Shakespeare Company claimed victory with this announcement, true to form, with a flash mob organized in the Great Court of London's British Museum (Shakespeare 2012), BP's sponsorship of which they were also protesting, drawing a bright, bold connection between environmental activist protest and real measurable change in public perception, and celebrating a small but important dismantling of such "greenwashing" of corporate offenses through sponsorship of the arts.

In this essay I will look at this stepping across the line of decorum, this in-your-face action, this deliberate appropriation (and reworking) of the conventions of already established public spectacle. One of the compelling aspects of protest performance is that each event functions as an occasion in and of itself, and at the same time as an infiltration and a co-optation of (or a performative acknowledgment of and resistance to) the elements and aesthetics of already standardized occasions, like the production of a stage play, for maximum impact. In the following pages I consider examples of this phenomenon in which, like the Reclaim Shakespeare Company's protest of the RSC partnership with BP, radical activist performance groups have captured the world's attention through strategic and highly visible acts of engagement—and offer some initial responses and questions that I hope will add to and nuance our understanding of the ways in which radical performative acts of protest can be successful and efficacious in modes different from both traditional theater and traditional forms of environmental advocacy.

Some explanation is necessary before I continue. Protest performances are often theatrical in nature; some of them partake more fully in what is recognized as standard theater than others. That is, protest performances may involve skits, reenactments, and such properties as costume and music. Even public performances such as parades or traditions such as mumming are referred to as "street theatre" (Mount 2014, n.p.). Throughout the present volume, we see instances of such performances that Jack Santino terms "ritualesque," in that they are aimed at social change. In this chapter, I wish to extend that idea to more traditional theatrical presentations. Here, rather than street theater being recognized as "like real theater," we see the ritualesque use of theatrical performances, and will examine the porous boundaries within and among them.

In Seattle, Washington, where this essay was written, the landfill bins in apartment complexes hardly need emptying. Nearly everything plastic in Seattle—what plastic there still is, with the green packaging now widely available—is recyclable. Single-driver commuting, reports the *Seattle Times*, is way down as more and more students and workers use bikes or public transportation (Westneat 2013).

Nevertheless, while eco-friendly lifestyles have become increasingly easy and indeed celebrated in the popular media, the worst environmental offenses persist, and are ramping up all over the planet. Fracking, poisonous emissions, deforestation, overfarming and other resource decimation, dumping, wild animal displacement (Chaudhuri 2012, 46), and human-made ecological disasters on a global scale are prompting activist performers to get the attention not just of everyday consumers, but of the legislative and corporate powers that be, and they do this in ways that range from peaceful performance protests to guerrilla resistance.[1] There are certainly corners of mainstream dramatic theater that have been concerned with environmental issues for some time. Indeed, our Western canon of dramatic literature is filled with plays that address humans' relationship with nature. Think of Ibsen's *Enemy of the People*. Or the *Noah's Flood* plays from the medieval English mystery cycles. Theater historian Downing Cless (2011) in fact has traced ecological concerns through plays from the Greeks through Shakespeare to Brecht and Beckett.

But in the past two decades, theater scholars concerned with drama's engagement with ecological issues have challenged mainstream theater's efficacy in achieving real political and social action when it comes to the crises facing Earth and its atmosphere today. Eco-critical scholar Una Chaudhuri, in a foundational 1994 article in *Theater* magazine, leveled a provocative challenge to dramatists and audiences. In brief: don't just use nature and its ills as a backdrop, a macrocosm to deal with human stories (think *King Lear* on the heath telling the winds to crack their cheeks). To "use ecology as a metaphor is to block the theater's approach to the deeply vexed problem of classification that lies at the heart of ecological philosophy: are we human beings—and our activities, such as theater—an integral part of nature, or are we somehow radically separate from it?" (Chaudhuri 1994, 27).

In fact, the subdiscipline of eco-criticism in theater interrogates the very notion, in place at least since the Enlightenment and having its origins in our earliest human stories in the West, that culture is *distinct* from nature, and that the latter needs to be feared, braved, conquered, tamed, and exploited for human benefit. I call your attention to the divine mandate in the book of Genesis in the Hebrew Bible and the Christian Old Testament, that "Man Shall Have Dominion over the Earth" (Genesis 1:27–29). Instead, eco-criticism views the Western ideas of "nature" and "culture" as social constructions, an imaginary binary that denies both scientific evidence and the dangers of such a paradigm in order to justify a status quo and set of protocols that threaten to undo us all. Evernden argues that "the entity [nature] we take for granted as an objective reality has, in fact, a complex origin as a social creation" (Evernden 1992, 109). And as Glen Love puts it, "Ecological thinking . . . requires us to take the nonhuman world as seriously as previous modes of criticism have taken the human realm of society and culture" (Love 2003, 47).

Such a trenchant binary has pitted human beings and what we call nature against one another. The effects over the last few thousand years of this discursive and philosophical disregard for the Earth and its atmosphere, argue eco-critical scholars, has had dire consequences, from deforestation to pollution and global climate change, from animal and human displacement with the damming of rivers and the devastation of the land to global sea-level changes and flooding that are immersing islands formerly populated by human and nonhuman animals.

Taking their cue from early eco-critical scholars in the mid-1990s like Chaudhuri, Bonnie Marranca, and Erika Munk, followed by Theresa J. May, Wendy Arons, Elinor Fuchs, Cless, Sarah Standing, and Baz Kershaw, theater scholars and practitioners have been committing to using theater and performance to more forcefully deal with and to alert and educate audiences about the real environmental problems caused by human beings' behavior.[2] Downing Cless founded the Underground Railway Theatre in Boston, and Theresa May organized EMOS (Earth Matters on Stage), a regular eco-drama symposium and festival (Earth Matters on Stage n.d.).[3] Concomitantly, artists like Rachel Rosenthal, Holly Hughes, Deak Weaver, Moe Beitiks, and Isabella Rossillini have focused on human beings' treatment of the rest of nature and other living beings in their work (see especially May 2007).

Theater, as we know, is a powerful communication tool and, as Cless's work demonstrates, human beings have always looked to drama for the metaphors and narratives by which they can understand nature and its crises. Cless, in "Eco-Theatre, USA," reminds us, "Crisis, of course, is dramatic and dramatic metaphors are used by the media to describe environmental incidents" (Cless 1996, 79). Cless's article inventories several eco-theater pieces over the last decades, including Seattle Public Theater's 1991 play *Timber*, an adaptation by Bryan Willis of the Federal Theatre Project's tradition of the Living Newspaper that treated Deforestation (80–81), and community-specific plays like Cherrie Moraga's 1992 *Heroes and Saints*, about pesticides killing Latino field workers, and Kalamu ya Salaam's 1995 *The Breath of Life*, which treats a string of petrochemical plants in an area dubbed Cancer Alley poisoning largely African American workers in southeastern Louisiana. Cless concludes, "These pieces tend toward a high degree of theatricality, perhaps because puppetry, masks, commedia dell'arte, pageantry, and direct ways of implicating the audience . . . lend themselves easily to the sizeable ideas that the environmental crisis engenders and the changes it requires."[4] Plays that are issue oriented and focused on communicating with audiences commonly have "broad acting, with musical numbers and a strong plot," that is, they are not necessarily great art: not chewy, complicated, ambivalent, and open to interpretation. Other common elements are simplicity and directness (what he calls "rough style," drawing on Peter Brook's rough theater), episodic structure, audience involvement, documentary reference, and activist protagonists with whom we identify. I would add here a couple of more recent performances like the activist company Bread and Puppet's recent skits protesting fracking, and *The Way of Water*, by Caridad Svich, about the effects of the Deepwater Horizon spill on Gulf coastal communities, staged readings of which have been held all over the world in the past two years, including one in which I participated in the spring of 2012 at Bowling Green State University in Ohio (Svich 2012).

But a play concerned with nature may not be the best and most efficacious tool for change, and the jury is out on whether traditional theater can achieve change on the scale it desires. Nor does it promise to reach wide audiences outside of those who have bought tickets, presumably because many of them already support the production and the viewpoint it advances. Furthermore, it is worth noting here that what we in drama seldom like to admit is that the enterprise of live theater itself, in particular professional and academic theater, is not very "green." In an essay in Wendy Arons and Theresa J. May's recent collection *Readings in Performance and Ecology*, Ian Garrett writes that theater is in fact pretty *bad* at being green. "We approach theatrical production with a sense of imminent impermanence: we only expect our shows to last for a few short weeks . . . In building a home, the integration of sustainable materials and technologies can be the guiding design concept. Theatrical design looks to dramaturgy and primatizes serving the text of the dramatic work. There is no reason to expect these conceptual practices to align" (2012, 201–2). When we choose materials for Nora's kitchen counters, Garrett writes, "we are not thinking granite vs. lumber, but about the most cost-effective choice to serve the play" (202). He compares the four-by-eight sheet of Lauan plywood sourced from deforested Philippines mahogany, which cost $9.95 at Home Depot at the time of his writing, to the same size sheet of Forest Stewardship Council (FSC)–certified medium density fiberboard at $21.95. And our incandescent stage lighting is easier to control aesthetically than LED, but it's a terribly inefficient use of energy.[5]

Here's where a more radical mode of environmentally conscious theater comes in. According to eco-critical scholar Sarah Ann Standing, traditional environmental advocacy groups like the Sierra Club, the Natural Resources Defense Council, and the Nature Conservancy follow the rules governing due process for change laid out by the system. Groups like these lobby, write letters, and invest in public education. But because the system is slow, bureaucratic, time intensive, and requires immense amounts of labor, fund-raising, and other resources, they often need to find compromises to accomplish positive political action. Standing cites the recent example of the Sierra Club pulling out of the protest of Arizona's Glen Canyon Dam in order to assure the preservation of Echo Park in Dinosaur National Monument in Colorado (2012, 153–54). Radical activist groups, however, step outside these processes as structured and policed by the system. They include Earth First! Greenpeace, Earth Liberation Front, Friends of the Earth, and Sea Shepherd Society. Radical groups like this find their battleground outside of traditional social structures and rules, and their tactics include behavior that breaks the law. Standing points out that Earth First!'s motto is "No Compromise in Defense of Mother Earth," (148) and she cites activities such as marring fast food restaurant windows with glass-etching cream or slashing the tires of SUVs. Other radical acts of environmental protest that may come immediately to mind are the practice of People for the Ethical Treatment of Animals and Animal Liberation Front of throwing red paint on fur coats or the dousing of the butter cow with fake blood at the Iowa State Fair by Iowans for Animal Liberation in the summer of 2013 (Berman 2013). Aiden Ricketts (n.d.) refers to these performances as "Direct Action," "more deliberate in its theatrical component than traditional forms of protest such as marches and rallies [and] a highly visual form of protest that not only presents an image of dissent, as all protests do, but that also frequently involves very physical acts with immediate consequences"—and that empowers participants themselves to become agents of change.

Such performative acts are why the FBI classifies such groups as domestic terrorism, as it did with Earth Liberation Front in 2001 (Standing 2012, 48). Activist groups will respond that they're not hooligans committing untargeted and "ethically ambiguous" vandalism; they break laws they feel are unjust in order to expose them. Standing argues that radical groups also break the law with their performances to "make the illegal spectacular," insofar as their acts are "provocative, amusing, interesting, and, perhaps, more palatable, [and] as a result, also serve to bring into view a perspective the public might not be fully ready to consider or appreciate" (149).

Radical eco-activist performance, according to Standing, "finds roots in situationist art, agit prop, farce, and performance art, as well as Dada and Futurism. All of these artistic movements," she writes, "make powerful and paradigm shifting interventions in social and political culture. If we understand ecoactivism as artistic practice as well as political action, we can similarly frame such activism as attempts to shift our paradigms and *ways of seeing* (as well as stunts aimed at shaping political opinion)" (2012, 148).

The main case study in Standing's essay is the eco-action Crack the Dam in 1981, a performance event on the spring equinox in which the activist collective Earth First! infiltrated the top of the Glen Canyon Dam, an immense hydroelectric facility (the third highest in the world) that plugged the Colorado River and flooded the colorful canyon for which it is named with the man-made Lake Powell, the second-largest man-made lake in the United States. In addition to blighting the scenic natural landscape, the dam disrupted the natural ebb and flow of the Colorado River and has threatened destructive flooding when the facility is not able to accommodate snowmelt at a fast enough rate during years with higher temperatures. It goes without saying that, with global climate change, it would appear these years of higher temperature will, in fact, be occurring at an increasing rate.

Seventy-five Earth First! activists watched from a bridge three miles away that sunny March day as four men and one woman occupied the top of the dam and unfurled a 300-foot length of black plastic held together with rope and 1,000 feet of duct tape, 12 feet wide at the top and tapering down to a 2-foot point over the downstream side, making it appear as if Glen Canyon Dam had suffered an immense crack. The action was followed by an impassioned speech delivered by environmentalist Edward Abbey (author of *The Monkey Wrench Gang*) from the back of a pickup truck to the gathered crowd. Images of the crack flooded the wire services, disseminating news of the action across the country (Standing 2012, 151).

The now-famous protest did not have what we might consider a direct effect on the site in question. The dam still stands today, in spite of continued criticism and calls for decommission. But, importantly, it served as a model for eco-protest theater in the years to come. This was Earth First!'s initial eco-action, but the group's members went on to initiate the first U.S. tree-sitting protests when member Mikal Jakubal strapped himself to a Douglas fir in old-growth forest in Wilamette National Forest in Oregon, which was in the process of being clear cut by logging companies. Earth First! has since protested at dozens of sites, including ski resorts and nuclear power plants, and has inspired several other activist groups and countless individuals.

But perhaps most compellingly, five years ago, workers began tearing down the Glines Canyon Dam in Port Angeles, Washington, which for decades had been preventing salmon from getting to their ancient spawning grounds. This came in part because of a lawsuit brought to spectacular attention by an anonymous group in 1987, which itself infiltrated and simulated a crack with black paint down the front of the dam, a reprise of Earth First!'s initial action at the Glen Canyon Dam six years earlier (Standing 2012, 155n1).[6] In 2011, Earth First! member Mikal Jakubal came out as the painter of the crack (Bartett 2011). The dam removal was completed in 2014, and ecological restorations are in place to return the ecosystems destroyed by the dam and Lake Mills, which was formed by the flooding of the Elwha River (National Parks Service n.d.).

Another example is the work of a Berlin-based nonprofit group calling itself Fuck for Forest (FFF), which commits works of direct action by traveling to the Amazonian and Costa Rican rain forests being decimated by slash-and-burn deforestation and engaging in explicit sex, which they film and distribute as "Eco Porn" in the form of homemade videos to raise funds for education and awareness, and to buy up land in the Amazon for reforestation. The group, formed in Norway by Tommy Hol Ellingsen in 2004, raised $100,000 in its first year of existence. It moved to Berlin after members had public sex onstage at the Quart Festival in Kristiansand, Norway, and subsequently dropped their pants in a courtroom in the ensuing legal action. A splashy documentary of FFFs performance work was produced in 2012 by director Michal Marczak. It had a theatrical release in Germany and Poland followed by a series of screenings at several international film festivals. While the group has received some positive attention from radical environmentalists and sex-positive advocates, and one entertainment reviewer called the documentary a "fascinating, timely film" (Huddleston 2013), the bulk of the critical response has been negative, calling FFF a pack of unlikeable, dreadlocked hippies, "self-deluding crusties" (Bradshaw 2013), and their work naïve and ineffectual. One of the most awkward scenes in the film, which draws the attention of critics, is the final one in which FFF, having raised huge sums through its performances and film sales, attempts to deliver the money directly to members of the indigenous Amazonian communities most affected by corporate deforestation. The locals balk at accepting the money, instead asking the activists about conservation efforts and job creation initiatives for members of the community, leaving the FFF members speechless—and causing green advocate James Murray-White to wonder if this failed attempt at cross-cultural exchange leaves the whole enterprise "in tatters" (Barry 2013). Peter Bradshaw, film critic for the *Guardian*, called the moment a "catastrophic culture-clash" (2013). (Bradshaw, it should be noted, also complained that there wasn't enough actual sex in the film.)

FFF has distanced itself from the documentary, claiming that the director misrepresented the performers' aims and framed their activism as exploitative and nonefficacious; and that he misrepresented his own aims as a supporter when really he was just after a good show that would make him some money. FFF states on its website that Marczak encouraged them to stage scenes in which they would not have otherwise engaged because of the tight filming schedule, scenes that simplified and sensationalized what FFF maintains is a much more complicated agenda and set of practices (Fuck for Forest n.d.). Nevertheless, critics continue to dismiss FFFs work as naïve and problematic, and both mainstream environmentalists and gender studies advocates decry the group's sex parties in the Amazonian forests as doing more harm than good.

A final example involves the radical environmental protests of the World Trade Organization Ministerial Conference during the riots in downtown Seattle in November 1999. This was the largest public demonstration of economic globalization in the United States. Some 40,000 to 50,000 demonstrators took part (some estimates range upward of 100,000), representing dozens of environmental and anticapitalist groups as well as religious groups, labor organizations, and anarchists, loosely led by DAN, the Direct Action Network, which organized anti-WTO activity, including nonviolent resistance and rallying; other groups, like the anarchist black bloc, responded with more aggressive and violent vandalism. The protests centered on progressive critiques of global capitalism, which threatens to curb human rights and exploit the Earth's resources on a hitherto-unseen scale, impacting most harshly the peoples of underdeveloped countries as well as the world's most vulnerable ecosystems.

One group that captured the world's attention during the protest was the so-called blue-green alliance between pro-labor and pro-environment groups, the "teamsters and turtles" who critiqued the WTO's role in determining global fishing and shrimping practices. Some shrimping practices, such as the use of large, indiscriminate trolling nets in waters populated by several species of threatened sea turtles, had been banned by the 1973 U.S. Endangered Species Act, which prohibited the importation and sale of non-turtle-safe shrimp in the United States. But the WTO worked with the nations of Thailand, Malaysia, India, and Pakistan to convince the United States to overturn portions of the act, or to pay the fishing industries of these countries hundreds of millions of dollars annually in compensation for lost trade. In 1998, the WTO issued an interim ruling against the United States, saying it was in violation of the World Trade Organization and that its policies were a "barrier to free trade." The United States responded by weakening its guidelines pertaining to the importation of wild shrimp to come into compliance with the WTO (Sea Turtle Restoration Project n.d.).

At the November protests, hundreds of activists dressed as sea turtles, representing the Sea Turtle Restoration Project (STRP), founded in 1998 in West Marin County, California, took to the streets of Seattle to protest the WTO's endorsement of shrimping practices that result in the slaughter of endangered turtles. The homemade costumes, largely cut from a template designed by STRP's Ben White, were made of cardboard from appliance boxes and strapped together with nylon. STRP worked quickly to assemble and paint about 250 of these turtle shells and helmets, but the number of costumes was not nearly enough to accommodate the hundreds of performers who showed up to participate in the protest. In 2008 Stuart Townsend's film *Battle in Seattle*, a docudrama treating the performers and the WTO protests and starring Charlize Theron, Woody Harrelson, Tatum Channing, and others, debuted at the Toronto Film Festival. The film received somewhat positive reviews, though some activist groups claimed that, while it was well researched, the film sensationalized and simplified the goals and performances of the protestors (Crimethinc newsletter n.d.). The Turtles, as the protestors became known, became a symbol of the 2001 protests, and turtle costumes were accessioned by the Smithsonian and other institutions for their collections and exhibits.

The actions of the Turtles, along with the rest of the protests, had an immediate and site-specific effect. The meetings were delayed, the city was turned into a police state under veritable martial law, officers in riot gear attacked activists with tear gas, and demonstrators were rounded up and hauled to jail. The city went $3 million over budget in the cleanup, and estimates of damages to downtown property and lost sales hovered around $20 million (CBS News 2000). The anti-WTO groups claimed the "battle in Seattle" a success. The heretofore relatively unknown antiglobalization movement was now talked about by every national and international media outlet. The protests also inspired subsequent action at WTO meetings, meetings of the IMF/World Bank, and at the Democratic and Republican National Conventions. In 2007 the City of Seattle settled with 170 of the protestors for illegally arresting them without probable cause (McDonald 2007) and agreed to pay them a total of $250,000 in damages (Young and Brunner 2004).

But, notwithstanding the legal and ideological successes of the eco-protest performance, are the turtles actually safer? It's hard to say. The final 2001 ruling of the World Trade Organization allowed the United States to restrict importation of shrimp not certified turtle-safe and still be in compliance with the WTO once the country adjusted its policy, per article XX(g) of the GATT (the General Agreement of Tariffs and Trade put in place by the United Nations in 1947 and replaced by the WTO in 1995), to ensure that the restrictions were applied in a nondiscriminatory way. Currently, shrimp that comes into the United States must be caught by shrimpers using so-called trap-door turtle excluder device technology to allow " by-catch" turtles to escape (Wikipedia n.d.). In short, time will tell for the turtles.

As I indicated earlier, theater and awareness of the environment around us have been allied since the dawn of Western drama. But what is the line between *radical activist theater* and *radical theatrical activism*? Can one form succeed over the other? In what ways? And how do we define, gauge, and measure success? Eco-actions like Reclaim Shakespeare Company's guerrilla theater in and around the world-class Royal Shakespeare Company and high-profile direct actions at sites of man-made disasters have an impact we can put our finger on. FFF's brand of shocking, tastefully questionable explicit eco-porn and vandalism directed at individuals and small businesses, however, leave us not only wondering how we might track the success of such actions but querying the validity of these modes of performance.

Does eco-protest have to be aesthetically good to be successful? Clearly, anyone who spends a bit of time watching eco-protest performances notices for the most part a distinct level of artistic quality. While much of traditional stage theater aspires toward professional-quality production values, rigorous rehearsal, and skillful, nuanced performances, eco-protest performance is more often simple and direct, didactic, necessarily without dress rehearsal, and privileges the political message over the talent or aesthetic rigor of the performers. But it's not even so much a matter of "good art" versus "bad art" when it comes to success. Reclaim Shakespeare's polished delivery of blank verse modified by clever word play delivered before sophisticated arts consumers lays claim to success corroborated by real change. *Earth First!* can take down a 210-foot concrete dam with a few buckets of black paint. And 250 turtle shells cut out of refrigerator boxes can change the world's point of view on the de facto laissez-faire neoliberalization of global capitalism.

The ritualesque dimension of these events removes them from the traditional criteria for evaluation. Sarah Ann Standing writes that "aesthetics and efficacy are a false dichotomy" (2012, 147). She argues, citing the Glen Canyon Dam protest, that nonslick direct eco-actions are successful. They cause change. Citing Keven Michael DuLuca in *Image Politics: The New Rhetoric of Environmental Activism,* Standing states that such actions not only capture attention in the locality and specificity of the moment, but the leaders of these activist performances also understand how to "utilize the contemporary media."[7] DeLuca quotes Greenpeace cofounder Robert Hunter, who calls these media moments "mind bombs" (Standing 2012, 152). In the case of the Glines Canyon Dam protest, while it might take twenty years to build a hydroelectric facility and flood a canyon, a single ten-minute act of protest theater can be filmed by camera news crews, cut to fifteen or even five seconds of recyclable and easily disseminated news clip—and succeed in reversing the process and achieving dismantling. A veritable David and Goliath feat.

In her article about Seattle-based activist group Theater Squad (starting with their 2004 production of *Shadows of Exile*), Theresa J. May says that didactic agitprop theater may rally the choir, but it seldom persuades those who are less sympathetic and does little to educate them. At worst, they "feel shouted *at*, or bullied" (May 2012, 23). But, continues May, "while many activists and applied theatre practitioners might measure efficacy by information disseminated, policies changed, or increased public outrage, Jill Dolan reminds us that 'success,' even in overtly political performances, lies in feeling." According to Dolan, "the politics lie in the desire to feel the potential of elsewhere . . . in our willingness to attend or create performance at all, to come together in real places . . . to explore in imaginary [ways] . . . the potential of the 'not yet' and the 'not here'" (Dolan 2008, 20).

Baz Kershaw argues that art, in fact, can get in the way of real change, and it is precisely in the moment when spectators do not realize they are watching theater that change can take place. Kershaw looks to the work of DiY (do-it-yourself) performance artist John Jordan, who writes that protest theater picks up where traditional theater fails.

> Art has clearly failed historically as a means to bring imagination and creativity to movements of social change . . . What makes DiY protest so powerful is that [according to Jordan,] it "clearly embodies a rejection of the specialised sphere of old politics, as well as of art and everyday life" [here he's drawing on Guy Debord]. Its insistence on creativity and yet the invisibility of art and artists in its midst singles it out as an historical

turning point in the current of creative resistance. By making the art completely invisible, DiY protest gives art back its original and socially transformative power. (Kershaw 2009, 255)

Kershaw writes that, paradoxically, "the power of the art in performance is greatest when you do not overtly know you are seeing it" (2009, 256), echoing what Augusto Boal (1985) has termed invisible theater. But, as Kershaw points out, ecological activism is *riddled* with paradox. Indigenous tribespeople on Mare's Island, British Columbia, drove 400,000 steel spikes into the trees in the old-growth forest they wanted to save from a local logging company. Greenpeace plugged the underwater outlet pipe of a chemical plant in Lafayette, New Jersey, causing a buildup of toxic waste on the site that will take "hundreds, perhaps thousands, of years to clear" in order to prevent the waste from poisoning the Jersey coastline. "You have to make things worse to make them better," Kershaw writes (2009, 258).

Part of this, argues Kershaw, has to do with Peggy Phelan's claim in her book *Unmarked* that as soon as art becomes visible, it conforms to the systems in power and the dominant ideologies in place. Earth First!'s UK chapter evades such traps by refusing to *exist* in the traditional sense. Earth First! UK's Alex Plows stated: "EF! Does not exist at all—certainly not as a campaign group such as Friends of the Earth, with paid membership and policy making bodies. Instead, EF! Is an egalitarian, non-hierarchical 'disorganisation,' relying on grass-roots networking and local/individual autonomy rather than centralised policy control" (quoted in Kershaw 2002, 125–26).

As to the merits of the distinction between protest performance and traditional theater and whether one form is more efficacious than the other, fortunately, we are not obliged to make an either/or choice. Traditional stage drama with environmental themes, eco-protest performance, and a range of other forms of advocacy can all be employed as a targeted and multipronged effort to draw attention to what's at stake.

The modern Western view of the environment and the subscription to a nature/culture divide is a pretty difficult thing to dismantle. As noted earlier, eco-critical theorists trace the present ecological problems to the founding narratives of humanity. Overcoming thousands of years of entrenched cultural narrative about what makes human beings distinct from the rest of the world is a daunting challenge.

Whether we consider ourselves eco-critical scholars or environmental activists, we do need to think about how we can break out of the nature/culture binary and its reification in political and corporate practice if it means continuing to inflict trauma on the Earth and its atmosphere with hydraulic fracturing, drilling, strip mining, dumping, unfettered emissions, poisoning the Earth and its animals and, yes, humans, with pesticides in our fields and chemicals in our factories. Performative radical acts of eco-protest are, on the face of it, about saving something out there, but a closer look reveals it's about something much, much closer. Downing Cless reminds us in "Eco-Theatre USA" (1996) that the Greek root *eco* means "home." Eco-protest is not, then, about saving nature—something apart from culture—it's about saving us and where we live. Ritualesque public performances insist upon keeping the conversation going.

NOTES

I would like to gratefully acknowledge the following individuals for their generosity and assistance in composing this essay: Wendy Arons, Una Chaudhuri, Downing Cless, Baz Kershaw, Theresa J. May, Sarah Standing, and especially Angenette Spalink. The essay was presented in an earlier form as part of the autumn 2013 performing arts lecture series "Radical Acts," sponsored by the University of Washington School of Drama and Center for Performance Studies. I would like to thank my colleague Odai Johnson for inviting me to talk, and I am grateful for the question-and-answer session with the audience that informed this essay's development.

1. Chaudhuri writes that in the face of global warming, Al Gore stated, "These 'beautiful animals' [such as polar bears] are 'literally being forced off the planet. They're in trouble, got *nowhere else to go.*'" This idea of there being nowhere to go is what Chaudhuri calls zoöpathology—a "disease of the ties that bind humans to other animals" (Chaudhuri 2012, 46).

2. This genealogy is pulled largely from Cless 2011.

3. Cless writes, "In Boston I still am involved with the Underground Railway Theater, which I would not call a 'protest theatre' but which definitely has a mission of producing plays about social and environmental issues." (personal communication, 2013).

4. Cless writes that eco-theatre is "refractive rather than reflective," given that "straightforward realism negates future action by spectators" (1996, 80, referencing Boal 1985).

5. But, Garrett argues, maybe theatres can keep their incandescent lights but green their lobby, offices, rehearsal rooms, and shops; recycle old props and set pieces; reuse materials; and make sure shows are good enough to play to full houses for shorter runs versus partially filled houses for more performances. "Congregating people has a powerful effect on mitigating emissions" (208).

6. Standing reports that a similar action was conducted by protestors at a dam construction site in Iceland in 2005.

7. Site-specific protests, argues Standing, benefit the places and communities immediately concerned. Standing writes, "Eco actions integrate the performative and the real in a manner similar to street performance" (2012, 154). She cites Jan Cohen-Cruz, who says that a performance like this "'creates a bridge between imaginary and real actions, often

facilitated by taking place at the very sites that the performance makers want transformed" (Cohen-Cruz 1998, 1).

REFERENCES

Barry, Doug. 2013. "Fuck for Forest Chronicles Activists' Frustrating Naïveté (NSFW)." *Jezebel*, May 26. Accessed October 12, 2013. http://jezebel.com/fuck-for-forest-chronicles-activists-frustrating-naïve-509920513.

Bartett, Bruce. 2011. "The Elwha's Last Dam Summer." *Seattle Met*, July 22. Accessed October 14, 2013. http://www.seattlemet.com/travel-and-outdoors/olympic-national-park/articles/elwha-river-dam-august-2011/1.

Berman, Taylor. 2013. "Iowa State Fair Butter Cow Doused with Fake Blood by Vegan Activists." *Gawker*, August 12. Accessed October 11, 2013. http://gawker.com/iowa-state-fair-butter-cow-doused-with-fake-blood-by-ve-1116661523.

Boal, Augusto. 1985. *Theater of the Oppressed*. New York: Theatre Communications Group.

Bradshaw, Peter. 2013. *Fuck for Forest* review video. *Guardian*, April 22. Accessed October 13, 2013. http://www.theguardian.com/film/video/2013/apr/22/fuck-for-forest-video-review.

CBS News. 2000. "WTO Protests Hit Seattle in the Pocketbook." January 6. Accessed October 14, 2013. http://www.cbc.ca/news/world/wto-protests-hit-seattle-in-the-pocketbook-1.245428.

Chaudhuri, Una. 1994. "'There Must Be a Lot of Fish in That Lake': Toward an Ecological Theater." *Theater* 25 (1): 23–31.

Chaudhuri, Una. 2012. "The Silence of the Polar Bears." In *Readings in Performance and Ecology*, ed. Wendy Arons and Theresa J. May, 44–57. New York: Palgrave. http://dx.doi.org/10.1057/9781137011695.0010.

Cless, Downing. 1996. "Eco-theatre USA: The Grassroots Is Greener." *TDR* 40 (2): 79–102. http://dx.doi.org/10.2307/1146531.

Cless, Downing. 2011. *Ecology and Environment in European Drama*. London: Routledge.

Climate Radio. 2012. "Shakespeare Reclaimed?" November 19. Accessed October 11, 2013. http://climateradio.org/shakespeare-reclaimed/.

Cohen-Cruz, Jan. 1998. Introduction to *Radical Street Performance: An International Anthology*, ed. Jan Cohen-Cruz, 1–6. London: Routledge.

Cooper, Charlie. 2012. "All the World's a Stage—And All the Men and Women Merely Environmentalists Who Hate BP." *Independent*, October 3. Accessed October 10, 2013. http://www.independent.co.uk/arts-entertainment/theatre-dance/news/all-the-worlds-a-stage-and-all-the-men-and-women-merely-environmentalists-who-hate-bp-8194854.html.

Crimethinc newsletter. n.d. Accessed October 13, 2013. http://thecloud.crimethinc.com/pdfs/whatabouttomorrow-print.pdf.

Dolan, Jill. 2008. *Utopia in Performance: Finding Hope at the Theater*. Ann Arbor: University of Michigan Press.

Earth Matters on Stage. n.d. Accessed June 10, 2016. http://emosfestival.wordpress.com.

Evernden, Neil. 1992. *The Social Creation of Nature*. Baltimore: Johns Hopkins University Press.

Fuck for Forest. n.d. Accessed October 12, 2013. http://www.fuckforforest.com/news/Freenews-839.

Garrett, Ian. 2012. "Theatrical Production's Carbon Footprint." In *Readings in Performance and Ecology*, ed. Wendy Arons and Theresa J. May, 201–9. New York: Palgrave. http://dx.doi.org/10.1057/9781137011695_18.

Huddleston, Tom. 2013. *Fuck for Forest* review. *Time Out*, April 17. Accessed October 14, 2013. http://www.timeout.com/london/film/f-ck-for-forest.
Kershaw, Baz. 2002. "Ecoactivist Performance: The Environment as Partner in Protest?" *TDR* 46 (1): 118–30.
Kershaw, Baz. 2009. *Theatre Ecology*. Cambridge: Cambridge University Press.
Love, Glen. 2003. *Practical Ecocriticism: Literature, Biology, and the Environment*. Charlottesville: University of Virginia Press.
May, Theresa J. 2012. "Meditations on the Pain of Others: Becoming Theatre Squad." *Theatre Topics* 22 (1): 23–37. http://dx.doi.org/10.1353/tt.2012.0006.
May, Theresa J. 2007. "Beyond Bambi: Toward a Dangerous Ecocriticism in Theatre Studies." *Theatre Topics* 17 (2): 95–110.
McDonald, Colin. 2007. "Jury Says Seattle violated WTO Protesters' Rights," *Seattle PI*, January 29. Accessed October 14, 2013. http://www.seattlepi.com/local/article/Jury-says-Seattle-violated-WTO-protesters-rights-1226824.php.
Mount, Toni. 2014. *Everyday Life in Medieval London: From the Anglo-Saxons to the Tudors*. Stroud, Goucestershire: Amberley.
National Parks Service. n.d. "Elwah River Restoration." Accessed April 25, 2014. http://www.nps.gov/olym/naturescience/elwha-ecosystem-restoration.htm.
Ricketts, Aiden. n.d. "Theatre of Protest." Accessed October 14, 2014. http://www.thechangeagency.org/_dbase_upl/RickettsTheatreOfProtest.pdf.
Sea Turtle Restoration Project. n.d. "WTO: The Story of the WTO versus the Sea Turtles." Accessed October 14, 2013. http://seaturtles.org/article.php?id=68.
Shakespeare, William. 2012. "'Out, Damned Logo!' Theatrical Flash Mob Hits British Museum." *YouTube*, November 18. Accessed October 12, 2013. http://www.youtube.com/watch?v=e9cznrBq7rQ.
Standing, Sarah Ann. 2012. "Earth First!'s 'Crack the Dam' and the Aesthetics of EcoActivist Performance." In *Readings in Performance and Ecology*, ed. Wendy Arons and Theresa J. May, 147–55. New York: Palgrave. http://dx.doi.org/10.1057/9781137011695_13.
Svich, Caridad. 2012. "The Way of Water." Accessed October 14, 2013. http://caridadsvich.com/plays/fulllength/the-way-of-water/.
Westneat, Danny. 2013. "Cars Losing Grip on Seattle." *Seattle Times*, September 24. Accessed October 14, 2013. http://seattletimes.com/html/localnews/2021890245_westneat25xml.html.
Wikipedia. n.d. "Shrimp-Turtle Case." Accessed October 13, 2013. http://en.wikipedia.org/wiki/Shrimp-Turtle_Case.
Young, Bob, and Jim Brunner. 2004. "City to Pay Protesters $250,000 to Settle WTO Suit." *Seattle Times*, January 17. Accessed June 10, 2016. http://community.seattletimes.nwsource.com/archive/?date=20040117&slug=wto17m.

13

The Material Culture of Remembrance in Ireland
Roadside Memorials as Contested Spaces

Barbara Graham

ALONG THE ROADWAYS AND LANES OF IRELAND the erection of permanent roadside memorials to victims of traffic accidents has become a growing trend over the last fifteen to twenty years. This chapter explores the phenomenon of the emergence of these memorials in a particular part of the eastern border area and examines ambiguous attitudes of both sympathy and antagonism to their presence in the landscape. Central to reactions to the memorials are issues of containment and displacement, the idea that remembrance is no longer bounded and regulated within what people perceive as the "norm" or "traditional," resulting in a difficulty in conceptualizing the place of these memorials in overall remembrance practices. This resonates with Douglas's (1966, 22) ideas about the necessity of drawing prohibitive boundaries around the sacred, and the dangers of "crossing forbidden boundaries." It is argued that the "out of place" materiality of roadside memorials disturbs people's ideals of tradition by frustrating "cherished classifications" (37). I trace the perceived origin of the practice and its diffusion into popular culture and place it within a historical context of wayside commemoration that is arguably a continuing, if fluctuating, form of remembrance in Ireland (MacConville and McQuillan 2005, 2010; NicNéill 1946).

The data used in this analysis are drawn from several months of fieldwork during which I documented sixteen memorials in counties Down, Louth, and Armagh, and conducted numerous interviews and discussions with bereaved families, clergy, civic authorities, and the general public.

Fifteen of the memorials considered here are polished stone slabs set into walls or fences, and one is a large flower display fashioned into the shape of a cross. Together the memorials commemorate seven women, twelve men, and one ten-year-old boy. Seven of those killed were teenagers, nine people were in their early twenties, one woman was thirty, and one man was in his forties. The survey did not include memorials erected to commemorate political deaths in the recent violence in Northern Ireland, artifacts that necessarily involve views that require wider considerations in relation to that conflict. MacConville and McQuillan (2010, 202) documented attitudes to these and found they could "evoke conflicting and highly charged responses." This survey sought to elucidate cross-border commonalities of opinion, both negative and positive, to a phenomenon that is present in many countries around the world. The marking of places on the roadside through this particular form of memorial is perceived by many as representing a geographical, emotional, and spiritual displacement of remembrance. A roadside plaque, as opposed to the headstone in a graveyard, places acts of remembering outside of wider social involvement and the control of the established churches (something that has been noted by Clark and Franzmann 2002 and Hartig and Dunn 1998 in relation to Australian memorials and Everett 2000 in consideration of Texas shrines).

The underlying impetus for uneasiness in regard to the wayside memorials stems from the cultural perception of how the dead should be remembered, as it is ultimately the place of the dead that is being contested and played out in the differing rituals associated with the roadside and graveyard. Roadside memorials have sparked debates on their nature as "shrines" and as displays that are rejected by many individuals and clergy as uncomfortable manifestations of individualist and even pagan practice. Indeed, an opinion article in the *Irish Independent* complained that many memorials resembled mini-shrines and suggested that it may be time to "call a halt" to such "ostentatious" displays (*Irish Independent* 2007). While younger people in this area are more accustomed to the physical presence of the roadside plaques, there remains, across all age groups, a conviction that the roadside does not facilitate the accepted remembrance process.

"TRADITION" AND "NORM"

The determination of what is acceptable centers on rites and practices associated with local churchyards and cemeteries. To place a loved one's remains physically in the landscape involves a practical undertaking that is entwined for many people with spiritual and religious beliefs; but even for those who profess no religious adherence, there is a cultural imperative to observe traditional rites in relation to the dead. What constitutes the "traditional" way of dealing with the dead and remembrance is often understood as what is "normal" practice. For the Christian churches this entails a church funeral service (or sometimes a service in the deceased's home) followed by a proscribed ritual of committal at a graveside, either in a churchyard or civic cemetery. This involves a coming together of people within the authority of the church, a precise demarcated time and space in which to enact rituals, and formulaic language and behavior. The final enactment in this process is the erection of a memorial headstone (or the adding of a name to an existing stone). These are rites that create an acknowledged structure, an important part of which is boundedness and containment—physical, emotional, and ritual. The roadside markers are viewed as frustrating those boundaries. They do not have the "invariance" that Hobsbawm and Ranger (1983, 2) argued is a characteristic of "traditions," nor do they (people believe) possess what Otto and Pedersen (2005, 13) called an "explicit link to the past." The initial objections to the memorials are, however, articulated in terms of the alien nature of their physical placing in the landscape.

CONTAINMENT AND GEOGRAPHICAL SPACE

The geographical space that is used for roadside memorials is public space that has been personalized. Yocom (2006, 69) says that erecting roadside memorials is a way of "claiming space" and it is precisely that appropriation of space that is problematic. Their presence is an example of private grief in the public and can been viewed as what Smith (1999, 105) called an "intrusion of another's sacred space" into what is public or neutral. People see them as impossible to avoid or, as many people put it, "in your face." Geographical spaces and particular places play an important part in the consciousness and memory of the individuals and families in this area. Senie (2006, 46) argues there is "pervasive evidence that we believe the ground we walk on holds the content of its history"—and in this way we have direct access to what happened there. The desire to have that access, or to try to re-create a connection that was severed suddenly and traumatically, is part of the rationale given by families who have erected the memorials.

It is necessary to understand the context in which these roadside markers generate uneasy emotions. Modern burial practices in the area dictate that for most people it is still customary to be buried in the family parish, even if someone has lived away from the area for many years. Evidence from early and late medieval Ireland suggest this practice may be a remnant of the importance that was attached to "interring the corpse in the territorial church to which it belonged. Cemeteries had territorial and dynastic associations" ; and being buried with one's ancestors was a means of claiming one's "position in the map of the community, to proclaim connections and to reinforce status by underlining continuity with the past" (Leigh Fry 1999, 191, 194). That separation from the living family at death "was balanced by incorporation with one's ancestral group at burial" (Tait 2002, 65–66). The graveyard is a physically and spiritually contained space, a community of the dead. The headstone that is erected over a grave marks the site of the physical body. There are fusings of physicality of body, place, and artifact that are interrelated with spiritual concepts of an afterlife, with reciprocity between the living and the dead, and with rites enacted within culturally acceptable modes of behavior. The blurring of the parameters, which leads to "fuzzy" boundaries, is the unsettling and unacceptable nature of the roadside remembrance. These memorials exist in stark contrast to the family grave as there is an absence of a body. Typical of comments made by people were: "There's nothing there by the road. The body's not there. Why would you want to be going to someplace like that? I don't see the point of it." Yet people also tempered their objections with sympathy for the bereaved: One young woman, whose attitude was typical of the ambivalence the memorials generate, said: "I don't like them. They are very intrusive. But I don't know how I would react if someone belonging to me, or a child of mine, died that way. There is one outside our work. It's huge, like a big shrine. Two teenagers died there in a car crash. It's very sad, really, but it's over the top."

There is an overall sense that the "space" is being intruded upon and that it should not be sacralized. Yet even among families who have erected memorials or are associated with them, there are differing attitudes. Some families explained that they wished people to think about careless and drunk driving, to remind them of the damage this can cause. This conforms to what Santino (2006a, 1; 2006b, 12–13) calls the performative nature of the memorials, whereby their purpose is to transmit a moral message or warning. Two of the memorials documented explicitly mentioned that the person commemorated had been killed by a drunk driver; both of these plaques are in South Armagh. Other people felt they wanted to be close to the spot where someone died, and one mother spoke of how she had visited the site of her daughter's death each night for a year. She talked about the performative aspect of the memorial and expressed the hope that making the tragedy public might effect a change in drivers' behavior. There was

The Material Culture of Remembrance in Ireland 243

Figure 13.1. A memorial to a young man killed when his car crashed into railings along the seashore at Narrow Water, Co. Down.

also a strong desire on her part to be at the place of death as she had not been with her daughter when the accident happened. "I go to her grave but she was alone here and I want her to know that I am with her. I can talk to her both places. But I want her to know she isn't alone."

Not all families, however, visit these memorials, or even were instrumental in their placing. Along a short stretch of the County Down coast are three memorials to road traffic victims. One was erected by friends after a young man of twenty crashed his car. The dead man's brother said that he would not have wanted such a reminder of what happened and admitted that he does not visit the site. He feels it is just too sad: "My father doesn't go there either but my mother does. She and his friends used to go every week, but not so often now. It's just at his birthday or anniversary [of his death] or whenever we are getting flowers for the graves; then extra ones will be bought to go at the wall." Many people who said they felt no need to place memorials believed that a constant reminder of the way of death was too disturbing. They preferred visiting a grave where, as one man explained: "Everyone can have a bit of peace." For the bereaved, though, there is an element of wanting to "cleanse" these sites of the tragedy (Thomas 2006, 27); and paradoxically families can achieve this either through erecting a

Figure 13.2. An elaborate memorial set into a wall at the foot of a large tree near Faughart, Co. Louth on the Irish border. Four young teenagers were killed when their car crashed into the tree.

memorial or not doing so. There is a disjuncture or deviation from the perceived "norm" of death due to its suddenness and the young age of the victims, and an effort has to be made to make the death peaceful again. As Santino (2006b, 10) argues, the key to the phenomenon of these memorials

The Material Culture of Remembrance in Ireland 245

Figure 13.3. Detail of religious and secular objects hanging on tree branches at the Faughart memorial; large rosary beads, a crucifix and a keyring.

is the nature of the deaths: sudden, tragic, and accidental. They can therefore by viewed as a response to the disturbance of equilibrium and natural order.

For the mother in the example above and other mothers and fathers, that desire to render a death peaceful (postmortem) has to be realized in a visible, material form, because otherwise these sites would be just anonymous places in the landscape. The site is therefore personalized and sacralized. Clark and Franzmann (2002, 15) argue that the sacralizing of the roadside by erecting a memorial indicates "the spiritual significance of place," but it is significant only for the bereaved who have foregrounded their private grief onto public space. For many other people a memorial would prove "too much a reminder," and the "cleansing" of the death place is instead achieved by allowing it to revert to its public status and reclaim its anonymity in the landscape.

While the blurring of the geographical boundaries is contested, the crossing of ritual boundaries also causes negative reactions to the memorials. Roadside shrines are not generally recognized, encouraged, or used by the churches, but the transitory placing of flowers at a site is acceptable. Catholic priests in the area say they have never been asked to officiate at a roadside memorial site. When a fatal road accident occurs, a member of the clergy is usually called to say prayers at the roadside and to bless the body. The site has, in a way, been sacralized by the clergy through prayers, but it is a transient act of ritual that does not confer any lasting sacredness to the site. Permanent markers are seen as inviting too much personal attention. The practice is perceived among Presbyterian clergy in the area as an aspect of Catholic iconography. Within the Catholic communities, for their part, there was a strong aversion to the individualization of grief through these memorials. Asked what they thought about the wayside memorials, people responded: "It's like worshipping a site where someone died . . . That can't be right" or "It's too personal, as if someone wants special attention." The churches dislike the individualism of the roadside memorials because they conflict with doctrine about equalizing in death. The wayside markers are viewed as making remembrance untidy and uncontained as they are breaking physical and ritual boundaries. The personalization evident through roadside memorials draws the dead into the world of the living in ways that cannot be accommodated within the prevalent cultural norms. But it also disrupts societal norms of imagined equal status in death.

The continued attention by family and friends to roadside sites is ritualistic but secular in that it does not entail anointed officers of any established church. The families of the dead still take part in the church rituals of funerals and burials; their attention to both forms of ritual suggests ambiguity and paradox in their belief and practice. Indeed, Inglis maintains that there was never an unquestioning acceptance of orthodoxy among Irish Catholics and there were always "myriad ways of being a Catholic" (1998, 204). Two Catholic priests with whom I spoke admitted privately they did not like the idea of the memorials but are reluctant to make any public criticism. This unwillingness to pass censure on the memorials also applies to secular authorities who must determine their legal status. Even the opinion writer in the *Irish Independent* tempered criticisms with acknowledging the bereaved: "The feelings of the bereaved should not be dismissed lightly . . . but is this the best way to remember a loved one? . . . For good reason we commemorate the dead in graveyards. Parks and other public places, including the roadside, are for the living" (*Irish Independent* 2007).

While the memorials are technically illegal, they are never interfered with. One local councilor in Newry admitted that there is a "gray" area in the planning laws whereby applications to erect permanent plaques may be bounced back between the Department of the Environment and the local council: "We actually have only been asked on one occasion for permission to erect a plaque. And we gave permission. It was the children of a man who had died, and out of respect for them we saw no reason to deny them. But generally people don't ask, but we don't bother with them unless they are a hazard." Louth County Council has no official policy on roadside memorials. An officer from the Roads Division said that if the council were asked for permission to erect a memorial it would initially refuse, but officials would then immediately negotiate with the family over the height and width of the proposed memorial and its distance from the road. The boundaries between religious and secular discourse are therefore becoming blurred. Decisions on granting permission for roadside memorials will consider the feelings and ritual requirements of the bereaved, and the parameters of discourse are not so tightly contained as may be generally assumed. MacConville and McQuillan (2009, 136) found that local councils in other parts of Ireland (between Dublin and Sligo) "facilitated" the memorials, and they believe that this accommodation of the markers reflects "a cultural emphasis of remembrance of the dead." More recently MacConville and McQuillan (2010, 195–207) reviewed attitudes to the memorials and found some disquiet but no public criticism within the Republic of Ireland.

The roadside memorials also display negative performative powers in demanding attention by nature of their physicality. There is a resistance to being drawn into these roadside scenes, of not having a choice about it. Santino (2006b, 6) recognizes that the spontaneous shrines draw in an "undifferentiated public." It is this undifferentiation that is at the root of much of the unease expressed by people. The removal of choice is another aspect of noncontainment and how personal and public boundaries are breached and disregarded by the siting of these plaques. As MacConville and McQuillan (2010, 200) have recognized, roadside memorials are not "neutral artefacts"; they "disrupt and disturb notions of private and public, secular and sacred through their material form and location."

People felt they had no choice whether or not to participate in the messages being communicated by the memorials; they were compelled into an involvement with them. They had not given their consent to what they resented as an intrusion into their feelings and reactions. Just as the shrines communicate in material ways the nature of loss, through their physical presence and through artifacts left beside them (Thomas 2006, 36), so also they communicate in nonmaterial ways in affecting the thoughts and feelings of the viewing public. But are roadside memorials a new practice, as many people believe them to be?

INFLUENCES PAST AND FUTURE

A number of people consulted on the wayside markers attributed their rise to the unprecedented outpouring of public grief seen after the death of Princess Diana in 1997. Everyone interviewed was of the opinion that the memorials constitute an imported, foreign practice. Wayside shrines are common in southern Europe (Greece and Spain), in parts of Latin America, and in the southern United States. Grider (2006), commenting on roadside memorials in New Mexico, has argued that they are essentially manifestations of folk Catholicism.

Roadside shrines to religious figures are not uncommon in parts of Ireland where little grottos to Our Lady or a local saint may be tucked into a wall or hedge and regularly adorned with flowers, rosary beads, and prayer sheets. This practice can be traced back to pre-Christian times when particular spots in the landscape were associated with different gods or goddesses. The placing of artifacts at modern roadside memorials, and on graves, can be viewed as an extension of the prehistoric practice of placing items within a burial. In modern practice these grave goods are displayed aboveground where they can be changed, renewed, tidied, and cleaned. Senie (2006, 43) believes that certain objects left at shrines "may be relics of the dead or gifts for them" and that they reveal "an array of personal relationships with the dead." The erecting of roadside memorials in Ireland can be seen as just one of the diverse ways that some of the living continue a relationship and dialogue with the dead.

While the rise of roadside memorials is viewed as perhaps being influenced from outside the country, the perception that these memorials are a relatively recent phenomenon in Ireland does not equate with the evidence. There is a tradition in Ireland of marking the sites of sudden deaths with crosses and cairns (MacConville and McQuillan 2005, 28). And Gillespie (1997, 20) recounts that wayside crosses were common in early modern Ireland. As late as the 1930s the Irish Folklore Commission recorded people who remembered wayside cairns and the custom of adding a little stone to them as you passed by (MacConville and McQuillan 2005, 28). Nic Néill (1946, 49–63) contends that the practice of marking a place where a death occurred in the open was once widespread. Her study, based on records from the Irish Folklore Collection for 1938–1939 and collections made by the Irish primary schools studies undertaken in 1937–1938, showed that in Ireland a cairn was usually erected at such a place of death and that each passerby would add a pebble to the mound. "The act of putting a stone on a cairn was regarded as doing good to the person on whose cairn it was laid" (Nic Néill 1946, 50). Recorded reasons for casting stones onto such a cairn and saying a prayer for the dead included a fear of ghosts at such death places. The votive offering of a stone along with a prayer was said to ensure that a ghost would stay in the ground and not follow the living (Nic Néill 1946). A study undertaken by Crimmin (2005), who maintains a website to catalogue roadside memorials, found examples of roadside memorials dating back to the nineteenth century. There are currently more than 800 memorials recorded on the site, the earliest one in County Wexford. It carries a date of 1908 and was erected after a twenty-one-year-old man was killed by a motorcar.

There is however, even earlier evidence of marking places of death in the landscape and of naming places to commemorate deaths. In the mythical epic The Cattle Raid of Cooley (which takes place across the Cooley Mountains in County Louth in the fieldwork area), there are at least seven references to memorials that were erected to mark the spot where a warrior was slain in battle (O'Rahilly 1976).[1] There are details of headstones erected where people were slain or drowned (32, 153, 159) and three instances of multiple headstones erected after battles (72, 77, 78). The placing of markers in the landscape to commemorate deaths is not an unbroken tradition. The contemporary memorials can be viewed as a resurgence of this practice, but the historical context of previous markers has to be considered. The mythical warriors of the epic tales were elite heroes and the marking of their places of death is perhaps more accurately placed in conjunction with the prehistoric cemeteries of previous centuries. The wayside crosses and cairns of earlier centuries were opportunities for the general population to commemorate people at junctures in history when individual burial places and headstones were not the norm for the general population.

CONCLUSION

It has been seen that there are a number of reasons why these roadside memorials are deemed to be "out of place." A headstone or plaque in a graveyard is not contentious by its placement, but by the roadside it is an object that is geographically out of place. The roadside is also a site of displacement for the emotional and spiritual. The landscape can be memorialized in headstones, and these are contained and ritualized within a religious setting or a secular civic graveyard. The roadside memorial, set out on a roadway, surrounded by the daily noise and bustle of life, is a reminder of suddenness, despair, and violence. It is the antithesis of belief in a quieter and happier afterlife. For people who criticize the memorials and feel uneasy about them, roadside memorialization does not resolve the grief felt at a death or help complete the circle of life. Rather, it freezes you in time and space, upsets the balance, and distorts the physical, mental, and emotional processes of both the living and the dead. At the roadside there is no resolution, but a tension and anxiety that something is not quite finished, and a fear perhaps that the dead cannot rest properly while this reminder is starkly staring at us all.

Within graveyards the dead are contained in a particular physical and ritual space. There are behaviors expected of and enacted by visitors that suggest an underlying uniformity to the remembrance of the dead. To have the bones of relatives and friends in graveyards is a celebratory fixing of families and communities in the landscape. The roadside allows no celebration; what is fixed here is a trap in time and space with no outlet due to the isolation and public aspect of the site. The roadside is not something in which everyone in a particular social network can be involved (this could include extended family, friends, and religious groupings)—most people have no experience of it. The roadside plaque is also suggestive of an individualism that is not readily accommodated within prevailing cultural values and is uncomfortable for people who have no association with the person being remembered. Yet no one knows everyone else who is buried in a cemetery: it is the geographical and ritual unboundedness, the disconnection from proscribed places of kin and neighborly gatherings, that makes the roadside plaques too intimate for their setting.

As Francis, Kellaher, and Neophytou (2005, 177) have suggested, the cemetery is an important site for "the creation of culture and memory." In a cemetery the "notions and practices of kinship"—ongoing ties between the living and the dead—are articulated and reinforced. The grave is a familiar place and is symbolic of a certain resolution and acceptance of death. It is visited and maintained within the support of family, friends, and the churches.

It is also a place of ease and communication with the dead. But whereas Clark and Franzmann (2002) have theorized that the wayside markers perform a spiritual function for people who are disaffected with established churches or who find the cemetery "unsatisfying as a focal point for mourning" (14), the situation with the Irish memorials is different. By visiting both the roadside and the graveyard, the bereaved families and friends are "going beyond the management of mourning practices and spaces provided by the traditional authorities of church and state" (Clark and Franzmann 2002, 15), but they are not abandoning these practices—rather, they are adding to them.

If memorials are "ways for people to mark their own history" (Senie 2006, 43), then it is the subverting of the traditional time and space in which to do this that leads to disharmony. Many people reluctantly accept that the roadside memorials are a feature of remembrance that will not disappear, and may grow in numbers. They are fixed features and as such make more of a cultural statement in terms of permanence. Their physical fixedness is akin to the permanence of the graveyard headstone. It is perhaps the similarity in form and sentiment to the headstone that underlies much of the disquiet about them. They are familiar on one level (because they are similar), yet they are displaced. This displacement causes tangled feelings that are difficult for people to articulate or conceptualize. What has been shown in this examination of the roadside memorials is that there is a need to have "private loss socially acknowledged and shared" (Senie 2006, 45). It is the way this is being enacted through the roadside markers that is unsettling for the people with whom I worked.

The evidence of the long, albeit interrupted, nature of the practice of marking sudden deaths by raising cairns at the death spot places the contemporary practice within a wider historical context. Nic Néill (1946, 50–53) found that in the 1930s there was still a custom of wayside cairns in Donegal, parts of Leitrim, Mayo, West Cork, and Kerry, but elsewhere it was described as a thing of the past or something that older people might do. It was spoken of in Connemara as "obsolete" and Nic Néill added: "In thirty years it might be as difficult to get traditions about it in Mayo and Kerry as it is today in Limerick and Tipperary" (51). If we view today's roadside memorials as a contemporary expression of an older custom, we must also acknowledge that motivations for their twenty-first-century manifestation have resonances with the past but also include new rationales. The cairns of old were not personalized through etchings or named plaques. The older custom and the new practice may share the desire of the bereaved to "cleanse" a site of tragedy or "fix" positive connotations onto a place, but today's memorials go beyond these concerns to embrace aspects of individualization along with moral messages to road users. Yet, whatever their future, or the attitudes to them, an underlying concern with all the people with whom I spoke was to portray a sympathetic attitude toward bereaved families and not to voice any public opposition to the memorials.

NOTE

1. The Cattle Raid of Cooley was written down sometime between the seventh and ninth centuries AD but purportedly relates to events in Ireland in the first century BC. It details the epic series of battles between Connaught and Ulster in which the main protagonists are Queen Mebh and Cu Chullainn.

REFERENCES

Clark, Jennifer, and Majella Franzmann. 2002. "Born to Eternal Life: The Roadside as Sacred Space." *Pointers* 12 (3): 14–16.

Crimmin, Jerry. 2005. Irish Roadside Memorials. http://homepage.eircom.net/~arantsli/intro.htm. Accessed February 10, 2014.

Douglas, Mary. 1966. *Purity and Danger: An Analysis of Concepts of Pollution and Taboo.* London: Routledge and Kegan Paul.

Everett, Holly. 2000. "Roadside Crosses and Memorial Complexes in Texas." *Folklore* 111 (1): 91–103.

Francis, Doris, Leonie Kellaher, and Georgina Neophytou. 2005. *The Secret Cemetery.* Oxford: Berg.

Gillespie, Raymond. 1997. *Devoted People: Belief and Religion in Early Modern Ireland.* Manchester: Manchester University Press.

Grider, Sylvia A. 2006. "Roadside Crosses: Vestiges of Colonial Spain in Contemporary New Mexico." In *Descansos: The Sacred Landscapes of New Mexico*, ed. Joan E. Alessi, 11–26. New Mexico: Fresco Fine Art.

Hartig, Kate V., and Kevin M. Dunn. 1998. "Roadside Memorials: Interpreting New Deathscapes in Newcastle, New South Wales." *Australian Geographical Studies* 36 (1): 5–20. http://dx.doi.org/10.1111/1467-8470.00036.

Hobsbawm, Eric, and Terence Ranger, eds. 1983. *The Invention of Tradition.* Cambridge: Cambridge University Press.

Inglis, Tom. 1998. *Moral Monopoly: The Rise and Fall of the Catholic Church in Modern Ireland.* Dublin: University College Dublin Press.

Irish Independent. 2007. "Time to Call a Halt to the Roadside Memorials." September 1. http://www.independent.ie/opinion/analysis/time-to-call-a-halt-to-the-roadside-memorials-26315008.html.

Leigh Fry, Susan. 1999. *Burial in Mediaeval Ireland, 900–1500.* Dublin: Four Courts.

MacConville, Una, and Regina McQuillan. 2005. "Continuing the Tradition: Roadside Memorials in Ireland." *Archaeology Ireland* 19 (1): 26–30.

MacConville, Una, and Regina McQuillan. 2009. "Remembering the Dead: Roadside Memorials in Ireland." In *Dying, Assisted Death and Mourning*, ed. Asa Kasher, 135–56. Amsterdam: Rodopi.

MacConville, Una, and Regina McQuillan. 2010. "Potent Reminders: An Examination of Responses to Roadside Memorials in Ireland." In *The Matter of Death: Space, Place and Materiality*, ed. Jennifer Hockey, Lorna Carol Komaromy, and Kate Woodthorpe,

195–207. London: Palgrave Macmillan. http://dx.doi.org/10.1057/978023028 3060_13.

Nic Néill, Máire. 1946. "Wayside Death Cairns in Ireland." *Béaloideas* 16 (1/2): 49–63. http://dx.doi.org/10.2307/20522127.

O'Rahilly, Cecile. 1976. *Táin Bó Cúailnge: Recension I*. Dublin: Dublin Institute for Advanced Studies.

Otto, Ton, and Poul Pedersen. 2005. *Tradition and Agency: Tracing Cultural Continuity and Invention*. Aarhus, Denmark: Aarhus University Press.

Santino, Jack. 2006a. Introduction to *Spontaneous Shrines and the Public Memorialization of Death*, ed. Jack Santino, 1–4. New York: Palgrave Macmillan.

Santino, Jack. 2006b. "Performative Commemoratives: Spontaneous Shrines and the Public Memorialization of Death." In *Spontaneous Shrines and the Public Memorialization of Death*, ed. Jack Santino, 5–15. New York: Palgrave Macmillan. http://dx.doi.org/10.1007/978-1-137-12021-2_2.

Senie, Harriet F. 2006. "Mourning in Protest: Spontaneous Memorials and the Sacralization of Public Space." In *Spontaneous Shrines and the Public Memorialization of Death*, ed. Jack Santino, 41–56. New York: Palgrave Macmillan. http://dx.doi.org/10.1007/978-1-137-12021-2_4.

Smith, Robert James. 1999. "Roadside Memorials—Some Australian Examples." *Folklore* 110 (1/2): 103–5. http://dx.doi.org/10.1080/0015587X.1999.9715990.

Tait, Clodagh. 2002. *Death, Burial and Commemoration in Ireland: 1550–1650*. London: Palgrave. http://dx.doi.org/10.1057/9781403913951.

Thomas, Jeannie B. 2006. "Communicative Commemoration and Graveside Shrines: Jim Morrison, Princess Diana, My 'Bro' Max, and Boogs the Cat." In *Spontaneous Shrines and the Public Memorialization of Death*, ed. Jack Santino, 17–40. New York: Palgrave Macmillan. http://dx.doi.org/10.1007/978-1-137-12021-2_3.

Yocom, Margaret R. 2006. "'We'll Watch out for Liza and the Kids': Spontaneous Memorials and Personal Response at the Pentagon, 2001." In *Spontaneous Shrines and the Public Memorialization of Death*, ed. Jack Santino, 57–97. New York: Palgrave Macmillan. http://dx.doi.org/10.1007/978-1-137-12021-2_5.

14

The Politics of Junk
Social Protest, "Outsider" Environments, and Ritualesque Display at the Heidelberg Project in Detroit

Daniel Wojcik

IN RECENT YEARS, THE PHENOMENON OF OUTSIDER ART has moved from the margins of cultural awareness toward the mainstream of the contemporary art world, captivating an international community of collectors, curators, dealers, scholars, and artists as well as the general public. Often characterized as "raw art" that is created spontaneously and for entirely personal reasons, outsider art historically has been associated with individuals who have no formal artistic training and exist outside of the dominant art world—psychiatric patients, visionaries and trance mediums, self-taught individualists, recluses, folk eccentrics, social misfits, and assorted others who are isolated or outcast from normative society, by choice or by circumstance. Unlike folk art, which is rooted in collective aesthetics and in the traditions of a particular community or subculture, outsider art is usually considered to be produced by people free of artistic training, "untainted" by the culture of the academy, and largely disconnected from broader culture or community (Dubuffet 1988; Cardinal 1972, 1994; Thévoz 1995; Maizels 1996; Rhodes 2000; Peiry 2001).[1]

Depictions of individuals identified as quintessential outsiders are frequently informed by recurring assumptions: insane and unrestrained, the outsider enacts pure and genuine forms of untutored creativity, reaches beyond the bounds of culture and societal norms, remains oblivious to the deadening hegemony and the pretense of the mainstream art world, and produces uniquely original works that evoke the tropes and qualities of the mystical. The term *outsider art* itself continues to be a subject of ongoing debate, promoted by some dealers and critics as a valid category and rejected by others as a deeply offensive concept that is elitist, patronizing, and dehumanizing, reinforcing romanticist ideas of the "artist as Other" while stigmatizing individuals as pathological or primitive in relation to normal people and culture.[2] Within the field of outsider art enthusiasm, there exists an ongoing representational practice of mystifying and fetishizing so-called outsiders and thus distorting the descriptions of such individuals, resulting in embellished tales that highlight the oddness of the artist's life, with an emphasis on eccentricity, deviance, and the individual's disconnection from history, society, and community. A common alternative strategy of representation, equally troubling, focuses primarily on the formalistic qualities of outsider art, celebrating the remarkable stylistic aspects of the work while ignoring the artist's biography almost completely, and thus severing the art from those who make it, and negating the voices of the creators and the deeper personal and cultural meanings (Ames 1994, 267–68).

A more humane and accurate understanding of those individuals classified as outsiders is offered by the emic and ethical perspective of folklorists and other theorists of expressive behavior, ritual, and cultural performance (Abrahams 1982; Babcock 1978; Bronner 2011; Csikszentmihalyi 1996; Falassi 1987; Jones 1994, 1997; Santino 2006b, 2011; Turner 1982). As an alternative to the decontextualized and romanticized misrepresentations of "outsiders," the approach advocated here emphasizes how individuals are connected rather than isolated by situating their lives and art within the matrix of vernacular traditions, ethnic heritage, religious worldviews, social interactions, personal motivations, public performances, and broader cultural contexts.

In this essay I examine the phenomenon of large-scale art environments built from debris and recycled materials—a mainstay in the outsider art compendium—and focus in detail on the Heidelberg Project, a public display of recycled objects in the inner city of Detroit. Created by so-called outsider artist Tyree Guyton, the environment has been condemned by various city officials and commentators, while at the same time celebrated by many others who support the project. I explore Guyton's motivations and the various contexts that inform his creative activities and discuss the social commentary that his environment provides. Guyton developed his Heidelberg Project as a form of street art, a public display that protests the collapse of his neighborhood. In the process he transformed his street from a blighted and dangerous part of the ghetto into an art environment, generating a grassroots-type of urban renewal. I analyze Guyton's environment, characterized by practices of bricolage, aesthetic recycling, and assemblage, as a performative site of contestation with explicitly "ritualesque" functions

(Santino 2011), and as a vernacular public display created to produce social change and transform the local community.

Seemingly isolated individuals who have created entire art environments have fascinated outsider art enthusiasts for decades and remain central to the field's conceptual core. These often monumental public displays are considered by many to exemplify the outsider genre, as their creators are frequently motivated by personal visions and artistic impulses that persist for years, in ways that are often viewed by onlookers as compulsive, if not neurotic. A sampling of those who have been acclaimed for creating such environments include Sabato (Simon) Rodia (1879–1965) and his towers in Watts, California; Ferdinand Cheval (1836–1924) and his *Palais Idéal* in southeastern France; Nek Chand (1924–2015) and his Rock Garden in Chandigarh, India; Tressa Prisbrey (1896–1988) and her Bottle Village in Simi Valley, California; and Howard Finster (1916–2001) and his Paradise Garden in Summerville, Georgia.

Although widely disparate in style and construction, these large-scale environments and folk sculpture parks are usually built from a bricolage of found objects and recycled materials. Beginning in modest ways, the projects often expand over the years as their creators continually add to the work through a process of ongoing accretion. Such spaces may become the life focus of their creators, an expression of the individual's energies, opinions, ideals, and dreams, or an attempt to construct a monument that outlasts death and renders the artist immortal. Entire homes and yards are transformed into vernacular art realms, for the expanding environments may grow to encompass the whole living space of their creators, which may eventually double as both a studio and artwork endlessly under construction, always in process. These environments are holistic and organic works that may combine architecture, sculpture, painting, landscape design, assemblage, and mottos and words of wisdom, thereby blurring conventional artistic categories.

The individualistic nature of many of these built spaces, involving ad hoc and unfamiliar construction techniques as well as the use of junk and discarded items, can disturb viewers and provoke controversy. While local hostilities may exist toward such places, the creators of these works are not necessarily isolated from their communities, as their constructions often reflect vernacular influences and are connected to local and social contexts as well as broader cultural views and issues (Beardsley 1995; Hernández 2013; Umberger 2007; Ward 1984). In many cases, these individuals have created art environments in order to directly engage their communities, provide social commentary, and express religious views or political concerns. For instance, Samuel Perry Dinsmoor's (1843–1932) Garden of Eden in

Lucas, Kansas, expresses populist views about the exploitation of workers and the "Crucifixion of Labor" by government, religion, the banking system, and corporate trusts. A number of African American art environments contain social commentary, such as the African American Heritage Museum and Black Veteran's Archive constructed by Charles Smith (b. 1940) in Aurora, Illinois. Motivated in part by ongoing war trauma and the death of his best friend while they were together in Vietnam, Smith's environment addresses racism and oppression while also commemorating the thousands of African Americans who died in the Vietnam War. Similarly, the artistic activities of Lonnie Holley (b. 1950), who constructed a two-acre yard art environment east of Birmingham, Alabama (now demolished), were initially related to grief and personal trauma, but also expressed his cultural heritage and addressed issues in his local African American community as well as broader problems such as poverty, drug abuse, racism, environmental destruction, and the mistreatment of children.

As unique as such environments may appear, they are necessarily rooted in social and cultural contexts, and sometimes are explicitly created to celebrate local culture, such as the Wisconsin Concrete Park built by Fred Smith (1886–1976) in Phillips, Wisconsin, that contains more than 200 embellished sculptures commemorating local history as well as national heroes and icons. In Chandigarh, India, the Rock Garden secretly and illegally built by Nek Chand from recycled debris and stones was initially condemned by bureaucrats and authorities yet was enthusiastically embraced by his fellow citizens for its homegrown style and connections to local traditions. As an oppositional alternative to the alienating and institutionally imposed modernist architecture of the city, Chand's seemingly outsider activities resulted in a folk environment imbued with cultural resonance that has had a restorative and transformative effect on the broader community, having been visited by millions of people and now celebrated throughout India and the world (Bhatti 1989).

Although these vernacular art environments initially may not appear to have much in common with ritual, festival, or celebration, upon closer examination they do exhibit some of the features of other public displays and cultural presentations, particularly murals and events characterized by the process of "folk assemblage" (Santino 2001, 37–74). Similar to protest marches, spontaneous shrines, processions, or activist demonstrations, these environments are performative displays that exist apart from institutional sanction, as grassroots expressions of symbolic action that may offer social critique. Like other public displays and performances discussed in this volume, such environmental constructions may involve the unauthorized claiming of public space or even its illegal appropriation (e.g., Chand's Rock Garden and Guyton's Heidelberg Project). These places may be politicized and valorized through symbolic action, and frequently exist as sites of contestation, generating hostilities from institutions and authorities that attempt to regulate their construction and the ideas expressed, in some instances actually ordering that the environments be demolished. In addition, vernacular environments, like other celebratory events and displays, may honor local events or figures; commemorate individuals or traumatic loss; and convey political commentary.

In some instances, these handmade constructions are created with the intent to transform attitudes and communities in ways that correspond to the ritualesque features that Santino (2011) identifies as an underlying facet of public displays and cultural events that are performed to accomplish social change and transformation.[3] Vernacular art environments tend to be fluid, ongoing, and ever-changing acts of creation, resembling other performative events that invite public spectatorship and participation. The construction of such environments is emergent and processual, with community members and visitors often bringing things to add to such sites and thus contributing to the construction process, much like the ongoing accretive activities and assemblage of objects that characterize the construction of spontaneous shrines and grassroots memorials (Everett 2002; Santino 2006a, 2006b; Margry and Sánchez-Carretero 2011; Wojcik 2008). In these ways, specific vernacular art environments share features and symbolic frames with other displays and cultural events, and in such instances they may be regarded as performative and participatory public displays, perhaps even "performative environments," with ritualesque aspects expressing the desire for social action.

THE HEIDELBERG PROJECT, AESTHETIC RECYCLING, AND SOCIAL PROTEST

Of the vernacular art environments that express political protest and have generated the promise of community transformation in ritualesque ways, Tyree Guyton's Heidelberg Project in Detroit has been one of most controversial. Like Chand's Rock Garden, sections of Guyton's project were built illegally on property that he does not own, and his appropriation of abandoned homes and vacant lots has provoked hostile responses from government authorities who have ordered the destruction of his constructions on several occasions. Guyton (b. 1955) began building his project in a rundown part of Detroit's lower east side, on Heidelberg Street, where he lived. It has overtaken two blocks of his largely abandoned neighborhood,

The Politics of Junk

Figure 14.1. Street view of Tyree Guyton's Heidelberg Project, Detroit, 1997 (Photograph by author)

a massive in-your-face display of recycled junk and discarded objects that he collected, reworked, and exhibited on his street. On dilapidated houses he painted polka dots and covered the structures with baby dolls, old appliances, furniture, and clothes; he hung old bicycles upside down from trees, all painted in bright colors and adorned with broken objects; and he piled and arranged configurations of tires, shoes, automobile parts, and vacuum cleaners on vacant lots and yards. Turning onto Heidelberg Street and entering Guyton's environment, one is confronted by an explosion of debris, as if the houses have been turned inside out and are spewing forth the commodities and junk of everyday life, a disorienting display that is simultaneously shocking, wondrous, and disturbing.

Guyton created these assemblages as a way to draw attention to the decline of his community. Over the years his constructions have addressed issues such as racism, poverty, homelessness, inner-city violence, war, politics, mass media bias, and social injustice in general. Like other environment builders who recycle junk and discards, Guyton has been called crazy, and his project has been criticized as a collection of garbage, an eyesore, and a health hazard (Darrach and Leonhauser 1988; Hodges 2011). His yard art installations have not only antagonized city officials but angered some of his neighbors, who are offended by what they regard as piles of trash that degrade the neighborhood, bring unwanted attention, reflect poorly on the local African American community, and are fire hazards. Parts of Guyton's environment have been bulldozed and demolished on orders by city authorities, while other constructions have been burned to the ground under suspicious circumstances. Despite the destruction of some of his installations and ongoing struggles over the years, his work has evolved into an internationally known art environment, described as a "Ghetto Guggenheim," which is now part of the identity of Detroit and attracts tens of thousands visitors each year (Alvin 2006).

Guyton began his project in 1986 in Detroit's McDougall-Hunt neighborhood, a part of the city that looked like the ruins of a town that had been bombed and abandoned, with boarded-up and ramshackle houses, vacant lots overgrown with weeds, gutted automobiles, and the remnants of structures burned to the ground. This was the neighborhood where Guyton grew up, in a house on the 3600 block of Heidelberg Street, his family struggling to survive on welfare, sometimes without food or electricity (Noriyuki 1995, E6). His mother raised the family by herself. As he described it to me an interview in 2006, "I grew up poor. I came from a big family, there were ten kids in my family. I was on my own. I never had shoes, I wore used ones. I grew up a loner. I played alone, did my own thing." Living in a six-bedroom house with twenty other people, he was a neglected child, one of many whose toys were discarded things, and at an early age he began salvaging found objects out of necessity. Cast-off things were used in creative ways. Guyton remembers playing with hubcaps, scraps of metal, old dolls, and anything else he could find. These experiences inform his assemblages today, which often are constructed from the objects he yearned for as a child. "We didn't have a phone, we didn't have toys to play with. So a lot of the stuff that I relate to is . . . stuff I didn't have, stuff that I wanted" (Plagens and Washington 1990, 64).

Guyton says he initially began creating art as a way to deal with the abuse and neglect he experienced as a child, explaining that the creative process has had a cathartic function throughout his life (Noriyuki 1989). The cast-off objects he salvaged for his projects mirrored his own childhood feelings of being discarded and worthless, and through the aesthetic recycling of found objects he found his own artistic voice. Guyton told me that began to see beauty and life in the discarded junk, and in translating his own experiences of abandonment and abuse into his art, he transformed worthless things into something of meaning and value. He discovered that the process of creatively reconfiguring recycled objects contributed to a reconstruction and reaffirmation of the self in response to the shattering effects of childhood trauma and ongoing adversity.

Guyton's project has not only helped him address the difficulties of his childhood, it is also directly related to the trauma that Detroit as a community experienced during the riots in 1967 and the subsequent decline of the city, the collapse of neighborhoods and white flight, plant closings, segregation, the abandoned structures, the poverty, murders, crime, inequality, neglect, and despair. In July 1967, at the age of twelve, Guyton witnessed the riots and watched as parts of the city burned. As he explained it to me, "The whole city was on fire, and I thought the world was ending . . . That changed me, and it changed Detroit, forever." After five days of violence and civil unrest in one of the most destructive riots in American history, more than 2,000 buildings had been looted and destroyed. A mass exodus from the inner city ensued, communities that were once racially integrated became segregated urban ghettos, and many people abandoned the city completely. In Guyton's view, and in the opinion of many others, city officials abandoned parts of Detroit as well.

The depopulation of the inner city of Detroit is staggering. More than 1 million people have moved away over the past four decades. The population dropped from a peak of 1.8 million inhabitants in the 1950s to 713,777 in 2010 and continued to decrease, the result of urban flight to the suburbs, the gasoline crises of the 1970s, and the decline of the American automobile industry (Seelye 2011). In his book *AfterCulture: Detroit and the Humiliation of History*, Jerry Herron, a native Detroiter and scholar of American literature and culture, comments on the tragic decline of the city: "Detroit, [the] one place that everybody else can agree on by agreeing they no longer want any part of it. Not when they think about what has gone on, and gone wrong, here: riots and white flight, plant closings and industrial collapse, murders and carjackings, assaults, arson, and drug wars . . . Neighborhoods collapsed . . . because half the goddam population left" (1993, 13–14). Guyton's neighborhood around Heidelberg Street was one of those that disintegrated in the aftermath of the riots. It quickly became a semiabandoned ghetto in which poverty, crime, hopelessness, and drug dealing were the rule. According to census figures, the mortality rate for African American males under the age of twenty-one in the neighborhood is now 55 percent, the unemployment rate is 75 percent, and more than 90 percent of those in the community are below the poverty line (Shibley et al. 2005, 157; Heidelberg Project ca. 2004, 2011). It is predicted that if the neighborhood continues to decline at its current rate, there will be nothing but vacant lots in the near future.

Prior to beginning his project, Guyton worked as a firefighter, was employed as an autoworker, and served in the army. He had been creating his small assemblages in the basement of his grandfather Sam Mackey's house, confronting the personal demons that haunted him. In 1986, at the age of thirty-one, as Guyton struggled with despair, it occurred to him that the public display of art on his street might be a possible solution to a desperate situation. During a home improvement project, he wiped his paintbrush on the street and realized how a streak of color could brighten up the drab environment. Soon after, as he tells it, the neglect and dereliction of his neighborhood literally began speaking to him. "When I started this Heidelberg Project, it was like the house next door was talking. Then the house across the street was talking. Then the crack house started to talk . . . Then I just got carried away and found myself running from this house to that house . . . You're not going to believe this. The street said to paint it, so I blocked off the street and starting painting" (Noriyuki 1989, 18). As he recalled in our interview, one of the first things he painted was a polka dot, as a circle of life representing the sun, moon, and universe; and then, with help from his wife Karen, Grandpa Mackey, and neighborhood children, he began building sculptures in vacant lots, painting abandoned buildings and covering them with toys, household appliances, car parts, shoes, dismembered dolls, signs, crosses, suitcases, stuffed animals, broken television sets, and other cast-off things.

The assemblages were created not only as a way to liven up the street but also to attract attention to the decaying neighborhood and the abandoned buildings, some of which were being used by crack cocaine dealers and prostitutes, Guyton explained to me. With Grandpa Mackey and Karen, he covered one crack house, for example, with colorful polka dots, put a big baby doll and blue inner tube on the roof, and a doghouse on the porch. Because of the attention the house received from the media and local Detroiters, the drug dealers began leaving the area (Darrach and Leonhauser 1988, 60; Alvin 2006). Guyton's assemblages and appropriation of local structures had effectively created a neighborhood watch program, and some supportive neighbors became involved in the project over time. Sometimes he listened to the music of John Coltrane and Thelonious Monk as he worked—and indeed Guyton's project might be seen as an improvisational visual riff on the art of jazz. His lyrical or jarring compositions of discarded junk eventually attracted an audience and community participation. As Guyton remembers it, "It really gave the neighbors something to do. They saw me getting out and cutting the grass in these vacant lots, and all of a sudden, they're coming to me with their cast-off old toys, car parts, whatever, and wanting me to incorporate them into my work. The people started sweeping up, then they started fixing up and painting, and all of a sudden people are having fun;

The Politics of Junk   263

Figure 14.2. Tyree Guyton and one of his transformed houses, Heidelberg Project, Detroit, early 1990s (Photograph by Ted Degener)

they're sitting out on the front porch again and saying this neighborhood has turned—from bad to good" (*PR Newswire* 1989).[4]

Although Guyton's efforts to transform his neighborhood were acknowledged by some, and he and Karen received a Spirit of Detroit Award in 1989, his project still generated hostility from a number of city council and community members who regarded his environment as a trash heap and blight on the neighborhood, a freak attraction for tourists and white suburbanites who cruised the street with locked car doors and who would never tolerate such a project in their own neighborhoods. As noted previously, Guyton had appropriated public property for much of his project, and although this was abandoned property, his actions were technically illegal. In response to neighborhood complaints, city officials ordered that some of his structures be destroyed or disassembled. In August 1989, without warning, the city demolished the Baby Doll House, an abandoned building formerly used by prostitutes until Guyton covered with it an unsettling display of broken, disfigured, and sometimes naked dolls and mannequins—hanging out of windows, perched precariously on the roof, crucified with nails through outstretched arms, dismembered, and sometimes in lewd

Figure 14.3. House with dolls, toys, and other objects, Heidelberg Project, Detroit, 1997 (Photograph by author)

positions. According to Guyton, his use of dolls was a commentary on child abuse, the shattered innocence of children, childhood prostitution, and the destruction of the young; and he believes the house was destroyed because of the issues it dealt with and its disturbing imagery (interview with author; Heidelberg Project n.d.; Alvin 2006).

Two months after the destruction of the Baby Doll House, a former crack house that Guyton had covered with tires and found objects (the Tire House) was also torn down. Then early on a Saturday morning in November 1991, again without warning, four houses were demolished by bulldozers sent by the mayor of Detroit, Coleman Young, who said the project was not art (Whitfield 2000, 190). Young's actions may have been motivated in part by Guyton's recent appearance on *The Oprah Winfrey Show*, which presented him as a nuisance to the neighborhood while also highlighting the deterioration of Detroit, perhaps embarrassing the mayor in the process. The demolition destroyed not only the houses but also a large number of artworks that Guyton had been storing for an upcoming show, including some of his grandfather's art. This destruction of the houses, art, and Guyton's other installations on vacant lots had a devastating effect. The following year, the death of his mentor and beloved collaborator Grandpa Mackey, who was heartbroken after the demolition, triggered a period of grief and soul-searching. Despondent and angry at the city, Guyton slowly began reconstructing his project. The process of creation again seemed to sustain him through difficult times and tragedies—his divorce from Karen Guyton after nine years of marriage; the loss of three brothers to violence and drugs; financial ruin; and a night spent with a .25 automatic in his hand, wanting to end a lifetime of pain (Noriyuki 1995, E6; Heidelberg Project 2011).

During this period of despair, he somehow gradually rebuilt the project, encouraged by his friends and supporters. Guyton first worked on his own house and then expanded to other abandoned structures, painting car hoods and plywood for his Faces of God and Faces in the Hood installations. His efforts received some recognition and financial support, yet his ongoing battles with the city continued, and he was cited for littering and creating an illegal dump site. In February 1999, Detroit mayor Dennis Archer declared the site unsanitary and a haven for rats. He ordered the destruction of three more houses, and about 40 percent of the project was demolished (Hodges 2011; Whitfield 2000, 191). This time, as the structures were being demolished, Guyton and his family and friends frantically tried to save some works, as did some of the city workers who had been ordered to disassemble the structures. In the midst of it all, Guyton grabbed a paint bucket and began to paint blue polka dots throughout the environment. When interviewed by reporters about the destruction, he gave them his defiant response: "I'm going to polka dot the whole fucking city next" (Moore 1999, 55). In a possible act of retaliation for challenging city hall, city officials claimed that Guyton's privately owned Canfield Project studio was hazardous to the community; it was demolished along with 200 of his artworks stored inside (Whitfield 2000, 191).

Guyton and those who support his project have repeatedly asked why, among the thousands of abandoned structures in the city, his assemblages often seemed to be at the top of the city's list for demolition during the 1990s. According to calculations in the late 1980s, there were approximately 15,000 vacant structures in Detroit, totaling more than 55,000 abandoned buildings and vacant lots; a survey in 2010 counted 33,529 empty houses and 91,488 vacant lots (Montemurri et al. 1989; Irwin 1990; Whitfield 2000, 192; Detroit Residential Parcel Survey 2010, 16–24). The targeted destruction of Guyton's rogue installations appears to have been motivated in part because they provided a symbolic commentary on Detroit's national reputation as a decaying, ruined city, and his spectacles of debris as ritualesque public display drew attention to a part of Detroit, and Detroit's past, that some city officials wanted to ignore or forget. When I spoke with Guyton about his relationship with city officials and the public responses to his project, he said,

> Some like it [his art], some hate it, some want to destroy it, some want to steal it. But I always get a response. They used to call me the "Voodoo Man of Heidelberg Street," some still call me crazy, they don't like all this. But there is a science to this madness, a system to this mess. I'm taking the junk of the city, making it special, and putting it in people's faces. The City of Detroit wanted to forget this part of town, that we are here. Let me get political with it—the governor, the city officials, they tried to tear it down, I've had lots of run-ins with all of them, and I've dealt with it. You have to stand up for what you believe. I chose to fight back . . . This is America, and I decided I'm going to call their asses out. And I did. Well, I won some battles, and they did too, but I'm still here. I've learned you got to be patient, it's like baby steps, a little bit at a time, to make things change.

Guyton is obviously no isolated outsider artist. He took art courses at Detroit's Marygrove College and the College for Creative Studies before dropping out of school in 1982. He says he has tried to forget his art school training. His inspiration for the project comes from dreams, his religious belief that he has a spiritual mission to renew his neighborhood, and from his Grandpa Mackey, a former house painter and handyman who put a paintbrush in Guyton's hand and supported him during times of despair. "My grandpa was my best friend," he told me. "He always encouraged me. There were bad times, I don't talk about those. But he was the one who always was there for me." Despite the outsider art label that often is attached to Guyton's environment, his work is a neighborhood-based, activist art project, and his public displays share some similarities with other African American art environments and reflect certain vernacular traditions, including the creolized visual language of yard shows, bottle trees, the aesthetic use of recycled material, and the protective use of certain objects. The aesthetic use of debris and recycled material traditionally has been a means of investing the African American yard and "home ground" with a sense of rootedness, and is characterized by specific themes (Gundaker 1998, 14–15)—all of which seem evident in Guyton's displays on Heidelberg Street: protection, personal virtuosity, community improvement, and honor to family and ancestors. Created in part as a means of guarding against drug dealers and the dangers of his neighborhood, Guyton's environment may reflect these traditions of safeguard and protection; in Robert Farris Thompson's opinion, Guyton's use of circular objects like tires, hubcaps, and clock faces is an expression of central African ideas of "motion" that not only activate dilapidated structures but also repel or "wheel away" criminals (1998, 43–44). Guyton's project exhibits other elements that Thompson (45) has identified as being central to the visual displays of African American yard shows, including "*motion* (wheels, tires, hubcaps, pinwheels); *containment* (jars, jugs, flasks, bottles, especially on trees and porches); *figuration* (plaster icons, dolls, root sculptures, metal images); and *medicine*," although instead of surrounding houses with traditional charms and healing herbs, Guyton has used discarded objects to protect and heal the neighborhood. The idea of the healing potential of art has been a part of Guyton's project from the start, as he notes: "It was my way of using art as a medicine to make a difference in that community" (Steele 2011).

When I asked Guyton about the possible African or African American influences on this art, he responded, "Well, I don't know. My grandfather encouraged me, he was the one who helped me in my art, and so I guess there *could* be connections." He then quickly added,

> But these are my own ideas too . . . This art is more about . . . shaping your world and bringing order into the equation. I had to create order, there was so much craziness here—crack houses, junkies, hoodlums, prostitutes, trash, ruins, fear after the riots in 1967. It was chaos down here. So what do you do? I realized even chaos has order, so I gave all this madness a new order . . . Most people here are trapped, they are cut off from that hope, the idea that things can change. So that's what I try to do, show that things can change . . . Working out here on the street is different, this is not the gallery, or the university, where people are all tight-assed about art, and afraid to get worked up . . . I'm *glad* you're talking to me about this. We need people to get excited, or angry, or whatever, to wake people up these days, to the problems here, and in the world.

Among his creations that involve political commentary and call for social change, Guyton's yard assemblage Clean This Mutha Up is dedicated to the City of Detroit and consists of rows of painted vacuum cleaners standing upright with gloves on their handles, a jab at the city's neglect of urban blight and decline of neighborhoods. Guyton says his sidewalks lined with shoes represent those standing in unemployment lines, while various piles and assemblages of thousands of shoes in vacant lots (A Lot of Shoes) symbolize the thousands of wandering homeless in the city of Detroit. He also represented the plight of the homeless by spreading hundreds of shoes across Heidelberg Street, to be run over by cars and to be beaten by the elements. After the 1991 demolition of much of his project, Guyton looked to the skies and incorporated the nearby trees into his environment as a safeguard, believing the city would not destroy the trees. His piece, Soles of the Most High, consists of hundreds of pairs of shoes hanging from the branches of a tree, a representation of the lynching of African Americans in the South, based on the childhood memories of his grandfather, who said that when he looked up at the lifeless hanging corpses, "All that could be seen were the soles of the shoes" (Heidelberg Project n.d.). Guyton has created other assemblages of shoes, including an old oven stuffed with shoes to represent those who suffered and died in the concentration camps of the Holocaust (Heidelberg Project, n.d.).

Although some assemblages represent human suffering or crimes against humanity, or memorialize those who have been killed, others address issues of civil rights, such as Guyton's painted bus, Move to the Rear, a tribute to Rosa Parks, a longtime resident of Detroit. After meeting the civil rights pioneer, he had a dream of creating art with a bus, and soon after, someone donated a passenger bus manufactured in 1955, the same year that Parks refused to surrender her seat to a white person on a bus in Montgomery, Alabama. Guyton painted the bus with polka dots, which for him symbolize diversity, racial and cultural differences, the hope for racial harmony, and the overall similarity among people (Heidelberg Project 2004). Guyton's Polka Dot House (also referred to as the Dotty Wotty House, and the New White House) was inspired by Martin Luther King Jr.'s vision of racial equality and harmony, significant in the context of the segregation and racial divide in Detroit. Polka dots are splashed across the other structures on Heidelberg Street and the street itself, enlivening with color an otherwise drab environment. Guyton also has painted polka dots on hundreds of abandoned structures throughout Detroit to draw attention to the empty buildings, and this motif has become his artistic signature, a tribute to his Grandpa Mackey inspired by his grandfather's love of jelly beans.

Guyton created his OJ House after the O. J. Simpson murder case in 1995, the most publicized criminal trial in American history. Guyton told me that the letters "OJ" painted all over the house stand for "Obstruction of Justice," and the house is a critique of the "media circus" and exploitation of the trial, the racist undertones in the coverage, the American obsession with celebrities, the media's larger neglect of the injustices and violence committed on marginalized people everyday, and the global obstruction of justice generally (see also Heidelberg Project n.d.). During the war in Iraq, Guyton began painting the word "war" on numerous displays, reflecting his belief that the war was initiated for the wrong reasons while important issues at home, such as poverty, health care, urban decay, and racism, were being ignored by the government. He says he tries not to preach to people about war through his art; he simply "puts the word out there. I don't tell people what it means. I want them to think about it. Some think it is only about the war in the Middle East. But it could be about the damn war that

Figure 14.4. Tyree Guyton's painted bus (a tribute to civil rights pioneer Rosa Parks) and his "Faces of God" and "Faces in the Hood" paintings on car hoods and plywood, Heidelberg Project, 1997 (Photograph by author)

goes on in our heads. Or the war in Detroit, the 1967 riots—that was a war, too." In 2011, Guyton completed an installation called Street Folk, which involved carpeting an entire block of Edmund Street near the Heidelberg Project with more than 10,000 discarded, donated, and painted shoes. Like his earlier piece A Lot of Shoes, he created this installation to draw attention to Detroit's large homeless population, and in this case he employed local homeless people to help him with the assemblage while encouraging those who needed shoes to take a pair.

The urban art displays of Guyton's Heidelberg Project share features with the folk assemblages described by Santino in his studies of political public displays, seasonal yard constructions, and spontaneous shrines that involve arrangements of discrete items to create a larger and more complex symbolic public statement with social, aesthetic, and political messages (Santino 1986, 160–65; 2001, 50–51). Characterized by juxtaposition and bricolage, such assemblages require observers to work through the layers of symbolic meaning evoked by disparate objects that are joined together in often incongruous or startling ways. At an early age, out of necessity, Guyton learned the do-it-yourself techniques of bricolage, resourcefully creating with things salvaged from the streets and trash.[5] While the concept of bricolage does not necessarily have connotations of subversion in its original usage, later revisions of the idea by cultural theorists link its techniques to resistance, whether in youth subcultural styles, oppositional tactics in the workplace, carnivalesque events, or the "textual poaching" of fans who rework the products of mass culture (Hebdige 1979, 102–27; de Certeau 1984; Jenkins 1992; St. John 2012, 199–232; Wojcik 1995, 11–20). The use of bricolage in these contexts is seen as a form of creative resistance offering a challenge to conventional uses and interpretations, as things are refigured and recontextualized through juxtapositions and assemblages that create new and potentially oppositional meanings; these creative and sometimes shocking recombinations may then destabilize established cultural boundaries or expose the ways dominant ideologies are constructed.

Like subcultural bricoleurs and creators of carnivalesque assemblages, Guyton recontextualizes objects—the hundreds of shoes scattered in the street or placed in an oven, the naked dolls crucified on houses, the Bible in a toilet, the discarded toys and stuffed animals nailed to trees—to disturb the normative contexts and meanings of things and, through inversion, excess, parody, chaos, and the grotesque, to subvert and critique the symbolic order. In this way, such displays may be perceived as a direct confrontation to societal order, invoking a "moral panic" and the labeling of Guyton's environment as a threat to ideas about art, neighborhood, and societal values in general. As a site of ideological contestation, the Heidelberg Project not only challenges elitist notions of what art is, who can make art, and how it is displayed, it is a commentary on notions of public and private space, art and trash, consumerism and materialism, and community and social justice.

The presentation of political views and social criticism in Guyton's environmental assemblages may have carnivalesque features, but his ongoing creative efforts are also clearly ritualesque in purpose and intent, involving the performative use of objects and symbols to effect social change. Carnivalesque events, in Mikhail Bakhtin's (1984) original conceptualization of the term, provide only temporary liberation from cultural norms and social oppression through inversion, parody, and licensed transgression; Guyton's environment represents a continuing attempt to transform things, an ongoing performative commentary and a day-by-day effort toward social action, reform, and the improvement of conditions, tangibly manifested in his neighborhood. Carnivalesque and ritualesque aspects of public displays frequently coexist in this regard and are not necessarily antithetical, with the ludic aspects of carnivalesque events potentially offering visions of social change, as Santino tells us: "Often, the carnivalesque qualities of public performative events are recognized, but their seriousness of purpose, the intention to raise awareness, change opinions and even the hearts and minds of spectators, has remained unremarked upon and has not been analyzed as a constitutive dimension of the event. Moreover, the presence of the ludic, of play, of the carnivalesque, does not negate their intention to make something happen, to change things, or to bring a new social reality into being" (2011, 62).

As a public display that is both ludic and liminal, Guyton's environment on Heidelberg Street is a "betwixt and between" site where alternative notions about reality are presented and where ideas of social change are generated. Through the processes of bricolage, assemblage, and the ludic recombination of recycled objects and debris, Guyton's displays transform the perception of specific spaces and blur the boundaries between "art" and everyday life. A visit to Heidelberg Street is necessarily participatory and expressive, as those who wander around the environment are immersed in the multisensory experience of the place. Neighbors, tourists, and curious Detroiters interact with the environment, with Guyton, and with each other—exploring, questioning, laughing, or criticizing—and they too become a part of the project, an active component contributing to the performance of the place, which constantly changes day by day and year by year. Heidelberg Street has now become a nexus of human activity and an oasis of hope in the urban ghetto, offering the possibility of community, change, and renewal.

From the beginning of his project, Guyton has invited the participation of community members. Some people in his neighborhood have responded and brought him things, especially the local children, who help on a regular basis and flock around Guyton as he works. Children have always been an important part of Guyton's environment, according to journalist Duane Noriyuki, who recalls the early years of the project: "It was interesting to me that children, more than adults, seemed to understand Tyree. They were drawn to the project without caring what it was, only that it was a whimsical distraction from daily life in the 'hood. The children were a part of his art, not only because they were invited to participate in its creation but also because seeing them play at Heidelberg transformed his work into living art. It was a much different experience when the children weren't there. At night, it was haunting, but when children were playing, it was entirely different, their play made it alive in a different way" (personal communication, November 17, 2011). Over the years, Guyton expanded his efforts to involve local children in making art at the site. He also began offering an after-school art program in the mid-1990s at the nearby Ralph Bunche Elementary School, in response to the fact that most Detroit public schools no longer had art programs.

In addition to introducing children to creative activities, Guyton says that his street displays are meant to transform his community in other ways, attracting people to his neighborhood and communicating with those who have never visited an art gallery or museum. As he told me:

> This is art in the real world, where people live, not in some gallery. Most people around here don't care about art in a gallery, maybe they never been to a gallery, so I put it right in front of their faces, expose them to color, shapes, forms. And it creates a brand-new conversation, it helps people to see in a new way. Not only the people who live here, but it brings in outsiders to this part of town, people who would *never* come here. They come from the suburbs, from all over the U.S., all over the world. And this is good for all of us. It is educating the world. And the people who live here get to meet new people, so they are not isolated or forgotten.

In recent years, as Guyton has received awards and recognition for his work. Support for his project has increased and resulted in various community events, including street festivals and concerts. There have been discussions of developing the environment and nearby lots into a "cultural village" for arts education, a community-based sustainable "green" urban area that will revitalize the neighborhood and perhaps serve as a model for other postindustrial "shrinking cities" (Heidelberg Project 2011; Shibley et al. 2005).

Initially created in an attempt to confront the personal traumas of childhood and the decline of his neighborhood, Guyton's Heidelberg Project has grown from a condemned collection of trash to become the third-largest tourist attraction in Detroit. For three decades, Guyton has collected objects regarded as worthless—perhaps analogous to the lives of those living in the ghetto, people who often feel that they have been cast off, beaten down, and broken—and given these abandoned things new life and meaning. In the process, he has transformed his neighborhood from a place where people were afraid to walk the streets into a safe haven of reconfigured objects and polka-dotted structures, a site of play and social commentary, a place where neighbors, curious Detroiters, and out-of-towners now congregate and interact. Those in support of the Heidelberg Project say that since its beginning more than thirty years ago, there have been no serious crimes reported on Heidelberg Street, and gang violence and drug trafficking there have been largely eliminated (Alvin 2006; Shibley et al. 2005; Heidelberg Project 2011). Guyton's grassroots effort at urban renewal expresses a singular vision of neighborhood empowerment and an affirmation of the inner city, and demonstrates how the creative process may serve as a source of healing and transformation for individuals and communities.

As Guyton has stated, "I can take anything and put meaning into it, but to take it beyond and use it as medicine to make a person well again, that is where the art is . . . I'm not here to argue aesthetics. I'm here to talk about how the project's working to bring life to the community" (Flores 2004).

Against all odds and in the face of ongoing animosity, Guyton's environment, like the creations of other environment builders, eventually resonated with some segments of the community through its expression of local concerns, social commentary, and neighborhood transformation. Despite the outsider art label and seemingly idiosyncratic nature of such environments, these displays are suffused with vernacular influences and embedded in local culture, as their creators, like other individuals who create things, draw upon traditional sources and ideas for inspiration and design elements. It is this interplay between individual creativity and vernacular vocabularies that makes these environments so evocative and yet so unsettling for some—a fusion of the familiar and unknown, reflecting hints of tradition that have been reshaped or overshadowed by the intensity of individual innovation, creative vision, or the desire to change the world. The power and controversy of such vernacular places reside in the multivalent meanings they evoke: as liminal spaces, folk heterotopias, illegal assemblages of trash, counterhegemonic critiques, illustrations of compulsive creativity, carnivalesque assemblages, empowering artistic achievements, or ritualesque sites of community transformation.

Instead of conceptualizing people as idiosyncratic outsiders or celebrating their perceived otherness and thus ultimately exiling to them to the outposts of society, the perspective offered here—with its focus on personal motivations, community influences, and broader sociocultural contexts—invites these artists in from the margins and reveals that they are motivated by concerns and emotions that may affect all of us. Although such individuals and the art environments they create are definitely outside the conventional parameters of public performative events, including them in our discussion of such events and ritualesque phenomena offers an expanded understanding of the varieties of public display and the politics of vernacular expression.

NOTES

This essay is based on the paper "Urban Decay, Public Display, and Protest Art in an African-American Neighborhood," presented at the Tenth Annual Conference on Holidays, Ritual, Festival, Celebration, and Public Display, held in conjunction with the Conference on Chinese Daily Ritual Practice, Willamette University, Salem, Oregon, June 2–4, 2006. I thank Jack Santino and Michael Owen Jones for their suggestions and helpful comments on this expanded version of that paper.

1. The expression *outsider art* was popularized with the publication of art historian Roger Cardinal's influential book *Outsider Art* in 1972, the title of which was proposed as an English equivalent for the French term *art brut*, a concept advanced by the modernist painter Jean Dubuffet in the 1940s and 1950s. For Dubuffet (1901–1985), art brut (raw art) was made by people free of formal artistic training whose production was "untainted" by the culture of the academy and existed outside of or against cultural norms as an "authentic" form of expression that exposed the pretentious and artificial nature of the contemporary Western art world.

Discussions and debates by folklorists about the definitions of folk art, fine art, outsider art, idiosyncratic art, self-taught art, tradition, community, creativity, material culture, and other relevant concepts are included in Bronner 1996, 2011; Feintuch 1995; Fine 2004; Georges and Jones 1995; Glassie 1989, 1999; Jones 1989, 1994, 1997; Pocius 1995; Santino 1986; Vlach and Bronner 1992; and Zug 1994, among others.

2. A sampling of debates and criticisms of the concept of outsider art include Borum 1993–1994; Cubbs 1994; Metcalf 1994; Jones 1994, 313–18; Russell 2001, 17–23; Fine 2004, 26–33; Maclagan 2009, 25–58; and Wojcik 2016.

3. Santino, drawing upon the linguist J. L. Austin's (1962) notion of "performative utterances" as pronouncements that achieve a social change, extends the concept of the performative to events that attempt to produce social transformation, address societal grievances, and create change in the surrounding society. For instance, he refers to spontaneous shrines as "performative commemoratives" to emphasize that these are not only places of memorialization but also may function as expressions of frustration and outrage in the wake of unexpected and traumatic death and become a politicized call to action to contest senseless violence (2006a, 2011).

4. For consideration of Guyton's project from a variety of viewpoints, see Heidelberg Project 2007.

5. Like other builders of art environments such as Chand, Rodia, and Prisbrey, Guyton embodies the concept of the *bricoleur* as a do-it-yourself inventor, a resourceful jack-of-all-trades creating with scrap, leftovers, and odds and ends. In Claude Lévi-Strauss's well-known explication of the notion, he specifically refers to the French vernacular environment builder Cheval and his *Palais* to illustrate this process of using available materials in new ways to create things from miscellaneous objects salvaged from a variety of sources (1966, 18–19).

REFERENCES

Abrahams, Roger. 1982. "The Language of Festivals: Celebrating the Economy." In *Celebration: Studies in Festivity and Ritual*, ed. Victor Turner, 161–77. Washington, DC: Smithsonian Institution Press.

Alvin, Julie. 2006. "Bringing Some Color to the Detroit Projects." *NY Arts Magazine*, July–August.

Ames, Kenneth. 1994. "Outside Outsider Art." In *The Artist Outsider: Creativity and the Boundaries of Culture*, ed. Michael D. Hall and Eugene W. Metcalf Jr., 252–72. Washington, DC: Smithsonian Institution Press.

Austin, J. L. 1962. *How to Do Things with Words*. Cambridge: Harvard University Press.

Babcock, Barbara A., ed. 1978. *The Reversible World: Symbolic Inversion in Art and Society*. Ithaca: Cornell University Press.

Bakhtin, Mikhail M. (Original work published 1965) 1984. *Rabelais and His World*. Trans. Helene Iswolsky. Bloomington: Indiana University Press.

Beardsley, John. 1995. *Gardens of Revelation: Environments by Visionary Artists.* New York: Abbeville.
Bhatti, S. S. 1989. "The Rock Garden of Chandigarh: Nek Chand's Testament of Creativity." *Raw Vision* 1 (Spring): 22–31.
Borum, Jenifer Penrose. 1993–1994. "Term Warfare." *Raw Vision* 8 (Winter): 24–31.
Bronner, Simon J. 1996. *The Carver's Art: Crafting Meaning from Wood.* Lexington: University Press of Kentucky.
Bronner, Simon J. 2011. *Explaining Traditions: Folk Behavior in Modern Culture.* Lexington: University Press of Kentucky.
Cardinal, Roger. 1972. *Outsider Art.* London: Studio Vista.
Cardinal, Roger. 1994. "Toward an Outsider Aesthetic." In *The Artist Outsider: Creativity and the Boundaries of Culture,* ed. Michael D. Hall and Eugene W. Metcalf Jr., 20–43. Washington, DC: Smithsonian Institution Press.
Csikszentmihalyi, Mihaly. 1996. *Creativity: Flow and the Psychology of Discovery and Invention.* New York: HarperCollins.
Cubbs, Joanne. 1994. "Rebels, Mystics, and Outcasts: The Romantic Artist Outsider." In *The Artist Outsider: Creativity and the Boundaries of Culture,* ed. Michael D. Hall and Eugene W. Metcalf Jr., 76–93. Washington, DC: Smithsonian Institution Press.
Darrach, Brad, and Maria Leonhauser. 1988. "With Blight Spirit, Tyree Guyton Transforms Trash into Murals and Crack Houses into Ghetto Galleries." *People Weekly* 30 (7): 58–60.
de Certeau, Michel. 1984. *The Practice of Everyday Life.* Trans. Steven Rendall. Berkeley: University of California Press.
Detroit Residential Parcel Survey. 2010. Detroit: Detroit Office of Foreclosure Prevention and Response, Community Legal Resources, and Data Driven Detroit. https://datadrivendetroit.org/files/DRPS/Detroit%20Residential%20Parcel%20Survey%20OVERVIEW.pdf. Accessed June 17, 2013.
Dubuffet, Jean. 1988. *Asphyxiating Culture and Other Writings.* New York: Four Walls Eight Windows.
Everett, Holly. 2002. *Roadside Crosses in Contemporary Memorial Culture.* Denton: University of North Texas Press.
Falassi, Alessandro, ed. 1987. *Time out of Time: Essays on the Festival.* Albuquerque: University of New Mexico Press.
Feintuch, Burt, ed. 1995. "Common Ground: Keywords for the Study of Expressive Culture." Special issue, *Journal of American Folklore* 108.
Fine, Gary Alan. 2004. *Self-Taught Art and the Culture of Authenticity.* Chicago: University of Chicago Press.
Flores, Taya. 2004. "Guyton Transforms Trash into Treasure." *Lantern,* January 28. http://www.thelantern.com/2004/01/guyton-transforms-trash-into-treasure/. Accessed November 17, 2011.
Georges, Robert A., and Michael O. Jones. 1995. *Folkloristics: An Introduction.* Bloomington: Indiana University Press.
Glassie, Henry. 1989. *The Spirit of Folk Art: The Girard Collection of the Museum of International Folk Art.* New York: Harry N. Abrams, in association with Museum of New Mexico.
Glassie, Henry. 1999. *Material Culture.* Bloomington: Indiana University Press.
Gundaker, Grey, ed. 1998. *Keep Your Head to the Sky: Interpreting African American Home Ground.* Charlottesville: University Press of Virginia.
Hebdige, Dick. 1979. *Subculture: The Meaning of Style.* London: Methuen.
Heidelberg Project. ca. 2004. *Heidelberg Project Pamphlet.* Detroit: Heidelberg Project.
Heidelberg Project, ed. 2007. *Connecting the Dots: Tyree Guyton's Heidelberg Project.* Detroit: Wayne State University Press.

Heidelberg Project. 2011. "The Heidelberg Project." https://www.heidelberg.org/. Accessed November 7, 2011.
Heidelberg Project. n.d. "The Living Canvas of Tyree Guyton." Detroit: The Heidelberg Project. Flier.
Hernández, Jo Farb, ed. 2013. *Singular Spaces: From the Eccentric to the Extraordinary in Spanish Art Environments*. San Jose: San Jose State University in association with SPACES—Saving and Preserving Arts Environments, Aptos, CA.
Herron, Jerry. 1993. *AfterCulture: Detroit and the Humiliation of History*. Detroit: Wayne State University Press.
Hodges, Michael H. 2011. "25 Years Later, 'Outsider Art' Vision Still Fuels Fame, Furor on Heidelberg Street." *Detroit News*, August 1.
Irwin, Jim. 1990. "Detroit Finds Rebuilding a Long, Hard Pull Upward." *Seattle Times*, April 22.
Jenkins, Henry. 1992. *Textual Poachers: Television Fans and Participatory Culture*. New York: Routledge.
Jones, Michael Owen. 1989. *Craftsman of the Cumberlands: Tradition and Creativity*. Lexington: University Press of Kentucky.
Jones, Michael Owen. 1994. "How Do You Get inside the Art of Outsiders?" In *The Artist Outsider: Creativity and the Boundaries of Culture*, ed. Michael D. Hall and Eugene W. Metcalf Jr., 312–31. Washington, DC: Smithsonian Institution Press.
Jones, Michael Owen. 1997. "How Can We Apply Event Analysis to 'Material Behavior,' and Why Should We?" *Western Folklore* 56: 199–214.
Lévi-Strauss, Claude. 1966. *The Savage Mind*. Chicago: University of Chicago Press.
Maclagan, David. 2009. *Outsider Art: From the Margins to the Marketplace*. London: Reaktion Books.
Maizels, John. 1996. *Raw Creation: Outsider Art and Beyond*. London: Phaidon.
Margry, Peter Jan, and Cristina Sánchez-Carretero, eds. 2011. *Grassroots Memorials: The Politics of Memorializing Traumatic Death*. New York: Berghahn.
Metcalf, Eugene W., Jr. 1994. "From Domination to Desire: Insiders and Outsider Art." In *The Artist Outsider: Creativity and the Boundaries of Culture*, ed. Michael D. Hall and Eugene W. Metcalf Jr., 212–27. Washington, DC: Smithsonian Institution Press.
Montemurri, Patricia, Zachare Ball, and Roger Chesley. 1989. "15,215 Buildings Stand Empty." *Detroit Free Press*, July 9, 8A.
Moore, Ryan. 1999. "Tyree Guyton: Demolition Man." *Juxtapose* 20 (May/June): 54–55.
Noriyuki, Duane. 1989. "To Stem the Darkness." *Detroit Free Press Magazine*, April 2.
Noriyuki, Duane. 1995. "A World Gone Mad." *Los Angeles Times*, May 5, E1, E6.
Peiry, Lucienne. 2001. *Art Brut: The Origins of Outsider Art*. Trans. James Frank. Paris: Flammarion.
Plagens, Peter, with Frank Washington. 1990. "Come on-a My House." *Newsweek*, August 6, 64.
Pocius, Gerald. 1995. "Art." *Journal of American Folklore* 108 (430): 413–31. http://dx.doi.org/10.2307/541654.
PR Newswire. 1989. "Creator of Post-industrial Art Honored by Detroit City Council; Sculpture Helps Rid Heidelberg Neighborhood of Dope Dealers." July 3. *LexisNexis Academic*. Accessed October 7, 2011.
Rhodes, Colin. 2000. *Outsider Art: Spontaneous Alternatives*. London: Thames & Hudson.
Russell, Charles. 2001. "Finding a Place for the Self-Taught in the Art World(s)." In *Self-Taught Art: The Culture and Aesthetics of American Vernacular Art*, ed. Charles Russell, 3–34. Jackson: University Press of Mississippi.

Santino, Jack. 1986. "The Folk Assemblage of Autumn: Tradition and Creativity in Halloween Folk Art." In *Folk Art and Art Worlds*, ed. John M. Vlach and Simon Bronner, 151–69. Ann Arbor: UMI Research Press.
Santino, Jack. 2001. *Signs of War and Peace: Social Conflict and the Use of Public Symbols in Northern Ireland*. New York: Palgrave Macmillan. http://dx.doi.org/10.1007/978-1-4039-8233-9.
Santino, Jack. 2006a. "Performative Commemoratives: Spontaneous Shrines and the Public Memorialization of Death." In *Spontaneous Shrines and the Public Memorialization of Death*, ed. Jack Santino, 5–15. New York: Palgrave Macmillan. http://dx.doi.org/10.1007/978-1-137-12021-2_2.
Santino, Jack, ed. 2006b. *Spontaneous Shrines and the Public Memorialization of Death*. New York: Palgrave Macmillan. http://dx.doi.org/10.1007/978-1-137-12021-2.
Santino, Jack. 2011. "The Carnivalesque and the Ritualesque." *Journal of American Folklore* 124 (491): 61–73. http://dx.doi.org/10.5406/jamerfolk.124.491.0061.
Seelye, Katharine Q. 2011. "Detroit Population Down 25 Percent, Census Finds." *New York Times*, March 22.
Shibley, Robert, Emily Axelrod, Jay Farbstein, and Richard Wener. 2005. *Reinventing Downtown: 2005 Rudy Bruner Award for Urban Excellence*. Cambridge, MA: Bruner Foundation.
Steele, Jazmine. 2011. "The Heidelberg Project Celebrates 25 Years." *Michigan Citizen* 33, no. 48 (October 9), A9.
St. John, Graham. 2012. *Global Tribe: Technology, Spirituality and Psytrance*. Sheffield, UK: Equinox.
Thévoz, Michel. (Original work published 1976) 1995. *Art Brut*. Geneva: Editions d'Art Albert Skira S.A.
Thompson, Robert Farris. 1998. "Bighearted Power: Kongo Presence in the Landscape and Art of Black America." In *Keep Your Head to the Sky: Interpreting African American Home Ground*, ed. Grey Gundaker, 37–64. Charlottesville: University Press of Virginia.
Turner, Victor, ed. 1982. *Celebration: Studies in Festivity and Ritual*. Washington, DC: Smithsonian Institution Press.
Umberger, Leslie, ed. 2007. *Sublime Spaces & Visionary Worlds: Built Environments of Vernacular Artists*. New York: Princeton Architectural Press.
Vlach, John Michael, and Simon J. Bronner. 1992. Introduction to *Folk Art and Art Worlds*, ed. John Michael Vlach and Simon J. Bronner, xv–xxxi. Logan: Utah State University Press.
Ward, Daniel Franklin, ed. 1984. *Personal Places: Perspectives on Informal Art Environments*. Bowling Green: Bowling Green State University Popular Press.
Whitfield, Jenenne. 2000. "Thoughts on Tyree Guyton's Heidelberg Project." *Southern Quarterly* 39 (1–2): 187–96.
Wojcik, Daniel. 1995. *Punk and Neo-tribal Body Art*. Jackson: University Press of Mississippi.
Wojcik, Daniel. 2008. "Pre's Rock: Pilgrimage, Ritual, and Runners' Traditions at the Roadside Shrine for Steve Prefontaine." In *Shrines and Pilgrimage in the Modern World: New Itineraries into the Sacred*, ed. Peter Jan Margry, 201–37. Amsterdam: Amsterdam University Press.
Wojcik, Daniel. 2016. *Outsider Art: Visionary Worlds and Trauma*. Jackson: University Press of Mississippi.
Zug, Charles G., III. 1994. "Folk Art and Outsider Art: A Folklorist's Perspective." In *The Artist Outsider: Creativity and the Boundaries of Culture*, ed. Michael D. Hall and Eugene W. Metcalf Jr., 144–60. Washington, DC: Smithsonian Institution Press.

About the Authors

ROGER D. ABRAHAMS was Hum Rosen Professor at the University of Pennsylvania. He has taught folklore and anthropology at Claremont College and the University of Texas at Austin. He was a former president of the American Folklore Society. Abrahams is one of the most influential folklorists of the twentieth and early twenty-first centuries. He has produced landmark research on African American verbal art, Anglo-American balladry, and carnivalesque gatherings throughout the Black Atlantic, as well as historical analysis using contemporary ethnographic and historical methodologies. His work has had enormous influence on many disciplines. He has been awarded the Lifetime Scholarly Achievement Award of the American Folklore Society, among his many honors. Abrahams died on June 20, 2017.

JOHN BORGONOVO lectures in the School of History at University College Cork. He specializes in modern Irish history, with special focus on the Irish Revolutionary period (1916–1923). Among his many books and articles is the research monograph *The Dynamics of War and Revolution: Cork City, 1916–1918*. He is associate editor of the acclaimed *Atlas of the Irish Revolution*, published by Cork University Press in 2017.

LAURENT SÉBASTIEN FOURNIER is a lecturer in social and cultural anthropology at the Aix-Marseille Université (France) and a member of the Institute of Mediterranean, European, and Comparative Ethnology (IDEMEC). His works concern the revitalization of local festivals in Europe, traditional games and sports, and the politics of intangible cultural heritage.

LISA GILMAN is professor of folklore and English at the University of Oregon. Her research interests include performance, music, dance, oral literature, intangible cultural heritage, war, trauma, gender, and sexuality in southern Africa and the United States. Her monographs include *My Music, My War: The Listening Habits of US Troops in Iraq and Afghanistan* (Wesleyan University Press, 2016), *The Dance of Politics: Performance, Gender, and Democratization in Malawi* (Temple University Press, 2009), and the coedited volume (with Michael Dylan Foster) *UNESCO on the Ground: Local Perspectives on Intangible Cultural Heritage* (Indiana University Press, 2015). She has published numerous articles on veterans' musical listening; dance, gender, and politics in Malawi; and other topics that explore relationships between creative arts and politics. She also produced the documentary *Grounds for Resistance* about the anti-war activism of US veterans of the Iraq and Afghanistan wars.

BARBARA GRAHAM is an anthropologist with a special research interest in material culture and death in Ireland. She has a background in archaeology and a PhD in anthropology from Queen's University Belfast. She has worked as a university tutor in anthropology and, in 2016, published *Death, Materiality, and Mediation: An Ethnography of Remembrance in Ireland* (Berghahn Books), a book based on research carried out along the eastern border area of Ireland. In 2010 she conducted research on memorial imagery and material culture in Hindu and Christian traditions as part of a British Council Scholarship to Chennai, India. She also has extensive research experience in the field of ageing and care and worked as a research fellow on international projects on dementia at the University of Stirling in Scotland. She is currently involved in community heritage projects and organizes archaeology tours to lesser-known sites along the Irish border.

DAVID HARNISH is professor and chair of the Music Department at University of San Diego. Author of *Bridges to the Ancestors: Music, Myth, and Cultural Politics at an Indonesian Festival* (University of Hawaii Press, 2006) and coauthor/editor of *Divine Inspirations: Music and Islam in Indonesia* (Oxford University Press, 2011) and *Between Harmony and Discrimination: Negotiating Interreligious Relationships in Bali and Lombok* (Brill Press, 2014), he is a double Fulbright and National Foundation Scholar and has consulted for the BBC, National Geographic, MTV-Fulbright Awards, ACLS, and the Smithsonian Institute. As a performer, he has recorded Indonesian, jazz, Indian, and Tejano musics with five different labels. He codirects Gamelan Gunung Mas at USD and serves as USD Academic Liaison for the Kyoto Prize Symposium.

SAMUEL KINSER is Presidential Research Professor, emeritus, at Northern Illinois University and the founder and director of the Center for Research in Festive Culture (www.festival-studies.org). Recent publications include "Once More the Festive Bears, Enduring Themes and Shifting Semes, 1100–1900" (Bra, Italy, 2015).

SCOTT MAGELSSEN IS associate professor and the director of the Center for Performance Studies in the University of Washington's School of Drama, where he heads the BA academic program. Scott is the author of *Simming: Participatory Performance and the Making of Meaning* (2014) and *Living History Museums: Undoing History through Performance* (2007). He edited *Theatre Historiography: Critical Interventions* with Henry Bial (2010), *Enacting History* with Rhona Justice Malloy (2011), and *Querying Difference in Theatre History* with Ann Haugo (2007). Magelssen edits Southern Illinois University Press's Theater in the Americas series and hosts the website theater-historiography.org with Henry Bial.

ELENA MARTÍNEZ has been a folklorist at City Lore since 1997, and since 2012 she has been the co-artistic director at the Bronx Music Heritage Center. She co-produced the documentary *From Mambo to Hip Hop: A South Bronx Tale* and was also a co-producer for the documentaries *We Like It Like That: The Story of Latin Boogaloo* and *Eddie Palmieri: A Revolution on Harlem River Drive*. Martínez curated the exhibition "¡Que bonita bandera!: The Puerto Rican Flag as Folk Art," was the assistant curator for the exhibit, *Nueva York: 1613–1945* at El Museo del Barrio (2010), and co-curated *Las Tres Hermanas: Art and Activism in the South Bronx*. She has been a contributor to *Latinas in the United States: A Historical Encyclopedia* (Indiana University Press, 2006), *Women's Folklore and Folklife: An Encyclopedia of Beliefs, Customs, Tales, Music, and Art* (ABC-CLIO, 2008), the *New York State Folklife Reader: Diverse Voices* (University Press of Mississippi, 2013), and *The Dictionary of Caribbean and Afro-Latin Biography* (Oxford University Press, 2016).

PAMELA MORO received a PhD in anthropology from the University of California, Berkeley in 1988. She is professor of anthropology at Willamette University in Salem, Oregon. Her research and teaching interests include the music of Southeast Asia, especially Thailand; the anthropology of religion; and sex and gender. She is author of *Thai Music and Musicians in Contemporary Bangkok* (UC Berkeley, Center for Southeast Asian Studies, 1993) and various articles on music and religion in Thailand and among Thai in America, as well as LGBT choral singing. She is also the author/editor of the textbook *Magic, Witchcraft, and Religion: A Reader in the Anthropology of Religion* (McGraw-Hill, 9th edition, 2013). Her current work uses historical sources to pursue ethnomusicology, especially vernacular music-making in the mid-nineteenth-century American West.

JACK SANTINO is professor of folklore and popular culture and has served as director of the Bowling Green Center for Popular Culture Studies. He was the Alexis de Tocqueville Distinguished Professor at the University of Paris, Sorbonne, 2010–2011. He was a Fulbright Scholar to Northern Ireland and has conducted research in Spain and France. His documentary film on Pullman Porters, *Miles of Smiles, Years of Struggle*, received four Emmy awards. His research centers on rituals and celebrations, with a particular focus on carnival and political and public ritual as reflective of political, social, and cultural identity. He is the author of numerous books and articles.

BEVERLY J. STOELTJE received her PhD degree in folklore/anthropology at the University of Texas at Austin in 1979 and taught there for six years. She has been a member of the faculty at Indiana University Bloomington since 1986. She has published on rodeo, ritual/festival, women of the West, beauty contests, gender, Asante Queen Mothers, the Asante courts, and the integration of chieftaincy with modernity.

DANIEL WOJCIK is professor of English and folklore studies and affiliate faculty in religious studies at the University of Oregon. His books include *The End of the World as We Know It: Faith, Fatalism, and Apocalypse in America; Punk and Neo-Tribal Body Art*; and *Outsider Art: Visionary Worlds and Trauma*, and he has published widely on the topics of apocalyptic belief, alternative spiritualities, visionary culture, subcultures, "outsider art," and vernacular artistic expression.

DOROTHY L. ZINN is associate professor of cultural anthropology at the Free University of Bozen-Bolzano. She has conducted fieldwork in Southern Italy, South Tyrol, and France and has published extensively on issues of political economy, with a focus on youth unemployment, clientelism, social protest, and immigration. With her attention to institutional and policy spheres, Zinn also has an interest in engaged forms of anthropology. Her book *La Raccomandazione* (Donzelli, 2001) won a Pitré international award and is forthcoming in English (Berghahn Books). Zinn is also a scholar of Italian ethnologist Ernesto de Martino, and she has produced two critically acclaimed English translations of his work: *The Land of Remorse* (Free Association Books, 2005) and *Magic: A Theory from the South* (HAU/University of Chicago Press, 2015).

Index

Abbey, Edward, 229
Abrahams, Roger D., ix, xi
absolutism, 5
acoustemology, 192
action: community, 201, 202n7; direct, 12, 228, 230, 233; eco-, 233, 236, 236n7; political, 90, 225, 228, 229; protest, 206; social, xi, 69, 88, 90, 225, 255, 258; symbolic, x, 5–6, 12, 14, 70–72, 76, 258; unofficial, 8
activism, 192, 228; community, 193–95, 197; ecological, 235; LGBT, 195, 198; participatory forms of, 189; political, 110n1; radical theatrical, 233, 236; spectacular, 191
Act of Union, 93–94
aesthetics, 55, 234, 255, 258–73
Africa Cup of Nations, 86
African American Heritage Museum, 257
African Americans, 52, 53, 257, 260; Afro-Trinidadians, 35, 36; cancer and, 227; Carnival and, 20, 21, 34; Indians and, 51; killings of, 10; liberties for, 50; mortality rates for, 261; unemployment rates for, 261
AfterCulture: Detroit and the Humiliation of History (Herron), 261
After Goodbye: An AIDS Story (film), 195
AIDS, xii, 158, 189, 190, 191, 195, 196, 197, 198, 199, 200, 201; medical marijuana and, 202n5
Al-Ahly, 85
Albizu Campos, Pedro, 119, 126 (fig.)
alcohol abuse, 125–26, 158
Alingoni Association, 168
Al-Jazeera, 86
All-for-Ireland League, 97
A Lot of Shoes, 267, 269
alternate society, establishment of, 4
Altieri, Mario, 219n7
Amoco Oil, 36
amoral familism, 208
Ampene, Kwasi, 77
Anabaptists, 32
Ancient Order of Hibernians, 100
Anderson, Benedict, 129

Angelou, Maya, 197
Anglican Church, 93
Anglo-Irish Treaty, 108
Animal Liberation Front, 228
Anthony, Kris, 196
antiauthoritarianism, 86
anticapitalism, 231
anticolonialism, 119
anticonscription campaign, 100, 103
antiglobalization movement, 217, 232–33
Antigua slave revolt (1736), 56
Antillean Confederacy, 117
antinuclear movement, 194, 208–9
Aponte-Parés, Luis, 122
Appadurai, Arjun, 207
Archer, Dennis, 265
Arons, Wendy, 226, 228
art, 90n5, 270; change and, 234; good versus bad, 233
art environments, 274n5; large-scale, 255, 256; vernacular, 257, 258
Asante, 74 (fig.), 73
Atlanta Olympics (1996), 46n29
Attali, Jacques, 189
Austin, J. L., 274n3
authoritarianism, 85, 89, 90n9
Avon Walk for Breast cancer, 189
awareness: cultural, 254; raising, 189, 190, 191, 193, 197, 200–201; spectacular and, 190

Babcock, Barbara, 11, 75
Baby Doll House, 263, 264, 264 (fig.)
Bad Behavior Sailors, 36, 37
bagpipe bands, 101–4
Bailey, George, 36
Bakhtin, Mikhail: on Carnival, 205, 211; carnivalesque and, 5, 42n2, 71, 75, 270; genre/hybridization and, 205; historical explanation and, 71; social protest and, 209
balance, 32, 68, 250; achieving, 89; harmony and, 146
Bali, 134, 140; Lombok and, 141, 143, 146, 148

Balinese, 135, 138, 139, 140, 143, 144, 151n7; Hindu, 132, 147; Sasak and, 139 (fig.), 141, 142, 143, 145, 146, 147, 148; worship with, 150n4
Banda, Hastings Kamuzu, 166, 170, 177
Banda, Joyce, 177, 177, 181, 183, 186n2; festival and, 179; funeral and, 180
Band Menace, 95–98
Banfield, Edward, 208
Baptist Church, 74
Barrack Street Band, 99, 110n1
Base Camp, 208, 210, 211
Basilicata, 205, 208, 209, 218n5, 219n10
Bat, 36, 46n29
Bataille, Georges, 152
Batara Alit Sakti, 151n6
Batara Gede Lingsar, 151n6
Batara Gede Rinjani, 151n6
Batara Gunung Agung, 151n6
Battle in Seattle (Townsend), 232
Bauman, Richard, 210
Bayazet II, 33
Beast, 36
Beckett, Samuel, 225
Beethoven, Ludwig van, 192
Beethoven—Symphony No. 9 (10000 Japanese), 192
Begin Ceremony, 140
behavior, xi, 72; antigovernment, 102; customary, 156; excessive, 153; expressive, 255; mourning, 136; performative, 161; proper, 94, 135; ritual, 5, 66; symbolic, 5
Beitiks, Moe, 226
Bellour, Hélène, 42n4, 43n5, 46n33
Belmont, Nicole, 158
Benjamin, Walter, 192
Berkeley, Wayne, 36
Berlin Conference, 167
Berlin Olympics (1936), 86
Bertrand, Gilles, 43n12
Besiktas, 83, 85
Besosa, Manuel, 118
Besosa, Maria Manuela, 118
Beteteh, 145
Biarsah, Anak Agung, 147, 151n7
Big Man, 56
Big Men and Big Drums, 60
black Atlantic world, 59–60, 61, 62
Black Governors, 60
black Indians, warrior tropes/practices and, 51
Blackpool Drum and Fife Band, 98, 99, 110n1
Black Veteran's Archive, 257

Bodu, Ignatius, 35
Boissevain, Jeremy, 156
bomba, 129
Bono, 189
Borgnovo, John, xi
Boru, Brian, 101, 102, 107
Bottle Village, 256
boundaries: crossing forbidden, 236; cultural, 270; geographical, 246; political, 167; ritual, 77, 246
BP. *See* British Petroleum
Bracetti, Mariana, 117, 118
Bradshaw, Peter, 231
Brant, Sebastian, 28, 31
brass bands, 59, 60, 99, 110n9; clashes between, 96, 97–98; formation of, 95; funerals and, 104–7; identity and, 96; IRA and, 104; politics and, 93, 96, 100; popularity of, 94–95; processions by, 108
Bread and Puppet (activist company), 227
breast cancer, xii, 190, 195, 198, 199, 200; outreach for, 197; story of, 196
Breath of Life, The (Salaam), 227
Brecht, Bertolt, 225
Brian Boru Pipe Band, 101, 102, 107
bricolage, 117, 255, 269
Briggs, Charles, 210
Brinker, Nancy, 196
British Army, 102, 106, 109; funerals by, 105; recruitment by, 99, 103; regimental band tradition and, 96, 99, 103; truce with, 107
British Museum, 222, 224
British Petroleum (BP), 222, 224
Bronx Council of the Arts Casita, 121
Brook, Peter, 227
Brown, Michael, 10
Budweiser, 125
burials, 53, 241, 242, 248; ceremonial, 57, 64; paramilitary, 105; politics and, 82; rituals and, 105–6; Second Line, 58, 64
Burke, Kenneth, 76
Burke, Peter, 42n2
butchers dance, 23, 25 (fig.), 32
Butter Exchange Band, 107, 110n1

cairns, 8, 249
calypso singers, 37
Camaradas, 113, 129
Campo Base, 208
canboulay parades, 19, 35
canboulay riots, 37–38
Cancer Alley, 227

Index 285

Canfield Project, 265
Cardinal, Roger, 274n1
Carnegie Hall, performing at, 195–98, 199
Carnival, x, xi, 3, 4 (fig.), 5, 46n33, 55, 60, 75; Afro-American interpretation of, 18, 19; Afro-Caribbean, 3, 20–21, 42n1; black, 51; *boeuf gras*, 9; controlling, 26; criticism of, 30–31; cultural specificity of, 161; dances at, 23, 24, 32; European, 37, 42n2, 54, 161; expansion of, 16, 34, 46n26; Fat Tuesday and, 19; as festivals, 5, 12, 17; of grief, 8–13, 12; integrity of, 39; interrelationship between individuals and, 211; local experience and, 21; music making and, 17–18; performance at, 21–22; popular culture and, 20; profination at, 54; reversal and, 152; riots and, 5, 44n19; ritualized confrontations at, 49; security at, 41; sentiments about, 46n25; social class and, 20, 206; social safety and, 12; South American, 3; special nature of, 21; as syncretic pageantry, 205; traditions of, xii, 14, 16, 21, 28, 36, 42n2; urban, 39
carnivalesque, xiii, 3, 5, 21, 23, 37, 42n2, 75, 128, 133, 200, 202n9, 270, 273; academic perception of, 160–62; elements of, 5, 14; expansion, 25; festivals and, 151, 152–56, 161; official and, 215–20; public performances and, 270; ritualesque and, 11–13, 151, 161, 205, 207, 209, 210, 215, 217, 218; social order and, 207; threatening and, 211
carnival model, 152–53, 154
Carnival players, 30; described, 26–28
Carnival plays, 17, 25, 28, 31, 46n25
Carr, E. Summerson, 68
Carsi (football fan club), protest by, 83, 85
casitas, 121, 122, 123
caste, 90n3, 136, 137
Catholicism, 32, 72, 139; folk, 211, 212, 214, 215, 248
Cattle Raid of Cooley, 249, 252n1
celebrations, ix, x, 3, 5, 162; black, 57; civic, 52; community-wide, 156; culture and, 153, 175; recollections of, 50; ritualized, 49; saints' day, 75; seasonal, 60; Trinidad-style, 42n1
ceremonies, 66, 76, 181; burial, 64, 106; carnival, 64; changing-over, 109; commemorative, 217; cremation, 135, 136; healing, 54; procession, 135; sacred, 4
Chand, Nek, 256, 257, 258, 274n5
change: art and, 234; cultural, 206; extra-ceremonial, 6; implementation of, 67, 191; ontological, 207; political, 135; social, 6, 12, 14, 128, 191, 193, 207, 224, 256, 270, 274n3; socioeconomic, 135
Channing, Tatum, 232
Charles V, Emperor, 33
Charlie Hebdo offices, 9, 12; shrines at, 7, 11 (fig.), 10
Chaudhuri, Una, 225, 226, 236n1, 236n2
Cheval, Ferdinand, 256, 274n5
Chewa, 167, 182
Chewa Heritage Foundation, 182
Chichewa language, 165
Chilimba, Allan, 183
Chisale, Claude Boucher, 181
Chitumbuka, 169, 172
Chiwanja cha Ayao, 183–84
Chock, Jeffrey, 42n4, 43n8, 46n33, 47n33
Christmas, 49, 55, 60
Christ Stopped at Eboli (Levi), 208
circumambulation, 137, 142, 143, 143 (fig.), 144, 145
Cirese, Alberto M., 212
citizenship, 120, 134; cultural, 128; Puerto Ricans and, 130n8
civic society, 52, 72, 106
civil disobedience, 93, 95, 261; bagpipe bands and, 101–4
civil rights, 194, 268
civil war, 82; British evacuation and, 108–10
Clark, Jennifer, 251; roadside memorials and, 240, 246
Clarke, J., 117
Clean This Mutha Up, 267
Cless, Downing, 225, 227, 236n3; eco-theatre and, 236, 236n4; Underground Railway Theater and, 226
Club Borinquen, 130n3
Coca Cola, song for, 192
Cohen, Abner, 70, 90n5
Cohen-Cruz, Jan, 236–37n7
collectives, 68, 115, 207
collectivism, 41, 156, 218
Coltrane, John, 262
Comaroff, Jean, 67
Comaroff, John, 67
commemoration, 213, 258, 274n3; of dead, 9, 240, 249, 250; roadside, 239, 240; war, 100
commercialism, Puerto Ricans and, 125–27
communication, 3, 5, 68, 78, 82; aural, 190, 192; community and, xi, 122; form and, 75, 192; global, 90; maritime, 61; multiple modes of, 14; nonmaterial, 248; oral/

gestural, 20; ritual, 75; symbolic, 73, 75–77, 78, 90n6; unofficial, 8; visual, 190
communitas, 11, 207, 210, 211, 217; ideological, 190; structure and, 157–58
community, 57, 58, 156, 202n7, 270, 274n1; building, 60, 193–95, 197; communication and, xi, 122; imagined, 129; LGBT, 194, 199, 202n8; nationalist, 95; power of, 128; Puerto Rican, 121, 122, 123; transformation of, 273
Compagnie della Calza, 44n16
Conference on Holidays, Ritual, Festival, Celebration, and Public Display, ix
conflict, 78–85; politics and, 79–80; resolving, 90
Confluence: at Carnegie Hall, 195–98; The Mixed GALA Chorus of the Willamette Valley, 193
Congo Square, 58
Connolly, James, 100
consciousness raising, 191; awareness and, 200–201
Constitution of the Registered Trustees of the Mzimba Heritage Association, 164
consumerism, 83, 85, 123, 127, 270
containment, 267; geographical space and, 241–48
Convention for the Safeguarding of Intangible Cultural Heritage (UNESCO), 151, 162, 166
"Conversation with Carnival about her Characteristics, A" (Sachs), 43n9
Coors, Puerto Rican flag and, 114, 125, 127
Cork: brass bands in, 93, 96, 97, 99, 100, 108, 109; IRA in, 104, 108; Irish Revolution and, 101; occupation of, 110; population of, 95; railway station, 102; recruiting campaign in, 103
Cork Exchange Band, 98
Cork Ex-servicemen's Federation, 100, 106, 107
Cork Men's Prison, 102, 105, 106
Cork Workingmen's Drum and Fife Band, 99
"Coronet Player Who Betrayed Ireland, The" (O'Connor), 97
cosmology, 73, 137, 143, 148, 160; agrarian, 151
Council of Hometown Clubs, 124
Council of Ministers, 214
County Armagh, memorials in, 239
County Cork, 104
County Down, memorials in, 239, 243
County Louth, 244, 249; memorials in, 239, 247

County Wexford, 249
Coup of Yauco, 130n4
Cowley, John, 43n5
Crack the Dam, 229
craftsmen's revolt (1347–1349), 23
cremation ceremonies, 135, 136
Crimmin, Jerry, 249
Cronin, Hannah, 99
Cronin, Maura, 93, 95
Crowley, Dan, 54
Cuban Revolutionary Party, 118
cultural activities, 166, 170, 173
cultural institutions, 7, 11, 154, 166
cultural practices, 164, 165, 166
cultural production, 50, 63, 122
cultural promotion, 164, 176, 184, 186; efforts at, 165–66
culture, 54, 59, 79, 153–54, 166, 246, 254; Balinese, 148; black Atlantic, 57–58; brass band, 93; Catholic, 72; celebrations and, 153, 175; consumer, 123; festivals and, 72, 152, 153, 155, 164; folk, 211–12; Georgian, 75; Latin American, 120; liminal/marginal situations and, 157–58; mass, 156, 270; material, 6–8, 13, 154, 274n1; memory and, 250; nature and, 159, 225, 235; normal people and, 255; pan-regional, 212; performance of, 128; political, 177–78, 229; popular, 8, 20, 21, 153; procession, 93, 94; Puerto Rican, 114, 115, 117, 120, 123, 125; rationality of, 153; rituals and, 72, 127; Sasak, 138, 148; social, 226, 229; street ballad, 96; symbolic, 127; youth, 83
Cumann na mBan, 105

Dada, 229
Dáil Éireann, 103
Dalmau, Micaela, 130n3
dances, 54, 57, 190; black, 55; butcher, 23, 25 (fig.), 32, 32 (fig.); Carnival, 23, 24, 32; funeral, 74; martial, 142 (fig.); narrative, 142; Ngoni, 170, 172, 173, 174, 179; ritual, 67; telek, 141 (fig.), 142, 142 (fig.)
Day, Susanne, 98
Days of Scanzano, 207, 211, 217
death, 4; commemoration of, 9, 240, 249, 250; political, 240; rites of passage and, 79; shrines to, 6, 9, 80; traditions/Jewish, 8; untimely, 90n7, 243, 244, 245, 248–49
death marches, playing, 59, 106
Debord, Guy, 234
Decca, 36

Index 287

Deepwater Horizon, 223, 224, 228
deforestation, 225, 226, 230
deities, 137, 143, 145, 146; descent of, 142; poetry-honoring, 144
Delaney, James, 99
Democratic National Convention, 232
Democratic Progressive Party (DPP), 179
Department of Culture, 166, 184
Department of the Environment, 247
Desfile Hispano, 124
Detroit: decline of, 261; homeless in, 269; riots in, 261, 269
development, 49, 62, 63, 70; commercial, 52; cultural, 154; economic, 154, 155; local, 154, 156; technological, 78
Diana, Princess, 248; funeral for, 81, 88
die Bursen, 26
die Genannten, 23
Dinosaur National Monument, 228
Dinsmoor, Samuel Perry, 256–57
direct action, 12, 228, 230, 233
Direct Action Network (DAN), 231
Doctors without Borders, 82
Dolan, Jill, 234
Dotty Wotty House, 268
Dragon, 36
drug abuse, 100, 158
drug trafficking, 261, 266, 272
Dubuffet, Jean, 274n1
DuLuca, Keven Michael, 234
Dundes, Alan, 191
Dunkirk, carnival at, 4 (fig.)
Dunn, Kevin M., 240
Dürer, Albrecht, 24

Earth Day, 6
Earth First!, 228, 229–30, 233, 235
Earth Liberation Front, 228
Earth Matters on Stage (EMOS), 226
Easter Rising (1916), 99, 100
Eastwood, William, 74–75
Ebola epidemic, 81–82, 87, 88, 89
Echo Park, 228
eco-actions, 233, 236, 236n7
eco-criticism, 25, 225, 226
ecological crises, 222, 225, 235
economic issues, 18, 54, 55, 122, 124, 125, 128, 184
eco-porn, 230, 233
"Eco-Theatre USA" (Cless), 236
education, 189, 193; art, 272; Puerto Rican, 125

Ehrbare Rat, 30
1812 Overture (Tchaikovsky), 192
El Barrio, 121, 122
El Congreso de Pueblo, 124
El Grito de Lares, 117
Ellingsen, Tommy Hol, 230
Elliot, Ray, 193
Ellis, Bret Easton, 202n8
El Morro, 122
El Mundo, 120
Elwha River, flooding of, 230
Emeterio Betances, Ramón, 117
emotions, 190, 250; expression of, 79; rituals and, 218; shared, 200
Enemy of the People (Ibsen), 225
Enlightenment, 71, 225
environmental groups, 209, 228, 231, 235
environmentalism, 224, 228, 230
environmental issues, 100, 226, 227, 235, 236n3, 257–58; theater and, 233
Erdogan, Recep Tayyip, 82–85
ethnic associations, 52, 172, 183
ethnic divisions, 53, 147, 148, 175–76
ethnic groups, 52, 133, 168, 169, 171, 176, 177; divisions among, 175; Mzimba and, 170; promoting, 166, 167; Zulu-related, 170
ethnic heritage associations, 166, 183–84
ethnicity, 35, 90n3, 147, 148, 185; politics and, 175–76; processions and, 134; regionalism and, 175–76
ethnic tensions, 164, 185, 186
events: cultural, 169, 178–79; mass, 201; meta-, 209; public, 5, 128, 192, 205, 209; ritual, 84–85, 89
Evernden, Neil, 226
Executive Committee (MZIHA), 168, 169, 171, 172
Executor, 37
ex-slaves, 21, 53, 62; Carnival and, 18, 19; fighting by, 63–64

Faces in the Hood, 265
Faces of God, 265
Fair Hill Band, 99, 108–9
Fair Lane Drum and Fife Band, 99, 110n1
Falassi, Alessandro, 86, 174
Falcón, Angelo, 125
fan clubs, 89; as activists, 85–86; protests and, 83, 88
Fancy Sailor, 36, 46n29
Fastnacht, 3, 29, 71
Fastnachtspiele, 17, 23–24, 45n25

Fat Tuesday, 17, 19
Faughart, memorial at, 245 (fig.), 244 (fig.)
Feast of Fools, 5
Federal Theatre Project, 226
festivals, xi, 5, 75, 127, 133, 173, 181; African-American, 50; Afro-Cuban, 53; Afro-Trinidadian, 43n7; carnivalesque and, 151, 152–56, 161; codification of, 153; culture and, 72, 152, 153, 155, 164; double system of, 18–19; East Indian-Trinidadian, 43n7; film, 230; financial aspects of, 153–54; form of, 76; invented, 155–56; local, 154, 156, 160, 161; as means of catharsis, 152; nationalist, 94; patron saint, 219n9; politics and, 152, 165; power and, 165; pre-Lenten, 3; processions and, 137–38, 138–46; repeated, 155–56; rites at, 138, 157; rituals and, 4–5, 71, 161, 181; saint-day, 72; Sasak, 142; slave, 63–64; studies of, x, 151, 152; temple, 136–37, 138; themes of, 156; theory/practice of, 162; utopia and, 152; violence in, 152
FFF. *See* Fuck the Forest
Fiat automobile factory, 208
FIFA Confederate Cup, 87
Finster, Howard, 256
Fireman character, 37, 38 (fig.)
First World War, 99–101, 103, 106, 109
Fitzgerald, Michael, 106
flags: historical, 114; Indonesian, 139 (fig.); Lares, 117, 118, 124 (fig.); national, 130n7; Nationalist Party, 114; symbolism of, 113; U.S., 118, 119, 120, 121. *See also* Puerto Rican flag
Flores, Juan, 119, 122
folk art, 115–17, 116 (fig.), 254, 274n1
folk assemblage, 116, 174, 257
folk Catholicism, 211, 212, 214, 215, 248
folklore, 153, 156, 206–7, 211; rites of passage and, 158; social relations of, 212
Folz, Hans, 18, 25, 46n25
Forest Stewardship Council (FSC), 228
Fournier, Laurent Sébastien, xii
fracking, 225, 228, 236
Francis, Doris, 250
Franzmann, Majella, 251; roadside memorials and, 240, 246
French Creole, 19, 34, 35
French Society for the Sociology of Religion, 158
Friends of the Earth, 228, 235
Frimpoma, Nana Abena: funeral of, 74 (fig.)
Fuchs, Elinor, 226

Fuck the Forest (FFF), 230, 231, 233
funerals, 51, 66, 74, 75, 77, 74 (fig.), 157, 158; brass bands and, 104–7; church, 241; Ebola deaths and, 81; jazz, 59; paramilitary, 105–6; republican, 104–7; royal, 81, 88; as spectacles, 104–7
Futurism, 229

gaduh, 143, 144, 145, 147, 148
Gaelic Athletic Association (GAA), 103
Gaelic League, 103
GALA choruses, 196, 197–98, 199, 202n9; contributions by, 195; mission statements of, 193
gamelan, 135, 136, 139 (fig.), 140, 140 (fig.), 141, 143, 144, 145, 150n3
Garden of Eden, 256–57
Gargantua and Pantagruel (Rabelais), 71
Garner, Eric, 10
Garrett, Ian, 227, 236n5
gasoducto protest, 121, 124 (fig.)
Gay and Lesbian Association of Choruses, 193
gay choral movement, 194–95
Gay Pride Parade, 13, 84
gay rights movement, 199
gaze theory, 191
General Agreement on Tariffs and Trade (GATT), 233
George, King, 99–100
Georgian Orthodox Church, 75
Gerena Valentín, Gilberto, 125
Gezi Park: Gay Pride Parade and, 84; protest at, 82–85; ritual events at, 84–85, 89
Ghanaian football team, attack on, 87, 88
Gillespie, Raymond, 249
Gilman, Lisa, xii, 77
Girard, René, 152
Glen Canyon Dam, protest at, 228, 229, 230, 234
Glines Canyon Dam, protest at, 230, 234
globalization, 68, 78, 88, 161, 164, 233; cultural, 165; economic, 165, 231
Gomani, Inkosi ya Makosi, 168
Gore, Al, on global warming, 236n1
Goya, 125
Graham, Barbara, xii
Gramsci, Antonio, 206
Grand Theft Auto, 83
gravesites, 8, 242, 243, 256
Great Court of London, 224
Great Voice, 56

Index

Greenmount Industrial School Band, 99
Greenpeace, 228, 234, 235
greenwashing, 223, 224
Greet Holy Water, 139 (fig.), 140, 140 (fig.)
grief, 246; carnivals of, 8–13, 12; responses to, 81, 88
Growler, 37
Guardian, 87, 231
guerrilla conflict, 101, 105, 107, 225
Guschwan, Matthew, 89
Guyton, Karen, 262, 263, 265
Guyton, Tyree, xi, xii, 263 (fig.), 264, 274n4, 274n5; assemblages by, 259, 265, 267–68, 269, 271; Canfield Project and, 265; environment of, 255–56, 260, 266, 267, 269–70, 271, 273; Heidelberg Project and, 258, 259, 260, 262, 263, 269, 272; Heidelberg Street and, 260, 261, 266; public responses to, 265–66
Gwo Ka, 60

Hahn, Stephen, 61
Haitian Revolution, 56
Halloween, ix, 6, 116
Handel, Friedrich, 106
Handelman, Don, 206, 207, 218
Harnish, David, xi, xii
Harrelson, Woody, 232
Hart, Richard, 55
Hartig, Kate V., 240
Havana, Carnival and, 57
headstones, 242, 249, 251; memorializing with, 241, 250
hegemony, 67, 72, 75, 254; Balinese, 146; challenging, 122; usurpation of, 11
Heidelberg Project, 255, 259 (fig.), 263 (fig.), 264 (fig.); growth of, 272; social protest and, 258–73; starting, 260, 261, 262
Heidelberg Street, 258, 260, 261, 266, 267, 272; visiting, 259, 271–72
heritage: cultural, 154, 155, 171, 185, 207, 212; ethnic, 166, 183–84, 255; model, 153–54; politics and, 183–84
Heroes and Saints (Moraga), 227
Herron, Jerry, 261
Hinduism, 135, 139, 148
Hobsbawm, Eric, 241
Hogan, Patrick, 109
holidays, ix, 3, 67; church calendars and, 49; slave, 50, 55, 60, 61, 63
Holland, Dorothy, 79
Hölle, 26, 44n15
Holley, Lonnie, 257

Honorable Council, 30
How to Survive the Loss of a Love (McWilliams, Cosgrove, and Bloomfield), 196
Hughes, Holly, 226
Huizinga, Johan, 85
Hunter, Robert, 234
Hurricane Katrina, 58
hybridization, 161, 205, 207, 210, 211, 215

Ibsen, Henrik, 225
identity: apprehension of, 67; asserting, xii, 191; brass bands and, 96; collective, 207; cultural, 101, 117, 123, 127, 153, 154, 165, 166, 185; ethnic, 123, 170, 175, 184–85; expression of, 79, 89; groups, 201; Italian, 206; local, 212; mobile, 124; music and, 109; national, 115, 122; Nationalist Party, 119; Ngoni, 171, 172, 180; performance and, 180; politics and, 95, 109, 175–76; Puerto Rican, 117, 120, 123–25, 127, 129; regional, 135, 175, 208; rituals and, 67, 69, 79; shared, 180; social, 62, 76; transformed, 85
ideology, 67, 72, 77, 85, 153, 184, 235, 269–70; modern, 71; political, 119
idiosyncratic art, definition of, 274n1
Illustrated London News, 43n5
Image Politics: The New Rhetoric of Environmental Activism (DuLuca), 234
independence, 99, 105, 107; Irish, 104; Ngoni, 176
Industrial Revolution, 94
inequality, 18, 200, 261
Inglis, Tom, 246
ingoma dancers, 170, 172, 171–72, 175
Intentona de Yauco, 118, 130n4
Iowans for Animal Liberation, 228
Iowa State Fair, 228
IRA. *See* Irish Republican Army
Irish Catholics, memorials and, 246
Irish Folklore Collection, 249
Irish Folklore Commission, 249
Irish Free State, 108, 110
Irish Independent, 240, 247
Irish National Land League, 95
Irish Party, 97, 100, 101
Irish Republic, 105, 107, 247
Irish Republican Army (IRA), 99, 101, 110; antitreaty, 109; brass bands and, 104; color guard, 105–6; guerrilla attacks and, 107; honor guard, 107; marching drills by, 102–3; police force, 108, 109; truce with, 107
Irish Revolution, 101

Irish Transport and General Workers Union, 100
Irish Volunteer Band, 101, 102, 104, 105, 106, 107, 108
Irish Volunteers, 99
Iron Ladies (film), 82
Islam, 135, 138, 139, 140, 148
Istanbul, 82–85, 89
It Gets Better Project, 195

Jab-Jab, 36
Jab Molassi, 36
Jakubal, Mikal, 229, 230
Jamaican "uprising" (1823–24), 55
James Connolly Drum and Fife Band, 100, 107
Jean, Carlo, 216
Jere clan, 174, 177
jíbaros, 120, 122, 123, 130n5
Johnson, Ellen Sirleaf, 82
Jones-Shafroth Act (1917), 130n1, 130n8
Jonkonnu, 5, 60
Jordan, John: on protest theater, 234–35
Juasohemaa, 78
Juris, Jeffrey, 217

Kachali, Khumbo, 176, 186n2
kalenda stick-fighting, 51
Kapchan, Deborah A., 207, 210
kebon odeq, 141, 143, 145, 146, 147; circumambulation by, 143 (fig.)
Kellaher, Leonie, 250
Keller, Adelbert von, 42n3
kemaliq, 141, 142, 142 (fig.), 143, 144, 145, 147, 148
Kerr, Dennis, 56
Kershaw, Baz, 226, 234, 235
Kertzer, David, 71, 170, 206, 212
King, Martin Luther, Jr., 268
King Lear (Shakespeare), 225
King Sailors, 36, 37, 46n30
Kinser, Samuel, xi, 43n5
Kiskeam Irish Volunteer Band, 104, 108
Krama Pura, 138, 145
Krolikowski, Alex M., 200
Kübler-Ross, Elisabeth, 196
Kungoni Annual Cultural Festival, 181
Kungoni Cultural Center, 181
Kurzman, Charles, 206

"La Borinquena" (anthem), 119
Lake Powell, 229
la ley de la mordaza, 119

Lamadrid, Enrique, 67, 90n1
la musica jíbara, 129
Land League, 95
Landship players, 60
Lane, Fintan, 93, 96
Langer, Suzanne, 69, 76
Laramie Project, 195
Lateran Pacts, 213
Latinos, alcohol dependence among, 125–26
Laurel, Juan Tomas Avila, 87, 88
Lave, Jean, 79
Le Breton, David, 158
Lempert, Michael, 68
Lent, 3, 5, 32, 71
Levi, Carlo, 208, 212
Lévi-Strauss, Claude, 117, 274n5
LGBT choral movement, 193–95, 199
LGBT choruses, x, 190, 193; performance by, 194, 195, 199–200; resistance and, 200
LGBT community: cultural legitimacy for, 199; honoring/uplifting, 194; mainstreaming, 202n8
Lhomwe, 167, 182–83
Lhomwe Festival, 183
Liberia, ebola epidemic in, 81–82
Limerick, 251; brass bands in, 97
liminality, 11, 12, 69, 157, 158, 159, 215, 273
Lingsar, 148; Balinese claim to, 141; procession at, 146–47; Sasak ethnicity/history at, 146–47
Lingsar temple festival, 137, 138, 139, 140, 143, 144, 145; researching, 147–48
Living Newspaper, 226
localism, 20, 21–22, 207
Lombardi, Don Filippo, 213, 214, 218
Lombok, xi, 134, 135, 137, 140, 151n6, 151n7; Bali and, 138, 141, 143, 146, 148
London, 79; ritual in, 81, 88, 89
London Olympics (2012), 222
Lord Kitchener, 37, 39 (fig.), 46n31
Louisiana Purchase, 58
Louisiana Superdome, 52
Louth County Council, memorials and, 247
Love, Glen, 226
Lucanians, 208, 209, 213, 215, 216, 219n10; folk culture and, 211–12; Scanzano and, 217; struggles of, 214
Luther, Martin, 33
Lutheranism, growth of, 31
Lycee Notre Dame de Sion, 90n8

Mabakti, 144
MacAloon, John, 4, 191

Index

MacClancy, Jeremy, 85, 86
MacConville, Una, 240, 247–48
MacCurtain, Tomás, 101, 106
Mackey, Sam, 262, 264, 266, 268
MacSwiney, Terence, 106, 107
Madonna of Loreto, 214, 218
Magelssen, Scott, x, xi, xii
Malawi, xii, 77, 164, 165, 166, 168, 171, 172, 173, 177; described, 167; ethnic groups of, 167; independence of, 177; Ngoni in, 186n1
Malawi Congress Party, 170
Malawi Voice, 183
Manchester Martyrs' Commemoration, 103
manifestation, 6, 7, 9, 42, 93, 121, 175, 240, 248, 251; embodiment of, 13 (fig.)
Manuel de folklore français contemporain (Van Gennep), 157
Manzanet, Jaran, 127
marching bands, 93, 96, 106, 219n9
marching drills, 102–3
March of 100,000, 209, 216, 217
Marczak, Michal, 230
Mardi Gras, 17, 19, 58, 60, 64, 71; brass bands and, 59; songs of, 51–52
Mardi Gras Indians, 51–52, 58, 60
Marine Square, 35
Maroon communities, 51, 55
Marranca, Bonnie, 226
marriage, 157; purpose of, 69–70
Martello, Davide, 84
Martí, José, 142n3
Martin, Carol, 46n28
Martin, Pamela, 196–97
Martínez, Elena, xi
Maseko Ngoni, 168, 175
Maseko, Ngwana, 168
masks, 26, 30, 31, 37
masquerades, 3, 6, 29, 37
Matera, 208, 213, 214
Mathew, Theobald, 94
Matory, J. Lorand, 62
Maximilian, Duke of Burgundy, 29, 33
May, Theresa J., 226, 228, 234
May Day, celebration of, 100
McDougall-Hunt neighborhood, 260
McGrath, Jack, 93
McNeill, William H., 190
McQuillan, Regina, 240, 247–48
McWilliams, Peter, 196, 202n5
media, 8, 191, 211, 268; competition for, 192; electronic, 194; multitude of, 10; popular, 196, 225

"Meet the Boys on the Battlefront" (song), 52
Meistergesang, 18
Melukar, 145
memorials, 122, 251–52; Balinese, 135; commemoration by, 240; containment/displacement and, 239; contemporary, 249; erecting, 241, 248; history and, 251; Irish, 246, 251; permission for, 247; priests and, 246–47; public opposition to, 252; roadside, 6, 8, 239, 240, 241, 243 (fig.), 245 (fig.), 244 (fig.), 246–51; secular authorities and, 247; traffic-accident, 239; war, 9
memory: culture and, 250; nationalist, 122
Mendak Kebon Odeq, 141, 144
Mendak Pesaji, 144, 145
Mendak Tirta procession, 139 (fig.), 140, 140 (fig.), 146, 148
Mensel, Robert, 194
Merabet, Ahmed, 10
Metaponto, 208, 211, 213, 214
MidAmerica Productions, 196, 197
Middleton, Kate, 70
Midnight Robbers, 36
Mighty Sparrow, 37
Miller, Audrey K., 200
MillerCoors, 125
Ministerial Conference (WTO), 231
Minshall, Peter, 36, 46n29
M'mbelwa IV, Inkosi ya Makosi, 164, 168, 169, 170, 174, 177; criticism of, 177; death of, 172, 180; legitimacy of, 181, 182; subchiefs and, 171
M'mbelwa V, Inkosi ya Makosi, 178
mobilization, 218; mass, 93, 101
modernity, 71, 88, 152, 208, 212; ritual, 158
Moko Jombie, 36
Mombera Kingdom, 177
momot, 143 (fig.), 146, 147
Monk, Thelonious, 262
Monkey Wrench Gang, The (Abbey), 229
Montignac (slave), 56
Moody, T. W., 95
Moraga, Cherríe, 227
Moral Basis of a Backward Society, The (Banfield), 208
Morales Ramos (Ramito), Florencia, 113
moralism, 25, 32, 72, 252
Moro, Pamela, x, xi, xii
Morton, Jelly Roll, 50
Mt. Hora, 164, 181, 184
mourning, 6, 8, 9–10, 106, 136; management of, 251; national, 214; public, 158; rituals, 105

movements, 69; brass band, 94; collective, 206; cultural forms in, 218; nationalist, 153; regionalist, 153; social, 201n3, 205, 206, 218
Move to the Rear, 268
Moylan, Seán, 104
Mpezeni, Inkosi ya Makosi, 168, 172, 182
Mua Mission, 181
Muhammad, Prophet, 10
Muir, Edward, 43n12
Mulhako wa Alhomwe, 182, 183–84
Mullen, Michael, 55
Muluzi, Bakili, 177
Mulvey, Laura, 191
mundillo, 115, 129
Munk, Erika, 226
Muñoz Marín, Luis, 119
Murray-White, James, 231
music, 55, 90n5, 133; Dominican, 113; effect of, 190–92; identity and, 109; Ngoni, 174; processional, 148; protest, 83; Puerto Rican, 113, 114, 129; spectacle and, 193–95; traditional, 129, 211; youth culture and, 83. *See also* songs
musical rivalries, 95–98
music making, 17–18, 190, 193, 201, 211
Muslims, 134, 135, 138, 139, 158
Mutharika, Bingu wa, 177, 179, 181, 182–83, 183
Mutharika, Peter, 183
mutual assistance clubs, 50, 52–53, 59–60
MZIHA. *See* Mzimba Heritage Association
Mzimba District, 164, 168, 176–77; Ngoni and, 167, 169; Ngonification of, 170–74; regionalism and, 178
Mzimba Heritage Association (MZIHA), 168–70, 176, 175–82; emergence of, 164, 169; festivals/other ethnic associations and, 182–84; Ngoni culture in, 176; organization by, 181; Umthetho Festival and, 184
Mzimba Ngoni, 167–68, 172, 176

Na Fianna Éireann, 101
Napier, David, 66
Narrow Water, memorial at, 243 (fig.)
Nassirya, shock over, 214
national anthems, protocols for, 102
National Dance Troupe, 166
National Institute of Health, 126
nationalism, 102; constitutional, 96; cultural, 120, 125, 128, 129; Irish, 93, 95, 97, 99; political, 120; popular, 95
Nationalist Party, 114; Puerto Rican flag and, 119, 129

National Mall, 9
National Puerto Rican Day Parade Inc., 125, 127
Natural Resources Defense Council, 228
nature: culture and, 159, 225, 235; as social construction, 226
Nature Conservancy, 228
NBC, protests at, 114
Nc'wala Festival, 172, 182, 184
Nelson's Harbor, 54
Neophytou, Georgina, 250
New England Symphonic Ensemble, 196
New Orleans, 16, 51; Carnival and, 57, 64; destruction of, 58; social openness of, 59
New White House, 268
New World, 3; African enclaves in, 52; black, 49, 52; liberal democracies of, 53; urban life in, 52
New York City: casitas in, 122; landscape of, 122; Puerto Ricans in, 115, 121, 122, 123
Ngaturang Pesaji, 144, 145
Ngilahang Kebon Odeq procession, 141, 143 (fig.)
Ngilahang Pesaji, 144, 145
Ngonde, 167
Ngoni, xii, 169, 181, 184; chieftaincy structure of, 170–71, 174; diversity of, 171–72; economic base of, 174; leadership of, 171, 176–77; migration of, 186n1; politics and, 176; settlements of, 167–69; symbols of, 174
Ngoniness, 170, 171–72, 174
Nguema, Teodoro Obiang, 87
Nic Néill, Máire, 249, 251
Nice, Carnival and, 40, 42n2
NIMBYism, 209, 214, 215,218n6
Ninth Symphony (Beethoven), 192
Noah's Flood, 225
Noriyuki, Duane, 271
norm, tradition and, 240–41
Northern Ireland: procession culture of, 93; ritual in, 79–81, 88; violence in, 240
Notre Dame Cathedral, 8
Notting Hill, 5, 90n5
Noyes, Dorothy, 161
nuclear waste storage, 208, 212
Nuremberg: Carnival and, 16, 17, 18, 20, 21, 23–34, 36, 41, 43n9, 43n12, 44n16, 45n25, 47n33; dramatic activities in, 42n3; elites of, 24; and Port of Spain compared, 22; religious dissention in, 32–33, 40; writing in, 44n15
Nurse, K., 42n1

Index 293

Obama, Barack, inauguration of, 70
O'Brien, William, 98, 110n1; Redmond and, 97, 99
O'Connell, Daniel, 93, 94, 95
O'Connor, Frank, 97
official, carnivalesque and, 215–17
OJ House, 268
Operation Bootstrap, 124
Oprah Winfrey Show, The, 264
Orange Order, 134
organizations, 133–34; development of, 49; fraternal, 50, 134; political, 212; religious, 134; temple, 145
Oring, Elliott, 115, 116
Orsino, Duke, 222
Orthodox Christian Church, 73
Ortiz, Fernando, 53
Osiander, Andreas, 31, 32, 33, 45n24; riot and, 33
other, 273; artist as, 255; self and, 210
Otto, Ton, 241
outsider art, 274n1; artistic training and, 254; enthusiasm for, 255; phenomenon of, 254; qualities of, 255
Outsider Art (Cardinal), 274n1
Öztürkmen, Arzu, 83, 84

padanda, 136, 144
padlocks, xi, 7 (fig.), 13; permanence and, 8; public display of, x; removal of, 7
pageants, 53, 133, 134, 205, 227
Palais Idéal (Cheval), 256
pamangku, 136, 138, 139, 141, 144, 146
Pan Am Airlines, 36, 46n32
Panca Sembah, 144
parades, x, xi, 43n5, 80, 127, 135; Camaradas, 129; *canboulay*, 19, 35; carnival, 162; commercially driven, 53; ethnic, 128; LGBT, 189; protests and, 84; Puerto Rican, 128; Schembart, 31, 32, 45n20; social conflict and, 110; Sunday, 96; as triumphal occasions, 13. *See also* Gay Pride Parade; Puerto Rican Day Parade
Paradise Garden, 256
paramilitary groups, 86, 107
Paramin Blue Devils, 43n8
Paris, Carnival and, 42n2
Parks, Rosa, 268
participation, 200; democratic, 128; divisiveness of, 195; embodied, 190; mass, 189, 190–91, 198; public, 258; transformation and, 68

"Patrick's Eve" procession, 109
Pedersen, Poul, 241
Pemendak, 140
Penaek Gawe, 140
Pengadagang, 140
Penglemek, 145
People for the Ethical Treatment of Animals, 228
Perang Topat, 143, 144
performance, x, xii, 5, 9, 14, 21, 44n15, 151, 194, 197, 270, 273; activist, 234; carnivalesque, 202n9; cultural, 164, 178, 178–79, 206–7, 213, 217, 255; dynamics of, 73–75; eco-protest, 229, 233, 235; emotional, 198–99; festivals and, 164; identity and, 180; mass participation and, 190–91; modes of, 233; musical, 84, 190, 198; patterns of, 63; politics and, 66, 68, 234; protest, 83–84, 224, 234, 235; recreational, 143; Rio-style, 3–4; rituals and, 68, 69, 73; spectacular and, 229; symbolic, 179, 180; theatrical, xi, 84, 224; Trinidadian, 3–4
performative, xi, 224, 228, 247, 257; concept of, 274n3; visual and, 13; social action and, 258
pesaji, 141, 144, 145
Phelan, Peggy, 235
Pierrot, 36
Pierrot-Grenade, 36
Pineda, Richard D., 128
Pinkster celebrations, 60
Pirckheimer, Willibald, 24
place: Puerto Rican flag and, 121–23; spiritual significance of, 246
Place Congo, 58
Place de la Bastille, 7
Place de la République, 9
plena, 114, 129
Plows, Alex, 235
poetry, 77, 144
Point Coupee Rebellion (1795), 56
police, 10, 12, 17, 83, 84, 85, 86, 87, 96, 97, 98, 101, 103, 106, 213, 217; clashes with, 102, 104, 107; IRA, 108, 109
political bands, 93–95
political conditions, changes in, 74
political dimensions, sharing, 14
political issues, 186, 256–57
Political Man, as Symbolist Man, 70
political messages, 174, 269
political parties, 97, 175–76, 217, 202n7
political prisoners, 102, 105, 121

politics, 23, 66, 69, 73, 74, 88, 270; brass bands and, 96, 100; burials and, 81–82; conflict and, 77–78; cultural, 165, 185; defining, 70; democratic, 218n3; ethnic, 175–76; festivals and, 165; forces of, 90; heritage and, 183–84; Irish, 93, 94, 95, 109; national, 165, 166, 173–79, 186; party, 177, 178, 181; performance and, 66, 68, 234; postcolonial, 164, 175; regional identity and, 175; rituals and, 66, 67, 68, 70, 71, 72, 73, 77, 78, 78–85, 86, 88, 90; social factions and, 41; violence and, 77–78
Polka Dot House, 268
Ponce, Carnival and, 116 (fig.)
Pont des Arts, padlocks on, 7
Pont Echevren, 7; padlocks on, 8 (fig.)
porosity, 16, 17, 18–22, 34, 35, 40
Port au Prince, 54
Port of Spain, 16, 43n8, 46n29; Carnival and, 17, 18, 19, 20, 34–42, 42n4, 43n6, 46n26; and Nuremberg compared, 22; parade in, 43n5; porosity of, 40
Port Royal, 54
Portland Gay Men's Chorus, 194
ports of call, development of, 62
postmodernity, 158, 159, 161
poverty, 186n4, 257, 261, 268
power: asserting, xii; festivals and, 165; government, 181–82; political, xiii, 164, 165; rituals and, 4, 68–70, 78, 165; symbolic, 70–72, 205; traditional, 181–82; transformative, 205
Power of Harmony, The (film), 195
prayers, 144
prejudice, 18, 41
Pride activities, strategy of, 199, 200
Pride Day, 5, 6, 14
priests, 141; common, 136; high, 136, 144; roadside memorials and, 246–47
Prior, Melton, 34, 43n5
Prisbrey, Tressa, 256, 274n5
processions, x, xi, 13–14, 96, 103, 147; Balinese, 135–38; brass band, 108; countercultural, 133; cremation ceremonies and, 135, 136; culture of, 93, 94; ethnicity and, 134; festival, 137–38, 138–46, 192; funeral, 106, 107; Hindu, 135; military, 133; motion/movement and, 134; organization of, 133–34; paramilitary, 102; royal, 133; social conflict and, 110; subcultural, 133; at temple festivals, 136–37; profane, sacred and, 161
propaganda, 102, 103, 105, 106, 189

protestors, 233; black female, 13 (fig.); as other, 215; police and, 84
protests, x, 86, 206, 208–9, 214; civic, 215; eco-, 233, 236; environmental, 205, 228, 231; expression of, 216–17; nationalist, 95; performance and, 83–84; political, xi, 67, 89; popular, 213; Puerto Rican, 128; ritual, 85, 89; ritualesque and, 216; site-specific, 236n7; social, 205, 209, 211, 258–73; symbols of, 10, 84; wartime, 99–100
public art, xii, 122
public displays, ix, xiii, 3, 6, 8, 134, 161, 258, 273; monumental, 256; paradigms of, xi; political, 269; stylized forms of, 49; unified theory of, x
Public Law 53 (1948), 119
public space, xiii, 109, 270; appropriation of, 263; disruption/temporary conversion of, 191; grief and, 246; politics and, 218; roadside memorials and, 241; uses of, 7, 11
Puerto Rican Day festival, x–xi, 113
Puerto Rican Day Parade, 113, 114, 115, 117; emergence of, 124, 128; Puerto Rican flag and, 125; space/identity at, 123–25
Puerto Rican flag, 113, 124 (fig.); casitas and, 122; civic duty and, 127–29; commodification of, 125–27; cultural pride and, 127; displaying, 114–15, 119, 120–21, 129; as enemy flag, 118; flag syndrome and, 125; as folk art, 115–17, 116 (fig.); history of, 117–19; Nationalist Party and, 119, 129; place and, 121–23; political significance of, 120–21; protesting, 126 (fig.); sales of, 126–27; symbolism of, 115, 120–21, 127
Puerto Rican Legal Defense Fund, 125
Puerto Ricans, 121; Americans and, 129; citizenship and, 130n8; colonial relationship with, 118; Puerto Rican flag and, 123
puertorriqueñidad, 115, 130n5
Pujawali, 138

Quarry Lane Band, 98, 110n1
Quart Festival, 230
Queen's Park Oval pageant, 46n27
Queen's Park Savannah, 39
queer youth, empowerment of, 195

Rabelais, 71
Race for the Cure, 197
racism, 20, 53, 100, 268
Raffeen Lodge, 100
rag trees/wells, 8, 13

Index 295

Rainan Karya, 143
Ralph Bunche Elementary School, 271
Ramón Sánchez, José, 128
Ranger, Terence, 241
Ratcliff, Jennifer J., 200
raw art, 274n1, 254
Readings in Performance and Ecology (Arons and May), 227
Reclaim Shakespeare Company, 223, 224, 233
recontextualization, reflexive, 209–13
Redmond, John, 100, 110n1; Fair Hill Band and, 99; O'Brien and, 97, 99
Reformation movements, 36, 40
Reggio Calabria, 215
regionalism, 153, 175–76, 178
Reilly, Montgomery, 118
religion, 67, 69, 72, 90n3, 90n5, 134, 250; public displays of, 133; transatlantic, 58; world, 139
remembrance, 128, 198, 239, 241, 246, 247, 250, 251; displacement of, 240; process of, 240; roadside, 242
Renwick Gallery, ix
Repeal Movement, monster meetings by, 94
Republican National Convention, 232
republicans, 96, 102, 107
Republic of Georgia, 74
Request to Leave, 145
resistance, 57, 67, 69; expressing, 82, 200; guerrilla, 225; symbolic, 72
resources: cultural, 60, 153, 154; decimation of, 225
rhyming, 26, 35
rhythms, 38, 39, 76
Ricketts, Aiden, 228
Right Sector, 86
Rio, Carnival and, 40, 42n2, 57
riots, 37–38, 102; antigovernment, 108; band, 97–98; carnivals and, 5, 44n19
rites of passage, 4, 54, 63, 66, 69, 82, 156, 157–60; cultural studies and, 158; death and, 79; festivals and, 157; folklore and, 158; pattern for, 160; prestructuralist value of, 159; rituals and, 157, 158; spectacles and, 157; usefulness of, 159–60
ritualesque, xi, xii, xiii, 3, 14, 68, 128, 224, 234, 236, 258, 265, 273; academic perception of, 160–62; carnivalesque and, 11–13, 151, 161, 205, 207, 209, 210, 215, 217, 218; elements of, 5; material culture and, 13; protests and, 216; rituals and, 156–60, 161; social order and, 207

ritual framework, 73–74, 76, 85, 89
rituals, xii, 3, 66, 77, 133, 134, 142, 148, 191, 250, 255; birth, 75; boundaries of, 77, 246; burial, 64, 106; carnivalesque, 75; Catholic, 4, 210, 213–15; community, 57, 128; concept of, 72, 161; culture and, 72, 127; described, 14, 73, 205; emotions and, 218; enactment of, 67, 241; festivals and, 4–5, 71, 161, 181; framework for, 70; funeral, 158, 241; games as, 86, 89; healing, 12; identity and, 67, 69, 79; instrumental, 75; legitimating, 80; local, 161; managing, 73; modern/postmodern, 159; mourning, 105–6; performance and, 69, 73, 159; politics and, 66, 67, 68, 70, 71, 72, 73, 77, 78, 78–85, 86, 88, 90; power and, 4, 68–70, 78, 165, 218; profane, 158, 160; protocol for, 146; public, x, 13, 88–89, 110; purpose of, 74, 75, 76; reflexive, 210; religious, 53, 76; rites of passage and, 157, 158; ritualesque and, 156–60, 161; sacred ceremonies and, 4; secular, 72, 90n4; social change and, 207; social conflict and, 110; social life and, 77; social media and, 90; symbolism of, 4, 12, 66; theatricalization of, 8; transformation and, 6, 66, 68–69, 77, 79–81, 160, 210
Rivière, Claude, 158
Roads Division, memorials and, 247
Roaring Lion, 37
Roberts, Justice, 70
Roberts, Kenneth, 56
Rock Garden, 256, 257, 258
Rodia, Sabato (Simon), 256, 274n5
Rogers, Everett, 191
Roller, Hans Ulrich, 43n10
Román, Maria, 127
Rondo, Elise, 46n29
Rosenthal, Rachel, 226
Rossillini, Isabella, 226
Royal Shakespeare Company (RSC), 222, 223, 224, 233
Rumphi District, 176
Rwanda, genocide in, 185

Sachs, Hans, 18, 45n25; poem by, 43n9; songs of, 24, 25
sacrifices, 135, 137, 138, 142, 152, 214
Sailor mas band, 37; Fireman from, 38 (fig.)
Saint Anthony Abbot, 219n10
St. Joseph's Day, 51
St. Patrick's Day, 109
Salaam, Kalamu ya, 227
Saldenha, Harold, 36

Salinas Hometown Club, 127
Salvador de Bahia, 16
Sandinista government, 86
San Fernando, Carnival characters and, 36
San Francisco Gay Men's Chorus, 194
San Mauro Forte, 219n10
Santino, Jack, 93, 156, 242, 258, 274n3; carnivalesque and, 128, 151, 205, 207, 270; ethnographic fieldwork and, 162; folk assemblages and, 116, 174; memorials and, 244–45; public displays and, 269; ritualesque and, 68, 151, 205, 207, 224; on rituals, 72; on shrines, 80; on unpredictable spectatorship, 191
Sanusi, Biarsah and, 147, 151n7
Sasak, 135, 137, 138, 140, 144, 150n4; Balinese and, 139 (fig.), 141, 142, 143, 145, 146, 147, 148; processions by, 141; tensions among, 139; worship with, 151n4
sasih lunar-solar calendar, 150n2
Satirani, Lombardi, 206
Savage Mind, The (Lévi-Strauss), 117
Scanzano protest, 205, 206, 211, 218n2; affective solidarity for, 217; carnivalesque/ritualesque and, 218; civic gravitas for, 215; cultural performance of, 207, 209, 210, 213; described, 208–9; expressive forms and, 210; folk culture and, 212; symbol of, 216
Scharmützel riot, 45n25
Schembart books, 28, 31, 32, 43n11, 45n23, 45n25
Schembartbücher, 17, 24
Schembart group, 26, 36
Schembart hell, 31 (fig.)
Schembartläufer, 26, 44n15
Schembart leaders, 27 (fig.), 30
Schembart manuscripts, 44n17, 44n19, 45n21
Schembart parades, 31, 32, 45n20
Schembart players, 32, 33, 35
Schembart runners, 28, 29, 30–31, 44n15, 44n16
Schielke, Samulie, 72
Schwenter, Pankraz Bernhaupt, 44n19
Sean Graham (betting office), 80
Sea Shepherd Society, 228
Seattle, battle in, 232–33
Seattle Public Theater, 226
Seattle Times, 225
Sea Turtle Restoration Project (STRP), 232
Second Line, 58, 59, 60, 64
secret societies, 52, 67
Seelig, Timothy, 195, 196, 197
segregation, 55, 261, 268

Seinfeld (television show), Puerto Rican flag and, 114
self-awareness, 17
self-government, 40, 94
selfhood, development of, 70
self-improvement, working-class, 94
Sena, 167
Senie, 241, 248
Shadows of Exile (Theater Squad), 234
Shaka Zulu, 167, 168
Shakespeare, William, 222, 223, 225
Shield Ceremony, 56
Ship of Fools (Brant), 28
shrines, 10, 11 (fig.), 90n7; communication by, 248; death, 80; healing, 13; as international phenomena, 8; religious figures at, 248; roadside, 6, 8, 240, 246, 247–51; self-motivated, 6; spontaneous, 8, 13, 247, 258
Sierra Club, 228
signifiers, 75; performing, 76; surplus of, 11, 76
Simon, E., 42n3
Simpson, O. J., 268
Sing for the Cure events, 196, 197, 198, 199, 202n6
Singhal, Arvind, entertainment-education strategy and, 191
Sinn Féin, 99, 100, 101, 104
Sirleaf, Ellen Johnson, 81
slave rebellions, 56
slavery, 19, 34, 49, 54, 55, 56, 61, 62; displacement and, 57; Protestant/Catholic attitudes toward, 62
slaves, 52, 55, 56, 57; cultural production and, 60–61, 63; developmental patterns among, 63; fighting by, 63–64; free blacks and, 49; independent enterprises and, 62; introduction of, 58; legal/religious status of, 62
Smalkaldic League, 34
Smith, Charles, 257
Smith, Fred, 257
Smith, Jeffrey Chipps, 42n3
Smith, Robert James, 241
Smithsonian Folklife Festival, 130n7
Smithsonian Institution, ix, 232
Smithsonian Office of Folklife Program, ix
Social Aid and Pleasure Clubs, 53
social bands, 93–95
social change, 6, 12, 14, 67, 74, 94, 128, 159, 191, 193, 224, 256, 274n3; rituals and, 207; symbols and, 270; visions of, 270
social class, 19, 21; boundaries/crossing, 22; Carnival and, 20, 206

Index

social commentary, 256, 272
social conflict, 110, 122
social context, xiii, 256
social creations, 225, 226
social criticism, 72, 270
social groups, 66, 70, 88
social issues, x, 9, 128, 166, 236n3
social justice, 125, 270
social life, 71, 77, 88, 152
social media, 68, 78, 82, 83, 88, 90
social movements, 201n3, 205, 206, 218
social order, 69, 76, 133, 152; carnivalesque and, 207; marriage and, 70; ritualesque and, 207
social protest, 205, 209, 211, 217; Heidelberg Project and, 258–73
social relationships, 70, 76, 90n4, 212
social sciences, 152, 157, 160, 205
social structure, 57, 67, 75, 136
society, 23; culture and, 226, 229
sociopolitical issues, 39, 66, 148, 273
Soko, Boston, 169, 172, 180, 182
Soko, Khumbo, 185
Soles of the Most High, 267
songs, 54, 96–97, 190, 192, 194; black, 55; improvised, 57; Mardi Gras, 51–52, 58; pop, 84; rhyme, 18; signature, 52. *See also* music
Sowards, Stacey K., 128
space: claiming, 241; containment and, 241–48; geographical, 241–48; living, 256; management of, 251; private, 270; profane, 137; Puerto Rican, 123–25; sacred, 137, 215, 216, 241; social, 58; time and, 76. *See also* public space
Spanish Creole, 34
Spanish-Cuban-American War (1898), 118
spectacle, 198; activist, 190–92, 200, 201; aural nature of, 192; etymology/idiomatic uses of, 191; music and, 193–95; public, 224; rites of passage and, 157; techniques of, 190
spectacular, 35, 40, 106 189, 190 191, 198, 230; aurally, 192; performance and, 229; visually, 199
spectatorship: public, x, 258; unpredictable, 191
Spirit of Detroit Award, 263
sports, 96; politics and, 86; as resource for domination, 86–88; rituals and, 87, 88
Standing, Sarah Ann, 226, 228, 229, 234
steelpan bands, 39, 40 (fig.), 46n32, 46–47n33
Stoeltje, Beverly, xi, 11, 74, 165
Street Folk, 269

Sufism, 72
Suleiman the Magnificent, 33
Sumberg, Samuel, 44n19
Susan G. Komen Breast Cancer Foundation, 196, 197, 201
Susanna (school play), 45n22
Svich, Caridad, 227
symbolic action, x, 6, 14, 76, 258; power relations and, 70–72; rituals as, 12
symbolism, xii, 4, 10, 70, 90, 156, 174, 258; communication and, 75–77; emergence of, 10; female, 146; interpretation/counterinterpretation of, 80; Irish, 110n8; Ngoni, 178, 180, 181, 182; party, 179; Puerto Rican, 113, 117, 123, 127; social change and, 270; transformation of, 76
Symbolist Man, as Political Man, 70

Take Back the Night, 6
Taksim, 83, 84
Tate Galleries, 222
Tchaikovsky, Peter, 192
technology, 68, 82, 88; development of, 78
telek dancers, 141 (fig.), 142, 142 (fig.)
Temel, Burga, 90n8
terrorism, 159, 228
Terzo Cavone, 214
theater: agitprop, 234; environmental awareness and, 233; guerrilla, 223, 233; protest performance and, 234–35; radical activist, 233; street, 6, 224; traditional, 234, 235
Theater magazine, 225
Theater Squad, 234
Theron, Charlize, 232
Thole, Aupson, 168, 169, 176, 180
Thompson, E. P., 206
Thompson, James, 55, 56
Thompson, Robert Farris, 56–57, 266
Thornton, John, 56
Timber (Willis), 226
Tire House, 264
Toelken, Barre, 129
Toronto Film Festival, 232
tourism, 134, 154, 160, 162, 208
Townsend, Stuart, 232
trade, 24; internal, 61; international, 63
trade unions, 101, 106, 209, 217
tradition, 274n1; invention of, 134, 170–74; norm and, 240–41; popular, 153
transformation, 6, 148; enabling, 77, 89; material, 67; neighborhood, 272; participation and, 76; personal, 218n2; political, 99; rituals

and, 6, 66, 68–69, 77, 79–80, 89, 210; symbolism and, 76
tribalism, 175, 185
Trinidad, 22; Carnival and, 16, 18, 34, 35–36, 42n1, 43n4; slavery and, 18; technological solutions in, 40
Trisandya, 144
Tuan Guru, 138–39
Tumbuka, 167, 169, 171, 174, 176, 185
Turner, Terence, 69
Turner, Victor W., ix, 157–58
Turtle Creek Chorale, 195, 196
turtles, endangered, 231–32
Turtles (protestors), 232
Twelfth Night (Shakespeare), 222
Twin Cities Gay Men's Chorus, 194

U2 (band), 189
Ulster Unionism, procession culture of, 93
ultras (football fans), 84
Ultras Ahlawy, 84
Umthetho Festival, xii, 164, 170–74, 175–76; cultural identity and, 178, 185; emergence of, 165, 172; ethnic identity and, 184–85; goals for, 182; Ngoni and, 167, 171; politics and, 175–81
Underground Railway Theater, 226, 236n3
unemployment, 125, 261
UNESCO, 151, 154, 162, 166
Unionist Party, 119
United Nations, GATT and, 233
Unmarked (Phelan), 235
U.S. Congress, Puerto Rico and, 119
U.S. Endangered Species Act, 231
U.S. flag, 118, 119; displaying, 120; Puerto Rico and, 121
U.S. Marines, 119, 121

vandalism, 228, 231, 233
Van Gennep, Arnold, 156, 157, 158, 160
Vega, James de la, 122
vejigantes, 115, 116 (fig.)
Velez Alvarado, Antonio, 130n3
Venice, 16; Carnival and, 24, 43n12
vernacular expression, 255, 266, 273
Vesey, Denmark, 56
Via Crucis procession, 214
Via Verde *gasoducto*, 121
Victor, 36
Victoria Barracks, 109, 110
Vienna Nationalbibliothek, 45n24
Vietnam Veterans Memorial, x, 9

Vietnam War: African Americans and, 257; controversy regarding, 9
violence, 10, 78, 77–78, 80, 151n4, 152, 261; brass bands and, 96; commemoration of, 240; domestic, 190, 191; endemic, 98; gang, 272; political, 78, 81, 110n2; threat of, 215
"Virtual Choir" (Whitacre), 192
voluntary associations, power/order and, 56
votive offerings, 13, 249

Walloons, 29, 30, 33
Walsh, Martin, 43n8
War of Independence, 108
warriors, 56, 60, 61, 174; Ngoni, 182; walking, 137
Way of Water, The (Svich), 227
Weaver, Deak, 226
weddings, 66, 68, 69–70, 75
Welschen/Weschen, 29, 44n18
West Indians, 3, 90n5
Westminster Abbey, funeral at, 81
Wetu Telu, 138, 139, 146, 151n4, 151n5
When We No Longer Touch (Anthony), 196, 202n6
Whitacre, Eric, 192
White, Ben, 232
White Knights, 86
Wild Indians, 35, 51
William, Prince, 70
Williams, Betty, 210–11
Willis, Bryan, 226
Wisconsin Concrete Park, 257
Wojcik, Daniel, xi, xii
World Bank, 232
World Health Organization, epidemics and, 82
World Shakespeare Festival, 222
World Trade Organization (WTO), 231, 232, 233
World War II, 37, 38, 124

Yao, 167, 183
yard assemblages, 259, 266–67
Yocom, Margaret R., 241
Yoruba, 55, 56, 77
Young, Coleman, 264

Zamalek, 84
Zapatistas, 216
Zinn, Dorothy, xi, xii
zoöpathology, 236n1
Zwangendaba, Nguni, 168

www.ingramcontent.com/pod-product-compliance
Lightning Source LLC
Chambersburg PA
CBHW051528020426
42333CB00016B/1834